S61

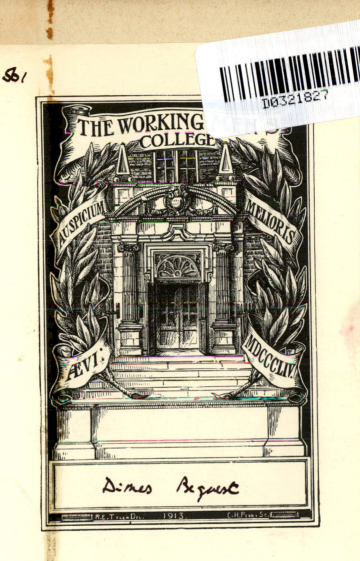

Dines Bequest

All communications with regard to the
Society should be addressed to
THE HON. SECRETARY
English Place-Name Society
University College
Gower Street
W.C. 1

ENGLISH PLACE-NAME SOCIETY.   VOLUME XVIII

GENERAL EDITORS
ALLEN MAWER *and* F. M. STENTON

THE
PLACE-NAMES OF MIDDLESEX
APART FROM
THE CITY OF LONDON

CAMBRIDGE
UNIVERSITY PRESS
LONDON: BENTLEY HOUSE
NEW YORK, TORONTO, BOMBAY
CALCUTTA, MADRAS: MACMILLAN
TOKYO: MARUZEN COMPANY LTD

ENGLISH PLACE-NAME SOCIETY.   VOLUME XVIII

THE PLACE-NAMES OF MIDDLESEX

APART FROM
THE CITY OF LONDON

29364

By
J. E. B. GOVER, ALLEN MAWER
AND F. M. STENTON
WITH THE COLLABORATION OF
S. J. MADGE

CAMBRIDGE
AT THE UNIVERSITY PRESS
1942

The collection from unpublished documents of material for this volume has been made possible by a grant received from the British Academy

PRINTED IN GREAT BRITAIN

PREFACE

THE present volume on the *Place-names of Middlesex* was originally planned as a volume on the place-names of the City of London and the County of Middlesex. War circumstance has compelled the editors to confine the volume to the County of Middlesex, for while the material for that county had to a very large extent been collected before the gradual closing of archives made work upon unpublished documents impossible, work upon the material for the City of London was not in the same advanced stage of preparation. Fortunately for the Survey, the sub-editor, Mr J. E. B. Gover, had for some years past been collecting Middlesex material, alike from printed and unprinted sources, and the Survey had also received from Dr S. J. Madge a very generous offer to place at its disposal the vast mass of material which he himself had been collecting for many years past upon the same theme. That material has now, in accordance with Dr Madge's own desires, been presented to University College for deposit in the Library where it will be available for consultation by future generations of scholars. The combined work of Mr Gover and Dr Madge has enabled us, even in war time, to prepare a volume upon the place-names of Middlesex on the same lines as those usually followed. There have been considerable difficulties in checking references from printed sources, still more from unprinted sources, but these difficulties should not seriously affect the accuracy of the volume as a whole.

In that part of the volume which is concerned with London (other than the City), we have been helped very greatly by Miss Jeffries Davis, sometime University Reader in the History of London. Amid many difficulties she has placed her unique knowledge at our disposal and given unstintingly her time and energy in criticising, correcting and supplementing the material for that area. Unfortunately, time did not permit of her dealing fully with it all but we trust that, in relation at least to the City of Westminster, the work of the late Mr C. L. Kingsford has made errors on the part of the editors less likely.

For this county no outline map showing the usual division into Hundreds and parishes has been prepared. The constant changing of parochial areas, the development of the modern boroughs and other factors would deprive any single map of most of its significance in relation to this county—a series of maps would be required. Distribution maps (see pocket at the end) have as usual been provided showing the distribution of (i) the chief habitational suffixes, (ii) the chief elements indicating the presence of woodland.

In the preparation of the volume extensive use has as usual been made of unprinted sources—the Bibliography will show how much work has been done upon records at the Public Record Office and at the British Museum. In work on muniments at Westminster Abbey we are much indebted to the Keeper, Mr Laurence Tanner, and his assistant, Miss Powell, and, in work on documents at St Paul's, to Mr Gerald Henderson. Full use was made of documents for Harrow and Pinner preserved in the Middlesex Guildhall, and we are much indebted to Miss Cameron of the Records Department there. For further documents relating to Harrow preserved in the Library of Lambeth Palace we are grateful for help given us by Miss Churchill, the Librarian. The Warden and Fellows of All Souls College have allowed us facilities for working through documents relating to Edgware, Kingsbury and Willesden. Unfortunately we were only able to consult those documents at a time when the College had placed the older among them in places of safety where they were no longer accessible. For material for Ruislip we turned to King's College, Cambridge, but unfortunately here again we were too late and the only document in their archives of which use has been made is a valuable Survey for 1565 to which Dr Madge was given access some few years ago. Once again we wish to thank the officers in charge of the Tithe Awards for facilities for consulting documents in their possession. Dr Madge in his part of the work stands specially indebted to Mr Walton of the Middlesex Guildhall for access to Enclosure Awards and to the officers in charge of the map-room in the British Museum.

Full use has been made of the printed material to be found in the publications of the Public Record Office, the old Record

Commission and various local Societies. Much material has also been derived from numerous parish histories and other volumes such as the Records of St Bartholomew's Priory, edited by E. A. Webb. These volumes are of varying quality, but they include a great deal of useful material.

For information upon various points we are indebted among others to the Town Clerk of the Borough of Ealing and to the Rev. W. S. Scott, Curate in Charge of St Peter's, Cranley Gardens.

In the reading of the proofs and in the treatment of cruces we have unfortunately, through the exigencies of war, been deprived of the help of Professor Ekwall which has been placed at our disposal from the earliest stages of the Survey. With other friends we have been more fortunate—Professor Tait and Professor Bruce Dickins have once again given us very valuable aid.

In the final stages of the preparation of the volume the facilities provided by the Institute of Historical Research, first through the kind offices of Miss Jeffries Davis and later of Mr Parsloe, assisted by Mr de Beer, have been specially useful. Miss Davis has in her turn been very greatly helped by the facilities placed at her disposal by the authorities and staff of the Bodleian at a time when that Library is itself working under great difficulties. The library of University College, including the special collection in the London History room, has been out of action since September last. This circumstance and the restrictions upon the use of the Reading Room at the British Museum have also made the help of the London Library of special value at the present time. Without the opportunity of using these libraries it would have been very difficult to complete the volume.

In these difficult days the editors owe very special thanks to Miss Armstrong, the Director's secretary, for her untiring devotion to the work of the Society.

A. M.
F. M. S.

1 *July* 1941
Stansteadbury,
Stanstead Abbots

CONTENTS

MAPS

INTRODUCTION

IT is a curious anomaly that Middlesex, the smallest of the ancient shires of England, bears a name which apparently denotes one of the major divisions of the Saxon settlers in Britain. Middlesex is obviously a name of high antiquity, and it is well-recorded, for it occurs in at least three pre-Alfredian documents[1], of which one, a charter of 767, is preserved in a contemporary text. Geographically, its meaning is plain. The Middle Saxons must have owed their designation to the fact that they occupied the country between the East Saxons of Essex and the early Saxon colonies established on either side of the middle Thames. Their name is clearly parallel to that of the Middle Angles, who inhabited the country between East Anglia and the Mercian settlements in the Trent basin. The only difficulty in this explanation lies in the smallness of the area to which, in historic times, the name Middlesex has been restricted.

The difficulty is less than it seems to be, for there are facts which suggest that the county of Middlesex is only a fragment of a much larger territory originally occupied by the Middle Saxon peoples. Towards the north, the boundary of the county is late and artificial. Its course is largely determined by the practical convenience of including the more southerly estates of the abbey of St Albans within Hertfordshire, where the monastery itself was situated. Towards the south, the name Surrey, which means 'southern region,' indicates with some force that this district had originally been the southernmost province of the primitive Middle Saxons[2]. Towards the west, the hunting-rights possessed in the Chilterns by the twelfth-century citizens of London may well go back to a time when these wooded hills formed the Middle Saxon frontier[3]. Like the Middle Angles, the Middle Saxons have no independent history, and it is unlikely that any single family ever rose to predominance among

---

[1] *Infra* 1. There is a fourth example in BCS 182, but this document is only known from a twelfth-century copy.
[2] See PN Sr xii–xv.
[3] *Norman London* 6 (Historical Association Leaflet No. 93).

them. Without a ruling house to hold them together, early peoples always tended towards disintegration. By the end of the sixth century, Surrey appears to have become debatable ground between the kings of Kent and Wessex. London had become the chief town of the East Saxon kingdom[1], and it is probable that the whole of Middlesex had fallen, like London, under East Saxon lordship by that date.

In any case, it seems clear that the district now called Middlesex was an early field of Saxon settlement. In view of the small area covered by the county, the number of ancient names which it contains is remarkable. The tribal names *Geddingas*, now Yeading, and *Gillingas*, now Ealing, belong to the oldest stratum of English nomenclature. *Gumeninga hergæ*, the original name of the tribal heathen sanctuary at Harrow, is obviously primitive. Wembley and Fulham contain ancient personal names of Germanic origin which never became adopted generally in England. Tyburn, Neasden, and Astlam contain substantives rarely, if ever, found independently in Old English sources. No parallel is known to the mysterious prefix in *Linga Haese*, the eighth-century name of Hayes near Harlington. No absolute date for the beginning of the settlement can be obtained from these names. But they agree very well with the archaeological evidence[2] which suggests that the Saxons were in occupation of Middlesex by the early part of the sixth century.

That the county was thoroughly settled before the Alfredian age is clear. There are many names in Middlesex, less obviously archaic than those which have just been quoted, which plainly belong to the earlier rather than the later stages of Anglo-Saxon history. Uxbridge, Waxlow, and Uxendon, which mean respectively the bridge, the *leah*, and the hill of the folk or people known as the *Wixan*, must have arisen at a time when the names of ancient tribes still had reality for those who used them. The stream-name *Lidding* is a formation of an early type. But the most interesting side-light on the early history of the county comes from the identification of Barnet Gate, formerly Greens-gate or Grinsgate, in Hendon with the boundary-point (*to*)

---

[1] Bede, *Historia Ecclesiastica* ii, 3.
[2] Such as that furnished by the cemetery at Shepperton, on which see J. N. L. Myres in *Oxford History of England* i, 371.

Grendeles gatan, which occurs in a late tenth-century charter. The name means 'Grendel's gates.' The exact sense of the compound, and, in particular, the nature of the 'gates,' is uncertain. But the name proves at least that stories about Grendel, the monster whom Beowulf slew, were current in early times on what is now the boundary between Middlesex and Hertfordshire[1].

The conditions of early settlement in Middlesex were mainly determined by local variations of soil within the great expanse of Tertiary deposits which fill the basin between the chalk hills of Hertfordshire and Surrey[2]. In many parts of the county, and especially in the south, the nature of the ground permitted agriculture upon a considerable scale, and gave rise to many coherent villages. But to the north and north-west of London, the stretches of woodland which had given a forest background to the Roman city limited the range of early Saxon cultivation. The distribution maps included in this volume illustrate these conditions very clearly. In the north-east of the county, Enfield Chase preserves something more than a memory of this ancient woodland. The local names of this part of the county, with few exceptions, are late, but one of them is of outstanding interest. There can be no doubt that the name of Camlet Moat in Enfield Chase represents the *Camelot* of Arthurian legend, applied as a literary reminiscence to a lodge in this wilderness of clay and woodland.

Among the less distinguished names of this woodland country, there is one which throws light on an obscure episode in the campaign of 1016 between Cnut and Edmund Ironside. According to the Abingdon version of the *Chronicle*, king Edmund, after an indecisive battle at Sherston in Wiltshire, collected a new army for the relief of London, which the Danes were then besieging. The *Chronicle* states that he marched to London, keeping to the north of the Thames, came 'out through *Clæighangra*,' and relieved the garrison. Up to the present, no name corresponding

---

[1] The name Grim's Ditch, which like Grendel's Gates is of mythological interest, is discussed below p. 11, with references to examples of the name in other counties. The earthwork itself is described by R. E. M. Wheeler in *London and the Saxons*, 62 *et seqq.*

[2] On these variations see *Royal Commission on Historical Monuments; London*, III, 10 *et seqq.*

to *Clæighangra* has been noticed anywhere on the probable line of Edmund's march. But an Assize Roll of 1294 refers to a place called *Clayhangre extra villam de Toteham*, now, apparently, represented by Clayhill Farm in that parish, which may reasonably be identified with the site indicated by the *Chronicle*. If the identification is correct, it would seem that Edmund, anxious to conceal his approach from the Danes at London, kept behind the screen of the Middlesex woodlands until he reached the line of Ermine Street at Tottenham, and then descended quickly on the city. It is a strong argument for this identification that it explains the surprise of the Danes at Edmund's appearance, which is implied by the language of the *Chronicle*.

The names in the county generally call for no particular comment. It is the case with Middlesex as with Essex and Hertfordshire, that apart from some river-names there are practically no names of Celtic origin. There are no traces of Scandinavian influence except in the name of the Anglo-Scandinavian *Gunnhild* who was the sometime lady of the manor of Gunnersbury (*infra* 91). Even the early centralisation of government in the Cities of London and Westminster had little influence in gallicising the names of the county as distinct from those of the City itself. The only name-type that is distinctively frequent in post-Conquest days is the formation of manorial names by the addition of the element *bury* to the name of the sometime holder of the manor, as in Canonbury (*infra* 125) and the just mentioned Gunnersbury, or its addition to the name of a vill as in Edgware Bury (*infra* 51). In this respect Middlesex groups itself very definitely with the counties of Essex and Hertfordshire where the same method of manorial nomenclature is even more common.

NOTES ON THE DIALECT OF MIDDLESEX
AS ILLUSTRATED IN ITS PLACE-NAMES

OE *æ* usually becomes *a* in ME and ModEng as in *Hatch End*, *Barnet*, with occasional *e* in ME.

OE *e* (*æ*) before nasals generally becomes *e* but occasionally *a* in ME and ModEng in the various names containing **denu** and **fenn**, which sometimes give forms *dane* and *fan(n)*. See also *Endiff* and the forms of *Walham Green*.

OE *ǣ*, whatever its source, gives ME forms in *e* and *a*, ModEng [*i·*] or [*ei*], or, with shortening, [*e*] or [*æ*]. See under *Broad Mead*, *Clendish*, *Cowleaze*, *Hatton*, *Heathrow*, *Laleham*, *Steyne*, *Stratford*.

eald (Angl *ald*) appears in ME as *eld*, *ald*, *old*, the *eld*-form being among the earliest. In ModEng (under the influence of StEng) we have *old*, never *eld*. *Aldwych* is a modern reconstruction.

weald (Angl *wald*) becomes ME *weld* (with occasional ME *wald*), ModEng *wild* (with irregular *weald*). *See Harrow Weald*, *Wildwood*.

OE *ēa* becomes ME *ě* as in *Hendon*, *Enfield*, but occasionally *a* as in *Ratcliffe*.

OE *ēo* becomes ME *ě* as in *Fleet*, *Preston*, but *o* (with occasional *e*) in *Dormers Well*.

OE *u* has become *e* between point consonants in *Teddington*, cf. PN W xx, PN Nt xxii.

OE *ȳ* becomes ME *e*, *i*, *u*, but *e* and *u* are *more* common than *i*. *e* has survived in *Bedfont*, *Kempton*, *Kensington*, *Kenton*, *Stepney*, *i* in *Kilburn*, *u* in *Ruislip*. In *Littleton* and names in *Hill* the influence of StEng forms has prevailed.

ȳ as found in OE **hyð** gives ME *huthe*, *hethe* and occasional *hithe*.

Voicing of initial [*f*] to [*v*] is sporadically found in ME as in early forms for *Finchley*, *Finsbury*.

cealc, *ceald* become ME *chalk*, *chald* as in *Chalkhill* and *Chacott* (now *Chalk Farm*), with occasional *cheld*.

BIBLIOGRAPHY AND ABBREVIATIONS

a.	*ante.*
Abbr	*Placitorum Abbreviatio*, 1811.
Abingdon	*Chronicon Monasterii de Abingdon*, ed. J. S. Stevenson (Rolls Series), 1858.
AC	*Ancient Charters* (Pipe Roll Soc.), 1888.
Acres	W. M. Acres, *London and Westminster*, 1923.
AD	*Catalogue of Ancient Deeds.* (In progress.)
AD	Unpublished Ancient Deeds (PRO).
Add	Additional MSS (BM).
AddCh	Additional Charters (BM).
AFr	Anglo-French.
Agas	*Civitas Londinium*; an Elizabethan map attributed to R. Agas (reproduced London Topographical Soc.).
Aliens	*The Returns of Aliens in London*, ed. R. E. and E. F. Kirk (Huguenot Soc. 10), 4 vols., 1900–8.
Allgood	H. G. C. Allgood, *History of Bethnal Green*, 1884.
All Souls	Documents in the possession of All Souls College, Oxford.
Andrews	J. Andrews, *The Country 65 miles round London*, 1777.
ASC	Anglo-Saxon Chronicle.
ASCharters	*Anglo-Saxon Charters*, ed. A. J. Robertson, 1939.
Ass	Assize Rolls, nos. 536–8, 542–3, 546–9 (PRO).
ASWills	*Anglo-Saxon Wills*, ed. D. Whitelock, 1930.
Baker	W. K. Baker, *Acton*, 1913.
Barratt	T. W. Barratt, *The Annals of Hampstead*, 3 vols., 1912.
BCS	W. de G. Birch, *Cartularium Saxonicum*, 3 vols., 1885–93.
Beaver	Alfred Beaver, *Memorials of Old Chelsea*, 1892.
Belv	*Manuscripts of the Duke of Rutland at Belvoir Castle* (HMC), 1905.
Bk	Buckinghamshire.
BlBk	*The Black Book of Hendon* (LMxAS (NS) 6).
BM	British Museum.
BM	*Index to Charters and Rolls in the British Museum*, 2 vols., 1900–12.
Bowack	John Bowack, *The Antiquities of Middlesex*, 1705.
Bowles	Bowles, *A Map for 20 miles round London*, 1730.
BPR	*The Register of Edward the Black Prince*, 4 vols., 1930–3.
Bracton	*Bracton's Note Book*, ed. F. W. Maitland, 3 vols., 1887
Bridges	*Report of the Committee of Magistrates respecting the Public Bridges in the County of Middlesex*, 1826.
Brittain	F. Brittain, *South Mymmes, the Story of a Parish*, 1931.
BT Supplt	*An Anglo-Saxon Dictionary based on MS Collections of Joseph Bosworth: Supplement* by T. N. Toller.
Bushell	*Church Life on Harrow Hill*, ed. F. Done Bushell, 1909.
c.	*circa.*
C	Cambridgeshire.
Cai	*Admissions to Gonville and Caius College*, ed. Venn, 1887.
CantYB	*Year Books of Probate in the Prerogative Court of Canterbury*, ed. J. and G. F. Matthews, 5 vols., 1902–7.

Capgrave	John Capgrave, *Chronicle of England* (Rolls Series), 1858.
Cary	John Cary, *Map of London and Suburbs*, 1793, 1808.
Ch	*Calendar of Charter Rolls*, 6 vols., 1903–27.
ChancP	*Chancery Proceedings in the Reign of Elizabeth*, 3 vols., 1827–32; *Chancery Proceedings* (PRO Lists and Indexes, nos. 7, 39, 47), 1896–1922.
ChelseaSurv	W. H. Godfrey, *The Parish of Chelsea* (LCC Survey of London), 4 vols., 1909–27.
Chertsey	*The Cartulary of Chertsey Abbey* (Surrey Rec. Soc.), 1915, 1931.
ChR	*Rotuli Chartarum*, 1837.
ChronStAlb	*Chronica Monasterii Sancti Albani* (Rolls Series), 12 vols., 1863–76.
ChwAcct	*St Martin in the Fields, The Accounts of the Churchwardens*, ed. J. V. Kitto, 1901.
Cl	*Calendar of Close Rolls*. (In progress.)
Clerkenwell	The Cartulary of Clerkenwell Nunnery (Cott. MS Faust. B. ii) (BM).
Cobbett	*Memorials of Twickenham*, ed. R. S. Cobbett, 1872.
Cor	*Calendar of the Coroners' Rolls of the City of London*, 1300–1378, ed. R. R. Sharpe, 1913.
Cor	Coroners' Rolls for Middlesex, nos. 94, 96, 97 (PRO).
CottCh	Cottonian Charters (BM).
Cox and Hall	T. Cox and A. Hall, *Magna Britannia and Hibernia*, 6 vols., 1729–31.
CR	Pipe Roll, Chancellor's Copy.
Crawford	*The Crawford Collection of Early Charters*, ed. A. S. Napier and W. H. Stevenson, 1893.
Crispin	J. Armitage Robinson, *Gilbert Crispin, Abbot of Westminster*, 1911.
Croniques	*Croniques de London* (Camden Soc. 28), 1844.
Cruchley	G. F. Cruchley, *London and its Environs*, 1838.
Ct	Court Rolls (unpublished).
CtRequests	Court of Requests (PRO).
Cur	*Curia Regis Rolls*. (In progress.)
D	Devon.
Davenport	*Records of Old Stanmore*, ed. Percy Davenport, 1935.
Daw	Edmund Daw, *Map of the Parish of St Mary Abbots, Kensington*, 1858.
Db	Derbyshire.
DB	Domesday Book.
DeedsEnrolled	Enrolment of Deeds at the PRO.
DEPN	E. Ekwall, *The Oxford Dictionary of English Place-names*, 1936.
DeSalis	Rachael de Salis, *Hillingdon through Eleven Centuries*, 1926.
dial.	dialectal.
DKR	*Reports of the Deputy Keeper of the Records*. (In progress.)
DNB	*Dictionary of National Biography*.
Draper	Warwick Draper, *Chiswick*, 1923.
Druett	*Pinner through the Ages*, ed. W. W. Druett, 1937.
Du	Durham.
Dugd	W. Dugdale, *Monasticon Anglicanum*, 6 vols., 1817–30.
DuLa	Duchy of Lancaster Documents in PRO.
DunBev	*Sanctuarium Dunelmense et Sanct. Beverlacense* (Surtees Soc. 5), 1837.
Dury	Bowles and Dury, *Environs of London*, 1771.

Eales	A. R. T. Eales, *A Lecture on the History of Elstree*, 1922.
ECP	*Early Chancery Proceedings* (PRO Lists and Indexes, nos. 12, 16, 20, 29, 38, 39, 47, 48, 50, 51, 54), 1901–33.
EDD	*English Dialect Dictionary*, 6 vols., 1898–1905.
EEW	*The Earliest English Wills* (Early English Text Soc. 78), 1882.
EHN	O. S. Anderson, *English Hundred-names*, 3 vols., 1934–9.
EHR	*English Historical Review.* (In progress.)
Ellis	Henry Ellis, *The History and Antiquities of Shoreditch*, 1798.
Elmes	J. Elmes, *A Topographical Dictionary of London and its Environs*, 1831.
EnclA	*Middlesex Enclosure Awards* (printed in various parish histories and in Bridges).
EnclA	Enclosure Awards (Mx Guildhall).
EPNS	English Place-name Society.
Ess	Essex.
Evans	E. T. Evans, *History of Hendon*, 1898.
Evesham	Evesham Cartulary (Cott. MS Vespasian B xxiv, 49, 51) (BM).
FA	*Feudal Aids*, 6 vols., 1899–1920.
Faden	W. Faden, *The Country 25 miles round London*, 1795.
Faithorne	William Faithorne and Richard Newcourt, *Map of London*, 1658 (reproduced Ln Topographical Soc.).
FaulknerB	T. Faulkner, *History and Antiquities of Brentford, Ealing and Chiswick*, 1845.
FaulknerCh	T. Faulkner, *An Historical and Topographical Description of Chelsea*, 2nd ed., 2 vols., 1829.
FaulknerFu	T. Faulkner, *An Historical Account of Fulham including the Hamlet of Hammersmith*, 1813.
FaulknerKe	T. Faulkner, *History and Antiquities of Kensington*, 1820.
Fees	*Book of Fees*, 3 vols., 1922–31.
Feilitzen	Olof von Feilitzen, *The Pre-Conquest Personal Names of Domesday Book*, 1937.
Feret	C. J. Feret, *Fulham Old and New*, 3 vols., 1900.
FF	*A Calendar of Feet of Fines for London and Middlesex*, 1197–1569, ed. W. J. Hardy and W. Page, 2 vols., 1892–3.
FF	Feet of Fines, unprinted, 1569–1700 (PRO).
Fine	*Calendar of Fine Rolls.* (In progress.)
Firth	J. B. Firth, *Middlesex*, 1906.
For	Forest Proceedings (PRO).
France	*Calendar of Documents preserved in France*, 1899.
G	C. and J. Greenwood, *Map of the County of Middlesex*, 1819; *Map of London*, 1827.
Gascoyne	J. Gascoyne, *Map of the Parish of Stepney*, 1703.
Gatty	C. T. Gatty, *Mary Davies and the Manor of Ebury*, 2 vols., 1921.
GDR	Gaol Delivery Rolls, nos. 35–40, 43 (PRO).
Gesta	*Gesta Abbatum Monasterii Sancti Albani* (Rolls Series, 3 vols.), 1867–9.
Gl	Gloucestershire.
Gladstone	F. M. Gladstone, *Notting Hill in Bygone Days*, 1924.
Griffiths	R. Griffiths, *Map of London and its Environs*, 1760.
Guildhall	J. E. Price, *Descriptive Account of the Guildhall*, 1886.
H	W. Harrison, *The Description of Britaine* (Holinshed's Chronicle), 1577, 2nd ed., 1586.
Ha	Hampshire.

HammSurv	*The Parish of Hammersmith* (LCC Survey of London, 1915).
Harben	H. A. Harben, *A Dictionary of London, being notes, topographical and historical, relating to the streets and principal buildings in the City*, 1918.
Harl	Harleian MSS (BM).
HarlCh	Harleian Charters (BM).
HarrowRec	*Records of the Grammar School, founded by John Lyon* 1572, ed. E. J. L. Scott, 1886.
Hatton	Edward Hatton, *A New View of London*, 2 vols., 1708.
HCMag	*The Home Counties Magazine*, vols. 1–14, 1899–1912.
HendonSurv	*Surveys of the Manor of Hendon* (LMxAS (NS) 6, 7).
HMC	Historical Manuscripts Commission.
Hoefnagel	The plan of London, engraved by Hoefnagel from drawings made c. 1555, first published in Braun and Hogenberg's *Civitates Orbis Terrarum*, 1572 (reproduced Ln Topographical Soc.).
HornseyCt	*The Court Rolls of the Bishop of London's manor of Hornsey*, 1603–1701, ed. W. McB. and F. Marcham, 1929.
HornseyRec	S. J. Madge, *The Early Records of Harringay alias Hornsey*, 1938; *The Medieval Records of Harringay alias Hornsey*, 1939.
Horwood	R. Horwood, *Plan of the Cities of London and Westminster*, 1792–1799.
Hust	*Calendar of Wills in the Court of Husting, London*, 1258–1668, ed. R. R. Sharpe, 2 vols., 1889–91.
Inq aqd	*Inquisitiones ad quod damnum*, 1803. *Inquisitions ad quod damnum* (PRO Lists and Indexes), 2 vols., 1904–6.
Ipm	*Calendar of Inquisitions post mortem.* (In progress.)
IpmR	*Inquisitiones post mortem*, 4 vols., 1806–28.
IPN	*Introduction to the Survey of English Place-names*, 1923.
ITRec	*Calendar of the Inner Temple Records*, ed F. A. Inderwick, 5 vols., 1896 ff.
K	Kent
K	C. L. Kingsford, *The Early History of Piccadilly, Leicester Square and Soho*, 1925.
KCD	J. M. Kemble, *Codex Diplomaticus*, 6 vols., 1839–48.
KCR	*Three Rolls of the King's Court* (Pipe Roll Soc. 14), 1891.
Kelly	*The London Post Office Directory*, 1940.
Kennedy	James Kennedy, *The Manor and Parish Church of Hampstead*, 1906.
Kent	*An Encyclopaedia of London*, ed. William Kent, 1937.
Knighton	H. Knighton, *Chronicon* (Rolls Series), 2 vols., 1885–9.
L	John Leland, *Itinerary*, ed. L. T. Smith, 5 vols., 1906–10.
L	Lincolnshire.
La	Lancashire.
Lambeth	Unprinted documents in Lambeth Palace Library.
LBk	*Calendar of Letter Books of the City of London, A to L*, ed. R. R. Sharpe, 1899–1912.
LBkMem	*Memorials of London and London Life* (translated from the City Letter Books), ed. H. T. Riley, 1868.
LCCDeeds	*Catalogue of Deeds relating to London and Middlesex, bequeathed by the late H. A. Harben, Esq. to the London County Council*, n.d.
LCCN	London County Council, *Names of Streets and Places in the County*, 1929, with Supplts. (In progress.)

Lei | Leicestershire.
Lewis | S. Lewis, *The History and Topography of St Mary, Islington*, 1842.
Lib | *Calendar of Liberate Rolls.* (In progress.)
LibAlb | *Liber Albus* (*Munimenta Gildhallae Londoniensis* 1) (Rolls Series), ed. H. T. Riley, 1859.
LibCust | *Liber Custumarum* (*Munimenta Gildhallae Londoniensis* 2, i, ii) (Rolls Series), ed. H. T. Riley, 1859.
LiBlBk | *The Black Books of the Honourable Society of Lincolns Inn*, 4 vols., 1897 ff.
LibReg | John Bacon, *Liber Regis*, 1786.
Lloyd | J. H. Lloyd, *History, Topography and Antiquities of Highgate*, 1888.
LMxAS | *Transactions of the London and Middlesex Archaeological Society.* (In progress.)
Ln | London.
LnEng | *A Book of London English* 1384–1425, ed. R. W. Chambers and Marjorie Daunt, 1931.
LnIpm | *Abstracts of Inquisitions post mortem for the City of London* 1485–1603, ed. G. S. Fry and S. J. Madge, 3 vols., 1896–1908.
LnTopRec | *London Topographical Record.* (In progress.)
Lockie | John Lockie, *Topography of London*, 1810.
Londin | *The Register of Ralph de Baldock, Gilbert Segrave, Richard Newport and Stephen Gravesend, Bishops of London*, 1304–1338 (Canterbury and York Soc.), ed. R. C. Fowler, 1909–12.
LP | *Letters and Papers, Foreign and Domestic*, Henry VIII, 21 vols., 1864–1932.
LRMB | Land Revenue Miscellaneous Books, vols. 220, 262 (PRO).
Lysons | Daniel Lysons, *Environs of London*, 5 vols., 1795–1811; *The County of Middlesex*, 1800.
M | Robert Morden, *A Map...for 20 miles round London*, 1686.
Machyn | *Diary of Henry Machyn* (Camden Soc. 42), 1848.
Madge | S. J. Madge, *The Domesday of Crown Lands*, 1938.
Map | See Addenda xxxiii.
MapCh | *A Map of Chelsea, Surveyed in the year* 1664 (by James Hamilton), continued to 1717 (by John King) (FaulknerCh, Vol. i).
Mayors | *Calendar of Early Mayor's Court Rolls*, 1298–1307, ed. A. H. Thomas, 1924.
McClure | Edmund McClure, *British Place-names in their Historical Setting*, 1910.
MDan | Middle Danish.
ME | Middle English.
Milne | Milne, *Map of London Environs*, c. 1820.
MinAcct | *Ministers' Accounts* (PRO).
Misc | *Calendar of Inquisitions Miscellaneous.* (In progress.)
MLR | *Modern Language Review.* (In progress.)
Mogg | Edward Mogg, *Map of London and the Environs*, 1817.
Moll | H. Moll, *Map of London and the Environs*, c. 1710; *Map of Middlesex*, 1724.
Moore | N. Moore, *The History of St Bartholomew's Hospital*, 2 vols., 1918.

Morgan	*London etc., actually surveyed by William Morgan his Majesty's Cosmographer*, 1682 (reproduced in Ln Topographical Soc., 1904).
Moulton	*Palaeography, Genealogy and Topography.* Selections from the collections of H. R. Moulton, 1930.
MP	Mathew Paris, *Chronica Majora* (Rolls Series), 7 vols., 1872–83.
MTRec	*A Calendar of the Middle Temple Records*, ed. C. H. Hopwood, 1903.
MxNQ	*Middlesex Notes and Queries*, 4 vols.
MxRec	Documents preserved at Middlesex Guildhall.
N	John Norden, *Map of Middlesex*, 1593.
NED	New English Dictionary.
Nelson	John Nelson, *The History of St Mary, Islington*, 1811.
Nf	Norfolk.
NI	*Nonarum Inquisitiones*, 1807.
O and M	(a) *A large and accurate Map of the City of London.* By John Ogilby: His Majesties Cosmographer. (b) *London Survey'd: or, an Explanation of the large Map of London*, by John Ogilby and William Morgan, His Majesty's Cosmographers, 1677 (reproduced by the Ln and Mx Arch. Soc., 1894, 1895).
OBrit	Old British.
OE	Old English.
OFr	Old French.
OFris	Old Frisian.
Ogilby	John Ogilby, *Britannia...an Illustration of the Kingdom of England and Dominion of Wales, a Geographical and Historical Description of the Principal Roads thereof*, 1675.
Orig	*Originalia Rolls*, 2 vols., 1805–10.
O.S.	Ordnance Survey Maps.
OxfordCh	*Facsimiles of Early Charters in Oxford Muniment Rooms*, ed. H. E. Salter, 1929.
P	*Pipe Rolls* (Record Commission, 3 vols.), 1833–44. Pipe Roll Society. (In progress.) *Great Roll of the Pipe* for 26 Henry 3, ed. Cannon, 1918.
Palmer	Samuel Palmer, *St Pancras*, 1870.
Pap	*Calendar of Papal Registers.* (In progress.)
ParlSurv	Parliamentary Surveys (PRO).
ParReg	*Middlesex Parish Registers, Marriages*, ed. W. P. W. Phillimore and others. (In progress.) *The Parish Registers of St James, Clerkenwell*, ed. Robert Hovenden, 6 vols., 1884–94. *The Parish Registers of Kensington*, ed. F. N. Macnamara, 1890. *The Parish Registers of St Dunstan's, Stepney*, ed. Thomas Colyer-Fergusson, 3 vols., 1898 ff. *The Parish Registers of St Martin in the Fields*, ed. Thomas Mason, 2 vols., 1898–1936.
ParRegFr	*Registre des églises de la Savoye, de Spring Garden et des Grecs*, ed. W. Minet (Huguenot Soc. 26), 1922. *Registre des quatre églises du Petit Sharenton, de West Street, Pearl Street, Crispin Street*, ed. W. and S. Minet (Huguenot Soc.), 1929.
Parton	John Parton, *History of St Giles*, 1822.
Pat	*Calendar of Patent Rolls.* (In progress.)

PC   *New Remarks on London, collected by the Company of Parish Clerks*, 1732.
PCC   *Wills Proved in the Prerogative Court of Canterbury* (British Record Society). (In progress.)
Pinks   W. J. Pinks, *The History of Clerkenwell*, 1865.
Pleas   *Calendar of Plea and Memoranda Rolls*, ed. A. H. Thomas. (In progress.)
PN BedsHu   *The Place-names of Bedfordshire and Huntingdonshire* (EPNS), 1926.
PN Bk   *The Place-names of Buckinghamshire* (EPNS), 1925.
PN D   *The Place-names of Devon* (EPNS), 2 vols., 1931–2.
PN ERY   *The Place-names of the East Riding of Yorkshire* (EPNS), 1937.
PN Ess   *The Place-names of Essex* (EPNS), 1935.
PN EW   J. B. Johnston, *The Place-names of England and Wales*, 1915.
PN Herts   *The Place-names of Hertfordshire* (EPNS), 1938.
PN in -*ing* E. Ekwall, *English Place-names in -ing*, 1923.
PN K   J. K. Wallenberg, *The Place-names of Kent*, 1934.
PN NbDu   A. Mawer, *The Place-names of Northumberland and Durham*, 1920.
PN NRY   *The Place-names of the North Riding of Yorkshire* (EPNS), 1928.
PN Nt   *The Place-names of Nottinghamshire* (EPNS), 1940.
PN Nth   *The Place-names of Northamptonshire* (EPNS), 1933.
PN Sx   *The Place-names of Sussex* (EPNS), 2 vols., 1929–30.
PN W   *The Place-names of Wiltshire* (EPNS), 1939.
PN Wa   *The Place-names of Warwickshire* (EPNS), 1936.
PN Wo   *The Place-names of Worcestershire* (EPNS), 1927.
Poll   *A parochial list of the Freeholders Poll for the County of Middlesex in the year* 1802, 1803.
Porter   T. Porter, *Mapp of the most famous Cities London and Westminster*, c. 1660 (reproduced Ln Topographical Soc.).
Potter   S. Potter, *The Story of Willesden*, 1926.
PRO   Public Record Office.
QW   *Placita de Quo Warranto*, 1818.
R   John Rocque, *An exact Survey of the Cities of London, Westminster and Southwark and the country c. 10 miles round*, 1741–5; *A plan of the Cities of London and Westminster*, 1746 (reproduced Ln Topographical Soc.); *A Topographical Map of the County of Middlesex*, 1754.
RamseyChron   *Chronicon Abbatiae Ramesiensis* (Rolls Series), 1886.
RBE   *Red Book of the Exchequer*, 3 vols., 1896.
Recov   Recovery Rolls (PRO).
RecStBarts   *The Records of St Bartholomew's Priory, West Smithfield*, ed. E. A. Webb, 2 vols., 1921.
Redford   George Redford, *The History of Uxbridge*, 1818.
Reg   *Regesta Regum Anglo-Normannorum*, ed. H. W. C. Davis, 1913.
Rental   Rentals at the PRO and BM.
RH   *Rotuli Hundredorum*, 2 vols., 1812–18.
RN   E. Ekwall, *English River-names*, 1928.
Robins   Wm. Robins, *Paddington Past and Present*, 1853.
RobinsonEd   Wm. Robinson, *The History and Antiquities of Edmonton*, 1819.

RobinsonEn	Wm. Robinson, *The History and Antiquities of Enfield*, 2 vols., 1823.
RobinsonH	Wm. Robinson, *The History and Antiquities of Hackney*, 2 vols., 1842–3.
RobinsonSN	Wm. Robinson, *The History and Antiquities of Stoke Newington*, 1820.
RobinsonT	Wm. Robinson, *The History and Antiquities of Tottenham*, 1818.
S	John Seller, *A Mapp of the Cityes of London and Westminster*, 1680; *The County of Middlesex*, 1710.
Saxton	J. Saxton, *Map of Middlesex*, 1575.
Seale	R. W. Seale, *Map of the County of Middlesex*, 1775.
Select Pleas	*Select Pleas* (Selden Soc. 1, 2), 1888–9.
Sess	*Calendar of the Sessions Books*, ed. W. J. Hardy, 1689–1709.
ShoreSurv	*The Parish of St Leonards, Shoreditch* (LCC Survey of London), 1922.
Simpson	R. Simpson, *Some Account of the Monuments in Hackney Church*, 1884.
S.J.M.	*ex inf.* Dr S. J. Madge.
Smith	*St John the Evangelist, Westminster: Parochial Memories*, ed. J. E. Smith, 1892.
Smith	T. Smith, *The Parish of St Mary-le-Bone*, 1833.
s.n.	*sub nomine.*
So	Somerset.
SP	*Calendar of State Papers Domestic.* (In progress.)
Speed	John Speed, *Map of Middlesex*, 1610.
SR	Lay Subsidy Rolls (PRO).
St	Staffordshire.
Star Chamber	*Proceedings in the Court of Star Chamber* (PRO Lists and Indexes 13), 1901.
StEng	Standard English.
StepneyMem	*Memorials of Stepney Parish*, ed. G. W. Hill and W. H. Frere, 1890–1.
StGilesSurv	*The Parish of St Giles in the Fields* (LCC Survey of London), 2 vols., 1912, 1914.
StMargSurv	*The Parish of St Margaret, Westminster* (ib.), 2 vols., 1926, 1933.
StMartSurv	*The Parish of St Martin in the Fields* (ib.), 3 vols., 1935, 1937, 1940.
Stockdale	J. Stockdale, *A New Plan of London, xxix miles in circumference*, 1797; *Map of Middlesex*, 1798.
Stow	John Stow, *A Survey of London*, ed. C. L. Kingsford, 2 vols., 1908.
StPancSurv.	*The Parish of St Pancras* (LCC Survey of London), 2 vols., 1936, 1938.
StPauls	MSS in the possession of the Dean and Chapter of St Paul's.
StPaulsCh	*Early Charters of the Cathedral Church of St Paul's, London*, ed. Marion Gibbs (Camden Soc. Third Series 58), 1939.
StPaulsDB	*The Domesday of St Paul's* (Camden Soc. 69), 1858.
StPaulsMSS	*Historical MSS Commission Ninth Report*, Part i, 1883.
Strype	John Strype, *A Survey of the Cities of London and Westminster*, 1720.
Studies[2]	E. Ekwall, *Studies in English Place-names*, 1936.

Sugden	E. H. Sugden, *A Topographical Dictionary to the Works of Shakespeare and his Fellow Dramatists*, 1925.
Survey	*Surveys of manors* printed in the Histories of Faulkner and Robinson. *v.* Addenda xxxiii.
t.	*tempore.*
TA	Tithe Award.
Tax	*Taxatio Ecclesiastica*, 1802.
Templars	*Records of the Templars in England in the Twelfth Century*, ed. B. A. Lees (British Academy Record Series), 1935.
Tengstrand	E. Tengstrand, *Genitival Composition in OE Place-names*, 1940.
Tengvik	G. Tengvik, *OE Bynames*, 1938.
Thorpe	Benjamin Thorpe, *Diplomatarium Anglicum*, 1865.
Tomlins	T. E. Tomlins, *A Perambulation of Islington*, 1858.
Tomlinson	E. M. Tomlinson, *A History of the Minories*, 1907.
Val	*The Valuation of Norwich*, ed. W. E. Lunt, 1926.
VCH	*Victoria County History of Middlesex*, vol. ii, 1911.
VE	*Valor Ecclesiasticus*, 6 vols., 1810–34.
Wa	Warwickshire.
Walcott	M. E. C. Walcott, *Westminster*, 1849.
Walden	Registrum de Walden, 1387 (Harl MS 3697) (BM).
Walford	Edward Walford, *Greater London*, 2 vols., n.d.
WAM	Westminster Abbey Muniments.
W and C	H. B. Wheatley and P. Cunningham, *London Past and Present*, 3 vols., 1891.
WDB	Westminster Domesday Book (*WAM*).
Weinbaum	M. Weinbaum, *London unter Eduard I und II*, 1933.
Westlake	H. F. Westlake, *St Margaret's, Westminster*, 1914.
Whitaker	C. W. Whitaker, *A History of the Urban District of Enfield*, 1911.
White	W. White, *A Directory of Middlesex*, 1845.
WI	*Wills and Inventories* (Surtees Soc. 2, 38), 1835–60.
Wilkinson	Robert Wilkinson, *The Parish of St Mary Islington*, a map, 1817.
Willdey	G. Willdey, *New Map of 30 miles round London*, 1720.
Williams	E. Williams, *Early Holborn*, 2 vols., 1927.
Winton	*Wykeham's Register* (Hants. Rec. Soc.), 2 vols., 1896–9.
WmCharities	*The Parochial Charities of Westminster*, 1890.
Wo	Worcestershire.
Wollaton	*Manuscripts of Lord Middleton at Wollaton Hall* (HMC), 1911.
Works	*Public Works in Medieval Law* (Selden Soc. 32, 40), 1913, 1923.
Worsley	*Master Worsley's Book*, ed. A. R. Ingpen, 1909.
YearBk	*Year Books of Edward II* (Selden Soc. 19, 26, 33), 1904–16.

PHONETIC SYMBOLS USED IN TRAN-
SCRIPTION OF PRONUNCIATIONS OF
PLACE-NAMES

p	*p*ay	ʃ	*sh*one	tʃ	*ch*urch	ei	fl*ay*
b	*b*ay	ʒ	a*z*ure	dʒ	*j*udge	ε	Fr. jam*ai*s
t	*t*ea	θ	*th*in	ɑˑ	f*a*ther	εˑ	th*ere*
d	*d*ay	ð	*th*en	ɑu	c*ow*	i	p*i*t
k	*k*ey	j	*y*ou	a	Ger. m*a*nn	iˑ	f*ee*l
g	*g*o	χ	lo*ch*	ai	fl*y*	ou	l*ow*
ʍ	*wh*en	h	*h*is	æ	c*a*b	u	g*oo*d
w	*w*in	m	*m*an	ɔ	p*o*t	uˑ	r*u*le
f	*f*oe	n	*n*o	ɔˑ	s*aw*	ʌ	m*u*ch
v	*v*ote	ŋ	si*ng*	oi	*oi*l	ə	*e*v*er*
s	*s*ay	r	*r*un	e	r*e*d	əˑ	b*i*rd
z	*z*one	l	*l*and				

Examples:

Chiswick [tʃizik], Holborn [houbən],
Yeading [jediŋ].

NOTES

(1) The names are arranged topographically according to the Hundreds. Within each Hundred the parishes are dealt with in alphabetical order, and within each parish the names of primary historical or etymological interest are arranged similarly, but in a large number of parishes these are followed by one, or two, or three further groups of names. These groups, so far as they are represented, always appear in the following order: (i) minor names of topographical origin found largely in the second name of persons mentioned in the Subsidy Rolls and similar local documents; (ii) names embodying some family name of Middle English or Early Modern English origin; (iii) minor names of obvious origin, or minor names for which we have only very late forms, about whose history it is unwise to speculate. All three types are represented under Harrow (*infra* 55–6).

Street- and road-names are given in a note immediately following the interpretation of the parish name, e.g. the street-names of Hendon are given in a note at the end of the article on Hendon itself *infra* 56, and similarly the street-names of Acton *infra* 82. The long lists of street-names in most of the metropolitan boroughs are set forth in separate articles at the end of all the names of the borough, e.g. Kensington street-names *infra* 130–2, Shoreditch street-names *infra* 147–8.

(2) Owing to the constant revision alike of the 1-inch and 6-inch Ordnance Survey sheets for this area, necessitated by the continuous urban and suburban developments, no attempt has been made to differentiate those names which are recorded respectively on the 1-inch and 6-inch sheets, and the map used for the most part as the basis of the work is the original 6-inch Ordnance Survey map.

(3) Place-names now no longer current are marked as (lost). This does not necessarily mean that the site to which the name was once applied is unknown. We are dealing primarily with names and the names are lost. These names are printed in italics when referred to elsewhere in the volume.

(4) The local pronunciation of the place-name is given, wherever it is of interest, in phonetic script within square brackets, e.g. Ruislip [rɑislip] (*infra* 46).

(5) In explaining the various place- and field-names summary reference is made to the detailed account of such elements as are found in *The Chief Elements in English Place-names* by printing those elements in Clarendon type, e.g. Ruislip, *v.* **rysc, hlype**. In this volume Clarendon type is used also for reference to those same elements and other additional ones recorded and explained on pp. 195 ff.

(6) In the case of all forms for which reference has been made to unprinted authorities that fact is indicated by printing the reference to the authority in italic instead of ordinary type, e.g. 'c. 1250 *St Pauls*' denotes a form derived from a MS authority in contrast to '1619 LCCDeeds' which denotes one taken from a printed text.

(7) Where two dates are given, e.g. '832 (c. 1250),' the first is the date at which the document purports to have been composed, the second is that of the copy which has come down to us.

(8) Where a letter in an early place-name form is placed within brackets, forms with and without that letter are found, e.g. *Kelleb(o)urn* means that forms *Kellebourn* and *Kelleburn* are alike found.

(9) All OE words are quoted in the West Saxon form unless otherwise stated.

ADDENDA ET CORRIGENDA

For addenda with appended initials we are indebted to

A.C.W.	Mr A. C. Wood.
L.W.H.P.	Mr L. W. H. Payling.
P.H.R.	Dr P. H. Reaney.
S.E.W.	Mr S. E. Winbolt.

VOL. II

The Place-names of Buckinghamshire

p. 194, under Stokenchurch. Add 'GURDON'S FM is to be associated with the family of Adam and Ralph *Gurdoun* (1319, 1323 *MertonRec*).'

VOL. III

The Place-names of Bedfordshire and Huntingdonshire

p. 214, *s.n.* BROADALL'S DISTRICT. Add '*j lake apud Brodholis* 1417 *Ct*, *v.* holh.' This makes it clear that the form in *-wall* is simply a faulty reconstruction of the final unstressed syllable (P.H.R.).

VOL. V

The Place-names of the North Riding of Yorkshire

p. 66, under KIRKDALE. Add 'HOWKELD MILL is *Hykelde al. Holbek Myll beside Wellbourne* 1545 LP' (A.C.W.).
p. 116, under FYLINGDALES. Add 'THORNEY BROW. Cf. *Thirneye in the parish of Fyleng* 1541 LP, *Thorney* 1545 ib.' (A.C.W.).
p. 252, l. 4. Add 'MOORCOTE is *Morecote* 1537 *MinAcct*' (A.C.W.).
p. 260, foot. Add 'HELM is *Helme* 1537 *MinAcct*' (A.C.W.).
pp. 270–4, under GRINTON add
    'HARKERSIDE is *Herkersyde* 1537 *MinAcct*.
    HAVERDELL is *Haverdale* ib.
    LOW WHITA is *Nether Whyttay* ib.
    SUMMER LODGE is *Somerlidge* ib.'   (A.C.W.)

VOL. VI

The Place-names of Sussex (Part I)

p. 157, under RUDGWICK. Add 'GASKYNS is *Gaskens al. Gastons* 1731 *Deed*, *v.* gærstun, 'paddock' (S.E.W.).
p. 182, *s.n.* WORMINGHURST. Add '*Worminghurste* 1605 *Deed*' (S.E.W.).
p. 227, *s.n.* HAWKSBOURNE. Add '*Auxborne* 1753 *Deed*' (S.E.W.).
p. 229, *s.n.* LANGHURST. Add '*Langherst, Langhurst* 1542 LP' (A.C.W.).

VOL. VII

The Place-names of Sussex (Part II)

p. 330, *s.n.* BROOKLAND. Add '*Broklandes* 1544 LP' (A.C.W.).
p. 381, *s.n.* MAYFIELD. Add '*Maighfold* 1588 *Writ*' (S.E.W.).
p. 531, under PEASMARSH, add 'HAZEL GROVE is *Haselgrove* 1547 LP' (A.C.W.).

VOL. VIII

The Place-names of Devon (Part I)

p. 88, *s.n.* Moreton. Add '*Moore al. Moore Town* 1544 LP' (A.C.W.).

p. 300, under Diptford. Add 'Thorn Fm is *Thorne in Dipford* 1507 Ipm' (A.C.W.).

VOL. IX

The Place-names of Devon (Part II)

p. 524, under Wolborough. Add 'Hennaborough, cf. *Henbury Woode in Wolborough* 1545 LP' (A.C.W.).

p. 636, *s.n.* Bruckland. This is Higher Bruckland. Lower Bruckland is in Musbury and is recorded as '*Brokeland in Musbury* 1545 LP' (A.C.W.).

p. 647, *s.n.* Bucehayes. The Rev. F. C. Butters calls our attention to the fact that the forms identified with this would better fit Broadhayes in this parish. Broadhayes is still one of the chief houses in Stockland and it often appears in the Church Registers and on the Tithe Map as *Bo(a)rdhayes*.

VOL. XII

The Place-names of Essex

p. 26, *s.n.* Warleys. Add '*Osbert de Warle* 1371 FF.'

p. 37, *s.n.* Perry Spring. Add '*Perryfeld* 1431 EAS xxii.'

p. 38, *s.n.* Roffey. Add '...*del Roughey* 1287 EAS xxii (p), *Rookheagh* 1383 ib.'

p. 61, n. 1. Add '*Deweshall or Daweshall* 1507 Ipm' (A.C.W.).

p. 139, *s.n.* Wealdside. Add '*Welside* 1553 Pat.'

p. 141, *s.n.* Summers Hill. Add '*Somers in Botyllesden* 1507 Ipm' (A.C.W.)

p. 156, *s.n.* Gt and Little Ilfords. Add '*Great Ilford Marsh* 1722 DKR xli.'

p. 171, *s.n.* Hassenbrook. Add '*Harsynbroke* 1436 Cl.'

p. 226, *s.n.* Ray Wick. Add '*Raywick (Farm)* 1705 DKR xli.'

p. 229, *s.n.* Morris Fm. Add '*Mareyses* 1435 Cl.'

p. 262, under Bacons. Add '*Bacons* 1508 Ipm' (A.C.W.).

p. 298, *s.n.* Scarlett's Fm. Add '*Scarlettes* 1509 Ipm' (A.C.W.).

p. 308, *s.v.* beorg. Burrow Hill should be transferred *s.v.* burh.

p. 318, under Layer Breton. Add 'Phips is *Peppes in Layer Breton* 1542 LP' (A.C.W.).

p. 322, *s.n.* Butler's Fm. Add '*Buttelers* 1536 LP' (A.C.W.).

p. 327, under Ardleigh add 'Brickhouse Fm is *The Brickhouse* 1722 DKR xli.'

p. 352, *s.n.* Thorpe-le-Soken. Add '*Thorpe Sancti Pauli* 1254 EAS xviii.'

p. 379, *s.n.* Roverstye Fm. Add 'This is probably to be associated with the farm of John *Thrower* (1360 Ct).'

p. 411, under Belchamp St Paul's add 'Claredowns Fm, Paul's Hall and Woodbarns Fm (6″) are *Claredowns, Paul's Hall Fm* and *Woodbarnes* 1720 DKR xli.'

p. 411, *s.n.* Colne Green. Add 'Cf. *Colecroft* ib.'

p. 415, *s.n.* Willoughby's Fm. Add 'It is *Willoughbys* 1726 DKR xli.'

p. 535, *s.n.* Strethall Field. Add '*Stratehalefeld* 1483 Rental, *Stretillfeilde* 1529 Ct. The second element is clearly healh.'

p. 540, *s.n.* St Aylotts. Add '*Seynt El(l)ottes* 1556 Pat.'

p. 544, *s.n.* Wendon Lofts. Add '*Upwenden* 1254 EAS xviii.'

VOL. XIV

THE PLACE-NAMES OF THE EAST RIDING OF YORKSHIRE AND YORK

p. 28, *s.n.* FOOTHEAD GARTH. Add '*Westhorn(e) al. Fothatgarth* 1543 LP, *al. Fothetgar* 1544 ib.' (A.C.W.).

p. 65, NOTE. Under EAST, SOUTH, WEST GATE add '*Est-, South-, Westgate* 1540 *MinAcct*' and under NEWBEGIN add '*Newbyggynge* ib.' Also add 'FOOTBALL GREEN is *Foteball Grene* ib.' (A.C.W.).

p. 216, NOTE. Add 'BARROW LANE is *Barowelane* 1536 *MinAcct*' and *s.n.* PRESTONGATE add '*Prestongate* ib.' (A.C.W.).

VOL. XV

THE PLACE-NAMES OF HERTFORDSHIRE

p. 269, under Harpenden, *s.n.* NEW ZEALAND. Sir John Russell tells us that New Zealand, field and name alike, are only some 60 years old. When the land was re-distributed at that time, the owner, Sir John Lawes, left it to the men to find a name for it. One of their number was about to migrate to New Zealand, which in those days was rather a notable thing to be doing, and in celebration of the event the men decided to call this small area New Zealand.

VOL. XVI

THE PLACE-NAMES OF WILTSHIRE

p. 279, *s.n.* QUIDHAMPTON. The forms dated 1196 P, 1242 Fees (both) and 1325 Ipm refer to Quidhampton in Bemerton (PN W 226) (A.C.W.).

p. 354, l. 4, *s.n.* BRICK HILL COPSE. For *infra* read *supra*.

VOL. XVII

THE PLACE-NAMES OF NOTTINGHAMSHIRE

p. 16, *s.n.* FINKHILL ST. Cf. also Finkle St in Benington (L) and *Finkell Lane* 1707 (lost) in Swineshead (L) (L.W.H.P.).

p. 25, *s.n.* BOLE. Mr F. Williamson notes for us a further parallel in the lost *Bolun* in the Derbyshire DB.

p. 85, *s.nn.* DEADMAN'S GRAVE and LADY'S GROVE. Add '*Deadmangrythe Copy, Ladygrthe in Langwithis* 1540 *MinAcct*' (A.C.W.).

p. 95, *s.n.* INKERSALL FM. Mr F. Williamson suggests that the curious form *Inkersall* may have been influenced by Inkersall (Db) some 12 miles away.

p. 109, *s.n.* STEETLEY. Mr F. Williamson notes that Steetley itself is in Derbyshire. It is only Steetley Wood that is in Nottinghamshire.

p. 139, *s.n.* BAGTHORPE. Add '*Bagthorp, Bagthorpe feld* 1538 *MinAcct*' (A.C.W.).

p. 223, *s.n.* CAR COLSTON. Add '[*vulgo* kousən]' (L.W.H.P.).

p. 228, *s.n.* ORSTON SPA. The old [spɔ·] pronunciation is still used locally (L.W.H.P.).

p. 228, *s.n.* SCARRINGTON. Add '[*vulgo* skæritn]' (L.W.H.P.).

p. 229, *s.n.* LUNNON. This is not a farm but the site of a hamlet where about ten families lived as recently as twenty years ago. The cottages were mud and thatch and the place was often jocularly referred to as 'Little London.' As the cottages fell empty they were condemned and became ruinous (L.W.H.P.).

p. 230, *s.n.* WHATTON BRIDGE. The name is now used for the bridge carrying the main Nottingham-Grantham road over the New Smite. The old wooden bridge, which is still called 'The Long Bridge,' carries the footpath from Aslockton to Whatton over the Old Smite. It is a long wooden structure built to carry the path well over the area likely to be flooded before the cutting of the New Smite in 1881. *longum pontem* is descriptive of this bridge (L.W.H.P.)

p. 252, *s.n.* KINGSTON ON SOAR. Mr F. Williamson calls attention to the gypsum quarries close at hand in which finely figured alabaster is sometimes found. The *cynestan* may possibly have been a stone from these quarries.

MAP OF NOTTINGHAMSHIRE. In the south-west corner for 'R. Dove' read 'R. Derwent.'

VOL. XVIII

THE PLACE-NAMES OF MIDDLESEX

p. xxii. Add 'Map. This reference may simply indicate a map of London at the date given; but it may be one of a special area, usually reproduced by the London Topographical Soc. or by Clinch, e.g. 1708 (the Cavendish-Harley estate, Marylebone); c. 1710 (West London, Ln. Topographical Soc. publication lvi); 1795 (the Duke of Bedford's estates, ib. lxvi). Parish maps are often cited under the name of the book in which they are reproduced, e.g. 1745 ShoreSurv denotes Chassereau's map of Shoreditch (also, larger, in Ellis); 1820 FaulknerKe, a parish map prefixed to that work.'

p. xxvi, *s.v.* Survey. Expand to '*Manorial Surveys* cited by their dates, as follows:—1544: FaulknerCh, 312. 1540, 1550: RobinsonH i, 314, 325. 1567: Strype, Bk iv, 101 (Finsbury). 1611: Nelson, 134 (Newington Barrow). 1652: RobinsonH i, 409. 1794: T. Smith, 44.'

p. 18. STADBURY should be under Sunbury parish.

p. 28, *s.n.* SYON HO. Professor Bruce Dickins notes the reference (*in*) *monasterio Syon quem vulgus vocat Scheene* (c. 1440) in T. Gascoigne's *Loci e Libro veritatum* (ed. Thorold Rogers) 170, an early example of confusion between the monastery of Syon and that of Sheen (Sr) to which Aungier (*History and Antiquities of Syon Monastery* 21) calls attention. Dickins also notes the reference (c. 1440) in Audelay's *Poems* (EETS (OS) 184) in the poem addressed to St Briggita to *Bregitsion*.

p. 50, n. 1. After this note was placed under Edgware the bounds of *Loðereslege* were worked out more fully and it is clear that it should have been placed under Hendon (cf. *infra* 220) rather than under Edgware.

p. 69, *s.n.* WEIR HALL. Wainhall in Chinnor (O) has early forms *Winehel(l)e* 1086 DB, *Wylehale* 1198 FF, *Wirhale, Wilehal'* 1207–8 Cur, *Wylenhale* 1303 AD vi, and if the name Weir Hall is of manorial origin, this might possibly be the home of the family of Richard de *Wylehale*.

p. 78, under South Mimms, add 'KITTS END is *Kykesend* 1523 Brittain, *Kyckes ende* 1545, 1569 FF, *Kitts or Kicks End* 1771 Dury, *Kicks End* 1801 EnclA.'

p. 84, under Bethnal Green street-names. Add 'CYGNET ST (1890 LCCN) was earlier *Swan Street* 1746 R.'

p. 93, NOTE. Before 'the extra parochial' add 'and the part of St Sepulchre's outside the City,' and after 'Glasshouse Yard' add 'ecclesiastically in the parish of St Botolph Aldersgate.'

p. 95, footnote. Add 'In that area Fogwell Court PC 180 (later Foxwell Ct 1746 R) survived in the 18th century.'

p. 102, *s.n.* COUNTERS BRIDGE. According to Bridges (186) it is sometimes called *Compton Bridge* from Bishop Compton (1632–1713) who, as lord of the manor of Fulham, probably rebuilt it.

p. 108, under Hackney street-names. Add 'LODDIGES RD. Cf. *Loddige's Nursery* 1827 G.'

p. 111, under Hampstead street-names. Add 'ETON AVENUE, FELLOWS RD, KING'S COLLEGE RD, KING HENRY'S RD and OPPIDANS RD are all on an estate belonging to Eton College, founded, with King's College, Cambridge, by Henry VI.'

p. 125, *s.n.* CANONBURY. For 'granted...Dugdale vi, 297' read 'given land in Islington before 1253 (RecStBarts i, 341–2, 485) by Ralph de Berners. The priory had two benefactors of that name and the donor may have been the one who lived t. Hy 2, not the one who died in 1297.'

p. 127, *s.n.* NEW NORTH RD. Read '1823 Map (S. and B. Percy, *History of London*) was constructed c. 1820 under an act of 1812 (Lewis 404).' It had not been begun by 1817 (Wilkinson).

p. 147, n. 2. Add 'It survived as the name of a building, *Wenlocks Barn*, till 1817 (Wilkinson).'

p. 150, last line. Add 'It became known as *Mile End Old Town* c. 1691 when the name *Mile End New Town* was given to another hamlet further west, adjoining Spitalfields (StepneyMem xi). This is an early instance of the use of 'town' to denote a newly built-up area. Cf. *infra* 135, 143.'

p. 156, *s.n.* GREAT HERMITAGE ST. Add 'This is mentioned in the 14th century (Hust ii, 147, 228), cf. plan of the area c. 1590 (LnTopog. Soc. Publication 61).'

p. 161, *s.n.* BRONDESBURY. The alternative name *Bromeswode* in the 1346 entry seems to be due to confusion with another St Paul's manor, viz. *Brownswood* (*infra* 122).

p. 175, l. 10, *s.n.* ARNE ST. The new name commemorates T. A. Arne (1710–78), the musical composer, who is buried in St Paul's, Covent Garden (LCCN).

p. 181, l. 2 from bottom, *s.n.* PIMLICO RD. Add '*Rombelowe* was originally a meaningless refrain to a sea-chanty and came to be used as a comic place-name, *v.* NED (*s.v. rumbelow*) which quotes *londe of Rombelowe* (1530 *Hick Scorner*) and *Rumbelo fayr* (1549 *Complaynt of Scotland*).'

MIDDLESEX

provincia quae nuncupatur *Middelseaxan* 704 (8th) BCS 111,
(*in*) *Middil Saexum* 767 ib. 201, *provincia Middelsaxanorum*
831 ib. 400, (*on*) *middel Seaxan* 962 ib. 1097, *Middel-*
Seaxum c. 1000 Asser, *Middelseaxe* c. 1150 (ASC (E) *s.a.*
1011)

Middelsexe c. 1050 (ASC (C) *s.a.* 1011), *Middelsex* 1072–6
StPaulsCh, *Midelsexe* 1086 DB, *provincia Midelsexorum* 757
(12th) BCS 182, (*in*) *Middelsexan* 959 (c. 1200) BCS 1050,
(*on*) *Middel Sexum* t. Edw Conf (c. 1200) KCD 855

For the significance of the name 'Middle Saxons' *v.* Introd.
xiii.

RIVERS AND STREAMS

Ash, R. (Thames, near Sunbury) is *little river Ash* 1738 Cox and
Hall. It is a back-formation from Ashford *infra* 11. Walford
(i, 177) speaks of it as a "small river called the Exe," clearly
another back-formation from some of the earlier forms of that
name. The earlier name *eclesbroc* is discussed under that name.
The place where the stream joins the Thames is called *Bourne-*
mouthe in a *Rental* of t. Ric 2. *v.* burna, muþa and cf. Bourne-
mouth (Ha). It is also referred to as *Charleton brooke* (1657
LCCDeeds) from Charlton *infra* 22.

Brent, R. (Thames, at Brentford)

(*innan, of*) *brægentan* 972–8 BCS 1290, *Bræingte, Brægente*
951–9 (13th) ib. 1351

Brainte, -y- 1203 FF, 1343, 1398 Works, (*le*) 1363 AD vi,
1599 *Recov*

Breynte 1274, 1294 *Ass*, 1381 Works, 1382 *Cor*, 1384 FF

Brent(e) 1274 *Ass*, 1545 *Ct*, *Brempte, Brembre* 1274 *Ass*

water of Braynte 1556 FF, *Brentbrooke* 1593 *All Souls*

This river-name goes back to OBrit *Brigantiā* (cf. Ekwall RN
s.n.). The meaning is probably either 'holy' or 'high' river.
As the Brent flows mostly through low country, the former is
more likely.

COLNE, R. (Thames, at Staines). Forms from Middlesex documents include *Collee* 1301 Works, 1478 BM, *Colne* 1351 Cl, *Colneystreme* 1433 Pat, *water of Colony* 1512 FF, *Cole* 1577, 1586 H, *aqua de Colney* 1620 Recov. For earlier and further forms *v.* PN Herts 2. For a discussion of the possible etymology *v.* RN 87. The forms *Collee, Colney* show addition of OE ea, ME *e(e)*, 'stream.' Between Uxbridge and Staines the Colne divides into many branches. *Quethelake* (sic) 1326 StPaulsMSS, *Smalbrok* 1483 Ct, *Swift Lake* 1636 Redford (Harmondsworth, Hillingdon and Uxbridge contexts) may refer to some of these, *v.* lacu, 'stream,' broc. *Quethelake* is probably an error of transcription for *Quechelake* from ME *queche*, 'thicket.' Cf. PN Herts 258.

COUNTERS CREEK (Thames, at Chelsea) is so named in 1826 (Bridges). The stream rises near the present Willesden Junction and enters the Thames at Chelsea Creek. It was earlier known as *Billingwell Dyche* 1437 Ct. Cf. also *Billyngwell* 1377 Works, *Byll-* 1410 Ct, *Billinges-* 1554 ib. 'Billing's spring or stream,' *v.* wielle. An alternative name may have been *Shyrredyche* 1490 Ct, the stream dividing Fulham from Chelsea and Kensington, *v.* scir and cf. Sherrick Green *infra* 163. For *counters*, *v.* Counters Bridge *infra* 102.

CRANE or YEADING BROOK (Thames, at Isleworth)

Fiscesburna 704 (8th) BCS 111, 793 ib. 265, *Fissesburnan*, *Ficesburne* (sic) 757 (12th) ib. 182, 265, *Fisseburn'* 1275 RH, *Fyssheburn* 1305 Pat
le Borne 1375 Cl, 1553 Pat
Cran Brook 1825 Bridges

At first 'fish's stream,' later simply 'stream' (*v.* burna). For the genitival compound *fiscesburna* see a full discussion in Tengstrand lxii, lxiii. *fisc* is probably collective and Tengstrand notes other examples in Surrey, Hampshire, Berkshire and Worcestershire contexts (BCS 955, 624 and 802, 1320). The modern Crane is a late back-formation from Cranford (*infra* 32). The upper part of the stream is Yeading Brook, a new formation from Yeading *infra* 40. Cf. Fishbourne (PN Sx 58), Fish Lake (PN D 6).

DEANS BROOK (Silk, near Edgware) is referred to as (*on, andlang*) *yburnan* in a charter of 972–8 (BCS 1290), *v. infra* 220, a name preserved in the 16th century as *Heybourne* (*land*) (1574 Hendon Surv). The old name may possibly be a compound of OE iw, 'yew' and burna, 'stream,' with early loss of *w* as in Iden and Ifield (PN Sx 318, 530). The present-day name is probably a new formation from Dean's Lane in Hendon *infra* 56.

DOLLIS BROOK (Brent). This is the name given to the upper part of the Brent above its union with Mutton Brook. For the name *v*. Dollis in Hendon *infra* 58. It is formed by the union of two streams near the present Woodside Park Station. In OE times the east and longest branch which rises in Hertfordshire was known as Brent (*supra* 1), while the shorter branch which rises near Highwood Hill was known as (*innan*) *tatan burnan* (972–8 BCS 1290), *v. infra* 219. This is '*Tata*'s stream,' *v*. burna, later spellings being *Tatebourn* 1358 AD iii, *Tadbourn*(e) 1546 Barratt's *History of Totteridge*, *Tadbourne* 1574 HendonSurv. The same man probably gave name to Totteridge (Herts), see more fully PN Herts 149–50.

EDGWARE BROOK (Silk) is referred to as (*æfter*) *stan burnan* in 972–8 BCS 1290 (*v. infra* 220). 'Stony stream,' *v*. stan, burna. Note Stanmore near by. A later name is perhaps found in *Melcheburnfeld* 1277 *Rental*. This would seem to be another example of the stream-name found in Melchbourne (PN BedsHu 16), of uncertain etymology, which Ekwall (DEPN) interprets as containing ME *mielch*, *milch*, 'giving good milk,' from the pasturage in the neighbourhood.

FLEAM DITCH (lost) is *le Flemdyche* 1441 *MinAcct*, *le Fleame ditche* 1619 *Ct*, *brooke called the fleame ditch* 1686 *DuLa*, all three references coming from Enfield parish. This must have been the name of one of the watercourses of the Lea, forming the boundary between Essex and Middlesex. So similarly the unidentified *Flemdyche* (PN Herts 253) in the parishes of Amwell, Hoddesdon and Stanstead probably refers to the Lea where it divides Hertfordshire from Essex. The name is possibly identical in origin with Fleam Dyke (C), *v*. EHN i, 100, from OE *flēmena dīc*, 'dike or ditch of the refugees, fugitives.' Cf. similarly the

history of Flimwell (PN Sx 452) on the borders of Kent and
Sussex. The alternative possibility must not however be lost
sight of, viz. that we have here ME *fleme*, ModEng dialectal
fleam, 'mill stream.'

FLEET, R. (Thames, at Blackfriars) is *Fleta* 1110–13 StPaulsCh,
c. 1130 Guildhall, (*super*) *flietam* 1159 Templars, *aque de Flete*
1199 ChR, *Flete* c. 1200 *Clerkenwell*, 13th AD iv, 1253 Pat,
watercourse of Flete 1307 ib., *le Flit* 1562 Aliens. This is OE
fleot, here no doubt used in the sense of 'creek, inlet' or the
like. The name was given originally to the short navigable part
of the Holborn, but extended later until it was often used, as
now, for the whole course of the stream, cf. Pinks 375. It gave
name to Fleet St in the City.

HOLBORN, R. (Thames) is (*on*) *Holeburne*, *-a* 959 (13th) BCS
1351, 1094–7, 1169 StPaulsCh, *Oldborne* 1603 Stow. 'Stream
in the hollow,' *v.* holh, burna. The depression is still indicated
in part by the course of the present Farringdon Road. The
stretch between Holborn and St Pancras was known to Stow
(i, 13) as *Turnmill* (or *Tremill*) Brook. *v.* Turnmill St. *infra* 99.
The lower part of the stream was known as Fleet *supra*.

LEA, R. (Thames, at Bow). Forms from Middlesex documents
include (*on*) *lig(e)an* c. 880 BCS 856–7, *la Luye* c. 1200
RecStBarts, *aqua de Luye* 1274 Ass, *la Luwe* 1289 AD ii, (*iuxta*)
Luyam 13th AD v, *la Leye*, *aqua de Lye* 1345 Works, *water called
la Leye* 1427 AD vi. For a full list of forms *v.* Ekwall RN *s.n.*
He derives the name from a Celtic root *lug-* meaning 'bright'
or alternatively from *Lugus*, a god, 'river dedicated to *Lugus.*'
Melflet (1256 AD ii) seems to have been the name of one of the
channels of the Lea at Edmonton. This name is probably a
compound of 'mill' (*v.* myln) and fleot (*v.* Fleet *supra*). Note
also *Barbeflete* (1306 RecStBarts) in Enfield, probably the old
name of another channel. In 1593 (N) and 1680 (S) it is called
Mereditch, i.e. boundary ditch, seeing that it separates Essex
and Middlesex, *v.* (ge)mære.

MOSELLE, R. (Lea, at Tottenham) is *The Moselle* 1600
RobinsonT, *Moselle River* 1825 Bridges, no doubt a late back-
formation from the colloquial forms of Muswell Hill *infra* 123.
An old name may have been *Campsborne* 1608 HornseyCt,

cf. earlier *Campisborne closse* 1495 HornseyRec. This survives in Campsbourne Rd (near the Moselle), *infra* 122.

MUTTON BROOK (Brent, at Hendon) is *Mordins Brooke* 1574 HendonSurv, *Mutton Brook* 1819 G. In an OE charter of 957 (BCS 994) the stream is referred to as (*innan*) *fihte burnan*. The origin of the present name is uncertain, but it is probably a corruption of the 16th-century form. In that document we have mention also of *Mordins pyghtell* (*v.* pightel), suggesting that *Mordin* may have been a man's name.

NEW RIVER is *flumen vocatum the newe River* 1625 Sess. This was an artificial watercourse constructed by Sir Hugh Myddelton in 1609–13 to bring water from springs near Amwell (Herts) to London. See further PN Herts 4. It was also known in part of its course as (*The*) *Boarded River* 1724 Moll, 1741–5 R.

PINN, R. (Colne, at Cowley) is referred to as *Pinner Brook* (1825 Bridges) and is no doubt a very late back-formation from Pinner *infra* 63. In 1206 (FF) it would seem to be referred to as the *burn of Ikeham* (cf. Ickenham *infra* 43). Another early name was possibly *Fullerith* 1434 HarlCh, the second element of this name being riþ, 'stream.' It is *le Broke* 1446 MxRec.

THE POOL (part of the Thames below London Bridge) is referred to as *la Pole in aqua Tamisie juxta Turrim London'* 1258 Cl, 1320 *Ass*, i.e. by the Tower.

PYMMES BROOK (Lea, at Edmonton) is earlier *Medeseye* c. 1200 *Clerkenwell*, (water called) *Medesing*(*g*)*e* 13th AD i, ii, 1250 ib. ii, *Medesange* 1257 ib., 1261 ib. i, *Medesenge* 1274 *Ass*, 13th AD ii, *Medishinga* 1303 StPaulsMSS. Ekwall (RN 284) derives this name from OE mæd, 'meadow,' and an element **sǣging*, related to OE *sīgan*, 'to drip, move, fall.' The whole name would mean 'slow-moving meadow stream.' The form from the Clerkenwell Cartulary (not known to Ekwall) suggests an alternative OE form **sǣge*, found perhaps in Seabrook (PN Bk 98). The present name derives from the family of Reginald *Pymme* of *Edelmetone* (Edmonton) (1303 LBk and other 14th-century records relating to that parish). His property is spoken of as *Pymmes land* in 1293 (AD iv). According to LG (24) it is John Gilpin's 'Wash of Edmonton so gay.'

SALMONS BROOK (Lea, at Edmonton) is so named in 1754 (R) and is perhaps to be associated with the family of John *Salemon* of Edmonton (1274 *Ass*).

SILK STREAM (Brent, at Hendon)

> *sulh, sulc, (æfter) suluc* 957 (13th) BCS 994, (*on, of*) *sulh* 972–8 ib. 1290
> *water called Solke* 13th AD i, *water called Selke* 13th ib. ii
> *Silke Bridge* 1622 Sess

This would seem to be the OE *sulh*, used topographically in the sense 'furrow, narrow gully,' etc. Cf. RN *s.n.* and Souldrop (PN BedsHu 42). *Sulkschot* (1321 *WAM*) was a piece of land by this stream, *v.* sceat.

STAMFORD BROOK (Thames, by Chiswick Eyot) is *Stamford Brooke* 1650 Feret, *Stanford Brook* 1741–5 R, 1819 G. Near by may have lived Walter de *Staunford* (1274 *Ass*). This was the old name for the stream which divided near its mouth the parishes of Acton and Chiswick and further north was spanned by Bollo Bridge, *v. infra* 82. It probably took its name from a 'stony ford' here (*v.* stan, ford), where the main Great West Road crossed the stream.

THAMES, R. Forms from Middlesex documents include *flumine Tamisie* 704 (8th) BCS 111, (*of*) *temese* 959 (13th) ib. 1048, *aqua de Tamis* 1235 *Ass*, *aqua Tamisie* 1274 ib., *aqua de Tamys* 1294 ib. For a full list of early spellings *v.* Ekwall (RN *s.n.*). The meaning is perhaps 'dark river.'

TYBURN (Thames, at Westminster)

> (*andlang*) *teoburnan*[1] 959 BCS 1048, *teoburnan* (13th) ib. 1351, (*into*) *theoburnan*, (*anglang*) (sic) *teoburnan* 979–1016 (14th) Crispin
> *Tyburn'* t. Hy 3 *WDB, Tybornewater* 1397 Works
> *Maribone broke* c. 1540 L, *Mariburne rill* 1586 H

This stream rose at Hampstead, flowed through Marylebone and, after crossing Oxford Street, divided the manor of Ebury (*infra* 167) from the rest of Westminster. Its mouth, afterwards the King's Scholars' Pond Sewer, is referred to as (*andlang*)

---

[1] This is the correct form (cf. Crispin 170) and not -*bernan* as in BCS 1048.

merfleotes, (*on*) *merfleote*, the estuary forming a boundary (*v.* Fleet *supra* 4 and (ge)mære) in the perambulation of Westminster in BCS 1048 (*v. infra* 222), when it formed part of the boundary of the Abbey lands.

The name has been fully discussed by Ekwall (RN 424) where it is explained as 'boundary stream,' a derivative of a lost OE *tēo* denoting a boundary, cognate with OFris *tia*, 'boundary (line).' Cf. also Teffont (PN W 193) for further details. For *Mariburne*, *v.* Marylebone *infra* 137. In 1491 (LBk) it is spoken of as *a gretebroke of water called Aybrooke*, *v.* eg and Hay Hill Fm *infra* 168.

WALBROOK (Thames, at Dowgate)

> *Walebroc* 1114–30 RamseyChron, 1193 P, c. 1200 StPaulsCh, 1261 BM, 1285 AD i, 1291 Tax, *bridge of Walebrok* 1291 LBk, *ditch called Walebroke* 1310 Hust
> *Wallebroch* 1193 P, *Wallebroke* 1282 LBk
> *Walbroc, -k* 13th, 14th StPaulsMSS, *ditch called Walbrookdyk* 1410 Hust, *bank of Walbroke* 1516 Ipm

This name, preserved in the street-name Walbrook in the City, probably goes back to OE *wēala brōc*, 'brook of the serfs or Britons,' *v.* wealh, broc. The rarity of spellings with a double consonant and the persistent medial *e* of the earliest forms are against connecting the first element with OE *weall*, 'wall.' Further, 'wall-brook' might suit a stream which ran by a town wall, but it would not be particularly apt for a stream which chanced at one point in its course to pass through the town wall. Professor Bruce Dickins notes the early attempt at interpretation in the Cambridge MS of Geoffrey of Monmouth (ed. Griscom, 212) '*super torrentem infra urbem qui postea de nomine ducit* (i.e. Livius Gallus) *britannice nautgallus, Saxonice uero galabroc nuncupatus fuit*.' Cf. Walla Brook (PN D 16).

WEALDSTONE BROOK[1] (Brent, near Wembley) is *le Weldebroke*

1453 MxRec, *Weyldbrooke* 1548 ib. The present form is a late formation from Wealdstone in Harrow *infra* 54. The old name was *liddinge*,... *torrentis lidding* 767 (12th) BCS 201, *Lyddynges water*, *water called Lyddyng* 1401 Cl, of uncertain etymology

---

[1] Sometimes known as Kenton Brook (cf. Kenton *infra* 53).

(cf. Ekwall RN *s.n.*). An alternative name for the upper part of the stream seems to have been *Gaderbroke, -brook* 1445, 1486 HarrowRec.

WESTBOURNE BROOK (Thames, at Chelsea). This stream rose on Hampstead Hill and flowed through Paddington to Hyde Park and thence to the Thames. (It is conveyed in a tube across the platforms at Sloane Square Station.) Near its source the stream is referred to as (*to*) *mærburnan* in the bounds of Hampstead (BCS 1351 *infra* 222), *v.* (ge)mære, burna. An alternative name for the upper part was probably Kilburn (*v. infra* 112). There seems to have been no special name for the lower part in medieval times. It is called *aquam de Knythebrugg'* in 1302 (*WDB*), *v.* Knightsbridge *infra* 169. In late times the stream was generally referred to as Bayswater Rivulet (*v. infra* 132). Cf. *the Rivulet* 1690 FaulknerCh, *Base Water Brook* 1717 LCCDeeds, *rivulet called Bayswater* 1808 ib. The present-day name, which does not appear until the 19th century, is a late formation from Westbourne in Paddington *infra* 133, the name of a place 'west of the stream' rather than a stream-name itself.

Except at its source the stream now runs entirely underground, apart from the stretch where it has been artificially dammed and widened to form the *Serpentine River* 1746 R. It was made c. 1730 (Lysons) and is so called from its winding course.

ROAD AND MISCELLANEOUS NAMES

ERMINE STREET. We have one reference to this street by its original name in an Edmonton document, where it is called *Erningestrate* 13th AD iv. For the history of this name *v.* PN Herts 6. It takes its name from the *Earningas* who also gave name to Armingford Hundred (C), through which Ermine Street passes. It is referred to as *via regia* 1228 RecStBarts (Enfield), *regia via in villa de Totenham* 1294 *Ass, Stonistrate* 13th AD ii (Edmonton), *the highway from Shordych to Ware* 1467 ib. vi, *The North Road* 1682 Morgan, and at the present day successive stretches are known as Bishopsgate, Norton Folgate, Shoreditch High St, Kingsland Rd, High St Stoke Newington, Stamford

Hill (*v. infra* 107), High Rd Tottenham, Fore St Edmonton (*infra* 68), Enfield High Way (*infra* 73), Hertford Rd.

WATLING STREET. Forms from Middlesex documents include (*on*) *wætlingan stræte*, (*of*) *wætlinga stræte* 957 (13th) BCS 994, (*on*) *wæclinga stræt* 972 ib. 1290, (*to*) *wætlinga stræte* 978 (18th) ib. 1309, *Wallinghestret* (sic) 1145 StPaulsCh, *highway called Watlyng street* 1548 Robins (Paddington context). It is referred to as *Oldestrete* in 1383 Works (Willesden context). The name means 'street of the *Wæclingas*,' the name of the people who gave name to *Wæclingacæstir*, i.e. St Albans, and the street was so called because it led thither. See more fully PN Herts 7, 86. The OE references given above relate to the road still commonly called Watling Street which starts at the Marble Arch and is now known in its early course as Edgware Rd, Maida Vale, Kilburn High Rd (cf. *Kylborne Streate* 1535 VE), Cricklewood Broadway, etc. In Kingsbury documents belonging to All Souls College it is called *Edgware high waie* (1574) and *London waie* (1632). In addition to these references there is an interesting reference in Ethelred's charter to Westminster Abbey (Crispin 168) to what is clearly the present Oxford St. It has been suggested that this name for Oxford St links up with Watling St in the City (cf. LnTopRec viii, 3), but the relation of the two streets bearing this name is entirely obscure. Watling St in the City is first called *Watlingstrate* in 1307 (Husting), but it is earlier known as *Athelyngstrate* in 1272 (ib.), *Athelingstrete* (1303 AD ii). See further Appendix iii.

MISCELLANEOUS ROADS

The Roman road running east from Aldgate to Colchester was clearly recognised as a stræt since the place where it crossed the Lea was known as Stratford (*v.* Bow *infra* 134). References to the medieval road include (*in*) *regalem viam extra Alegate* 1276 RH, *via regia de Stratford* 1345 Works, *The King's Way leading from Mile End to Stratford* 1549 RobinsonH, *Whitechappell strete* 1568 AD iv, corresponding to the present Aldgate High St, Whitechapel Rd, Mile End Rd, Bow Rd.

The main road corresponding to the Roman road to the west, through Brentford and Staines (Newgate, Holborn, Oxford St, Bayswater Rd, Holland Park Avenue, Uxbridge Rd, etc.) is called (*to*) *þære wide here stræt*, 'the wide army road,' in Edgar's charter to Westminster Abbey and *watlinga stræt* in Ethelred's charter (Crispin 168). Watling Street itself branched off from it at the foot of Edgware Rd (*v. supra* 9). Later it is *via regia qui ducit de London versus Tyborne* 13th StGilesSurv, *regiam viam in villa de Tyborne* 1373 Works, *le Higheway* 1571 Ct (Hayes), *Road from Uxbridge* 1794 Horwood, *the great road to Acton* 1652 FaulknerKe, *Uxbridge Way* 1664 ib., *The Road to Oxford* 1682 Morgan, *Tyburne al. Acton Road* 1740 LCCDeeds. See further Oxford St *infra* 138. The spot where it crosses the Pinn river is still known as Stratford Bridge (*v. infra* 42), cf. also *Strateschote* 1380 Cl (in Acton), a piece of ground which perhaps lay by this road. For the application of the name Watling Street to this road, *v.* Appendix iii.

The second main road to the west (Ludgate, Fleet St, Strand, Charing Cross, Haymarket, Piccadilly, Knightsbridge, Kensington Rd and High St, Hammersmith Rd, Chiswick High Rd, etc.) which joined the first at Brentford is *Akemannestræte* in Ethelred's charter. (Crispin 168), presumably so called because it was the recognised road to *Acemannes ceastre* or Bath (cf. PN BedsHu, Addenda xl and Appendix iii). For later names of its eastern sections see the Westminster street-names *infra* 174 ff.; note that the Haymarket as well as Piccadilly are *the waye to Colbroke* 1585 K. Further west it is *regia via de Hundeslaw* 1294 Ass, i.e. Hounslow, *Stanes way* 1438 Cl, *the waye to Colbroke* (i.e. Colnbrook, Bk) 1585 K, *Brentford Great Road* 1652 Faulkner Ke, *The highway from Brainford to London* 1678 Ct. In an Isleworth Court Roll of 1436 we have mention of *Stratfurlonge* (*v.* **furlang** *infra* 198) which was probably by the main Hounslow Road here, and in a Court Roll of Fulham of 1434 we have *le Streteshot* (*v.* sceat *infra* 203) which may have been by the present Hammersmith Rd, then part of Fulham parish.

Most of the other modern main thoroughfares of London and district such as the City Rd, Commercial Rd, Marylebone Rd and Euston Rd, Kings Rd (Chelsea), etc. are of modern construction or replace mere lanes or tracks. They will be noted under the boroughs in which they occur[1].

GRIM'S DITCH (Pinner and Stanmore parishes) is *Grimesdich*, *Grimmesdich* 13th AD i, ii, *Grimesdich* 1289 ib. ii, *Grymesdich* 1541 Druett. This is the remains of an old earthwork, formerly of much greater extent[2]. The same name occurs in Hertfordshire (cf. PN Herts 7–8) and in Wiltshire (PN W 15), where the name has been fully discussed. In 1902 W. H. Stevenson suggested (EHR xvii, 629) and Ekwall has further demonstrated that *Grim* is probably another name for Woden, to whose activities these ancient earthworks were attributed. Cf. such names as Devil's Dyke (PN Sx 287).

I. SPELTHORNE HUNDRED

Spelet(h)orne 1086 DB *et freq* to 1428 FA, *Spelesthorn(e)* 1169 ff. P, *Spellethorn* 1189 ib. 'Speech thorn-tree,' *v.* spel and cf. Spelloe Hundred (PN Nth 131). The site of the meeting-place is not known with certainty but may have been somewhere near Ashford, since in 1819 (G) the road which leads from Ashford to Kempton Park is named *Spelthorne Lane*[3].

Ashford

ASHFORD

Ecelesford 969 (c. 1100) Crawford, *Ecclesforde* 969 (14th) BCS 1264, 1042–66 (13th) *WDB*

---

[1] There seems to have been an ancient way which led from Hertfordshire towards Kingsbury, now represented by Dennis Lane, Honeypot Lane and Slough Lane in Stanmore and Kingsbury (*v. infra* 66, 62). It is referred to in *Eldestretehegge* 1401 Cl (Wembley context), *Eldestrete shote, Elderstretehaw* (sic) 1486 HarrowRec (Preston, Harrow). For a discussion of this ancient way, which passes the site of the meeting-place of Gore Hundred *infra* 49, see LMxAS New Series vii, 218 ff.

[2] *v.* Wheeler, *London and the Saxons*, 62 ff.

[3] Spelthorne Grove is marked on the modern 6″ map on the south side of the road from Ashford to Kempton, just west of Sunbury Common, and Spelthorne Cottage is similarly marked a quarter of a mile south of the same road, but as they do not appear on the old 6″ map (1862–70) they may both be antiquarian revivals.

Echelesford 1042–66 (13th) *WAM*, 1274 *Ass et freq* to 1383
  FF, *Echelford* 1274 *Ass*, 1285 FF, 1535 VE, *Echeleford* 1279
  QW, 1294 *Ass*, 1341 NI, *Echillesford* 1443 FF
(*æt*) *Exforde* 1062 (13th) KCD 812, *Exeforde* 1086 DB,
  Exford 1274 *Ass*, *Exeford* 1293 Ipm, *Exenford* 1294 *Ass*
Eglesford 1445 FF
Assheford 1488, 1517 FF, (*otherwise Echelford*) 1561 ib.,
  Echelford otherwise Assheford 1567 ib., *Echeford* 1563 *Recov*,
  Asheford al. Echeford 1606 PCC
Achilforde 1509 PCC

Ashford lies on the Ash river (*supra* 1), called *eclesbroc* in
the bounds of Sunbury (BCS 1085). On the basis of these forms
Ekwall (RN 141) suggests the possibility of the gen. sg. of a
personal name **Eccel*, a diminutive of the recorded *Ecca* as the
first element, hence '*Eccel*'s **broc**' and 'ford.' He notes there,
however, the occurrence of the element *eccles-* in other OE
stream-names, including *ecclesbroc* (KCD 682) in Worcestershire, and in his treatment of Ecchinswell (Ha) in DEPN he
notes a nearby *Ecclesburna* (BCS 674), Ecclesbourne, R. (Db)
(*Ecclesborne* 1298 Ipm) and an *ecles cumb* (BCS 927) in Somerset,
all of which suggest the possibility of *ec(c)les* as an early stream-
name.

NOTE. CLOCKHOUSE LANE. Cf. *Clockhouse Fm* 1865 O.S. EXEFORD
AVENUE is a modern name reproducing the DB spelling of Ashford.
Similarly ECCLESFIELD HO is a modern name.

FORD FM is *Ashford Ford Farm* 1697 DKR xli and was the home
of John *atte Forde* (1365 *Ct*).

CHATTERN HILL is *Chatern Hill* 1754 R, *Chattern Hill* 1819 G.

HENSGROVE FM. Cf. *Hengrove Pits* c. 1800 EnclA, c. 1840 *TA*
(Stanwell), *Hensgrove* ib. (Staines). The three parishes touch at
this point.

East Bedfont

EAST BEDFONT

Bedefunt, Bedefunde 1086 DB, *-font(e)* 1198 Cur *et passim* to
  1353 FA, with variant spellings *-funte, -founte, Bedesfounte*
  1315 Cl
Bedefons 12th BM

Estbedefont 1235 Fees *et freq* to 1441 FF, with variant
spellings *-funt(e)*, *-fount(e)*, *Bedestfont* (sic) 1235 Fees,
Estbedevonte 1336 Pat, *Bedfont east* 1593 N
Bedfunte 1279 FF, *Bedhunt* 1373 Pat
Chirchebedfounte 1405 FF, *Cherchebedfunte* 1407 ib.
Bedfond 1649 SP, 1754 R, *Belfound* 1806 Lysons

Bedfont is a difficult name. It is found twice elsewhere, (i) in
Bedford Well (PN Sx 427), (ii) in Bedmond (PN Herts 76),
the first element in both cases being in the form *Bede-*. It is
clear that the second element is OE *funta*, 'spring.' In DEPN
the name is interpreted as '*Bēda*'s spring,' but it must be noted
that it would be a strange coincidence if the somewhat rare
word *funta* were thus found compounded on three occasions
with the not very common OE personal name *Bēda*. We ought
perhaps rather to associate the first element with the element
bede (occasionally *bude*, *bide*, *byde*) which is so commonly found
compounded with *wielle* in the ME forms of certain place-
names. The forms for these names will be found under Biddles
Fm (PN Bk 216), Bidwell (PN BedsHu 128, PN D 410, 573,
PN Nth 222), Bedlar's Green and field-names Bedwell's, Beddell,
Beadle (PN Ess 35, 619, 623, 647), Bedwell (PN Herts 138, 224)
and Bedwell *infra* 37. All alike point to an element *byd(e)*
denoting a 'hollow or depression' which is allied to the OE
byden, 'tub, cask,' which is found in a topographical sense
'hollow' or the like in Bidna (PN D 102) and Beedon (Berks)
(cf. DEPN *s.n.*). Note also the history of Bydemill Brook
(PN W 4) and other similar names noted there. The absence in
Bedfont (except for one form for West Bedfont *infra* 21) of
any forms in *u*, *y*, *i* is a little disturbing but OE *y* in Middlesex
appears very commonly as *e* (cf. Introd. xvii). Hence probably
'spring in the hollow.' There is no large hollow here but there
may have been a small depression where the spring was. The
form *Bedhunt* is interesting as another example of the common
development of *funt* to *hunt* discussed under Chadshunt (PN Wa
249–50) and Cheshunt (PN Herts 220). *East* and *Church* to
distinguish from West Bedfont in Stanwell *infra* 21.

NOTE. DOCKWELL LANE. Cf. *Dockwell* c.1840 *TA*, probably 'dock-
grown spring.'

HATTON is *Hatone, Haitone* 1086 DB, *Hatton(e)* 1211 RBE *et freq, (next Bedefunte)* 1293 FF, *Haddo(u)n juxta Huneslowe* 1373 IpmR, *(by Houndeslowe)* 1400 Cl. 'Heath farm,' *v.* hæþ, tun. It lay at the extreme western edge of Hounslow Heath.

FAGG'S BRIDGE, FAWNES[1] and PATES[2] are to be associated with the families of George *Fagg* (1845 White), Alan *Foun* (1317 FF) and John *Pate* (1404 ib.).

Feltham

FELTHAM [feltəm]

> *Feltham* 969 (c. 1100) Crawford, 969 (13th) BCS 1264, 1100–35 (1330) Ch *et passim, Feltam* 1655 ParReg (Hillingdon)
> *Feltehā* 1086 DB, *Feltesham, Fultesham* 1274 *Ass*
> *Feltem* 1668 ParReg (Sunbury), *Felton* 1626 SP, 1675 Ogilby

The name is possibly a compound of feld, 'open space' and ham, with the same unvoicing of final *d* to *t* before *h* as in Up Waltham (PN Sx 77). See further Ekwall in *Studia Neophilologica* i, 97 ff. Neither form can be taken as representing an OE original with any accuracy. Each comes from a charter which is a fabrication of the Norman age. Alternatively, the first element might be a plant-name *felte*, a derivative of OE *felt*, 'felt,' found in certain plant-names and taken by Ekwall (DEPN) to be the first element of Feltwell (Nf).

RAY (lost) is *la Rye* 1257 FF (p), *Reye next Feltham* 1294 ib., *la Reye* 1311 AD iii, *Great, Little Rye* 1631 VCH, *Ray Close* 1801 EnclA. 'At the well watered or marshy land' from ME *atter eye, v.* eg and cf. Rye (PN Sx 536). The place was on the south border of the parish near Felthamhill (VCH 317).

BROOK FM. Cf. *Brokedych* 1369 Cl, *The Broke* 1438 ib. FELTHAMHILL. Cf. *la Hulle* 1369 ib., *Feltham Hill* 1593 N.

Hampton

HAMPTON[3]

> *Hamntone* 1086 DB
> *Hantune* c. 1130, 1163 OxfordCh, *Hantona* 1165, 1184 P

---

[1] *Fawnys* 1531 FF. [2] *Patys* 1550 ib.
[3] In DB Hampton is placed in Isleworth Hundred (*Honeslauu*), but in all subsequent records in Spelthorne. *Hamtonet* (1227 Ch) is referred to this place, but the identification is not certain.

Hamton 1202 Cur, 1223 Pat, 1230 Cl, 1235, 1294 *Ass*
Hampton 1237 Cl *et passim*, (*juxta Kyngeston*) 1293 FF, (*on Thames*) 1343 Pat

'Farm in the **hamm**,' *v.* tun. **hamm** must here have reference to the great bend in the river. Kingston lies just on the other side of the river.

BUSHEY PARK is *Bushie Parke* 1650 *ParlSurv, Bushey Parke* 1667 Sess. The forms are too late to decide whether this is simply a late name, 'bushy park,' or whether it is an old compound of **bysc** and (ge)**hæg**, 'bush-enclosure,' as in Bushey (PN Herts 64).

HAMPTON COURT is *Hampton Courte* 1476 Pat. The name was evidently given to the earlier manor house before the building of Wolsey's palace there.

HAMPTON WICK is *Wica* 13th AD ii, *Hamptone la Wyke* 1263 FF, (*a la Wyke*) 1289 ib., *Wik'* 1274 Ass, *Hamptonwicke* 1615 Sess. *v.* wic, 'dairy farm,' and cf. Hackney Wick *infra* 106.

POOLE'S PLACE is to be associated with the family of Samuel *Pool* (1688 ParReg).

HAMPTON COURT PARK is *The Greate Parke of Hampton* 1563 Sess. ROSEHILL is *Rose Hill* 1819 G. THE WILDERNESS. Cf. *The Lower Wilderness* 1754 R.

Hanworth

HANWORTH

Haneworde 1086 DB *et passim* to 1359 FF, with variant spellings *-wrde, -wurthe, -worth(e), Hanesworth* 1254 Val, 1274, 1294 *Ass*
Hanneworth 1389 BM, 1453 FF
Hanworth 1428 FA

v. worþ. The first element is OE *hana*, 'cock,' here possibly used as a personal name, since worþ is commonly compounded with personal names. Cf. (*on*) *hanan wurðe* 901 BCS 588 (Wilts) and Hanworth (L), DB *Haneworde*.

BUTTS FM may be associated with the family of Jane *Butts* (1789 ParReg) or the name may have referred to archery butts, *v.* **butte**.

HANWORTH PARK is so named in 1593 (N). LOW FM. We may possibly compare *Low Field* 1801 EnclA.

Laleham

LALEHAM

> *Læleham* 1042–66 (13th) *WDB*, *Lælham* 1062 (13th) KCD 812
>
> *Lelehā* 1086 DB, *Lelham* 1134 France, 1205 Cur, 1275 RH
>
> *Lalham* 1207 FF *et passim* to 1467 ib., *Estlalham* 1237 Cl, *Laalham* 1445 *HarlCh*
>
> *Lanham, Estlanham* 1274 *Ass*, *Lanam* 1341 NI
>
> *Laleham* 1274 *Ass*, 1294 FF, (*otherwise Lalam*) 1567 ib.
>
> *Lalleham* 1294 *Ass*, 1328 Fine
>
> *Laleton* 1547 FF

The first element is OE *læl*, 'twig, withe.' Hence 'ham by which, or (more probably) hamm on which "withies" grow.' The place is by the Thames.

GREENFIELD HO. Cf. *Green Field* 1754 R. HIDE (lost) is *Hidland* 1242 Fees, *-lond* 1353 FA, *Hydlaund* 1274 *Ass*, *La Hide of Laleham* 1328 Ch. *v.* hid. LALEHAM PARK is so named in 1819 (G). LYNCH CORNER. Cf. *Linches* 1329 *MinAcct* and *v.* hlinc.

Littleton

LITTLETON

> *Littleton* 1042–66 (13th) *WDB*, 1298, 1310 FF *et passim*
>
> *Litleton, -y-* 1184 P (p), 1235, 1280 FF, 1274 *Ass*, 1291 Tax, *Littil-* 1282 FF, *Litel-, Lytel-* 1336 Pat, *Littelton near Stanys* 1375 Hust, *Lyttelton* 1469 FF
>
> *Lutleton* 1204 FF, 1294 *Ass*
>
> *Litlinton* 1206 Abbr (p), 1242 Fees, *Lytlyn-* 1294 *Ass*, *Littlinton* 1321 FF, *Litlynton juxta Certesey* 1373 Ipm
>
> *Lut(e)lynton* 1274 *Ass*, 1347 FF, *Lutilynton* 1341 ib.
>
> *Lutelington* 1274 *Ass*, *-yng-* 1347 FF, *Luttel-* 1356 ib.
>
> *Littelyngton, Littelingeton* 1274 *Ass*, *Littelyngton* 1350 Ch, *Lytlyngton* 1428 FA, 1445 BM
>
> *Letelyngton* 1341 NI, 1351 Ch
>
> *Littleton al. Litlington* t. Eliz ChancP

The exact interpretation of this apparently simple name is not quite certain. Probably the differing ME forms arise from nom. *lyteltun* or *lytela tun* and dat. *lytelantun*, '(at the) small enclosure or farm,' *v.* tun. *Certesey* is Chertsey (Sr).

ASTLAM[1] [æsləm]

> *Estelham* 1291 FF
> *Hastelham* 1362 FF, *Astelesham* c. 1400 ECP, *Astelham* 1445 HarlCh, *Astlam al. Astleham* 1445 BM, *Astelam* 1517 FF, *Astlam* 1865 O.S.
> *Ashlam* 1650 FF
> *Aslem* c. 1840 TA, *Ayslem* 1850 EnclA

This is a difficult name and no certainty is possible. It may be (as suggested by Dr Reaney) that the first element is the rare word *ætsteall*, found once in an original OE charter of the 11th century (KCD 741) in the phrase *ætstealles beorh* and twice in rather difficult poetic contexts in *Waldhere* and *Guthlac*. The word is rendered 'station, camp' in BT Supplt *s.v.* For a full discussion *v.* Tengstrand 142–7. It is difficult to give any precise interpretation but we may note that the corresponding un-compounded *steall* would seem to be found in Stalham (Nf), *Stalham* 1044–7 (*a.* 1300) KCD 785. *steall*, like *ætsteall*, is one of those words of wide meaning—'place, position'—to which it is difficult to give any precise interpretation. Hence 'ham by the ætsteall.'

LITTLETON GREEN is so named in 1819 (G). THE SLIP is so named c. 1840 (*TA*), *v.* slipe.

Shepperton

SHEPPERTON

> (*in*) *Scepertune* 959 (c. 1100) BCS 1050, 1066 (14th) KCD 824
> (*in*) *Sceapertune* 1042–66 (13th) WDB
> *Scepirton* 1066 (12th) KCD 858, t. Wm 1 (12th) WAM, *Scepirtune* t. Edw Conf (13th) ib.
> *Scepertone* 1086 DB *et passim* to 1393 IpmR, with variant spellings *Shep-, Schep-, Sep-, (Nether)* 1490 FF

[1] Now covered by the new reservoir (1928).

Shiperton 1284 Pat, *Ship(p)ar(d)ton* 1650 *ParlSurv*
Schapertone 1534 LP, *Shup(p)ar(d)ton* 1650 *ParlSurv*

The first element is probably OE *scēaphierde*, 'shepherd,' hence 'shepherd farm' or 'shepherds' farm,' *v.* tun. There is rich pasture here by the Thames.

NOTE. BROADLANDS AVENUE. Cf. *Bradelond* t. Ric 2 *Rental*. GASTON BRIDGE RD. Cf. *le Garstone* ib. and *Gaston Bridge* 1819 G. *v.* gærstun, 'grassy paddock.' GREEN LANE. Cf. *le Greneweye* ib. HIGHFIELDS RD. Cf. *Highfield* c. 1860 O.S. MANYGATES RD. Cf. *Menegate* t. Ric 2 *Rental*, *le Manygate* 1445 *HarlCh*. Perhaps 'common gate,' from OE (ge)mæne. Cf. *le Menemere* 1445 ib.

DOG AIT is *Dockeyte* 1377, *Dokkeyte* 1432 Chertsey, *le Docket* 1605 *LRMB*, *Dog Ayte* c. 1840 *TA*. 'Islet overgrown with dock,' *v.* iggoð.

SHEPPERTON GREEN is so named in 1754 (R). It may be identical with *Upsheperton* 1294 *Ass*, *Uppersheperton* 1517 FF, since it lies away from the river a mile north of Shepperton church.

STADBURY (lost) is *Stadbury* 1302 *WDB*, 1650 *ParlSurv*, 1819 G, c. 1840 *TA*, *Stadebery*, *Staddebury* t. Ric 2 *Rental*, *Stodbury* 1650 *ParlSurv*. In Greenwood's map Stadbury lies by the Thames, so the probabilities are that the name is a compound of stæð and burh, i.e. 'burh by the river-bank.' To what the burh may here refer we do not know. *v.* Addenda xxxiii.

COWEY STAKES is *Cowey Stakes* 1686 M, *Caway Stake* 1777 Andrews. HAMHAUGH POINT. Cf. *Ham farme* and *meadow* 1650 *ParlSurv*, *Hamhawe* 1657 PCC, *v.* hamm. HOE BRIDGE is *Hoebridge*, (*Hoe lane*, *Hoe close*) 1650 *ParlSurv*, *Hoo Bridge* 1800 Faden, *v.* hoh. Now Watersplash Bridge, cf. *infra*. LORD'S BRIDGE is *Lord Bridge* 1754 R. POOL END is so named c. 1840 (*TA*). WATERSPLASH FM. Cf. *Water Splash* 1810 G. There is a small stream here.

Staines

STAINES

Stána 969 (c. 1100) Crawford, *Stana* 969 (13th) BCS 1264, 1066 BM

(*æt*) *Stane* c. 1050 (*s.a.* 1009) ASC (C, D), c. 1150 (E), (*into*) *Stane* 1066 (13th) KCD 855

Stanes 1086 DB *et passim* to 1593 N, *Stanis* 1167 P, *Stanys* 1428 FA

Steynys, Staynys 1535 VE, *Staines* 1578 *FF*

'Stone,' *v.* **stan**. The reference is generally held to be to a Roman milestone near by, Staines being on or near the site of the Romano-British station *Pontes* where the London–Silchester road crossed the Thames. The development of the name is quite irregular. *Stan* should have become *Stone* and the change from singular to plural is also unexplained. For the vowel cf. Stains Fd *infra* 211 and Staine Hundred (C), DB *Stanes*.

NOTE. LEACROFT RD. Cf. *Leacroft Ho* c. 1865 O.S. WORPLE RD, *v. infra* 204.

GROVE BARNS is *Groveborn* 1376 IpmR, *Grovesbarne* 1417 ib., *Grovebarn(e)s* 1469 ib., 1564 FF, *Barngrovis* 1504 AD iii, *Growbarnes al. Holbarnes* 1546 FF and was perhaps near the home of Geoffrey de *la Grave* (1230 FF), *v.* **græfe, grafa**. Cf. also *Grovelond* 1450 *WAM*.

KNOWLE GREEN is *Knowl Green* 1680 S and was probably by the home of Richard de *la Knolle* (1294 *Ass*) and William *at Knoll* (1446 *WAM*), *v.* **cnoll**. There is a very slight elevation here, which would have been conspicuous amid the surrounding dead-level country.

PENTON HOOK is *Pentyhoke* 1535 FF, *Penton Hook* 1754 R. The name is probably to be associated with the field-names *Long Pentys* in the Laleham *TA* and perhaps also with *Punteyescroft* 1329 *MinAcct*.

YEOVENEY FM [jiˑvni]

Giueneya 1042–66 (13th) *WDB, Gyveneya* 1066–87 (13th) *WAM*, 1087–1100 Crispin

Iueneia t. Ric 1 BM *et freq* to 1316 FA, with variant spellings *Iven-* and *-ey(e), Yvenay* 1204 Cur, *Iveny* 1606 PCC

Heveneye 1235 *Ass, Eveney* 1593 N, 1680 S, *Eveney* 1777 Andrews

Jeveneye 1277 Misc, *Yeveneye* 1294 *Ass*, 1322 Pat, 1383 FF, *Yeveney* 1401 *SR, Yevene* 1675 Ogilby

'*Geofa*'s well watered land,' *v.* **eg**. Cf. *Geofanstige* (BCS

2-2

1074), a lost place near Bath (So), *geofandene* (BCS 116) near Ombersley (Wo) and Yeaveley (Db) (DEPN). The place stands on flat land between two branches of the Colne.

BILLET BRIDGE is to be associated with the family of Roger *Belet* (1333 FF). Cf. *Belletes tenement* 1463 VCH ii.

BIRCH GREEN is so named in 1754 (R). BONE HEAD. Cf. *Bourne Head Mead* 1842 *TA* and burna. CHURCH LAMMAS is so named ib. *v.* lammas. DUNCROFT HO. Cf. *Duncroft* c. 1825 O.S. SHORTWOOD is *Shortewood* 1485 *WAM*. STAINES BRIDGE is (*ad*) *pontem de Stanes* 1228 Cl, *Stanes brigge* 1313 LBk, 1489 Pat. STAINES MOOR is so named in 1675 (Ogilby). *v.* mor.

Stanwell

STANWELL

> *Stanwelle* 1086 DB *et passim*
> *Stanewell(e)* 1199 FF *et passim* to 1316 FA, *Stannewell* 1219
> 　　Abbr, 1291 Tax, 1547 FF, *Staneswell* 1258 FF
> *Standwell* 1595 PCC

'Stony stream or spring,' *v.* wielle. The soil here is gravelly.

NOTE. SPOUT LANE. Cf. *Spout Copse* 1843 *TA*. WATER LANE is *Watery Lane* ib.

HAMMOND'S FM was earlier *S(c)hepcote* 1399, 1428 IpmR, *Shipcote* 1428 ib. and is *Shipcotes otherwise Hamondys* 1452 ib., *Hamondes otherwise Tycheborn* 1544 FF. The earlier name is self-explanatory, *v.* cot(e). Robert *Hamond* is mentioned in connection with Stanwell in 1534 (FF). The family must have been in the district a century earlier.

HITHERMOOR FM is *Hither Moor* 1843 *TA* and is doubtless so named in distinction from a *Further Moor* marked in R (1754) between the site of this farm and Stanwellmoor *infra* 21. The two marshes appear as *Lesmores* in 1198 (FF).

LEYLANDS. Cf. *Laylond* 1367 Cl, *Leylond* 1546 *Rental*. Perhaps 'fallow land,' *v.* læge.

POYLE

> *Pulla* 1210–12 RBE, 1353 FA, *villa de Puilla* 1235 Fees, *la Puille* 1259 FF

Poyle 1238 FF (p), 1426 IpmR, *la Poyl(l)e* 1274 *Ass*, 1299, 1318 Ipm

La Penle (sic) 1329 FF

Pyle 1819 G

Although the above spellings refer (with one exception) to a place, not a family, the name is no doubt manorial in origin. Walter de *Pulla* held half a fee here in 1210–12 (RBE), Thomas de *la Puille* is mentioned in 1259 (FF) and Walter de *la Poylle* in 1274 (*Ass*). The original form of the surname must have been de *l'Apulie*, i.e. of Apulia (Italy). *Puille*, *Poylle* are forms in which the name Apulia commonly occurs in ME, the initial *l'a* having been taken to be the French definite article.

RIDSWORTH (lost)

    Ruddeswurth 1243, 1268 FF, 1277 Misc, *-worth* 1415 Pat, *Rudesworth* 1258 FF, 1415 Pat

    Reddeswrth 1245 FF

    Rodesworth 1279, 1446 FF, *Roddes-* 1375 Pat, *Rodesworthe al. Colbrockende* 1583 Sess

    Ryddesworthe near Colebrooke t. Eliz ChancP, *Ridsworth* 1657 PCC

Probably 'Rudd's farm,' v. worþ. Cf. Rudham (Nf), *Rudeham* 1086 DB, *Ruddaham* 1163 BM, which contains the strong form *Rudda*. The name is now lost, but two references above suggest that this was the name of the small part of Colnbrook (Bk) which lies east of the river Colne in Middlesex. For the sound development *u* to *i* in the neighbourhood of point consonants cf. PN W xx, and for similar *u* to *e* cf. Teddington *infra* 24.

STANWELLMOOR is (*super*) *moram de Stanewell* 1274 *Ass*, *Stanwellemore* 1363 Pat, with reference to the flat marshy land here by the Colne, v. mor. It was the home of Walter de *la More* (1226 FF).

WEST BEDFONT is *Westbedefund* 1086 DB, *-font* 1189–1212 BM, *-funte* 1201 FF *et freq* to 1274 *Ass*, *-founte* 1316 FA, *Westbudefunte* 1266 FF. v. East Bedfont *supra* 12. *West* to distinguish it from that place.

HEATH COTTAGES recall the home of William *atte Hethe* (1367 Cl).

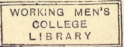

COLLAS FM and LINTELL'S BRIDGE are to be associated with the families of John *Colas* (1443 FF) and *Lenthal* (1600, 1748 ParReg), *Lintell* (1750, 1786 ib.). Cf. *Lintills* 1843 *TA*.

MAD BRIDGE is *Mad bridg* 1686 M, *Met*, *Mad or Mead Bridge* 1826 Bridges. Probably 'bridge by the *mead* or meadow.' MILL MEAD (Kelly) is *Mill Meade* 1843 *TA*. OAK COTTAGES. Cf. *The Oak* ib. THE SLIPS is *the Slip* ib. *v.* slipe. STANWELL PARK. Cf. *The parke, the Greate Parke* 1546 *Rental*.

Sunbury

SUNBURY

> *Sunnabyri* 959 (13th) BCS 1050
> (*æt*) *Sunnan byrg*, (*into*) *Sunnanbyrg, Sunnan burges bōc* 960 BCS 1063[1], (*æt, to*) *Sunnanbyrig* 962 ib. 1085
> *Suneberie* 1086 DB, *Suneberi(a)* 1198 Cur, t. John Weinbaum, *Sone-* 1316 FA
> *Sunneberi* 1198 Cur, *-bir'* 1274 Ass, *Sunnesbyr'* ib., *Sonnebery* 1291 Tax, *-bury* 1341 NI, *Sonnesbury* 1314 Pat
> *Sundebur'* 1294 Ass, *Sundbery* 1550 PCC
> *Sonbury* 1428 FA, *Sunbury* 1535 VE, *Sumbury* 1745 R

'*Sunna*'s burh or stronghold,' cf. Sonning (PN in *-ing* 68) in Berkshire.

NOTE. PORT LANE is so named in 1754 (R), perhaps because leading to Staines. *v.* port.

CHARLTON

> *Cerdentone* 1086 DB, *Cherdinton* 1232 FF, 1235 Fees, 1274 Ass, *-dyn-* 1294 ib., 1316 FA, *Cherdyngton* 1268, 1309, 1523 FF, *Cherdingtone* 1274 Ass
> *Chardynton* 1294 Ass, *-yng-* 1341 NI, 1517 FF, *Charyngton* c. 1465 ECP
> *Sherdyngton* 1392 SR, *Shardington* 1592 ib.
> *Charlyngton* 1539 FF, *Charleton* 1550 Pat, *Charleton al.* *Chertington* 1594 LCCDeeds, *Charlton* 1610 Speed
> *Charton* t. Eliz ChancP

Probably '*Cēolrēd*'s farm,' as suggested in DEPN, *v.* ingtun. For interchange of *d* and *l* cf. Harlington *infra* 37.

[1] Endorsed *Sunnanburga talu, Sunnanburge, Sonebury*.

UPPER and LOWER[1] HALLIFORD

(to) *halgan forde* 962 BCS 1085

halgeford 969 (c. 1100) Crawford, 1208 FF, 1274 *Ass*, *-forte* 969 (13th) BCS 1264, *Halegeford* 1206 Abbr, 1268 FF, *-eghe-* 1268 ib., *-eg-* 1286 ib., *-egh-* 1298 ib.

Halheford 1252 FF, *Halehe-* 1274 *Ass*

Haluford 1259 FF, *Haleweford* 1274 *Ass*, *Hallewe-* 1280 FF, *Uphaleweford* 1274 *Ass*

Hal(l)eford 1274 *Ass*, *Uppehalleford* 1294 ib., *Uphalleford* 1417 BM

Halkeford 1274 *Ass*, *Halgford* 1294 ib., 1389 FF, *Halghe-* 1316 FA, 1326 FF, *Norther-* 1306 ib.

Netherhalford 1349 FF, *-halghford* 1351 ib., *Uphalford* 1445 BM

Heloughford al. Halforde 1545 LP, *Hawlford* 1576 ParReg, *Uphawlford* 1676 *FF*

Lower hallingford 1558 ChancP

Halford al. Hallowford 1650 Madge, (*al. Hollowford*) 1651 ib.

Halliford 1801 EnclA

'The holy ford,' *v.* **halig, ford.** The reason for the name is unknown.

KEMPTON (PARK)

Chenetone 1086 DB, *Kenetune* t. John Weinbaum, *Kenetone* 1219 FF, 1229, 1234 Cl, 1274 *Ass*, 1293 Ipm

Keninton 1228 Ch *et freq* to 1316 FA, with variant spelling *-yn-*, *Keniton* 1230 P, 1244 Cl, 1249 FF, *Kenytun Park* 1251 Pat

Kenyngton 1274 *Ass*, 1328 Ch, 1341 Works, NI, (*by Kingeston*) 1395 Pat, (*Froide*) 1442 Pat, *Keynyng-* 1341 Works

Kunyton 1274 Cl

Cold(e)kenyn(g)ton 1340 Pat, 1345 Orig, 1357 *Ct*, 1421 FF, *Colkenyngton* 1535 VE, *Colkennington al. Kempton* 1594 SP

Kinton in Sonbery 1587 LCCDeeds

Kenton 1593 N, 1610 S, 1754 R, *Kempton Park* 1665 SP, *Kempton* 1803 *EnclA*

'Cǣna's farm,' *v.* **ingtun** and cf. Kenton *infra* 53. The reason for the epithet *Cold* is unknown. The soil is gravelly.

---

[1] Lower Halliford is in Shepperton.

FRENCH PLACE (so named c. 1865 (O.S.)) is probably to be associated with the family of William *French* (1754 ParReg).

MOUNT PLEASANT is so named c. 1865 (O.S.). *v. infra* 207.

Teddington

TEDDINGTON

> *tudintún* 969 (c. 1100) Crawford, *Tudingtune* c. 1000 (13th) *WAM*
>
> (*æt*) *Tudincgatunæ* c. 970 BCS 1174[1]
>
> *Tudinton* 1198 FF, 1235, 1274 *Ass*, -*yn*- 1298 FF
>
> *Todinton* 1274 *Ass*, -*yn*- 1316 FA, 1336 Orig
>
> *Tudington* 1274 *Ass*, *T*(*h*)*odyngton* 1341 NI, 1443 FF, *Tuddington* 1593 BM, 1618 ParReg (Brentford)
>
> *Tedinton* 1294 QW, -*yng*- 1428 FA, *Tedington* 1686 M, *Teddington* 1754 R

'*Tuda*'s farm,' *v*. ingtun. For the modern vowel cf. Tedfold (PN Sx 150) and Introd. xvii.

NOTE. BURTON'S LANE. Cf. Francis *Burton* 1825 ParReg. SHACKLEGATE LANE. Cf. *Shacklegate* 1819 G and Shacklewell *infra* 107.

UDNEY FM[2] is to be associated with the family of Robert *Udney* found in the parish t. George II (Lysons).

BLACKMORE FM[3] is so named from the novelist Richard *Blackmore*, who died here in 1900 (*v*. DNB). BROOM HALL, BROOMHILL. Cf. *le Brome, le Bromweye* 1380 *Rental, Broomhill* 1819 G. TEDDINGTON GROVE is so named ib.

II. ISLEWORTH HUNDRED

In DB this is referred to as *Honeslauu hundredum* from Hounslow *infra* 26. The meeting-place was presumably at the mound or barrow which once must have existed at this place. In all subsequent records it is called Isleworth Hundred (*Ystleswurð* 1176 P, *Ysteleswurde* 1182 ib.) from Isleworth *infra* 27.

---

[1] It is by no means certain that this place should be identified with Teddington. If it should, then the name denotes 'farm of *Tuda*'s people.'

[2] Surviving in UDNEY PARK RD.

[3] Surviving in BLACKMORE RD.

Heston

HESTON [*vulgo* hesən]

Heston(e) 1123–33 OxfordCh *et passim*, *Hestune* c. 1130 ib.,
  Eston 1176 P, *Eston al. Heston* 1443 FF
Histon(e) 1392, 1401, 1592 *SR*, 1409 Pat
Heyston 1493–1500 ECP, *Heston al. Heyston* 1577 *FF*
Heeston 1542 LP, 1544 *FF*, *Heason* 1600 ParReg (West
  Drayton), *Hessen* 1602 PCC, *Hesson* 1635 ParReg (Brent-
  ford)

'Farm in the brushwood (district),' cf. Hayes *infra* 39. It is
about four miles distant from that place, *v.* tun.

NOTE. GREEN LANE. Cf. *Grenewey Lane* 1558 Pat.

LAMPTON is *Lamptonfeld* 1376 AD v, *Lampton* 1426 *Ct*, *Lamton-
feld* 1438 ib., *Lambton* 1611 ParReg, *Lampton* 1633 *FF*. Probably
'lamb farm,' *v.* tun, with unvoicing of *b* to *p* before the voiceless
consonant. It is perhaps worth noting that Osterley (*infra*) is
close by. Cf. Lambton (PN NbDu 131).

NORTH HYDE is *Northhide* (1710 S) and was the home of John
de *Northyde* (1243 FF), de *la Northhide* (1274 *Ass*) and *atte
Northhyde* (1355 FF). 'North hid', cf. Hyde Park *infra* 168. The
hamlet lay in the extreme north of the parish.

OSTERLEY PARK

Osterle, Ostrele 1274 *Ass*, *Osterlye* 1294 ib. (p), *Osterlegh* 1299
  ib., *Osturle* 1376 AD v
Esterlee 1294 *Ass* (p)
Oysterle 1302 *Ass*, *Oisterle* 1342 Cl, *Oysterley* 1342 Pat
Osterley Parke House 1576 Sess
Austerleie 1586 H, *Austerley* 1609 ParReg

'Sheepfold clearing,' *v.* eowestre, leah. Cf. Osterhills (PN
Herts 90) and Austerley (PN NbDu 153).

SCRATTAGE

Cracheheg' 1274 *Ass*, *Crachehegg'* 1294 ib.
Crecheeche, Cregeshegg' 1274 ib.
Crac(c)hehage 1436 *Ct*, *Crachehach lane* 1438 ib.
Cratchedfelde 1547 Pat

Scratchhedge 1659 PCC, *Scrathedge* 1661 ParReg, *Scratedge* 1710 S, *Scratage* c. 1815 EnclA

This name repeats itself in the old name for the site of Temple Mills *infra* 107. It is a compound of the common word *hedge* (ME *hegge*) and ME *cracche*, *crecche*. This last word (*v.* NED *s.v. cratch* sb.[1]) is used of a 'hurdle' or 'wooden grating,' and *cracche-hegge* is perhaps descriptive of a hedge or enclosure made of hurdles. The later forms show the same development of inorganic *s* which is noted in PN Sx 190, *s.n.* Poles Pitch, and PN Ess 180, *s.n.* Scaldhurst.

SPIRT LANE. Cf. *Spert* 1795 Lysons, *Spirt Lane* 1819 G. We may compare *Spertemed* 1380 *Rental*, *Spartmede* t. Hy 6 ib. in Twickenham. This would seem to be the word *spirt*, 'jet of liquid,' etc. found in Spurt Street (PN Bk 138), Spurtham (PN D 642).

SUTTON is *Sutton* 1438 *Ct*, and was the home of Jordan de *Sutton* (1286 *Rental*). 'South farm,' *v.* sup, tun.

BEAVER'S FM[1], BUTCHER'S GROVE[2] and THORNBURY HO are probably to be associated with the families of Andrew *Beaver* (1806 ParReg), Richard *Butcher* (1680 ib.) and Philip *Thornbury* (1773 ib.).

MOUNT PLEASANT is so named c. 1865 (O.S.). *v. infra* 207. THE SLIP is so named c. 1840 (*TA*). *v.* slipe. It survives as the name of a street.

Hounslow

HOUNSLOW[3]

Hundeslawe 1217 Pat, 1274 *Ass*, 1275 RH, -*lauwe* 1242 Fees, -*lowe* 1275 RH, 1294 *Ass*, 1295 Ch
Houndeslowe 1341 NI, 1353 FA, (*within the parish of Heston*) 1519 FF
Haundeslowe 1394 FF, *Hondeslowe* 1428 FA
Hounslawe 1406 FF, *Hownslo*(*we*) 1534 ib., 1545 PCC
Hunslow 1593 N

[1] *Great Beavers* 1819 G, surviving in BEAVER'S RD.
[2] So named in 1754 (R).
[3] There was no parish of Hounslow before the middle of the 19th century. It lay partly in Heston, partly in Isleworth, the dividing line being the main Bath road.

'*Hund*'s hill or tumulus,' *v.* **hlaw**. Cf. *hundes hlæw* BCS 687 (Berks). The first element is OE *hund*, 'dog,' here probably used as a personal name. For earlier forms *v.* Isleworth Hundred *supra* 24.

Hounslow Heath is *brueria de Hundeslaue* 1275 RH, *Houndes-loweheth* 1382 *Cor*, *Hounselo Hethe* 1545 LP.

Isleworth

Isleworth [aizəlwə·θ]

> *Gislheresuuyrth* 695 (late copy)[1] BCS 87
> *Gistelesworde* 1086 DB
> *Istlesworde* 1100–35 (1330) Ch, *Ystleswurða* 1176 P, *Ysteles-wurde* 1177 ib., *-wurtha* 1180 ib.
> *Histelehurd* 1123–33 OxfordCh, *Histelewrde* 1163 ib.
> *Istleworth* 1231 Cl *et freq* to 1675 Ogilby, with variant spellings *Istel-*, *Ystel-*, *Istil-*, *Histle-*
> *Yisteles-*, *Yhisteleworth* 1275 RH, *Yistelworth* 1306 FF, *Yisil-* 1306 ib., *Yistilworthe* 1333 ib.
> *Thistel(le)worth* 1313, 1416 Pat, *Thystel-* 1477 AD vi, *Thissil-worth* 1522 DunBev, *Istleworth al. Thistleworth* 1629 PCC, *Thistleworth* 1641 SP, *Thistlewood* 1650 Madge
> *Isletworth* 1348 *SR*, *Isleworth* 1463 PCC, *Isellworth* 1576 *SR*, *Isselworth* 1576 PCC
> *Isleworth vulgo Thistleworth* 1675 Ogilby

The identification of the first form, which occurs in a list of early gifts to the nuns of Barking, is not certain. If it is correct the first element is a personal name *Gislhere*, with later *t* developing between the consonants *s* and *l*. Cf. Bülbring, *Altenglisches Elementarbuch*, § 535. The form *Gistel-* developed to *Yistle-* and *Istle-*. The occasional development of earlier *Is(s)leworth* to *Thistleworth* is curious and so is the modern pronunciation with initial [aizəl] rather than [isəl].

Note. Church St is *Church Row* 1754 R. Heath Rd is *Heath Lane* ib., leading to Hounslow Heath. Inwood Rd. Cf. *Inwoods* c. 1840 *TA* and *infra* 205. Linkfield Rd. Cf. *Lynkefeld* 1431 *Ct*, *Link Fd* c. 1840 *TA* and Linkfield (PN Sr 306), from OE *hlinca feld*, 'open land marked by the presence of linches' (*v.* hlinc). Maswell Park Rd. Cf. *Mas(s)ewelle*

---

[1] The form itself would seem to be good OE.

1485 *Ct, Mesewelfurlong'* ib., *Maswell stile* 1498 ib. MILL PLATT is so called in 1745 (R). Cf. *Millehawes* 1376 AD v and *v.* haga, plott. PARK RD. Cf. *Parkehill, -feld* 1558 Pat. POUND LANE is so named in 1754 (R), *v.* pund. ST JOHN'S RD was *Brassil Mill Lane* ib. SYON LANE is *Sion Lane* ib., leading to Syon Ho *infra.* UNION RD was *Cut Throat Lane* ib. WARPLE RD is *The Warple* ib., *v. infra* 204. WOOD LANE is so named ib. An interesting lost name is *Cootedhegelane* 1436 *Ct*, i.e. 'cutted hedge lane.' Cf. *The Cuttydhegge* (1401 Cl) in Harrow.

BABER BRIDGE[1] is *Baber Bridge* 1593 N, *Babersbridge* c. 1800 Lysons and takes its name from a farm called *Babbewrth* 1268 Pat, *-worth* 1274 *Ass.* Cf. also *Babbeuuorthepond* 1301 Pat, 1302 *Ass, Babbeworthpond* 1370 Pat, *-ponte* 1376 AD v, *Babermead* 1553 Pat. '*Babba*'s enclosure,' *v.* worþ. For the modern development cf. Abinger (PN Sr 259) and for the personal name cf. *Babbehegge* 1294 *Ass* in Ealing.

ISLEWORTH AIT. Cf. 2 *islands called Eughtes* 1558 Pat, from OE iggoð, 'islet.' Cf. *infra* 201.

MOGDEN[2] is *Mokedene* 1426, 1431 *Ct*, t. Hy 6 *Rental, Mokden* 1436 *Ct*, 1498 *Rental, Mogden* 1491 *Ct.* The second element is denu, 'valley.' The forms are late but the first element is probably the OE personal name *Mocca*, recorded from Surrey and from Mercia.

SMALLBURY is *Smalborow* 1436 *Ct.* Cf. *Smalborowelane* 1438 ib., *Smalleboro Grene, Smalleborowe Closes* 1547 Pat, *Smallbury Green* 1680 S. The forms suggest that the original second element was OE beorg, 'barrow.' 'Hill' is hardly possible here.

SYON HO [zaiən] takes its name from the *Monasterium S Salvatoris et S Brigittae de Syon* founded by Henry V in 1414 (*v.* Dugdale vi, 542). Cf. *abbatissa de Syon* 1428 FA, *Istelworth Syon* 1564 FF, *Eslworth Sion* 1602 AD vi. Norden (1593) says "Syon in remembrance of that hill in Jerusalem," but the authority for that statement is unknown. *v.* Addenda xxxiii.

WORTON HALL is *Worton* 1274 *Ass* (p), 1357 FF, 1376 AD v, *Wortton* 1535 VE. 'Herb or vegetable enclosure,' *v.* wyrt, tun, and cf. Worton (PN W 248).

---

[1] Marked on the old 1″ O.S. map (c. 1825), the name does not appear on present-day maps. The bridge was that which carried the main Bath road over the Crane just to the west of Hounslow.
[2] Surviving in MOGDEN LANE.

WYKE GREEN and HO. Cf. *la Wyke* 1238 FF, *Wike* 1243 ib., *Wykeheth* 1557 Pat. *v.* wic, 'dairy farm.'

GUMLEY HO takes its name from a glass manufacturer of the end of the 17th century (Walford i, 58). HOLME COURT. Cf. *Holmefelde* 1557 Pat and holm. QUEEN'S BRIDGE is *Quenebryg'* 1450 *Ct.* SILVER HALL is so named in 1694 (Lysons). SPRING GROVE. Cf. *Spring Grove House* 1819 G. SYONHILL FM is *Sion Hill* 1794 Lysons. Cf. Syon Ho *supra* 28. WARREN FM. Cf. *warren of Thistillworth* 1399 Pat. WOODLANDS[1] is *Wodelond* 1485 *Ct.*

Twickenham

TWICKENHAM [twiknəm *olim* twitnəm]

Tuican hom, Tuiccanham 704 (8th) BCS 111
Tuicanham, (in) Tuicanhamme 793 (10th) BCS 265
Tuuiccanham 941 (13th) BCS 766, 948 (c. 1250) ib. 860
Tuuicaham 948 (c. 1250) ib. 861
Twikeham 1216 FF, *Twykenham* 1279 ib., 1301 Ipm, 1316
    FA, *Twik-* 1291 Tax, *Wickenham* 1650 Madge
Twekynham 1396 FF
Twyckname 1560 FF, *Twicknem* 1651 ParReg (Teddington)
Twitnam(e) 1644, 1721 ParReg (Northolt), *Twittenham* 1698
    ib. (Heston)

Probably '*Twic(c)a*'s hamm.' There is a well-marked bend in the river here. Ekwall (DEPN *s.n.*) suggests the gen. sg. of a hypothetical OE word **twicce*, related to *twicene*, 'fork or junction of roads or ways.' The meaning would be 'river fork' with reference to its situation at the junction of the Thames and Crane, but the genitival compound 'hamm of the river-fork' seems, however, a very unlikely one.

NOTE. CROSS DEEP GARDENS. Cf. *Cross-deepe* 1680 S. The name must have referred to a deep pool in the river near by. MAY RD was *Stacon Lane* in 1754 R. Cf. *Steaken* 1682 Cobbett and *Staten* (sic) *Field* 1784 Walford. MEREWAY RD. Cf. *The Mearway* 1650 *ParlSurv.* It is near the parish boundary, *v.* (ge)mære. ORLEANS RD is so named from Orleans Ho *infra* 30. It was earlier *Folly Lane* (1754 R), *v. infra* 205. RICHMOND RD, leading to Richmond, was earlier *Ferry Lane* (ib.).

---

[1] Surviving in WOODLANDS RD.

EEL PIE ISLAND was earlier *one ayte called the parish ayte* 1608 Cobbett, *The Aight* 1784 Walford and may be identical with *Gose Eyte, Goseeyte* t. Hy 6 *Rental.* '(Goose) islet,' *v.* iggoð *infra* 201. The present-day name is probably a quite modern humorous nickname from picnicking parties here. Cf. Eelpie Bridge (PN Nt 48).

FULWELL is so named c. 1450, 1458 *Rental.* The forms are too late for certainty. The name may be descriptive of a full or of a foul (*v.* ful) spring.

MARBLE HILL is *Mardelhylle* 1350 *MinAcct, Marble Hill* 1650 *ParlSurv.* The early spellings are insufficient for any etymology to be suggested, though it is clear that the 17th century and present-day spellings must be due to folk-etymology.

STRAWBERRY HILL. Cf. *Strawberry Hill Close* 1691 Cobbett. Austin Dobson (*Horace Walpole* 113–4) notes that the house as first built by a retired coachman about 1698 had been nicknamed *Chopped Straw Hall*, but that Walpole, in looking through some old deeds when he bought the house in 1748 and rebuilt it, found reference in one of the deeds to *Strawberry Hill Shot* and adopted the name for his new house.

WHITTON is *Wytton* 1274 *Ass* (p), 1300 Ipm, 1301 Cl, *Whitton* 1352 AD iii, 1354 FF, *Whytton* 1357, 1379 ib., *Whyttondoune* 1431 *Ct.* Probably 'white farm,' *v.* tun.

COLE'S BRIDGE is to be associated with the family of Agnes *Coale* (1607 ParReg) and Jane *Cole* (1690 ib.).

BROOK HO. Cf. *The Broke* 1436 *Ct.* CAMBRIDGE HO is so named from Richard Owen *Cambridge* who lived here c. 1750 (Walford i, 83). HEATH HO. Cf. *The Heath* 1675 Ogilby. HOSPITAL BRIDGE is so named in 1754 (R). KNELLER HALL takes its name from the painter, Sir Godfrey Kneller, who lived here (*v.* DNB). MARSH FM. Cf. *le Mersshefurlang* 1466 AD i, *in marisco de Twykenham* t. Hy 6 *Rental.* ORLEANS HO. Louis Philippe, Duke of *Orleans*, lived here in exile (Walford i, 86). TWICKENHAM PARK is *Twikenham park* 1593 N.

III. ELTHORNE HUNDRED

Helet(h)orne 1086 DB, 1192 P, *Elle-* 1168, 1189 P, 1235 *Ass*, *Ele-* 1169 P, 1235, 1274 *Ass*, 1316, 1428 FA, *Elles-* 1176 P, *Helle-* 1235 *Ass*. Perhaps '*Ella*'s thorn tree.' This was probably, like Spelthorne *supra* 11, some conspicuous thorn tree or bush, but the site is not known. Elthorn Park in Hanwell is quite a modern name and there is no authority for assuming that the meeting-place was in Hanwell parish, which is indeed at the extreme east end of the hundred[1].

Brentford

Brentford

Bregunt ford 705 BCS 115

(*æt*) *Bregentforda* 781 (11th) BCS 241, c. 1050 ASC (*s.a.* 1016 C)

(*æt*) *Brægentforda* c. 1050 ib., (ib. D), (*æt*) *Brentforda* c. 1050 ib. (*s.a.* 1016 C), c. 1150 ib. (*s.a.* 1016 E)

Breinford, -y- 1222 StPaulsDB, c. 1300 QW *et freq* to 1341 NI

Brainford, -y- 1222 StPaulsDB (p), 1222 FF *et freq* to 1274 *Ass, Braynes-* 1284 Winton, *West-, Estbraynford* 1294, 1332 FF, (*Old*) 1476 FF, (*Newe*) 1521 ib.

Branford 1352 Pap, 1669 Cai, *Old Branford* 1697 ParReg

Brayntforth 1556 FF, *West Brayntford al. Newe Brayntford* 1598 *Recov*

Olde Braneford 1563 Sess, *Ould Brainford* 1655 ParReg

Brentford 1593 N

'Ford over the river Brent' (*supra* 1). This must have been just above the spot where the Brent joins the Thames, where the main Bath road crosses the stream. The *t* was early dropped in the consonantal sequence *-ntf-*, being re-introduced at a later date through the influence of the river-name itself.

NOTE. THE BUTTS is so named in 1664 (FaulknerB). The street must have been near old archery butts, *v.* butte. BOSTON RD leads to Boston Ho *infra* 32. Cf. *Bordestonlane* 1408 *Ct*. HALF ACRE. Cf. "*half an acre* lying in long shoote butting on the kings highway" 1528 FaulknerB.

[1] *ex inf.* Dr S. J. Madge. Anderson (EHN iii, 55) wrongly assumed the authenticity of this name.

THE HAM is *The Hame* 1584 DKR xxxviii, *v.* hamm. The street is on the site of former flat meadowland here. HIGH ST. Cf. *the kings highway* 1528 FaulknerB. TOWN MEADOW. This street must be on the site of meadowland adjoining the village of Brentford, *v.* tun.

BOSTON HO

> *Bordeston* 1377 Hust, 1535 VE, *Bordestonlane* 1408 Ct
> *Borstonelane* 1462 Ct, *Burston* 1547 Pat, 1572 FF
> *Boston* 1593 N

The forms are too late for any certainty. The meaning may be '*Bord*'s farm,' *v.* tun. Cf. Bordesley (PN Wo 365, PN Wa 29), Bozen Green (PN Herts 189).

BRENTFORD BRIDGE is *Braynford brigge* 1463 AD v.

Cowley

COWLEY

> *Cofenlea* 959 (13th) BCS 1050, *Cofanlea* 998 (13th) Thorpe,
>   *Coflei* 1214 Cur
> *Covelie* 1086 DB, *Coueleg'* 1204 FF *et passim* to 1440 FF,
>   with variant spellings *Cove-* and *-legh, -lee, -ley(e)*
> *Cowelee* 1294 Ch, *Cowle* 1428 FA, *Cowley* 1535 VE

'*Cofa*'s clearing or wood,' *v.* leah. Identical in origin with Cowley (PN Bk 64, PN D 455). Cf. also Coventry (PN Wa 160).

NOTE. LAMMAS LANE. *v.* lammas.

COWLEY PEACHEY is *Couele Peche* 1358 Ipm, *Coulepecche* 1371 FF, *Cowleypechey* 1560 FF. Bartholomew *Pecche* was granted land in Cowley and Ickenham in 1252 (Ch).

COWLEY GROVE is so named in 1819 (G). COWLEY HALL is *Couelehalle* 1439 FF, *Cowley Hall* 1521 FF, *v.* heall. COWLEY MILL is so named in 1680 (S). LITTLE BRITAIN is no doubt a nickname, *v. infra* 206. It is so named in 1819 (G).

Cranford

CRANFORD

> *Cranforde* 1086 DB *et passim*
> *Cramford(e)* 1199 Cur, 1235 Ass, *Craum-* 1247 FF, 1542 LP,
>   *Crampford* 1575 PCC

Craunforde 1211 RBE, 1316 FA, *Craune-* 1341 NI
Craneford 1294 *Ass*, 1410 FF, 1428 FA, 1584 PCC

'Crane- or heron-frequented ford.' For the river Crane *v. supra* 2.

CRANFORD BRIDGE is *Craneford Bridge* 1593 N. CRANFORD PARK is so named in 1754 (R). WATERSPLASH FM. Cf. *Watersplash Mead* c. 1840 *TA*.

West Drayton

WEST DRAYTON

Drægtun 939 (13th) BCS 737, (*of*) *Drægtune* c. 1000 AS Charters
Draitone 1086 DB *et passim*, with variant spellings *Dray-, Westdrayton* 1465 IpmR, *Draighton* 1572 ParReg (Heston)
Dreygton 1274 *Ass*, *Dreyton* 1314 Pat, 1316 FA, 1326 StPaulsMSS
Dratton 1322 Pat
Dreaton 1684 Sess

v. **dræg, tun**. The site of this place, by the many branches of the Colne, would be consistent with Ekwall's suggested interpretation of *dræg* as a spot where a boat might be dragged overland to avoid a river bend. *West* probably to distinguish from Drayton in Ealing *infra* 91.

* NOTE. WISE LANE may take its name from the family of Thomas *Wise* (1764 ParReg).

SWAIN'S FM is to be associated with the family of *Swain* found in Stanwell ParReg in the 18th century.

DRAYTON MILL is so named in 1686 (M). A mill here is mentioned already in DB.

Greenford

GREENFORD

(*et*) *grenan forda* 845 BCS 448 (endorsed *to grenanforda*)
Greneford(e) 1066 (13th) KCD 824, 1086 DB *et passim* to 1448 FF, (*Magna*) 1254 Val, 1274 *Ass*, 1316 FA, (*Muche*) 1572 PCC, *Grenford* 1214 Abbr, 1483 FF, *Greneforth* 1354

ib., *Grynforthe the more* 1521 PCC, *Grynford* 1561 Sess, *Greyneforde* 1564 FF, *Grinford* 1575 Saxton, 1608 PCC, *Gringforde* 1582 *SR*, *Gerneforde* 1593 N

Self-explanatory. *Magna* to distinguish from Greenford Parva, now Perivale *infra* 46.

NOTE. COSTON LANE probably takes its name from the family of Simon *Coston* (1625 *Ct*). OLDFIELD RD. Cf. *Oldefelde* 1545 ib. WESTMEAD RD. Cf. *Westmeade* 1625 ib.

HORSENDON HILL is *Horsendun* 1203 FF, *-dune* 14th *AddCh*, *in bosco de Horsedon*, *Horsindon* 1302 *WDB*, *Horsington Hill* 1819 G and was the home of John de *Horsindune* (1262 AD iii). The persistent *n* shows that this name is probably to be interpreted as 'Horsa's down or hill pasture' (*v.* dun) from OE *Horsan dūn* rather than 'horses' down' (OE *horsa dūn*).

STICKLETON (lost) and STICKLETON BRIDGE, now GREENFORD BRIDGE

> *Stickelyndon* 1294 *Ass* (p), *Stikelynton* 1331 FF, *-ingdon* 1373 IpmR, *Stikelendon* 1399 ib.
> *Styclyngdonbrigg*, *Styclyndon Brigge* 1343 Works
> *Stikeldon* 1385 FF, 1389 IpmR, *Stekyldon* 1395 FF
> *Sticleton bridge* 1625 *Ct*

The name probably goes back to an OE (*æt*) *sticolan dūne*, 'at the steep hill or down.' Cf. Sticklepath (PN D 27, 166). The 1343 context shows that the bridge must have been the present bridge over the Brent here, so that the hill must have been the steep hill by which the road ascends westwards to Greenford village.

KNAPP'S COTTAGES and RAVENOR HO[1] are to be associated with the families of Philip *Knapp* (1783 ParReg) and Symon *Ravener* (1591 ib.).

BRABSDEN GREEN is *Brabstone Green* 1745 R, *Brabsden Green* 1865 O.S. Cf. *Brabsons*, *Brabsons meade* 1545 *Ct*. GREENFORD GREEN is *Grenefeld Grene* 1538 FF, 1540, 1551 Recov, *Greenford Green al. Greenfield Green* 1558 ECP, *Greenford Greene* 1625 *Ct*.

---

[1] Surviving in RAVENOR PARK RD.

Hanwell

HANWELL

Hanewelle 959 (13th) BCS 1050, 1066 (13th) KCD 824, 1086
   DB *et passim* to 1344 FF
Hanawella 998 (13th) Thorpe
Hanwell 1402 FF

This is probably a compound of OE *hana*, 'cock' and **wielle**,
'spring, stream.' Hence 'cock-frequented spring.' Identical in
origin with Hanwell (O).

BRENT BRIDGE is *Breyntbregge* 1339 Works, *Brynt bridg* 1530
LMxAS v. CUCKOO FM. Cf. *Cuckoo Grove* 1754 R. THE
GROVE. Cf. *Groveend greene in Hanwell* 1625 *Ct*. HANWELL
HEATH is *Hanwell hethe* 1537 *Ct*. PARK FM. Cf. *Parkecloses* 1537
ib., *le parke corner* 1625 ib.

Harefield

HAREFIELD [*olim* hɑ·vəl]

Herefelle 1086 DB, *Herefeld* 1206 Abbr *et passim* to 1342 NI,
   with variant spelling *-feud*, *Heresfeld* 1219 P, *Hereveld* 1311,
   1372 FF
Herrefeld 1115 StPaulsMSS (p), 1176 P, 1213, 1247 FF
Harefeld 1223 FF, 1242 Fees, 1294 *Ass*, *-feud* 1274 ib.
Herfeld(e) 1301 Ipm, 1316 FA, 1350, 1431 FF
Harfeld 1393 IpmR, 1402 EEW, 1428 FA, *-veild* 1560
   ParReg (Ickenham), *-vil* 1625 ib. (Hillingdon), *-vill* 1657 ib.
   (Ickenham), 1682 Morgan, 1724 Moll

'Army open space,' *v.* **here**, **feld**. It is impossible to say at
what particular period the name may have arisen or just what
its significance may be. For the late spellings with *v*, see
Introd. xvii.

BAYHURST WOOD is *Baynhurste* 13th LMxAS iii, *wood called
Bayhurst* 1522 ib. Probably '*Bǣga*'s wooded hill,' *v.* **hyrst**.

BRACKENBURY FM is *manor of Brakenburgh* 1485 Ipm, *Braken-
borough* 1488 FF, *Brockenborrowes* 1593 N. This is probably a
name of manorial origin. Thomas *Brakenborgh* is mentioned in
connection with the parish in 1388 (*Cor*) and the same man was

witness to a Harefield deed in 1394 (AD v). The family must have come from Brackenborough (L).

BREAKSPEAR is *Breakespeare* 1593 N. This name also is of manorial origin. In 1371 William Swanlond granted a lease for 60 years to William *Brekespere* of a house and land in Harefield (Lysons 111). The family, however, were in the neighbourhood much earlier, a Nicholas *Brakespere* being mentioned in connection with Ruislip in 1246 (Select Pleas).

COPTHALL FM is *Coppydhall* 1532 FF, *Copthall* 1819 G. 'Hall with a roof rising to a cop or peak,' *v.* coppede, heall. Cf. Copt Hall (PN Ess 24).

HAREFIELD MOOR is *Herfeld Moor* (sic) 1394 Works and was probably the home of John de *la More* (1235 *Ass*). The 'moor' (*v.* mor) is the flat marshy land in the Colne valley here.

KNIGHTSCOTE FM is *messuage called Knyghtcotes in Herefeld* 1404 FF. The name may be a compound of cniht and cot(e), cf. Knightsbridge *infra* 169. More probably it is manorial in origin, from the family of William *Knyghtcote*, citizen of London, who held premises in Harefield in 1380 (FF). The family may have come from Knightcote (Wa).

MOORHALL FM is *More Halle* 1361 Ipm, *Morhalle* 1339 Cl, 1395 FF. It lies at the edge of Harefield Moor *supra*.

BOURNE FM[1], HILLEND, LODGE FM[2] and HAREFIELD PARK[3] were probably the homes of Avice de *la Burne* (1265 LMxAS iii), Roger *atte Hulle* (1388 *Cor*), Thomas de *la Loge* or des *Loges* (1274 *Ass*) and Robert *atte Parke* (1388 *Cor*).

CRIPP'S FM[4], DEWES FM[5], DUCKS HILL[6], SHEPHERDSHILL FM and WOODCOCK HILL[7] are probably to be associated with the families of John *Crips* (1302 Cl) and Richard *Crippes* (1563 *SR*), Richard *Dawe* of Uxbridge (1397 Cl), *Duck(e)* (1577 etc. ParReg), *Shipard, Sheperd, Shepard* (1649 etc. ib.) and John *Wodecok* (1402 Cl).

---

[1] *Bourn Farm* 1754 R, *v.* burna. The place is by the Pinn (*supra* 5).
[2] *Lodge* 1819 G.   [3] *Harvill Park* 1680 S.
[4] *Cripps Farm* 1819 G.   [5] *Dews Farm* 1754 R.   [6] *Ducks Hill* ib.
[7] Cf. *lands called Wodecokkes, Wodecokkes Denne* 1485 Ipm.

Broadwater Fm is *Broad Water Farm* 1819 G. The Colne is wide here, with many channels. Broomfields is *Broom Field* c. 1840 *TA*. Colney Fm is *Colneye by Woxbrugge* 1360 Pat, *Konnees* 1461–83 ECP, *Colney* 1561 FF, *Conneye Farme* 1664 *SR*. 'Colne marsh,' *v*. eg. It is not far from Uxbridge. Cow Moor is *Cowe More* 1561 Sess. Crows Nest Fm is *Crows Nest* 1754 R. Deadmans Grove is so named in 1819 (G). Flagmoor Covert. Cf. *Flagmore* c. 1840 *TA*. Gospel Oak Covert (cf. *Gosple Oak* 1754 R) is on the parish boundary, cf. Gospel Oak *infra* 141. Harefield Grove is so named in 1819 (G). Highway Fm is so named in 1754 (R). Cf. *the kings highway from Woxebrugg to Watford* (13th LMxAS iii). Newyears Green is so named in 1754 (R). Weybeards is so named in 1819 (G). Widows Cruise Covert may be a nickname of the complimentary type, *v. infra* 207.

Harlington

Harlington

> *Hygereding tun* 831 BCS 400
> *Herdintone* 1086 DB, *-ton(e)* 1207 Abbr, 1235 Fees, 1235, 1239 FF, *-ing-, -y-* 1274 *Ass*, 1291 Tax, 1331 FF, 1353 FA, *Hirdyngton* 1311 FF
> *Hurdinton, -en-, -ing-, -yn* 1274 *Ass*, 1301 Ipm
> *Hordingeton* 1274 *Ass*, *Hurdelynton* 1524 *SR*
> *Herlyngdon* 1362 Pat, *Herlyngton al. Herdyngton* 1564 FF
> *Hardlyngton* 1475 FF, *Hardyngton* 1495 ib., *Harlyngton* 1521 ib., *Hardington al. Harlington* 1535 VE, *Arlington*[1] 1691 Archaeologia xii

'*Hygered*'s farm,' *v*. ingtun. For interchange of *d* and *l* cf. Charlton *supra* 22.

Bedwell Cottages. Cf. *Bidwell* 1592 *Ct*, *Bidwell Meadow* 1819 EnclA. For this name cf. Bedfont *supra* 12. There is no major hollow here, the hollow can only be that of the spring itself.

Dawley

> *Dallega* 1086 DB *et passim* to 1416 FF, with variant spellings *-legh, -ley(e), -lee, Dalleye next Hirdyngton* 1311 FF

---

[1] Sir Henry Bennet, Baron Arlington of *Arlington*, Mx, took his title from this place (*Complete Peerage*, i, 217).

Daulee 1199 Cur, *Danleg* (sic) 1238 FF
Dawley courte 1592 *Ct, Doyley* 1710 S

The name seems to be a compound of OE **dal**, 'dole, part, share,' etc. and **leah**, 'clearing,' with reference to a piece of land shared out between various settlers. The first element cannot be **dæl**, 'dale, valley,' as suggested by Ekwall (DEPN *s.n.*), since the surrounding country is dead level.

KINGS ARBOUR is so named in 1710 (S). See IPN 162 n. 1 for a note on the site by O. G. S. Crawford. PINKWELL and WEST END are so named in 1754 (R). WESTFIELD COTTAGES. Cf. *West Fd* 1819 EnclA. WOOLPACK FM. Cf. *Great, Little Woolpack* c. 1840 *TA*.

Harmondsworth

HARMONDSWORTH [*olim* hɑ·mzwə·θ]

Hermodesworde 1086 DB, -*w(u)rth*, -*worth* 1235, 1274 *Ass*,
    1275, 1295, 1317 FF
Heremodesw(o)rth(e) 1222 StPaulsDB, 1274 *Ass*, 1291 Tax,
    Hermodisworth al. Hermondisworth 1430 Pat
Ermodhesworth 1260 Cl
Hermereswurthe 1294 *Ass, Hermoursworth* 1566 FF
Hermondesworth 1316 FA, 1318, 1390 FF, *Here-* 1360 AD vi
Hermesworth 1408 Pat, *Harmesworth* 1485 PCC, 1552 FF,
    1593 N, 1597 *Recov, Harmsworth* 1664 ParReg (W. Drayton), 1715, 1723 ib. (Stanwell)
Harman(n)esworth 1436 Pat, 1553 FF
Harmondsworth vulg. Harmsworth 1675 Ogilby, *Harsworth*
    1732 ParReg (Harlington)

'*Heremōd*'s farm,' *v.* **worþ**. Cf. Hamsworthy (PN D 156). For the old spelling and pronunciation cf. the surname *Harmsworth*.

NOTE. MOOR LANE is *le Morlane* 1337 *Rental, Morelane* 1483 *Ct*.

HEATHROW is (*la*) *Hetherewe* t. Hy 5 *Ct, Hetherowfeyld* t. Hy 8 *MinAcct, Hitherowe* 1547 Pat, 1553 FF and was perhaps the home of Richard de *Bruera* (13th *AD* 3236) and John *atte Hethe* (1342 NI). The name probably referred to a row of houses at the western edge of Hounslow Heath. *v.* **ræw**.

LONGFORD

Longeford(e) 1294 *Ass* (p), c. 1410 *Ct*, 1431 FF
Langeford(e) 1327 FF (p), 1355 Works, c. 1410 *Ct*
(*water called*) *le Longeforth* 1430 FF, *Lang(e)forth* 1430 Pat,
   1535 VE

Self-explanatory.

PERRY OAKS is *Pyrye* 1337 *Rental*, 1355 Works, 1411 AD iii,
Pury 1355 Works, *Puryplace* 1553 FF, *Peryplace* t. Hy 8
MinAcct, Perry Oaks 1754 R. 'The pear tree,' *v.* pirige. The
Oaks would seem to be a late addition, when the original
name was no longer understood.

SIPSON

Sibwineston, Sybwynston early 13th *AD*
Sibodeston' 1214 Cur
Sybbeston c. 1310 *Ct, Sibbeston* 1318 FF
Subbeston 1339 *Rental,* t. Hy 5 *Ct*
Sibeston 1342 FF, *Sibston* 1391 ib., 1402 AD iii, *Sybeston*
   c. 1410 *Ct*
Shybbeston 1547 *Particulars for Grants* (PRO), *Shepiston al.*
   Sypson 1593 N, *Sipson* 1638 CantYB

Probably '*Sibwine*'s farm,' *v.* tun.

PALMER'S FM is to be associated with the family of Richard
Palmer (1390 FF).

COLLEGE FM belongs to Winchester College. KING'S BRIDGE is
so named in 1825 (Bridges). MOOR BRIDGE is *Moor Bridg* 1720
Willdey. SOUTHCOTE (lost) is *Suckot* 1265 Misc, *Suthcote juxta
Colebrok* 1342 FF, *Suthcoterewe* 1430 Pat, *Southcoterowe* 1483
Rental, v. cot(e), ræw, 'row.' It was evidently near Colnbrook
(Bk).

Hayes

HAYES

(*on*) *linga hæse* 793 BCS 265[1], *Hæse* 831 ib. 400, *Haes* 1248
   Select Pleas
Hyse 832 (12th) BCS 402
Hesa 1086 DB[2], *Hese* 1232 Ch *et passim* to 1516 FF

---

[1] Endorsed *hyse* 11th, *lingahese* 12th. *lingahese* in MS Lambeth 1212 (13th).
[2] HESA RD is a modern revival of this form.

Heyse 1229 Bracton, 1498 FF

Heese 1456 PCC, 1541, 1561 FF, *Heesse* c. 1500 StarChamber, 1570 *Ct*, *Hease* 1504 FF, *Hesse al. Hayse* 1565 BM, *Heese al. Hayes* 1643 HMC vi

Heys 1498 FF, 1682 Morgan

Hayes 1524, 1560 FF, *Hayse* 1551 ib., *Hayes al. Hese* 1648 *Recov*

This is OE *hese*, 'brushwood,' etc. The country round here was formerly open land overgrown with bushes, shrubs and rough undergrowth. *linga* remains an unexplained addition.

BOTWELL is *Bote wælle* 831 BCS 400[1], *Botewell* 1266 Pat, 1274 *Ass*, *Boteswell* ib., *Bodwell* c. 1480 ECP, *Batwellhethe* 1551 FF. BCS 400 is a contemporary text, so that the first element cannot be the reduced gen. sg. of the OE personal name *Bōta*. Ekwall suggests (DEPN *s.n.*) that it may be connected with the OE word *bōt*, 'healing, mending, remedy,' *bote* being a qualifying genitive, the meaning of the compound being 'healing spring,' or the first element may be an unrecorded OE feminine name *Bōt*. *v.* wielle.

YEADING [jediŋ]

(*in regione quæ dicitur*) *Geddinges* 757 (12th) BCS 182

Geddingas 793 BCS 265, (*æt*) *Geddincggum* 825 ib. 384

Geddinges 1211 RBE (p), 1274 *Ass*

Yedding(g)s 1325 FF, *Yeddyng* 1331 ib., *manor of Geddyng otherwise called Yeddyngesmaner* 1541 FF, *Yedinge Grene* 1571 *Ct*

'The people of *Geddi*,' *v.* ingas and PN in -*ing* 52–3. For *in regione*, *v.* Introd. *supra* xiv.

BULLS BRIDGE and WHITTINGTON'S FM are to be associated with the families of Isotta *Bull* (1576 Sess) and Richard *Withington* (1547 *SR*).

COLDHARBOUR FM is *Cold Harbour Farm* 1819 G. *v. infra* 206. FROGMORE is so named in 1663 (ParReg). HAYES END is *Heese ende* 1571 *Ct*, *Heys End* 1675 Ogilby. It is a hamlet at the extreme

---

[1] Endorsed *bote wællan boc* (contemporary), *Boteuuelle* (12th).

western end of the parish. PARK FM. Cf. *in parco de Heuse* (sic) 1274 *Ass*. WOOD END is *Wodehende* 1531 FF. There is no wood here, but in DB the manor of *Hese* contained woodland for 400 swine.

Hillingdon

HILLINGDON[1]

Hildendun(e) 1078–85, 1162–91, 1206 *Evesham*, c. 1160 (14th) ChronEvesham, *Hildendone* c. 1120 *Evesham*, *Hyldedon* 1236 Pat, *Hildesdun* 1237 ib.

Hillendone 1086 DB, -*don* 1229 FF, -*in*-, -*yn*- 1248 Pap, 1265 Pat, 1274 *Ass*, 1291 Tax, 1317, 1404 FF, *Hilen*- 1235 *Ass*, *Hilin*- 1252 BM, *Hylen*- 1268 Pat

Hilledon 1237 FF

Hylingdon 1274, 1294 *Ass*, -*yng*- 1352 FF, *Hillingdon* 1291 Tax, 1294 *Ass*, -*yngdone* 1341 NI, 1494 FF, *Illyngton* 1507 Pat, *Hyllington al. Lighlington* 1535 VE, *Hillington* 1555 PCC

Holyngdon 1378 Cl, *Hulynden* 1388 FF, -*doun* 1401 Cl

Helindon 1402 EEW, *Helyngton* 1439 Pat, -*don* 1452 FF, *Littelhelyngdon* 1466 IpmR, *Litell*, *Gret Helyndon* 1486 Pat, *Helingdon* 1606 PCC

'*Hilda*'s hill,' *v.* dun. *Hilda* would be a pet form of OE personal names in *Hild*- such as *Hildric*, *Hildwulf*. Cf. Hildenborough (PN K 178).

NOTE. CHARVILLE LANE is probably to be associated with the family of Mary *Sharvell* (1755 ParReg). It is called Sharvel Lane in Ickenham *infra* 44. LONG LANE is so named in 1754 (R). PAGE'S LANE is perhaps to be associated with the family of Margery *Page* (1566 ParReg). PARKFIELD AVENUE. Cf. *Oldeparke* 1434 *Harl*, *Parkfield* 1865 O.S. ROYAL LANE is so named c. 1764 (De Salis). *Royal* is a corruption of *Rihille* 1434 *Harl*, cf. Royal Fm (PN Sr 208). RYEFIELD AVENUE. Cf. *Rye feilds* 1682 Morgan.

COLHAM GREEN [kɔləm]

Colanhomm 831 BCS 400, *Colnham* 1211 RBE, 1434 BM, *Colneham* 1593 N

Colehā 1086 DB, *Coleham* ib. *et passim* to 1349 FF, *Colham* 1235 *Ass et freq*, *Collam* c. 1467 ECP, *Collom* 1523 FF,

[1] Hillingdon East and West now distinguish the old parish from that part which is in Uxbridge.

Collamgrene 1578 PCC, *Colham garden*, *Colham parke* 1592 Ct, *Collumbe* 1593 N, *Collume Green* 1670 ParReg

'*Cola*'s hamm.' Although Colham is by the river Colne the first form shows that it cannot contain that word as first element. For *Green* cf. Roger de *la Grene de Coleham* (1294 *Ass*).

LITTLE LONDON is *Little Londons* 1659 De Salis, a common term for a new or tiny settlement.

PIELD HEATH is *Peeld Heath* 1592 *Ct*, 1599 De Salis, *Peelde Heath* 1670 ParReg, *Peal Heath* 1747 De Salis. The NED gives as one of the meanings of *pealed*, 'bare of herbage, as ground,' which may be the sense required here.

STRATFORD BRIDGE is so named in 1589 (Redford). This is the bridge which carries the main Bath road (*supra* 10) over the Pinn River. *v.* stræt and cf. Bow *infra* 134.

YIEWSLEY

Wiuesleg' 1235 *Ass* (p), *Wyvesle* 1406 Cl
Wynesle 1281 Abbr, *-lee* 1383 FF, *-ley* 1504, 1506 FF
Wewesley 1593 N, 1636 Redford, 1675 Ogilby
Yewsley 1819 G

In view of the modern form it seems likely that the *n* in some of the earlier forms should be read as *u* (*v*). The first element may be a personal name, the strong form of *Wifa*, found in Wivenhoe (PN Ess 403). Hence '*Wife*'s wood or clearing,' *v.* leah. The later phonological development is difficult of explanation.

GOULD'S GREEN[1], HERCIES FM[2], HUBBARD'S FM[3], KEANE'S COTTAGES, MOORCROFT HO[4] and PHILPOT'S FM are to be associated with the families of John *Golde* (1373 De Salis), Walter *Hercy* (1453 FF), Ralph *Huberd* (1327 Pat), Margery *Keene* (1581 ParReg), William *Morecroft* (1515–18 ECP, 1523 FF) and Roger *Felpot* (1434 *Harl*).

BARNES FM is *Barnes* 1659 De Salis. It is possibly to be associated with Robert *Barnes* (1661 ParReg). CONY GREEN is *The*

---

[1] *Gould(e)s grene* 1592 *Ct*.   [2] *Hercyes maner* 1466 IpmR.
[3] *Hubbards* 1659 De Salis.
[4] *Morecrofte(s)* 1579, 1599 De Salis, 1592 *Ct*.

Cony Green 1659 De Salis. HIGHFIELD is so named in 1754 (R).
HILLINGDON HEATH is *Heth* 1551 FF. HONEY HILL is so named
c. 1825 (O.S.). *v. infra* 205. STARVEHALL FM is *Starveall* c. 1865
O.S., a common nickname for poor soil, *v. infra* 206. WARREN
FM. Cf. *Warren House* 1754 R.

Ickenham

ICKENHAM

    Tichehā 1086 DB, *Ticheham* ib., 1177 P (p), *Tikeham* 1176 ib.
    (p), 1223, 1235 FF, 1235 *Ass*, *Tyke-* 1232 Cl, 1252 BM,
    Tikenham 1203 Cur, *Thike-* 1234 Cl, *Tyken-* 1301 Ipm,
    1305 FF, *Thiken-* 1356 Cl
    Ikeham 1203 Cur, 1206 FF, *Icham* 1220 Cur, *Yke-* 1219 Fees,
    Hikenham 1235 *Ass*, *Ikenham* 1236 FF, 1252 Ch, 1274 *Ass*,
    1291 Tax, 1316 FA, *Hykenham* 1387 FF, *Iknam* 1452 FF,
    Icknam 1737 ParReg (Northolt)
    Ikenhall 1300 Ipm

Probably '*Tic(c)a*'s ham,' the name being identical in origin
with Tickenham (So), *Ticaham*, *Ticheham* 1086 DB. For loss
of initial *t*, due to confluence with ME *at*, cf. Oakington *infra*
53, Elstree (PN Herts 74), earlier *Tiðulfes treow*, and Ibsley
(Ha) in DEPN (DB *Tibeslei*).

BEETONSWOOD FM is *Beetons Wood* 1754 R. Cf. *Bydonesmede*
1367 Misc. The place-name is perhaps to be associated with
the family of Ralph de *Bidun* (c. 1200 RecStBarts), a tenant in
Ickenham at that date.

GUTTERIDGE WOOD is *Great Headge Wood* t. Jas 1 ECP, *woods
called Great Hedge* 1610 *Depositions*, *Grutedge Wood* 1754 R.
The modern form is no doubt corrupt. Cf. dialectal [gə(r)t] for
great.

SWAKELEYS is *Swaleclyves maner* 1466 IpmR, *Swalcliff* 1486 Pat,
1532 FF, *Swacliffe* 1591 *FF*, *Swackleis Parke* t. Eliz ChancP,
Swacliff al. Swakeley 1593 *Recov*, *Swakeleys* 1593 N, the estate
taking its name from the family of Robert de *Swalclyve* who
held premises in Ickenham in 1327 (FF). The family may have
come from Swalecliffe (K), Swalcliffe (O) or Swallowcliffe (W).
For the present-day form cf. the late spellings of Swallowcliffe
(PN W 192).

CANNON'S FM is probably to be associated with the family of Henry *Canoun* of Ruislip (1310 AD iv) and Christopher *Can(n)on* of Ickenham (1592 *Ct*), MILTON FM with that of James *Milton* (1845 White).

HILL FM is so named in 1819 (G). LONG LANE FM. Cf. *Long Lane* ib. SHARVEL LANE. *v.* Charville Lane *supra* 41. TIPPER FM. Cf. *Tybberfeild, Typperhill* 1565 *Kings*, in the neighbouring parish of Ruislip.

Northolt

NORTHOLT

(*æt*) *norð healum* 960 BCS 1063
Northala 1086 DB, *-hale* 1214 FF, 1274 *Ass*, 1288 FF, *Norhale* 1211 RBE, 1231 FF, 1265 Pat
Northall(e) 1235 *Ass*, 1275 FF, 1291 Tax, 1316 FA, 1341 NI, *Norhall*[1] 1299 AD iv
Northold 1593 N, *Northolt* 1610 Speed, *Northall al. Northolt* 1631, 1649 CantYB i, iv
Northoll 1706 ParReg (Hillingdon)

'The north healh(s) or angle(s) of land,' in contrast to Southall *infra* 45. For the dat. pl. form cf. Halam (PN Nt 167).

DOWN BARNS is *Ladon'* 1202 Cur (p), *la Dune* 1211 RBE (p), *la Doune* 1279 QW, 1351, 1369 FF, 1377 Ch, *Downe* 1399 AD ii, *Downebarnes* 1535 VE, *v.* dun. The farm stands on a slight elevation in flat country.

WEST END is *West End* 1660 PCC and was the home of Richard *atte Westende* (1274 *Ass*). It is at the west end of the parish.

ILIOT GREEN is to be associated with the family of Robert *Elyot* (1525 *SR*).

COURT FM is so named in 1754 (R). WOOD END is *Wodende* 1464 Cl.

---

[1] *Norhalla* (1130 P) is possibly an earlier example of this spelling.

Norwood-cum-Southall[1]

NORWOOD GREEN

(*apud*) *Northuuda* 832 (12th) BCS 402[2]

Northwude 1235 *Ass*, -*wode* 1254 FF, (*next Braynford*) 1353 FF, *Norwode* 1235 *Ass*, 1453 AD i, *Southall al. Norwoode* 1615 Sess, *Norwood Green* 1724 ParReg (Ashford)

Self-explanatory, but it is not clear in relation to what place it is *north*.

SOUTHALL

Suhaull 1198 Cur, *Suhall* 1233, 1246 FF

Sudhale 1204, 1206 Cur, 1211 RBE, *Suhale* ib. (p), 1250 FF, *Shuhal* 1245 ib., *Suthale* 1274 *Ass*

Suthall(e) 1261 FF, 1316 FA

South(h)alle 1345 FF, 1419 *SR*, *Southall* 1415 *SR*, 1447 FF

Southold(e) 1578 Saxton, 1675 Ogilby, *Southolt* 1710 S

'The south healh or nook.' *South* to distinguish from Northolt *supra* 44.

DORMERS WELL FM is *Dermodeswell* 1235 *Ass*, 1247 FF, 1307 GDR, *Dermundeswell* 1235 *Ass*, 1307 GDR, *Dormandeswell* 1571 FF, *Dormanswell* 1596 *Recov.* '*Dēormod*'s or (possibly) *Dēormund*'s well or spring,' *v.* wielle. Cf. *Deormodes wican* in the bounds of Hampstead (*v. infra* 221).

NORTHCOTT (lost) is *Nortcote* 1249 FF, *North-* 1250 ib., 1398 Works, 1496 FF, *Norcote or Northcote* 1593 N, *Northcott al. Southall* 1754 R. *v.* cot(e). The name denoted that part of the present Southall which lies on the main road to Uxbridge, i.e. to the north of the original village of Southall.

WAXLOW FM is *Buxle* 1249, 1294 FF, 1286 *Rental* (p), *Woxeleye* 1294 *Ass*, *Wexleyes hedge* 1625 *Ct*, *Wexley* 1754 R, 1822 O.S., *Waxlow* 1819 G. The initial *B* in the earliest forms may be a clerical error for *W*. If so, the name should probably be associated with Uxbridge (*v. infra* 48). The second element is leah,

---

[1] A parish formed in 1864 from Norwood, a chapel of ease to Hayes, and Southall, a former hamlet of Hayes.

[2] The identification is almost certain. Hayes is mentioned in the same charter (*v. supra* 39).

the whole name being descriptive of land where the *Wihsan* had made a settlement.

HILL HO was the home of John *atte Hulle* (1382 *Cor*).

MOUNT PLEASANT is so named in 1754 (R). *v. infra* 207. OVER-SHOT MILLS is *Overshall* (sic) *Mill* 1819 G. WARREN FM is so named ib.

Perivale

PERIVALE

Greneforde 1086 DB, *Greneford(e) parva* 1254 Val, 1291 Tax, *parva Greneford* 1294 *Ass*, *Little Greneford* 1386 FF
Pyryvale 1508 FF, (*otherwise Lyttle Greneford*) 1566 ib.
Peryvale 1524 LP, 1564 FF, *Parva Greneford al. Peryvale* 1545 *Ct*, *Perevall* ib., *Perevell* 1568 FF, *Perryvale* 1637 *Recov*
Purevale 1593 N

Originally *Little Greenford* in distinction from Greenford or Great Greenford *supra* 33. The present name is not found before the beginning of the 16th century and would seem to be a ME compound of *perie*, *pirie*, 'pear tree' (OE **pirige**) and *vale* (from OFr *val*).

Ruislip

RUISLIP [rɑislip]

Rislepe 1086 DB, -*lep(e)* 1230 FF *et freq* to 1483 ib., with variant spellings *Rys*-, *Risselep(e)* 1241 CR, 1252 Ch, 1343 FF, *Risshe*- 1292 Cl (p), 1381 Pat (p), *Rysshe*- 1307, 1400 FF, *Rysse*- 1315 ib., *Rissee*- 1356 YearBk
Ruslep 1227 Pat, *Russelep(e)* 1229 Pat, 1291 Tax, 1294 FF, 1365 BM, *Russhe*- 1247 *Ass*, 1341 NI, 1342, 1349 FF, *Rush*- 1315 ib., *Russlep* 1293 FF
Risslipe 1246 FF, *Rishlip* 1310 ib., *Rysslypp* 1550 PCC
Reslepe 13th, 1328 StPaulsMSS, *Resslep* 1363 Cl, *Reslipp* 1628 ParReg (Ickenham)
Ruysshlep 1341 Pat, *Ruyssheleppe* 1435 *MinAcct*, *Ruyslep* 1437, 1438 Pat
Rislelepp (sic) 1462 Pat

Ryselypp 1530 FF, *Rieslyppe* 1553 ib., *Ryslip* 1593 N, *Rislipp*
   al. Islipp 1701 BM
Ruislip(p) 1597, 1621 PCC

This name is probably a compound of OE **rysc, risc,** 'rush'
and **hlype,** 'leap.' The application of the second element here
is uncertain. It may refer to a spot where the little river Pin
could be crossed. Ekwall (DEPN *s.n.*) would take the second
element to be **slæp,** 'slippery spot,' etc., but the absence of any
medieval spellings with *a* and the numerous forms with medial *e*
between *l* and *l* and *sh* and *l* tell against this. The modern *ui*
preserves a ME orthography for the sound [y], cf. *buy, build,*
bruise, etc. (NED).

NOTE. CATTLIN'S LANE runs past ST CATHERINE'S END FM. *Catlin's*
is probably a popular corruption of *Catherine's.* For the latter cf. *manor*
of Riselip al. Katherine End 1729 Lysons (210). The reason for the
name is unknown. WILTSHIRE LANE is *Wylchers strette* 1565 *Kings.*

EASTCOTE is *Estcotte* 1248 Select Pleas, *Estcote* 1296 ib., 1323
AD iv, *Ascote* 1356 Works, 1593 N, 1710 S, *Astcote* 1435
MinAcct, Eastcote 1819 G. 'East cot(e).' The hamlet lay to
the east of Ruislip. There was also a Ruislip *Westcott* (1780
MxNQ i).

HAYDON HALL is *Heydons* 1611 PCC, *Haydon Hall* 1819 G and
probably takes its name from the family of John *Heydon* (1382
Cor). The family appear frequently in the parish in the 15th
century as *Haydon* (e.g. t. Hy 5 *Ct*, 1436 *MinAcct*).

KINGS END is so named in 1550 (*CtRequests*). It was then held
by King's College, Cambridge. This may, however, be only a
coincidence, since the surname (*le*) *Kyng* is found in the parish
as far back as 1296 (Select Pleas) and again as *Kyng* in 1436
(*MinAcct*). Cf. *Kinges wythys shottes* 1565 *Kings.*

NORTHWOOD is *Northwode* 1435 *MinAcct,* 1437, 1438, 1441 Pat,
Norwo(o)de 1565 *Kings.* This was originally the name of a wood
and farm lying to the north of Ruislip, the present town dating
chiefly from the construction of the railway c. 1880.

PARK WOOD was probably near the home of Richard *del Parke*
(1246 FF). A *park* is mentioned at Ruislip as early as DB.

PRIORS FM. Cf. *Priores feilde* 1565 *Kings*, *Priors Field* 1754 R, *Pryor Farm* 1819 G. The name recalls the small priory of Ruislip, a cell dependent on the abbey of Bec in Normandy.

SOUTHCOTE FM is *Suhtcote* 1296 Select Pleas (p), *Suth-* 1342 FF, *South-* 1343 ib. *v.* cot(e). It is north of Ruislip and it is difficult to say in relation to what place it is described as South.

BOURNE FM, BURY STREET[1], FIELD END[2] and HILL FM[3] were probably the homes of John *atte Bourne* (1382 *Cor*), Agnes de *la Strette* (1248 Select Pleas), William de *Felde* (ib.) and John de *Hulle* (ib.). *v.* burna, burh (manorial), and feld.

CLACK FM[4], JOEL STREET FM[5], KEWFERRY FM, WOODMAN'S FM and YOUNG WOOD are to be associated with the families of Willyam *Clacke* (1598 ParReg), Elizabeth *Jewell* (1758 ib.), Johanna *Kevere* (1296 Select Pleas), Charles *Woodman* (1845 White) and Thomas *Young* (t. Hy 5 *Ct*).

BRACKEN BRIDGE HILL (1819 G) is *Brokenbridge Hill* 1565 *Kings*. CANNON BRIDGE is *Canons bridge* ib. and may derive from a family name, cf. Cannon's Fm in Ickenham *supra* 44. CHENEY STREET is *Chayham strete* 1365 BM, *Chaynye strete* 1565 *Kings*, *Cheney Street* 1754 R. COPSE WOOD. Cf. *Copshawe* 1436 *MinAcct*. *v.* haga. GREENLANE FM is *Green Lane Farm* 1819 G. HIGH GROVE is so named ib. MISTLETOE FM is possibly to be associated with *Mylstye shotte* 1565 *Kings*, the modern form being due to folk-etymology. *Mylstye* is 'mill-path,' *v.* stig. POORS FIELD is *Puersfeld* 1436 *MinAcct*. POTTERSTREET HILL. Cf. *Potters Hill Street* 1800 Milne. WINDMILL HILL is *Wyndmylnhull* 1436 *MinAcct*.

Uxbridge

UXBRIDGE[6]

> *Oxebruge* c. 1145 *Evesham*, 1198 Cur, *-bric* 1208 ib., *-brigg* 1235 *Ass*
>
> *Wixebrug'* c. 1145 *Evesham*, *Wyxebrigge* 1220 FF, 1274, 1294

---

[1] *Burye strete* 1565 *Kings*. [2] *Feilde ende* ib. [3] *Hill Farm* 1819 G.
[4] Cf. *Clackes lane* 1565 *Kings*, *Clack Lane* (present day).
[5] For *street*, *v. infra* 68.
[6] Until the late 19th century Uxbridge, though an ancient market town, was a chapel of ease to Hillingdon and was part of that civil parish. The present Uxbridge parish consists of little more than the town itself.

Ass, -bruge 1294 GDR, *Wixebrigge* 1274 *Ass*, 1277 Pat,
-*brugg'* 1294 *Ass*

Wxsebrig' 1198 Cur, *Wxe-* 1274 *Ass*

Uxebrigg(e) 1200 P, 1235, 1274 *Ass*, 1515 FF, -*brugg(e)* 1219
P, -*bregge* 1230 StPaulsCh, -*brige* 1311 Ipm, -*bridge* 1560 FF

Woxebruge 1219 FF *et passim* to 1433 FF, with variant
spellings -*brigg(e)*, -*bregg(e)*, *Woxbregge* 1310 Ipm, *Wox-
brygge* 1415 Pat, *Wokesbrygge* 1434 PCC, *Woxbridge* 1493
FF

Wuxebr' 1235 *Ass*, -*brug(g)* 1242 Cl, 1294 *Ass*, *Wuxbrigge*
1422 Pat

Wexebrigg(e) 1274 *Ass*, -*brugge* 1294 Ch, -*bregg* 1428 FA

Woxenbrugg 1389 Pat, *Woxenbrugge al. Uxbridge* 1398 IpmR

Wokysbregge 1467 Pat, *Wooxbryge* 1547 FF

This name must be taken with Uxendon (*infra* 54) and
probably with Waxlow (*supra* 45). The first element is probably,
as suggested by Ekwall (DEPN *s.n.*), a tribal name *Wixan*, found
in the 7th-century Tribal Hidage (BCS 297). As the three places
are all rather far apart it would seem that members of this tribe
must have been widely spread over the county. Other members
probably settled in the neighbourhood of Whitsun Brook (PN
Wo 16). The second element is brycg, 'bridge.' There is an
ancient bridge over the Colne here. See further Introd. xiv.

NOTE. HIGH ST may be *the Markett Place* 1589 Redford. VINE ST
was earlier *Blind Lane* or *Woolwind Lane* ib. WINDSOR ST was *street
called the Lynch* ib., *v.* hlinc. The main road is referred to as *London
Road* (1636 ib.). Unidentified names include *street called Frogmore*
1553 Pat, *Wood Lane* 1589 Redford.

FRAYS FM[1] and RABBS FM[2] are to be associated with the families
of John *Fray* (1430 FF) and Henry *Rabbe* (1383, 1388 ib.).

IV. GORE HUNDRED

Gara, Gare 1086 DB, *Garhdr'* 1168 P
Gorhundr' 1235, 1274 *Ass*, *Gore* ib., *la Gore* 1316, 1428 FA
Goare 1593 N

[1] Cf. *Frayesbridge* 1624 Redford.   [2] *Rabbesfarme* 1637 LCCDeeds.

This is the OE **gara**, 'gore, triangular or wedge-shaped field or piece of land,' cf. Kensington Gore *infra* 169. The site of the Hundred meeting-place was at Gore Fm in Kingsbury *infra* 62. Near by there is mention of a place called *le Motehegg* 1445, 1486 HarrowRec, i.e. 'moot-hedge,' *v.* gemot, hecg. See LMxAs New Series vii, 218 ff. for a full discussion.

Edgware

EDGWARE[1]

(*innan*) *Ægces wer* 972–8 BCS 1290
Eggeswera 1168 P, *-were* 1176 RecStBarts, 1183 P *et passim* to 1411 FF, *Heggeswere* 1197 ib., *Eggeswar* 1475 PCC, *Edgesware* 1543 LP
Egeswere 1199 FF *et freq* to 1341 NI
Heggwere 1202 FF, *Eggwere* 1270 AD ii, *Eggewere* 1294 Ch *et freq* to 1389 Pat, *-ware* 1310, 1475 ib., *Egewar* 1537 FF
Egeswurth 1235 Ass
Egewere c. 1250 AD ii, 1290 Cl, 1310 Pat
Eddgeware 1489 *All Souls*, *Edgeware* 1495 Pat, 1541 FF, *Edgware* 1531 LP
Edgewarth 1545 LP, *-worth* 1546 ib., 1703 ParReg (S. Mimms)
'*Ecgi*'s weir or fishing pool,' *v.* wer.

NOTE. BARNFIELD RD. Cf. *Barnfeld* 1277 *Rental*. BROADFIELDS AVENUE. Cf. *Bradfeld* 1281 *Ct.* MILLFIELD RD. Cf. *Mulepondfeld* 1277 *Rental*.

BROCKLEY HILL is *Brokeley Hill* 1593 N, *Brockley hills* 1682 Morgan, cf. *Brockle Wode* 1544 *All Souls*. It is possible that the first element of the compound is identical with *Brokholes* 1277 *Rental*, 1306 RecStBarts, *Brokhole* 1277 *Rental*, 1307 GDR, *le Brocholes by Eggeswere* 1354 Pat, 'badger-holes'.

---

[1] The present parish of Edgware includes the ancient estate of *æt Loceres leage* (this form is clearly corrupt) 957 (13th) BCS 994, *Loþereslege* 959 (c. 1100) BCS 1050, *loþereslege* 969 (c. 1100) Crawford, *Lohðeres leage*, *Loðeres leaga* 972–8 BCS 1290, *v. infra* 219, 220. This is probably '*Hlōðheres* clearing or wood,' *v.* leah, the form in BCS 994 being corrupt. *v.* Addenda xxxiii and Appendix i.

HILL HO is *Hill House* 1819 G and may be near the home of Robert de *la Hulle* (1281 *Ct*).

PIPERS GREEN is *Purcells al. Pipers* 1632 *All Souls* and is to be associated with the family of William *Pypard* (1295 ib.). *v.* Purcell's Fm *infra*.

BOYS HALL. Cf. *Boyes* 1545 DKR x, *Boyesland* 1574 Hendon Surv. BROADFIELDS[1] is *Bradfeld* 1281 *Ct*, *Brodefeld* 1309 *All Souls*, *v.* feld. BURNT OAK. Cf. *Burnt Oak Close* and *Field* 1754 HendonSurv. DEACONS HILL takes its name from an old chantry here, granted by Henry VIII to All Souls College, Oxford. EDGWARE BURY is *Ye Berrey in Edgware* 1657 Eales, *Edgworth Berry* 1754 R. Cf. *Berifel* 1277 *Rental*, *Berylandes* 1496 *All Souls* and *v.* burh (manorial). THE FORTUNE. Cf. *Fortune* 1754 R and Fortune Gate *infra* 161. NEWLANDS is *Newlandes close* 1535 *All Souls*, *New Lands* 1845 *TA*. PENNYWELL. Cf. *Pennywell Felde* 1552 Pat. PURCELL'S FM[2] is *Purcells al. Pipers* 1632 *All Souls*. *v.* Pipers Green *supra*. SHEEPHOUSE is *Sheephouse Farm* 1845 *TA*. Cf. *Shepecotewyk* 1277 *Rental*, *v.* wic. STONE GROVE is so named in 1819 (G). WOODCOCK HILL is *Woodcocke Hill* 1574 *All Souls*.

Harrow

HARROW

gumeninga hergae (dat.) 767 BCS 201, (*æt*) *Hearge* 825 ib. 384[3]

Hergas, (*apud*) *Hergan* 832 (c. 1250) BCS 402, *Herges* 1086 DB, 1232 Cl, 1235 *Ass*, *Her(e)ghes* 1232 Cl, Pat, 1235 *Ass*, FF, 1265 Pat, *Hareghes* 1258 FF, 1294 *Ass*

Her(e)wes 1234 Ch, 1249 FF, 1251, 1269 Pat, 1261 Ch, 1270 Ipm, 1272 FF

Hergeg' 1240 FF, *Hergh* 1243 ib., 1270 Ipm (p), *Heregh'* 1294 *Ass*

Har(e)wes c. 1250 MP, 1291 Tax, 1294 *Ass*, 1307 Cl, *Harwys* 1295 Ipm

Har(e)we 1278 FF, 1294 *Ass*, 1313 Ch, 1316 FA, 1341 NI, *Haruwe* 1348 FF, *Hargwe* 1397 Pat

Harghe 1299 Pat, *Harwo* 1347 ib., *Harogh'* 1368 FF, *Harowe* 1369, 1377 ib.

---

[1] Surviving in BROADFIELDS AVENUE. [2] Surviving in PURCELLS AVENUE.
[3] Endorsed (*H*)*earg* (10th), *Herga* (12th).

Harow(e) atte Hille 1398 IpmR, 1468 FF, (*on the Hull*) 1400 Pat, (*of the hyll*) 1421 FF, *Harowe on the Hill or Harwe on the Hull* 1426 Pat, (*upon le Hill*) 1474 ib.

This is OE *hearg*, 'heathen temple or shrine,' cf. Harrowden (PN Nth 125). Harrow is on a prominent isolated sand-capped hill, rising to about 300 ft. above the Middlesex plain, the ground falling away steeply on all sides. There must have been a site of ancient heathen worship here, perhaps on the site of the present church which stands on the summit of the hill. The early and persistent use of a plural form side by side with the singular one is curious. *gumeninga* would seem to be the gen. pl. of some tribal or folk-name, cf. *linga hæs* (*supra* 39). Nothing further is known of it.

NOTE. CROWN ST, so named from an inn. HIGH ST is *Harwestrete* 1453 *MxRec*. WEST ST is *le Weststrete* ib.

ALPERTON [*olim* æpətən]

Alprinton 1199 FF (p)
Alperton(e) 1282 *MxRec*, 1294 *Ass* (p), 1322 *Cor*, 1446, 1469 FF, *Halperton* 1407 ib.
Apurton 1342 FF, *Talpurton* 1390 ib., *Alpurton* 1350 *AD*, 1400 FF
Aperton al. Alperton 1578 *FF*, *Apperton Green* 1819 G

The forms are too late for any certainty. The name may go back to an OE *Ealhberhtingtun*, 'farm of *Ealhbeorht*,' *v.* ingtun. Cf. Alpraham (Ch), *Alburgham* DB, *Alpram* 1259 Ct (DEPN).

FORTY FM[1] is *Wembleyfortye* 1446 *MxRec*. Cf. *Forty Green* 1754 R. For the sense cf. Forty Hill *infra* 73. The farm was near Wembley just by Wealdstone Brook.

GREENHILL is *Grenehulle* 1334 *MxRec*, *Grenehill* 1563 *SR*, *Green Hill* 1675 Ogilby, *Girnell* 1675 MxNQ iv and was probably the home of Henry de *Grenehulle* (1282 *MxRec*), Richard de *Grenhulle* (1307 *GDR*) and John de *Grenehill* (1479 FF). As there is no appreciable hill here, it may be that the name is manorial rather than local in origin, Henry having come from elsewhere.

---

[1] Surviving in FORTY LANE.

HARROW WEALD

> *Weldewode*, (*in campo*) *del Welde* 1282 *MxRec*, *le Weldewode*
> 13th AD ii
>
> *Weld(e)* 1294 *Ass*, 1361, 1382, 1391 AD i, *le Weld(e)* 1410
> IpmR, 1453 *MxRec*, *le Weyld* 1548 ib.
>
> *Wald* 1294 *Ass*, (*in*) *Waldis* 1303 AD iii, *Walda* 1446 *MxRec*
> *Harewewelde* 1388 *Cor*, *Harrow Weelde* 1553 FF, *Harrow*
> *Wilde* t. Eliz ChancP, *The Wilde* 1564 PCC, *Harrowe Weale*
> 1603 PCC, *Harro Wild* 1662 ParReg (Stanmore)
>
> *v.* **weald**, 'forest, woodland.' For the forms *v.* Introd. xvii
> and cf. PN Sx 1–2, PN Sr 9.

KENTON is *Keninton* 1232 FF, *Keny(g)tone* 1282 *MxRec*, *Kenyng-ton in parochia de Harghes* 1307 GDR, *Kenynton* 1323 AD iv, *Kenyngton next Harogh'* 1368 FF, *Kenton al. Kynyton* 1548 Pat. Identical in origin with Kempton *supra* 23. KENTON LANE FM is so named in 1819 (G).

NORTHWICK PARK is a modern district name, taking its name from the *Northwick* family, lords of the manor of Harrow since 1797.

OAKINGTON is *Tokint'* 1194 Cur, *Toketon* 1235 *Ass*, *Tokinton*, -*y-* 1236, 1240, 1247 FF, *Tokingdon* 1274 *Ass*, -*yngton* 1508, 1587 FF, *Okington* 1594 FF. 'Toc(c)a's farm,' *v.* ingtun. For loss of initial *t* cf. Ickenham *supra* 43. For the personal name cf. Tockenham (PN W 272) and *toccan sceaga* (BCS 181).

PRESTON is *Preston* 1194 Cur (p), 1232 FF, 13th AD iv (p), 1356 HarrowRec, 1593 N. 'Farm of or belonging to the priest(s),' *v.* preost, tun. A priest is mentioned as holding land in Harrow parish in DB.

ROXBOROUGH is *Rokisborw* 1334 *MxRec*, *Rokesbergh* 1446 *Lambeth*, *Roxbourgh* 1462 *MxRec*, *Roxborrow Field* 1754 R, *Ruxborough* 1800 EnclA. It is close to Roxeth *infra*. 'Rook's or rook's hill or barrow,' *v.* beorg.

ROXETH

> (*et*) *Hroces seaðum* 845 BCS 448
>
> *Roxhe* 1235 *Ass* (p), *Roxeye* 1330 Cl, *Roxehay* 1508 FF,
> *Roxsey* 1524 ib.

Roxeth 1280 Pat, 1321 *MxRec*, 1680 S
Roxheth(e) 1282 *MxRec*, 1422 FF
Rokeshese 1294 *Ass*

'seaþ of a man named *Hrōc*,' i.e. 'rook,' cf. *Hroc* (Feilitzen 294). OE *sēaþ* meant 'pit, well, lake.' This might be rendered 'rook's pit,' but such a compound is extremely unlikely and is made still more improbable by the existence of the nearby Roxborough (*supra* 53). The first form shows the word in the dat. pl. Here the name may have referred to the slight hollow or depression in which are springs giving rise to the river Crane (*supra* 2).

SHEEPCOTE FM is *field called Longshoyte al. Shipe Cotefelde* (sic) 1548 Pat, *Shipcott ferme* 1682 *MxRec Sheepcote* 1800 EnclA. The alternative 16th-century name is a compound of 'long' and sceat, 'corner, angle,' *v. infra* 203.

SUDBURY is *Suthbery* 1282 *MxRec*, *Sudbery, Sudbur'* 1294 *Ass*, *La Suzberi* 1299 AD iv, *Sudbury* 1382 Cl, *Southbery* 1398 IpmR, *Sodbury* 1424 Pat, *Sutbury* 1474 ECP. 'South manor,' *v.* burh (manorial) and Introd. xvi. It lies to the south-east of Harrow. In early times there is mention of a *Norburyhyll* 1513 Harrow-Rec, *Northburie feild* 1581 ib., perhaps deriving from the manor house of Harrow itself.

UXENDON FM[1] is *Woxindon* 1257 FF (p), 1274 *Ass*, 1377 FF, 1389 IpmR, *Woxedon* 1274 *Ass*, *Wxindon* 1275 RH, *Woxendon* 1282 *MxRec*, 13th AD ii (p), 1307 *Ass* (p), *Oxindon* 1298 Pat (p), *Oxendon* 1563 SR, *Uxendon* 1593 N, *Oxendon al. Woxendon* 1602 *Recov*. For a discussion of the first element of this name *v.* Uxbridge *supra* 48. The second element is dun, 'down, hill.'

WEALDSTONE is *Weald Stone* 1754 R. Near by may have lived John *atte Stone* (1282 *MxRec*), John Stute de *Stone* (1548 ib.). It was perhaps originally a boundary mark separating Harrow Weald from the rest of Harrow parish. The growth of the place dates from the opening of the London and Birmingham railway in 1838, before which date there were only a few houses here.

---

[1] Surviving in UXENDON AVENUE.

WEMBLEY [*olim* wemli]

(*æt*) *Wemba lea* 825 BCS 384 (endorsed *Wembanlea* 10th, *Wambelea* 12th)

Wambeleg' 1249 FF, -*le* 1282 *MxRec*, 1294 *Ass*, -*ley*(*e*) 1334 *MxRec*, 1401 Cl

Wembele 1282 *MxRec*, 1368 *Cor*, *Wemblegrove* 1418 Harrow-Rec

Wemlee 1387 HarrowRec, *Wemley* 1508 FF, *Wembley* 1535 VE, *Whemley Grene* 1562 FF

Wymeley al. Wemley 1562 FF

'*Wemba*'s or *Wæmba*'s clearing,' *v.* leah. The personal name is not on record, but would be a nickname derived from OE *wamb*, 'belly.' Ekwall (DEPN *s.n.*) notes *Wamba*, the name of a Gothic king.

WOODCOCK HILL is *Woodcocks Hill* 1754 R. On the same map the present Woodcock Hill Fm is marked as *Ruff Leas Farm*, i.e. (probably) 'rough pasture,' *v.* læs.

BROOKSHILL[1], DOWNS FM and GROVE FM[2] may have been the homes of William *atte Broke* (1282 *MxRec*, 1294 *Ass*), Henry de *la Doune* (1307 FF) and Henry *atte Grove* (1282 *MxRec*). The second may be of manorial not local origin, Henry having come from Down Barns *supra* 44, not far distant.

BAMFORD'S CORNER, BONNERSFIELD LANE, DABBSHILL LODGE, FLAMBARDS[3], HONEYBUNN'S FM, LYON'S FM and PARKER'S FM are to be associated with the families of Mary *Bamford* (1619 LCCDeeds), Richard *Bonnour* (1282 *MxRec*), William *Dabbe* (1543 ib.), Edward *Flambard* (1354 FF), Thomas *Honeybunn* (1802 Poll), William *Lyon* (1274 *Ass*) and William *Parker* (1448 *MxRec*). The *Lyon* family continued in the neighbourhood till the 17th century (cf. John *Lioun*, *Lyoun*, 1370 HarrowRec, John *Lyon* of Preston, yeoman, the founder of Harrow School in 1572).

BARN HILL is *Barnhills* 1800 EnclA. THE BUTTS is so named in 1731 (Walford). *v.* butte. COPSE FM. Cf. *Weald Coppice Farm*

[1] *Brooks hill* 1680 S.
[2] *Roxhethgrove* 1446 *MxRec*. Cf. Roxeth *supra* 53.
[3] *Flambardes* 1448 *MxRec*, 1487 Ipm. Cf. Flamston (PN W 393).

1800 EnclA. DEADMAN'S HILL. Cf. *Dedemans lane, Dedmans slade* 1548 *MxRec.* EAST CROFT. Cf. *Westcroft* 1282 ib. EAST LANE is *Estlane* 1548 ib. THE HERMITAGE is *le Armytage* 1548 ib., *le Ermytage* t. Hy 8 ib. HUNDRED ELMS FM. Cf. *Hundred Elms* 1754 R. MOUNT PLEASANT is so named in 1819 (G). *v. infra* 207. OLDFIELD HO. Cf. *Oldfeld* 1548 *MxRec.* PRIESTMEAD is *Prestesmed(e)* 1506 *Lambeth*, 1548 *MxRec.*

Hendon

HENDON

> *Hendun* 959 (c. 1100) BCS 1050, 13th AD ii, *-don* 1199 FF
> *et passim*
> (*oþ*) *heandunes gemære* 972–8 BCS 1290, (*in*) *Heændune* (sic)
> 1042–66 (13th) *WDB*, (*in*) *Heandune* 1066 KCD 824
> *Handone* 1086 DB
> *Heindone* 1199 Cur, *Heyn-* 1291 FF, *Heendon* 1305 Pat,
> *Hyndon* 1344 ib., 1370 Cl, 1534 PCC

'At the high down,' *v.* heah, dun. The passage from BCS 1290 has reference to the bounds (*v.* (ge)mære) of *Loþereslege* and Hendon, *v. infra* 220. The old village of Hendon clustered round the church of St Mary, which stands on a prominent hill, visible for many miles from the west and south-west.

NOTE. ASHLEY LANE is so named in 1584 (HendonSurv). BANSTOCK RD. Cf. *Banstockfeild* 1574 ib., *Banstocks* c. 1840 *TA*. BELL LANE. Cf. *Bell Field* 1685 HendonSurv and bell. COLIN DEEP LANE. *v. infra* 57. COOL OAK LANE is *Colleck lane* 1574 *All Souls.* Cf. *Cowle Oak, Cool Oke Lane* 1574 HendonSurv. Curiously enough there is a *Cheldokfold* (1321 BlBk) in Hendon, deriving from OE ceald, 'cold.' It may possibly have reference to the same oak. DEANS LANE. Cf. *Denes* 1574 HendonSurv, *Dinns Lane* 1685 ib., and Deans Brook *supra* 3. DOWNAGE LANE. Cf. *le Doun(e)hegge* 1316 *WAM*, 1321 BlBk, *Dounedge* 1574 HendonSurv. A compound of dun, 'down, hill' and hecg, 'hedge.' DRYFIELD RD. Cf. *Dry Field* c. 1840 *TA*. HENDON WOOD LANE. Cf. *Hendon Woodes al. Hendon Park* 1550 Pat. HIGHFIELD AVENUE. Cf. *High feld* 1574 HendonSurv. HOMEFIELD RD. Cf. *Home Meadow* c. 1840 *TA* and ham. LILLY LANE is so named ib. MILLFIELD RD. Cf. *Mill Field* 1754 HendonSurv. OLDBERRY ROW. Cf. *Oldberries* 1574 ib. ORANGE HILL is so named c. 1840 (*TA*). RIDGEWAY. Cf. *Ridgwaie feld* 1574 HendonSurv. It runs south-east to north-west on the highest ground in the district. SANDER'S LANE. Cf. *Saunders* ib.

It is probably to be associated with the family of Richard *Saundre* (1321 BlBk). WISE LANE is to be associated with the family of Nicholas *Wise* (1548 HendonSurv).

BARNET GATE was earlier *Greensgate* 1574 HendonSurv, *Grinsgate* (*Wood*) 1754 R, c. 1840 *TA*, and is to be identified with the (*to*) *grendeles gatan* of 972–8 (BCS 1290), *v. infra* 220. '*Grendel*'s gate.' For other examples of Grendel, the man-eating monster of the Beowulf story, cf. Grimsbury (PN D 489), Gransmore (PN Ess 422) and *grendlesmere* (BCS 677) in Wiltshire (PN W 481). The place is on the county border adjoining High Barnet parish, Herts.

BLECHENHAM (lost) is *Blecceanham* 951–9 (13th) BCS 1351, *Bleccenham* 970 (14th) ib. 1264, *Blechenham* 1226, 1315 FF (p), *Blecheham in Hendon* 1302 *WDB*. '*Blæcca*'s ham.' Cf. Bletchley (PN Bk 17). The name was later entirely lost. The bounds in BCS 1351 (*v. infra* 220–1) show that the place must have been in the south part of the present Hendon parish.

BURTONHOLE FM is *Button Hole* 1754 HendonSurv, 1754 R, 1800 Faden, *Burton Hole* 1819 G. It may be that this is a place-name of the nickname type (*v. infra* 207), the reference being to a tiny or insignificant homestead. In that case the modern form must be a more dignified re-fashioning.

CLUTTERHOUSE FM is *Clyderhous*(*e*) 1445 FF, 1523 *SR*, *Clyderous* 1453 Pap, *Clitherhouse* 1535 VE, *Clytherhouse*, *Cletherhouse* 1547 LP, *Clitter House* 1649 CantYB iv, 1724 Moll, *Clutter House Farm* 1819 G. The origin of this name is not certain, but it may well be of manorial origin, deriving from the family of Robert de *Cliderhou* mentioned in 1311 (FF), the family having come from Clitheroe (La). If this is so, the forms are due to folk-etymology through the influence of the word 'house,' *Clyderhou's* becoming *Clyderhous*(*e*).

COLINDALE was earlier known as *Collyndene* 1550 *All Souls*, *Cullinge Deepe*, *Collin Deep Lane* 1584 HendonSurv, 1754 R, *Collen Deep* 1675 Ogilby, *Collins Deepe* 1710 S, and is probably to be associated with the family of John *Collin* (1574 Hendon Surv). *Deep* must refer to the valley of the Silk Stream at this spot. It must have been very near to, if not actually identical in site with, the *deopan fura* in the bounds of BCS 994, *v. infra* 220.

CRICKLEWOOD[1] is *le Crikeldwode* (sic) 1294 *GDR*, *Crikeledewod* 1321 BlBk, *Crikeledewode* 1394 *Cor*, *Crykyll Wood* 1509 *All Souls*, *Crekyll Woddes* 1525 *WAM*, *Crekle Woods* 1553 ib., *Cricklewood* 1680 S, *Krickle Wood* 1754 R. The early forms given here make it difficult to take the first part of this name to be a compound of British *cruc*, 'hill' and OE *hyll*, as suggested by Ekwall (DEPN *s.n.*), and in addition to the formal difficulty, though there is a hill here it is not of the abrupt distinctive type which we find in such places as Crich (Db). More probably the first element is a participial adjective derived from the dial. *crickle* (*v.* EDD), 'to bend, give way,' the adjective being descriptive of the outline of the wood.

DOLE STREET and DOLLIS FM. In 16th and 17th century records we find places called (a) *Dolstret(e)* 1523, 1547, 1563 *SR*, *Dole Street*, *Doldstreat* 1584 HendonSurv, (b) *Dalys* 1563 *SR*, *land called the Doles, tenement called Doles* 1574 HendonSurv, *Dallies* 1583 PCC, *Dallys* 1584 HendonSurv, 1622 Sess, *Dalis* 1593 N, *Dallehays* 1685 HendonSurv, (c) *Dollis Bridge* 1574 ib. It is difficult to reconcile all these spellings or to know whether there is any connection with Dollis Hill in Willesden (*infra* 161), a few miles away. There is a Sarra *Dol* mentioned in 1321 (BlBk) and the place may take its name from her family, though the 1574 forms suggest connection with ME *dole*, OE *dāl*, 'portion,' the reference being to *doles* or portions of the common field, *v.* **dal**.

FRITH MANOR is *Fryth in Hyndon* 1535 VE, *Frith al. Newhall* 1571 BM and was the home of Thomas *Attefrethe* (1274 *Ass*), de *la Frithe* (1294 ib.) and Valentine *atte Fryth* (1294 FF). *v.* **fyrhðe**, 'wooded country.' This was once a part of the old Middlesex woodland area.

GOLDERS GREEN is *Golders Greene* 1612, 1619 *FF*, *Goulders Green* 1680 S, *Groles Green* 1754 R, *Groles or Godders Green* 1790 Stockdale, *Goldhurst Green* 1795 Lysons. The first element is clearly a personal name. No surname *Golder* has been noted

---

[1] Partly in Willesden.

in any record relating to the parish, but in the BlBk we have mention of John *le Godere* (1321) and in 1371 (FF) of John *Godyer* of Hendon. Near by is Golders Hill in Finchley (*infra* 93) which is *Godereshill* t. Hy 4. It may well be that the green and hill alike took their name from this family *God(y)ere*, with later corruption to *Golder* in both cases.

HALE was the home of Ralph *in the Hale* (1294 *Ass*), John *in the Hale* (1310 *AddCh*). It is *Hale* 1525 FF, *Netherhale* 1588 *SR*. This is OE healh, 'angle, corner of land.' The hamlet lay in the north-west corner of the parish.

HIGHWOOD HILL is (*in*) *alto bosco* 1321 *Ct*, *Highwode, Hiwode* 1523 *SR*, *Highwodhyll* 1543 LP, *Heiwoodhill* 1563 *SR*, *Hyewoodhill* 1568 FF. The place lies high above Hendon near the Hertfordshire border.

HODFORD[1] is *Hodeford* 1296 Cl, 1318, 1321 FF, 1321 BlBk, 1337 Ipm, *Hoddesford* 1398 Ch, Pat. '*Hodda*'s ford.'

HYDE is *la Hyde* 1281 *Ct*, 1289 AD ii, *Hepeworthe Hyde* 1315 BM, *Hide* 1675 Ogilby. *v.* hid, 'measure of land,' and Hyde Park *infra* 168. William de *Heppeworthe* held land in Hendon parish in 1285 (*AddCh*). The family probably came from Hepworth in Suffolk or Hepworth in the West Riding of Yorkshire.

MILL HILL is *Myllehill* 1547 *SR*, *Milhill, Mylhyll* 1563 ib.

SHOELAND FM is *Schooland* 1384 *All Souls, Scholand* 14th AD i, *Sholands, Shoelands* 1574 HendonSurv. The name is probably identical in origin with Shoelands (PN Sr 210–11). See also PN Ess 584–5. The first element is either the OE *scēo*, 'shoe' or else *sceolh*, 'oblique, awry,' in either case with reference to the shape of a particular piece of land.

TEMPLE FORTUNE is so named in 1754 (R). Cf. *The Temples* 1574 HendonSurv. The Knights Templars held land in the parish in 1243 (FF). The meaning of *Fortune* is not clear, but cf. Fortune Gate in Willesden *infra* 161.

THE WELSH HARP (officially 'The Brent or Kingsbury Reservoir') is an artificial lake formed in 1835–9 by the damming of

---

[1] Surviving in HODFORD RD.

the Brent near its junction with the Silk stream at this point.
The popular name is from the old Welsh Harp Inn on the main
road here. WELSH HARP BRIDGE was *Braynt Bridge* in 1662
(Sess).

WILDWOOD FM. Cf. *The Weildes, Wildswoode, Weildswoode* 1574
HendonSurv. 'Woodland,' *v.* Harrow Weald *supra* 53. For the
present-day spelling *v.* Introd. xvii and cf. Wild Close in Hale
(Ha), *Weld, Weild Close corner* 1670 *For*, in the bounds of the
New Forest.

THE GROVE was the home of Ralph *atte Grove* (1321 BlBk). Cf.
Grovefeilds, South Grove 1574 HendonSurv.

BUNN'S FM[1] (6"), CHILDS HILL[2], DRIVER'S HILL[3], GIBBS GREEN[4],
GOLDBEATER'S FM[5], GOODHEWS FM[6], HOLDER'S HILL[7], LANGTON
LODGE, PAGE STREET[8], RAVENSFIELD HO[9] and RENTER'S FM[10] are
to be associated with the families of Simon *Bunde* (1434 Hendon
Surv), Richard *Child* (1321 BlBk) and Robert *Child* (1325
WAM), John *le Driver'* (1321 BlBk), John *Gybbe* (1525 *SR*),
William de Aldenham of London, *goldbetere* (1307 FF) and John
le Goldbetere (1321 BlBk), John *Godhewe* (ib.), Roger *le Holdere*
(1294 *Ass*), John de *Langeton* (1321 BlBk), John and William
Page (1294 *Ass*), Richard *Raven* (1330 HendonSurv) and John
le Renter (1309 FF).

BELMONT HO is so named in 1819 (G). BITTACY HO. Cf.
Bittasea Hill, Wood 1754 HendonSurv, *Bittersey Wood* c. 1840
TA. BRENT STREET is *Braynestreete* 1613 *FF, Brent Street* 1710
S, by the river Brent. For *street* in the sense 'hamlet,' *v. infra*
204. BURNT OAK BARN is so named c. 1840 (*TA*). BURROUGHS
is *land called Borowis in Hendon* 1529–32 ECP, *Burrowes* 1574
HendonSurv. Cf. *le Berwestret* 1316 ib., *Borowstrete* 1493 ib.
The first element is **beorg**, 'hill,' the 'high down' itself. COPT-

---

[1] Cf. *tenement of Bunnes, Bounes grove* 1574 HendonSurv.
[2] *Childes Hill* 1593 N.   [3] *Dryvers* 1574 HendonSurv.
[4] Cf. *Gibb feild* ib.
[5] Cf. *Goldbeters gardyn, mede* 1434 ib., surviving in GOLDBEATER'S LANE.
[6] *Goodhews* 1574 ib.
[7] *Oldershyll, Oldershilles* 1584 ib., *Holears Hill* 1680 S, *Hollars Hill* 1745 R,
Holders Hill 1750 Seale.
[8] *Page Streete* 1588 SR.   [9] *Ravenesfeld* 1316–29 *WAM*.
[10] *farm called Renters* 1566 Sess.

HALL is *Copt Hall* 1574 ib., *Copidhall* 1632 *All Souls*. Cf. Copthall Fm *supra* 36. COVENTRY FM is so named in 1754 (R). COWHOUSE FM is *Cowhous* 1398 Ch, *Cowys* 1535 VE. COW-LEAZE HO. Cf. *Cowelease* 1574 HendonSurv. *v.* læs. DIAL HO. Cf. *Dial Cottages* c. 1840 *TA* and *infra* 205. GUTTERSHEDGE FM. Cf. *Gutters Hedge* 1680 S. HOLCOMBE HO. Cf. *Hocumfeild* 1574 HendonSurv, *Hocome Hill* 1686 M. HYVER HALL is *Hivers Hill* (sic) 1754 HendonSurv. JEANETTS is *Jenates* 1574 ib. LAURENCE ST FM is *Larance St* 1680 S, *Laurence Street* 1754 R. MILESPIT FM is *Milespet* 1475 HendonSurv, *Myles pytt* 1547 *SR*, *Milspit* 1563 ib., *Milles pitt* 1588 ib. Cf. *land called Myles* 1574 Hendon Surv. MOATMOUNT. Cf. *Motefeild* ib., *Moat Mount* 1754 ib. Moatmount was surrounded by a moat in 1799 (Evans 261). THE PARK. Cf. *Hendon Parke* 1550 Pat. ROCKHALLS LODGE is *Rokeholtes* 1446 Pat, *Rookholtes* 1475 HendonSurv, *Rokeholdes* 1547 LP, *Rockhold* 1754 HendonSurv, *Rowkhowlls* 1617 Moore. Cf. Ruckholt (PN Ess 102). The name may be significant—'rook-woods'—or it may be manorial, from someone bearing the name *Rookholt*. SHEVESHILL is *Shefshill* 1505 HendonSurv, *Sheveshill* 1574 ib., *Shesshill* c. 1840 *TA*. SILK BRIDGE is *Silke Bridge* 1622 PCC. *v.* Silk Stream *supra* 6. STONYFIELDS is *Stonyfeilde* 1574 HendonSurv. WEST CROFT FM is *Westcrofte* ib. WOODFIELD[1] is *Wodefeld* 1325 *WAM*.

Kingsbury

KINGSBURY

> *Kynges byrig* 1044–46 KCD 843
> *Chingesberie* 1086 DB, *-biri* 1219 Pap, *Kingesbir'* 1199 Cur
>   *et passim* to 1316 FA, with variant spellings *Kynges-* and
>   *-bury, -beri, Kiggesbire* (sic) 1199 Cur
> *Kynkesbury* 1294 *Ass, Kynnesbur'* 1310 FF

'The king's manor or stronghold,' *v.* burh. Cf. Kingsbury (PN Herts 89). The manor was granted to Westminster Abbey by Edward the Confessor. In OE times the present parish of Kingsbury was included within the bounds of the manor of *Tunworth infra* 62.

The association of the place with a king goes back at least to

---

[1] Surviving in WOODFIELD AVENUE.

957 when the woodland in the parish is referred to in the phrase (*oð ðæs*) *cinges inwuda* (BCS 994).

NOTE. SLOUGH LANE. Cf. field called *Hony Slowe* 1574 *All Souls*. *hony* from its stickiness, cf. *infra* 205. WAKEMAN'S HILL AVENUE. Cf. *Wakemans Closes* 1545 ib.

CHALKHILL HO is (*æt*) *Cealchylle* 1044–66 KCD 843, *Chalchell'* 1199 Cur (p), *Chalehull* (sic) 1236 FF, *Chalkhulle* 1240 ib., 1383 SR, *Chalkehull'* 1294 *Ass*, *Chalkhill* 1441 AD iv. The OE form of this name shows that the first element must be *cealc*, commonly rendered 'chalk, limestone.' Elsewhere in the county we find *Chalkecroft* 1557 Pat (Hendon), 1441 *Ct* (Enfield), *Chalkfeld* 1552 Pat (Edgware), *Chalkefeld* 1557 ib. (Isleworth), *Chawkehill* 1539 *Rental* (St Pancras). Neither chalk nor limestone is to be found at any of these places. For a similar difficulty elsewhere, cf. *Caulke Cliff* (PN Nt 129). Potter (12) says "The Saxons named it so probably because the hard blue clay on the hillside seemed to have an appearance like chalk."

FRYANT FM is *Freryn Court* 1515–18 ECP, *Freren al. Kyngesbury* 1544 LP, *Friarn Manor* 1593 N, *Friant* 1754 R. 'Friars' court or manor.' According to Lysons (iii, 233) the manor belonged to the Priory of St John of Jerusalem, so the *freren* or brethren were the knights.

GORE FM[1]. Cf. *Goreslea* 1407 HarrowRec, *Goreden* 1445 ib., *Goorfeldes*, *Goormed* 1476 ib., *Gore lane*, *Gowerlanegate* 1565 ib. v. **gara, leah, denu, feld, mæd**. It is possibly *Gor* (1220 Cur) and here may have lived John de *Gore* (1307 FF). This was the Hundred meeting-place, v. *supra* 50.

ROEGREEN FM is *Wrogrene* 1574 *All Souls*, *Wroe croft juxta Wroe Greene* 1632 ib., *Rowe Green* 1680 S. It may be that we should compare *Wrolandes* 1399–1413 HarrowRec, 12 *acres called le Wroo* 1422 ib., *le Wrothe* 1476 ib., all in Kingsbury. The initial *w* is well established and it looks as if we have a derivative of ON *vrá*, 'nook, corner,' ME *wro*, but such a form would be surprising in Middlesex. The last form seems to be irregular.

TUNWORTH (lost) is (*æt*) *Tuneweorðe*, *Tunwæorðinga gemære* 957 (13th) BCS 994, *Heytoneworth* t. Hy 4 HarrowRec, *High Ton-*

---

[1] Demolished in 1937. The site is now occupied by the Odeon Cinema.

worth in the lordship of Kingsbury 1536 ib., *Tunworth* 1839 *TA.*
This seems to have been the earlier name for the manor later
known as Kingsbury (*v. supra* 61). Ekwall (DEPN *s.n.* Tunworth (Ha)) takes this to be a compound of **tun** and **weorþ**, but
semantically such a compound is exceedingly unlikely. There is
an OE personal name *Tuna.* **weorþ** is commonly compounded
with personal names and the text of BCS 994 is such that no
reliance can be placed upon it. We may note that *tatanburnan*
found in BCS 1290 (a 10th-century text) appears as *tateburnan.*
Hence probably '*Tuna*'s farm.'

GROVE FM[1] and HILLHOUSE FM[2] were the homes of Richard de
la Grave (1281 *Ct*), otherwise Richard *atte Grove* (1294 *Ass*),
and Richard *atte Hill* (1384 *All Souls*). *v.* **grafa, græfe.**

SALMON STREET is *Salmonstreete* 1632 *All Souls* and is to be
associated with the family of William *Salman* (1427 ib.). *v.*
infra 68.

BLACKPOT HILL is so named in 1819 (G). BUSH FM is so called
in 1754 (R). Cf. *Bussheshottes* 1528 HarrowRec and sceat.
KINGSBURY GREEN is *Kingsbury grene* 1574 *All Souls.* LEWGARS
is *Lewgars tenement* 1632 ib. RED HILL is so named in 1686 (M).
Cf. *Redhill croft* 1632 *All Souls.* TOWNSEND is so named in 1839
(*TA*). *v.* **tun.**

Pinner

PINNER[3]

> *Pinnora* 1232 Ch (p), *Pinora* 1232 FF
> *Pinnore* 1248 SelectPleas (p), *Pynnore* 1257 FF *et freq* to 1349
>   Orig, with variant spelling *Pinn-*, *Pinhore* 1253 FF
> *Pinnere* 1332 BM, *Pynner in the parish of Harrow* 1532 FF
> *Pynnor* 1483 FF

The second element is **ora**, 'bank, edge, slope,' etc. The
original village street slopes steeply up to the church from the
Pinn River, but there can be little doubt that that river-name
is a late back-formation (cf. *supra* 5). The first element may be

---

[1] Cf. *Groves, Grovefeild* t. Jas 1 ECP.
[2] *the Hill House* 1754 R. Cf. *Hill Croft* 1532 CtRequests, *Hilhousecroft*
1632 *All Souls.*
[3] A chapel of ease to Harrow until the 18th century.

the OE *pinn*, 'pin, peg,' but it is difficult to see how this could be used in a topographical sense here. Alternatively we may have this word used as a personal name, originally a nickname. Cf. the names *Pin* (Gl) and *Pinna* (Wo) recorded from DB (Feilitzen 344). Cf. also *pinnan rod* (KCD 767) and PN Wo 338, *s.n.* Pinton.

NOTE. LOVE LANE is *Lovelane* 1506 *Lambeth*. WARPLE WAY is *le Werpeweye* 1332 BM. Cf. *The Worple, Warple Hill* 1565, 1659 *MxRec* and *v.* worple.

HATCH END is *le Hacchehend* 1448 *MxRec*, *Hacheend* 1475 FF and was probably by the home of Roger *atte Hacche* (1307 *GDR*) and William *atte Hacche* (1393 FF). *v.* hæcc, 'gate, wicket,' etc. The reference may have been to a gate of Pinner Park. *End* has the sense 'quarter, district of a parish,' *v. infra* 198.

HEADSTONE

Hegeton 1348 *MinAcct*
Heggestone 1367, 1545 Bushell, *Hedgestone* t. Hy 8 *MxRec*, *Hegeston(e)* 1526, 1546 LP, 1605 *Rental*, 1612 *Recov*
Heggedon 1382 Bushell, *-ton* 1398 IpmR, 1438, 1459 *Lambeth*, 1446, 1453 *MxRec*
Hegton 1397 Pat
Hedsdon 1682 Morgan, *Hedston* 1754 R, *Headstone* 1819 G

The forms are late and their inconsistency makes any satisfactory suggestion impossible.

OXHEYLANE FM. Cf. *Oxhey lane* 1648 *AddCh*, so named because leading to Oxhey (PN Herts 106).

RAYNER'S LANE is a newly developed area (*post* 1930). According to Druett (218) the lane took its name from one *Rayner*, an old shepherd who lived at the solitary cottage here less than 40 years ago.

WAXWELL FM is *Wakeswell(e)* 1274 *Ass*, 1306 *Lambeth*, 1448 *MxRec*, *Waxwell* 1680 S. The first element may be a personal name as in Waxway (PN D 606). Hence '*Wæcc*'s spring,' *v.* wielle.

WOOD HALL is *Wodehall(e)* 1271 Pat, 1282 *MxRec*, *la Wodehalle* 1274 *Ass*, *Wodhall* 1349, 1354 FF. 'Hall or manor by the wood,' *v.* heall. It is near Woodridings *infra* 65.

DOWN's FM, EAST END[1], NOWER [nɑuə] HILL[2] and PINNER PARK[3]
were the homes of Richard de *Doune* (1282 *MxRec*), William *del
Esthende, atte Nesthende* (ib.), John *atte Nore* (ib.) and Richard
de *Parco* (ib.). *v.* dun, ende, ora, parke. ME *at then ore,* 'at the
bank,' has become *atte nore.*

CANNON FM[4], GATESHILL FM, PAINES BRIDGE and TERRILANDS[5]
are to be associated with the families of John *Canoun* (1282
MxRec), Thomas and Robert *Gates* (1563 *SR*), Edward *Payne*
(1662 Druett) and Ralph *Terry* (1282 *MxRec*).

BARROWPOINT HILL is *Borrowpoint Hill* 1686 M, *Perrie Point
Hill* 1733 Druett, *Barrow Point Hill* 1750 Seale, *Berry Pond Hill*
1800 EnclA. HOOKING GREEN is *Hooken Green* ib. PINNER
HILL. Cf. (*a*) *monte de Pynnore* 1334 *MxRec*. WESTEND FM is
le Westhend 1448 ib. WOODRIDINGS is *Woodredynge* t. Hy 8 ib.,
Woodreeding 1733 Druett. 'Clearing in the wood,' *v.* ryding.

Stanmore

STANMORE

> *Stanmere* 793 (12th) BCS 267, 1086 DB *et passim* to 1411 FF,
> (*magna*) 1235, 1274 *Ass, Stammere* 1219 Pap
> *Stanemere* 1279 QW, *Stannemere* 1332 Ipm
> *Great*(*e*) *Stanmare* 1392 Pat, 1565 PCC, *Stanmar the More*
> 1508 PCC, *Much Stanmer* t. Eliz ChancP, *Stanmer the
> More* 1563 *SR*
> *Standemore* 1562 PCC, *Standmere, Standmore* 1605 Daven-
> port
> *Stanmore the Great* 1574 PCC, *Stanmore* 1682 Morgan,
> 1710 S

'Stony mere or pool,' *v.* stan, mere. There are outcrops of
gravel on the clay soil here and the *mere* may have been one of
the ponds which still exist. *Great* to distinguish from Whitchurch or Little Stanmore *infra* 66.

---

[1] *Esthend* 1453 *MxRec, East End* 1793 Cary.
[2] *Nowre* 1548 *MxRec, Nower Hill* 1733 Druett. The farm is on a steep
hillside.
[3] *park of Pynnore* 1348 Pat.
[4] *Canons* c. 1486 ECP, 1733 *MxRec*.   [5] Now CHISWICK HO.

NOTE. DENNIS LANE is *Denyse Lane* 1578 Davenport. HONEYPOT LANE is *Honeypott lane* 1680 ib. with reference to the heavy clay soil here, *v. infra* 205. See also *supra* 11, n. 1. WEMBOROUGH RD. Cf. *Wyneberwe* 1277 *Rental, Wimborough* 1541 Druett, *Wynborough Bush* 16th ib. Possibly 'Wina's hill,' *v.* beorg.

BENTLEY PRIORY is *Benetleg*(*h*) 1243 Cl, 1306 Pat, *Bentleye* 1282 *MxRec, Binttle*(*y*) 1291 Tax, 1318 Ch, *Bentley* t. Hy 8 *MinAcct.* 'Clearing overgrown with bent grass,' *v.* beonet, leah.

THE GROVE was the home of Ricardus de *la Graue* (1221 Bracton) and Thomas de *la Grave* (1315 YearBk). *v.* græfe.

AYLWARDS and WARD'S FM are to be associated with the families of William *Aylewarde* (1578 Davenport) and Richard *Warde* (1601 ParReg).

BELMONT is *Bell Mount* 1754 R, *Belmount* 1822 O.S. BROOM-FIELD. Cf. *Bromefeld Grove, Bromefeild Halfe* 1552 Pat, 1590 AD iii. CULVERLANDS. Cf. *Culvercroft* c. 1840 *TA* and culver. HERIOT'S WOOD is so named ib. WARREN HO is *The Warren House* c. 1580 Davenport.

Whitchurch

WHITCHURCH

Stanmera 1086 DB, *alia Stanmera* 1106 Round, *Commune of London*

villa de Parvo (sic) *Stanmere* 13th RBE, 1235 Fees, (*parua*) 1235 *Ass, Stanmere parva* 1291 Tax, (*minor*) 1294 *Ass, Stanmer the lesse* 1513 PCC, 1563 *SR, Little Stanmer* 1540 DKR x, *Stanmare the lesse* 1553 Sess, *Little Stanmore* 1599 PCC

Whyzt Churche 1538 LP, *Whytchurche* 1551 FF

Whitchurch al. Little Stanmer 1590 AD iii, *Stanmer little called also Whytechurch* 1593 N

Originally *Little Stanmore*. The later name may have been given because of the colouring of the church walls, cf. Whitchurch (PN D 247).

NOTE. HANDEL WAY is a modern name recalling the association of Handel with the Duke of Chandos who lived at Canons *infra* 67.

CANONS PARK is *Canons* 1518–29 ECP, *Cannons* 1593 N, representing the six acres of land in Little Stanmore granted to the prior and *canons* of St Bartholomew's, Smithfield in 1331 (Inq aqd). Cf. *Barthilmewe Grove* 1552 Pat.

CLOISTERS WOOD is *Cloyster Grove* 1541 RecStBarts, *the wood hedge of Cloysters* 1680 Davenport. The origin of the name is uncertain. It is possibly to be connected with the ownership by the canons of St Bartholomew's, Smithfield.

MARSH FM is *Marshe* 1520 RecStBarts and was the home of Roger de *Marisco* (13th AD v).

PEAR WOOD is *Pary Wood* 1538 RecStBarts, *Pars Wood al. Pares Wood* 1590 AD iii and is possibly to be associated with the family of William *Parys* (1272 AD ii).

WOOD FIELD is so named c. 1840 (*TA*).

V. EDMONTON HUNDRED

Delmetone 1086 DB, *Ædelmeton* 1182 P, *Elminton* 1187 ib., *Emilton* 1189 ib., *Aedelmeston* 1194 ib., *Edolmeton* 1235 *Ass*, *Edelmeton* 1274 ib. The site of the Hundred meeting-place is unknown[1].

Edmonton

EDMONTON

Adelmetone 1086 DB, *Eadelmeton* late 12th BM, 13th AD ii
Edelmeton(e) 1202 FF *et passim* to 1550 ib., *-miton* 1306 Ipm,
   Edolmeton, Edulmeton 1235 Fees, *Eddelmethone* 1276 LBk,
   Edelmeltone 1329 AD i, *Edlemeton* 1534 FF
Edelmintone 1211 RBE, *Edelmenton* 1340 Pat, *Edelmynton*
   1397, 1406 FF, *-mon-* 1386 SR, *-myng-* 1432 FF
Edelmeston 1214 ClR, *-tun* 1235 Fees, *Edelmiston* 1407 IpmR
Edelington 1259 FF, *Edlington* 1264 Ipm, *Edelynton* 1397 FF
Edelmptone 1349, 1356 FF

[1] The parish of Hadley or Monken Hadley was in the Hundred until 1904 but was then transferred from Middlesex to Herts. *v.* PN Herts 75.

Edmenton 1369 AD i, 1392 FF, 1445 IpmR, *Edmun(d)ton*
1372 Pat, 1396 IpmR, *Edmanton* 1400 Pat, *Edmyngton* 1422,
1425 FF, *Edmynton* 1464 Pat

Edelmeton al. Edmonton 1464 IpmR, (*al. Edmondton*) 1544 FF
Elmuton, Edmuton 1550 FF

'*Ēadhelm*'s farm,' *v.* tun. The early forms show variation
between inflected and uninflected compounds *Eadhelmtun, Ead-
helmestun* and a form *Eadhelmingtun, v.* ingtun.

NOTE. ANGEL RD is so named from an inn of that name. BARROWELL
GREEN RD. Cf. *Berwelleslond* t. Hy 7 *Rental, Barrowell Green* c. 1840
TA. BROOKFIELD RD. Cf. *Brookefeild* 1636 *DuLa*. CHURCHFIELD
LANE. Cf. *Cherchefeld* 1387 *Walden*. FORE ST is *Forestreete* 1650
ParlSurv and was earlier *Heghestrate* 1342 FF. FOX LANE is so named
in 1819 (G). GREEN LANE. Cf. *Green Lane End* 1662 RobinsonEd.
HEDGE LANE is so named in 1608 (*LRMB*). MILLFIELD RD. Cf. *Mill-
feild* 1636 *DuLa*. SILVER ST is so named c. 1630 (ECP).

ARNOS GROVE ['aˑnouz] is *Arnold(e)s Grove* 1551 Pat, 1819 G,
Arno's Grove c. 1865 O.S. It may be that the name is to be
associated with the family of Margery *Arnold* (1344 FF).

BETSTILE[1] LODGE is *Bettestigle* 13th AD ii, *-stile* 1303 StPauls
MSS, *-style* 1370 BM, 1492 *StPauls*. Probably '*Betta*'s path,'
v. stigel.

BOWES[2] is *Bowes* 1396 StPaulsMSS, (*manor of*) 1412 FF and is
probably to be associated with the family of John de *Arcubus*
(1274 *Ass*), the name being of manorial origin. Cf. Bowes (PN
NRY 304).

BURY STREET is *Berystreate* t. Hy 8 *MinAcct, Burye streete* 1593
N. *Bury* is manorial (*v.* burh and Introd. xvi) with reference
to the manor house of Edmonton. *Street* here means 'hamlet,
row of houses,' as in other Middlesex names, *v. infra* 204.

CAUSEYWARE is *Caseware* 1710 S, *Cazaware* 1724 Moll and is
perhaps identical with *Chawsea* 1636 *DuLa*. It looks as if the
first element here was the ME *cauce, c(h)ausee*, 'causeway'
with reference to the Old North Road. The second element is
uncertain.

DANFORDS[3] (lost) is *Derneforde* 1275 RH, 1332, 1396 StPauls
MSS, 1412 FF, *Darnford* 1669 *StPauls, Great, Little Danfords*

---

[1] Surviving in BETSTILE RD.
[2] Surviving in BOWES PARK (district).   [3] Surviving in DURNSFORD RD.

c. 1840 *TA*. 'Secret or hidden ford,' from OE *dierne*, cf. Durn-ford (PN W 363). The name must have referred to a ford over the Pymmes Brook.

GROVELANDS. Cf. *le Grofe* t. Hy 7 *MinAcct*. It was known as *Cullands Grove* in 1795 (Lysons), 1819 (G). It may be that the name is to be associated with the family of Gilbert *Culling* (1235 *Ass*), Philip *Cullyng* (13th AD ii) and Robert *Culling* (1274 *Ass*), all mentioned in connection with Edmonton parish.

MARSH SIDE is *Mershside* 1608 *LRMB* and was by the home of John *atte Mersse* (1298 FF). Cf. also *le Common Mersh* 1608 *LRMB*, referring to the Lea marshes.

MINCHENDON[1] is *Mincenden* 1682 Morgan, *Mincington Hall* 1750 Seale, *Minchenden* 1795 Lysons. Cf. also *Menechenfeld* 13th AD i. The first element is myncen, 'nun.' The names probably refer to land in the parish held by the nuns of Clerkenwell. So similarly Minchinhampton (Gl), Mincing Lane (City).

PALMERS GREEN is *Palmers grene* 1608 *LRMB* and is to be asso-ciated with the families of Matthew *le Palmere* (1341 FF) and Richard *Palmer* (1598 Sess). It may be noted, however, that as early as 1205 (FF) there is mention of a field in the parish called *Palmeresfeld*, so the family may have been in the neighbourhood at a much earlier date. The surname *Palmer* means 'pilgrim.'

SOUTHGATE is *S(o)uthgate* 1370, 1372 AD i, *le South gate* 1608 *LRMB*. The hamlet grew up at the south gate of Enfield Chase (*infra* 73).

WEIR HALL. This is *Wirehall, Wyerhall* 1593 N and is probably to be associated with the family of Richard de *Wylehale* (1303, 1309 FF), de *Wesehale* (sic) (1307 ib.), de *Willehale* (1308 ib.), de *Wyllehale* (1332 ib.) and John de *Wyrhale* (1334 Pat, 1344 FF). It looks as if the original place-name was a compound of *wilig*, 'willow' and healh, 'nook, angle' (with later corruption), but since all the early forms are derived from personal names, it may well be that the place-name is of manorial rather than local origin. *v.* Addenda xxxiii.

---

[1] Surviving in MINCHENDON CRESCENT.

WINCHMORE HILL is *Wynsemerhull* 1319 AD ii, *Wynsmershull* 1395 Pat, *Wynsmorehyll* t. Hy 8 *MinAcct*, 1565 FF, *Wynsmore hill* 1543 ib., *Winchmore Hill* 1586 SP, 1593 N. The forms are too late for any certainty. The name may be for '*Winesige*'s or *Wynsige*'s boundary hill,' *v.* (ge)mære, hyll. The hamlet lay near the southern boundary of the ancient parish.

BARROWFIELD is *Barrow feld* 1608 *LRMB* and was probably the home of Peter de *la Berghe, la Berwe* (1235 FF, *Ass*). *v.* beorg, 'hill, barrow.'

BEAVER'S HALL[1], BOHUN FM, CLAPPERS GREEN, CLAVERING FM[2], DEEPHAMS FM[3], DYSON'S FM, FORDS GROVE[4], HUXLEY FM[5], NIGHTINGALE HALL[6], PICKETTS LOCK[7] and TANNERS END[8] are probably to be associated with the families of William *Bever* (1588 ParReg), Nicholas *Boone* (1608 *LRMB*), Stephen *le Claper*' (1272 FF), Thomas *Claveryng* (1385 ib.), Roger de *Depham* (1316 ib.), James *Dyson* (1802 Poll), Geoffrey and Ailward de *Forde* (1202 FF), Katheren and John *Huxley* (1630, 1656 Par Reg), *Nitingale, Nightingall* (1589 etc. ib.), *Picot* de Marisco (t. Hy 3 AD ii) and Thomas, son of *Picot* (13th ib. v) and Nathaniel *Tanner* (1650 NQ iii).

BOURNE HILL. Cf. *Bournegate way* 1658 *ParlSurv, Bournegate* 1686 *DuLa*. BROOK HO. Cf. *Brokcroft* 1274 AD ii. BROOMFIELD HO is *Bromefeyld* t. Hy 8 *MinAcct*. BUSH HILL is *Bussheyhill* 1549 Pat, *Upper Bushhill* 1608 *LRMB*. CONYBOROUGH HILL. Cf. *South Cunnyborough, North Cunnyborough* 1658 *ParlSurv*. *v.* coneyborough. COOKS FERRY is *Bleak Hall or Cook Ferry* 1754 R. CUCKOOHALL FM is *Cuckow Hall* 1750 Seale, *Cockow Hall* 1754 R[9]. EAST MARSH is *East marshe* 1608 *LRMB*. HIGH-FIELD HO[10] is *Heghefeld* t. Hy 3 AD ii, *le Heyfeld* 13th AD i, *le Highe feeld* 1608 *LRMB*. *v.* feld. HOPE HO may be *le Hope*

---

[1] *Beaver Hall* 1819 G. Surviving in BEAVER RD.
[2] *Claverynges* 1486 Pat, *Claveringe greene* 1608 *LRMB*.
[3] *manor of Dephams* 1459 ECP, *Diphams* 1486 Pat. The family probably came from Deopham (Nf).
[4] *Fordesgrove* t. Ed 3 Rental.
[5] *The House of John Huxley, esquire* 1636 *DuLa*, surviving in HUXLEY RD.
[6] Surviving in NIGHTINGALE RD.
[7] Cf. *Picketts feild* 1669 Ct. [8] *Tanners End* 1819 G.
[9] Surviving in CUCKOO HALL RD. [10] Surviving in HIGHFIELD RD.

c. 1290 AD i, c. 1300 ib. ii. *v.* hop, 'enclosure.' HOUNDSFIELD[1]
is *Houndesfeld, Hounsfeld* 1608 *LRMB, Hownesfeild al. Hunts-
feild* 1686 *DuLa. v.* feld and cf. Hounslow *supra* 26. HYDE HO
is *La Hyde* 13th AD iv, *le Hyd* t. Hy 8 *MinAcct. v.* hid. LONG-
HEDGE NURSERY. Cf. *Lang(e)hegh* t. Hy 3, 13th AD iv, *Langhege*
1274 ib., *Langhedge* 1608 *LRMB*. The original second element
may have been OE (ge)hæg, 'enclosure,' etc. *langhay* seems
later to have been replaced by *langhedge*. MILLBROOK[2]. Cf.
Melcroft, Melflet 13th AD i, *Millfeild* 1636 *DuLa*. MOOR PARK.
Cf. *le More* 1486 Pat, *Moor Park* 1664 SP, *v.* mor. OAKFIELD
COTTAGE[3]. Cf. *Okefeilde* 1608 *LRMB*. SHEEPSHEAD FM. Cf.
Sheeps Head Hall 1819 G. TILEKILN FM is *Tile Kiln Farm* 1754
R.

Enfield

ENFIELD

> *Enefelde* 1086 DB *et passim* to 1393 FF, with variant spelling
> *-feld* and occasionally *-feud, Enefeldgrene* 1420 *MinAcct*
> *Enesfeud, -fued* 13th RBE
> *Ainefeld* 1205 ClR, 1230 P (p)
> *Einefeld* 1214 Cur, *Eynefeud* 1235 *Ass, Eynfeud* 1275 FF
> *Enfeld* 1293 FF, *Ennefeld* 1452 ib.
> *Endfelde* 1323 Inq aqd, *Endefeld* 1523 Belv, *Endefeild* 1535
> VE, *Endfield* 1638 BM
> *Envill* 1460 Pat, *Envilde* 1507 ib., *Enveld* 1538 FF, *Enfild*
> 1564 PCC

Possibly '*Ēana*'s open space,' *v.* feld. Alternatively Ekwall
(DEPN) suggests the possibility of a lost OE **ēan*, 'lamb,'
cognate with Latin *agnus*. Cf. OE *ēanian*, 'to yean.' *Field*
(*v.* feld) here no doubt refers to a cleared space in the woodland
of which Enfield Chase was a part.

NOTE. BAKER ST is *Bakers Street* 1686 M, *Beaker Street* 1754 R and
is to be associated with the family of Thomas *Baker* (1413 Cl). BELL
LANE is so named from an inn. BULLSMOOR LANE is *Bellesmore* (sic)
lane 1619 Ct, *Belsmoor Lane* 1754 R, *Belsmoor Lane* 1786 Cary. The
modern vowel must be due to the neighbouring Bulls Cross *infra* 74.

[1] Surviving in HOUNDSFIELD RD.
[2] Surviving in MILLBROOK RD.
[3] Surviving in OAKFIELD RD.

BURY ST is *Burystrete* 1593 N. *v.* burh (manorial). CARTERHATCH
LANE is *Carters hatch lane* 1636 *DuLa* and is to be associated with the
family of Nicholas *Carter* (1574 ParReg). *v.* hæcc, here no doubt a
gate of the Chase. CHURCHBURY LANE. Cf. *Churchberryfeild* 1636 *DuLa*
and burh (manorial). COOPERS LANE is so named in 1754 (R) and is
perhaps to be associated with the family of John *Cooper* (1626 ParReg).
DUCK LEES LANE. Cf. *Duck's Leys* 1800 EnclA, *v.* læs. EASTFIELD
RD. Cf. *Estfeld* 1275 RecStBarts, *East Field Hoppet* c. 1800 EnclA and
v. hoppet. FLASH LANE. Cf. *The Flash* ib. and *v.* flash. HOE LANE is
so named in 1659 (RobinsonEn). MARDYKE RD. Cf. *Mar Dyke* c. 1800
EnclA. Where the Lea ran eastwards a straight ditch called the *Mardyke*
or *Markdyke* was cut to effect a regular division between Essex and
Middlesex (Whitaker 167). *v.* mearc. NORTHFIELD RD. Cf. *Northfield*
1619 *DuLa*. PHIPPS HATCH LANE. Cf. Edward *Phipps* (1730 ParReg)
and *supra* 64. RED LANE. Cf. *Redland* 1636 *DuLa*. RIDGEWAY is *The
Ridge Way* 1658 *ParlSurv*. SOUTHBURY RD. Cf. *Southbury Field*
c. 1800 EnclA. SOUTH ST is *South street* 1682 Morgan. STOCKING-
WATER LANE. Cf. *le Stokkynges, Stockynge, Stockyngflate* 1441 *Min
Acct*, *Stocken* 1636 *DuLa* and *v.* stocking. WELCH'S LANE is to be
associated with the family of Robert *Welch* (1594 ParReg). WINDMILL
HILL RD. Cf. *Wind Mill Field* c. 1800 EnclA.

BRIMSDOWN

> *Grymesdoun(e)* 1420, 1441 *MinAcct*, *Grymes downe* 1610,
> 1622 *DuLa*, *Grimsdowne Corner* 1686 ib.
> *Brymesdowne, Bromesdowne* 1610 *DuLa*, *Bromesdoune, Bryms
> Downe* 1622 ib.
> *Grymsdown, Brymsdown* 1686 *DuLa*

It would seem that the original initial consonant of this name
was *G*. In that case the name would mean '*Grim*'s down.' Cf.
Grim's Ditch *supra* 11. Here the name is probably a surname
with no mythological significance. There is no hill here and dun
must be used of open country as in Farndon (PN Nt 213).

CAMLET MOAT is *loggii* (*gen.*) *de Camelot* 1441 *MinAcct*, *North
Camelott Ground* 1649 LMxAS vi, *Camelot Moat, Camelott Way*
1658 *ParlSurv, Camlet Moat* 1822 Scott, *Fortunes of Nigel*. There
is an old moat and camp here. The name is clearly derived from
the Camelot of Arthurian legend. Fictitious names of such
origin are rare, but cf. Pendragon Castle (We). The site is
traditionally that of the ancient manor-house of Enfield (Lysons
ii, 282). This tradition is supported by the fact that it lies in a
meadow called Oldbury, i.e. old manor, *v.* burh.

CATTLEGATE[1] is *Cathale* 1216–26 BM, 1240 Ch, *Cathalgate, le Chathalegate* 1441 *MinAcct, Cattle Gate* 1605 *DuLa, Cathellgate* 1636 ib. 'Wild cat nook or corner,' *v.* healh. *Gate* refers to the northern entrance to Enfield Chase.

CLAY HILL, CLAYSMORE. Cf. William *atte Cleye* 1274 *Ass, Clayhyll* 1524 *SR, tenement called Clayes, Clayes More Grove* 1610 *DuLa, Clayhillgate* 1636 ib. A John *Clay* is also mentioned in 1420 (*MinAcct*). The place-name Clay Hill was probably originally descriptive. The history of Claysmore is uncertain. It may be of manorial rather than local origin, the place taking its name from the family of *Clay* whose name was ultimately of local origin. The two places are close together.

COCKFOSTERS[2] is *Cokfosters* 1524 *SR, Cock(f)fosters* 1610, 1622 *DuLa, house called Cockefosters* 1613 Sess. This name has been discussed in PN Herts 71 where it was suggested that the name might have referred to the house of the *chief foster* or *forester*. Cf. *tenement voc' Cockeparkers* 1548 *Ct* (in Harrow), *cockparker* being clearly a similar formation. The place was on the edge of Enfield Chase.

ENFIELD CHASE, CHASE SIDE, ENFIELD HIGHWAY, LOCK and WASH appear as *Enefeld Chacee* 1325 Inq aqd, *chace of Enefelde* 1373 Pat, *Chase Side* 1754 R, *Alta Via* t. Ed 3 *DuLa, the kings highe way leading from Waltham Cross toward London* 1610 ib., *Norhtlok* (sic) 1355 Misc, *The Locke* 1657 RobinsonEn, *Enfield Lock* 1710 S, *Enfield Wash* 1675 Ogilby. The last is at the spot where the Ermine Street crosses the Cuffley Brook, *v.* (ge)wæsc, 'ground washed over by water, ford.' *lok* must be OE loc, 'enclosure.'

FORTY HALL and HILL. Cf. *Fortyehill, Fortye Greene* 1610 *DuLa, Fortie greene, hill* 1619 ib., *Fortey green* 1636 ib., *Fortee hill* 1686 ib., which must have been by the home of John *atte Fortey* (t. Ed 3 ib.) and John and Hugh *Fortey* (1420 *MinAcct*). 'In front of the well-watered land' from OE *forð* and eg. Cf. Forty Green (PN Wo 202). Forty Hall and Hill are on ground rising gradually above the Lea marshes. Other examples in the county

---

[1] Partly in Northaw (Herts). Cf. PN Herts 114.
[2] Partly in East Barnet, Herts (cf. PN Herts 71).

of this compound include *land called Fortheye* 1289 AD ii (Whitchurch), *Fortye* 1392 Cl (Fulham), *Forty* 1574 Hendon Surv (Hendon) and *Vorte* 1480 RobinsonT. Cf. also Forty Fm *supra* 52.

PONDERS END is *Ponders ende* 1593 N, probably so called because it is the *end* or quarter of the parish (*v.* ende) of Enfield where lived John *Ponder* of *Enefeld* (1373 Pat). It is possible that an earlier member of this family was Luc' de *la ponde*, who is mentioned c. 1200 (*CottCh*) as a former holder of land in Edmonton. Ponders End is on the Enfield border of Edmonton. For such *er*-formation cf. PN Sx 35, *s.n.* Bridger's Pond.

RAMMEY MARSH is *Ramhey* 1538 *LRMB*. Cf. *olde Rammey bridge, Ramybridge, Rammey Reach* 1610 *DuLa*. The second element is probably eg, the place lying low in the Lea marshes.

TRENT PARK. This was an estate formed under the Enclosure Act of the Chase in 1776. It was granted on a lease by George III to his favourite doctor, Sir Richard Jebb, who gave it the name of *Trent* from Trent in Tyrol where the king's brother, the Duke of Gloucester, had recently recovered from a severe illness (LGS 90).

BRIDGEN HILL, BULLS CROSS[1], CAPEL HO[2], COOKSHOLE[3], CREWS HILL[4], DURRANTS[5], GOUGH PARK, SANDERS CORNER[6] and WOODHAM FM[7] are to be associated with the families of William *Bridgen* (1740 ParReg), Gilbert *Bolle* (1235 *Ass*), Sir Giles *Capel* (1547 FF), John *Cok* (1351 Pat), Sarah *Crew* (1742 ParReg), Adam *Durant* (1244 FF), Joseph *Gough* (1744 ParReg), John *Saunder* (1525 *SR*) and William *Wodeham* (1420 *MinAcct*).

BEECH HILL PARK is *Beech Hill* 1795 Lysons. BELMONT HO is *Mount Pleasant* 1658 *ParlSurv*, *Belmont* 1819 G. BOTANY BAY

---

[1] *Bellyscrosse* (sic) 1540 FF, *Bulls Cross* t. Eliz ChancP.
[2] *Capels* c. 1615 ECP, *Capel Ho* 1819 G.
[3] *Cooke-hall* 1680 S. Cf. *Cokesgrove* t. Ed 3 *DuLa*. Surviving in COOKS HOLE RD.
[4] *Crews Hill* 1819 G.
[5] *Durauntesplace* 1382 FF, *Durantes manor* 1402 IpmR, *Durance* 1593 N. Surviving in DURANTS RD.
[6] *Sanders Corner* 1686 *DuLa*, *Sander's Corner* c. 1865 O.S. At a corner of Enfield Chase.
[7] *lands and tenements late William Woodhams* 1610 *DuLa*.

is so named ib. It was so named in jest, it being for many years a remote and inaccessible spot (Whitaker 360). BULLBEGGARS HOLE, i.e. 'hobgoblin's hole,' is so named in 1823 (RobinsonEn). Cf. PN Herts 50. BURY FM. Cf. *Westberifeld, Southberyfeld* 1420 *MinAcct, Southburyfeld* 1610 *DuLa. v.* burh (manorial). BYCULLAH HO was so named by a retired Indian officer from a place of that name near Bombay (Whitaker 141)[1]. COLLEGE FM is *Colledges* c. 1525 *DuLa, Colletts al. Colledges* 1619 ib., *close called Colledges* 1636 ib. These forms suggest that the name has nothing to do with any *college.* EAST LODGE is *East Bailey Lodge* 1609 *DuLa.* Cf. *Eastbailly* 1485 Capgrave. FERNYHILL. Cf. *Fearney feild* 1622 *DuLa.* FILCAPS GATE is so named in 1819 (G). FOLEY COTTAGES is *Folly Cottages* 1771 RobinsonEn. *v. infra* 206. FOXHOLE HILL is so named in 1786 (Cary). FREEZYWATER is *Freezwater* 1768 RobinsonEn, *Freezy Water* 1819 G, originally the name of a pond here, so nicknamed from its bleak and exposed situation (Whitaker 172–3). GORDON HILL takes its name from a house formerly standing here, which belonged to the father of the notorious Lord George *Gordon* (ib. 362). GREEN STREET is *Grenestrete in Enfeld* 1472 Cl, *the Grene Street* 1563 *CtRequests.* GROVE HO is so named in 1823 (EnclA). HOLLYHILL FM is *Holly Hill* 1819 G. HOOKE HILL is *Hookes* t. Jas 1 RobinsonEn, *Greate, little Hooke Hill* 1658 *ParlSurv, Hooksgate* 1686 *DuLa.* There is a well-marked spur of land here, *v.* hoc. LEEGING BEECH is so named in 1658 (*ParlSurv*). Cf. *Leeging Oak Gutter* (old 6″). Possibly we have here a survival of ME *liggyng,* 'lying, i.e. fallen,' from OE *licgean.* LONG HILL is so named in 1658 (*ParlSurv*). LOSSICK HILL. Cf. *Lossick Way* ib. MAIDENS BRIDGE is *Maydenbridge* 1638 *DuLa.* MERRY HILLS. Cf. *Merry Hill Way* 1658 *ParlSurv.* This is on the parish boundary and may be a corruption of OE (ge)mære, 'boundary.' Cf. Merry Brook (PN Wo 13). MILL-MARSH is *Milnemers* 1306 RecStBarts, *Mellemersh* 1387 *Walden, Millmarsh* 1638 *DuLa.* MOAT WOOD. Cf. *Mottfeld* ib., *Moat* 1819 G. MONKEY MEAD is so named in 1658 (*ParlSurv*). It adjoins *Monken* Hadley (PN Herts 75) and the first element may be a corruption of *Monken.* MYDDELTON HO takes its name from Sir Hugh *Myddelton,* the engineer of the New River (Whitaker

---

[1] Surviving in BYCULLAH RD.

363). OAK LODGE is so named in 1823 (RobinsonEn). OLDBURY.
Cf. *Oldbury gardyn, Oldburycrofte* 1441 *MinAcct, Ouldberry* 1638
DuLa. *v.* burh (manorial). OLD PARK, LITTLE PARK are *the oulde
park* 1658 *ParlSurv, New Park al. Little Park* t. Hy 8 Lysons.
PLUMRIDGE FM. Cf. *Plumridge Hill* 1658 *ParlSurv.* POND
WOOD. Cf. *Old Pond* ib. SCOTLAND GREEN is so named in 1750
(Seale). SLOPER'S FM. Cf. *Slopers Pond* 1777 RobinsonEn.
SOUTH LODGE is so named in 1750 (Seale). SOUTH MARSH is
Southmerssh 1420 *MinAcct, South Marshe* 1568 FF. TURKEY
STREET is *Tokestrete* 1441 *MinAcct, Tuckey street* t. Jas 1 ECP,
Tuckhey str(e)ete 1610, 1622 *DuLa, Turkey street* 1805 O.S.
v. stræt for the meaning here. WEST LODGE is so named in 1702
(*DuLa*). WHITE WEBBS is *White Webbes* 1543 LP, *Whytewelles*
(sic) 1553 FF, *Whitewebes* 1558 ECP, *Whitwebb* 1593 N, *Whit-
webbgate, White Webbs now called White Webbs place* 1610 *DuLa*.
WILDWOOD. Cf. *Wildwood Green* 1686 M.

South Mimms

SOUTH MIMMS

> *Mimes* 1086 DB, 1274 RH
> *Mimmes* 1211 RBE, 1221, 1236 FF, 1291 Tax, *Mymmes* 1316
>   FA
> *Suthmimes* 1253 FF, *-mimmes* 1256 ib., 1274 *Ass, -mymmes*
>   1312 Ch, *South Mymis* 1423 Pat, *Southmyn(e)s* 1560 FF,
>   1610 Speed, *South Mymbes* 1593 DKR xxxviii

South in contrast to North Mimms in Hertfordshire (cf. PN
Herts 65). The name must remain an unsolved problem.

NOTE. BAKER ST is *Bakers Street* 1680 S. COOPERS LANE is to be
associated with the family of *Cooper* (1558 ff. ParReg). GALLEY LANE
is *Galowlane* 1475 *AddCh.* MUTTON LANE is so named in 1754 (R).
Cf. *infra* 99. SAWYERS LANE. Cf. *Sawyersstrete* 1475 *AddCh.* WATERY
LANE is *Water Lane* 1819 G.

DYRHAM PARK is *Derhams* 1475 Cl, *Durhams* 1593 N. John
Durham held land in South Mimms in 1411 (FF), probably a
descendant of Henry de *Durham*, taxed under Shenley (Herts),
an adjacent parish, in 1294 (*SR*). The family may have come
from Dyrham (Gl).

GANWICK CORNER is *Gannokk* 1475 *AddCh*, *Gannockes* 1547 LP, *Gannock Corner* 1605 *Rental*, *Galley Corner* 1754 R. Hitherto that name has been explained as a compound of OE *gamen*, 'game' and **ac**, 'oak,' 'games oak,' but Dr Angus McIntosh in the *Review of English Studies* (xvi, 54 ff.) suggests ME *gannok*, possibly denoting a stronghold or fortified place. He himself notes in his suggestive article that the name calls for further investigation.

OLD FOLD FM is *Oldefold* 1274 *Ass*, *Le Eldefolde* 1347 Gesta, *le Old(e)feld* 1375 Hust, 1398 IpmR, 1547 FF. 'The old (sheep) fold,' *v.* **falod**, with occasional later confusion with **feld**. Cf. Alfold (PN Sr 222) and *v.* Introd. xvii.

POTTERS BAR is *Potterys Barre* 1509 Brittain, *Potters Barre* 1548 Pat, and is to be associated with the family of Geoffrey *le Pottere* (1294 *Ass*) and William *Pottere* (t. Ed 3 *Rental*). The *bar* was one of the forest gates of Enfield Chase. Cf. Swanleybar Fm (PN Herts 66).

WROTHAM PARK is so named in 1754 (R). This house was built by the Byng family in 1750 and was so named from Wrotham (K), their ancient seat (Lysons 230).

BRIDGEFOOT HO is *Bridg Foot* 1710 S and was no doubt the home of William *del Punt* and de *Ponte* (i.e. 'of the bridge') (1281 FF).

BLANCHE FM[1], CLARE HALL[2], DANCERS HILL[3], EARLS FM, KNIGHTSLAND FM[4], MOSES HILL and SALMON'S FM[5] are to be associated with the families of Thomas *Blaunche* (1597 Brittain), *Clare* (18th ParReg *passim*), Henry *Dancer* (1601 Brittain), Thomas *Erle* of Barnet (1408 FF), William *Knight* (1628 Sess), John *Mosse* (1541 FF) and (possibly) *Salomon* le Couherde (1316 FF).

BENTLEY HEATH is so named in 1680 (S). Cf. Bentley *supra* 66. CLOCK HO is so named in 1822 (O.S.). DELL WOOD. Cf. *Dell Fd* and *Hole* 1841 *TA* and *infra* 197. DUGDALE HILL is *Dubdell* 1680 S. FENNYSLADE is *Fennyslade* 1658 *ParlSurv*. *v.* **slæd.**

---

[1] *Blanches* 1754 R.   [2] *Clare Hall* ib.
[3] *Dancershill* 1593 N.   [4] *Knights* 1822 O.S.
[5] *Salamanns* 1475 *AddCh*.

FURZEFIELD WOOD. Cf. *Furze Field* 1841 *TA*. HORNBEAM HILL
is *Hornbemes* 1441 *MinAcct* (the earliest quotation for *hornbeam*
in NED is dated 1577). LAUREL LODGE is so named in 1819 (G).
MIMMS HALL is *Mimmehall* 1437 ECP, *Mims Hall* 1682 Morgan.
PARKFIELD is *Parkefeilde* 1591 Sess. PILVAGE WOOD. Cf. *Great,
Little Pilvage* 1841 *TA*. SPOILBANK WOOD. This is the site of
a 'spoilbank' or heap of refuse formed at the time of the construction of the railway c. 1842. VINEGAR SPRING is so named
in 1841 (*TA*). WARRENGATE is so named in 1750 (Seale).

Tottenham

TOTTENHAM

> *Toteham* 1086 DB, 1128–34 BM, 1183 AC, *Totham* 1237 Cl
> *Totinham* 1227 FF, 1284, 1310 ib., -*tyn*- 1287 ib., *Totyngham*
> 1325 Cl
> *Thotenham* 1236 FF, *Totenham* 1189 *CottCh et passim* to
> 1543 FF
> *Tottenham* 1254 Pat, 1286, 1303 FF
> *Totenhamstrete* 1350 Ipm
> *Totnam* 1515 PCC, 1544 FF, (*Tottenham otherwise*) 1556 ib.
> *Tottenham otherwise Tottenham Highecrosse* 1569 FF

'*Totta*'s ham.' *strete* must have reference to the settlement
along the main road, Ermine Street, which ran through the old
village. *v. infra* 204. For *Highcrosse*, *v. infra* 80. Cf. further
Tottenham Court *infra* 143.

NOTE. AWLFIELD RD. Cf. *Awlefeild* 1619 RobinsonT. BROAD LANE
is so named in 1600 ib. GREEN LANE is so named in 1745 (R). LORD-
SHIP LANE is so named in 1600 (RobinsonT). Cf. the same name in
Stoke Newington *infra* 159. LORDSMEAD RD. Cf. *Lordsmead* ib. LOVE
LANE is so named in 1502 (*Ct*). MARSH LANE is *le Mershe lane* 1467
RobinsonT. PHILIP LANE is *Philip's Lane* 1745 R. Cf. *Phelippescroft*
1502 *Ct*. STONELEYS RD. Cf. *Stoneslese* 1467 RobinsonT, *Stone Leas*
1599 ib., *Stoneleys* 1600 ib. and *v.* læs. TURNPIKE LANE is *Turnpike
Road* 1813 ib. WEST GREEN RD was earlier *Black hope lane* 1619 ib.,
Blackup or Black Hope Lane c. 1780 ib. WHITE HART LANE was so
called in 1600 (RobinsonT) from the inn of that name. WOLVES LANE
is *Wolfyeslane* 1397 *Ct*. It is possible that the first element is the OE
personal name *Wulfwīg*.

BOUNDS GREEN is *le Boundes* 1365 *AD*, 1383 IpmR, *Boundsgrene*
1608 *LRMB* and is to be associated with the family of John
le Bonde (1294 *Ass*) and Walter *le Bounde* (13th AD ii).

BRUCE CASTLE is *Bruses* 1353 Ipm, 1418, 1459 Pat, *Le Bruses in Totenham* 1375 IpmR, *Breuses* 1487 Ipm. The name is derived from the association of the family of *de Bru(y)s*, afterwards Kings of Scotland, with a manor in Tottenham.

CLAYHILL FM is *Clay Hill* 1600 RobinsonT. This is probably *Clayhangre extra villam de Totenham* 1294 *Ass*, *Cleangre* 1255 Misc (*v.* hangra, 'wooded slope') and is to be identified with the hitherto unlocated (*þuruh*) *Clæighangran* ASC (C) *s.a.* 1016.

CLENDISH MARSH[1] is *Clendich* 1502 Ct, *Clendish Hills Marsh* 1600 RobinsonT. 'Clean ditch,' i.e. one clear of weeds or mud.

DUCKETTS[2] is the name of the manor of *Duket* 1346 FF, *Duketus* 1371 AD i, *Dukettes* 1372 ib., taking its name from the family of Laurence *Duket* (1232–7 AD i, 1294 ib. ii).

HANGER LANE[3] is *Hangars lane* 1745 R, preserving the name of the wood or wooded slope (*v.* hangra) referred to as *Hangre Totenham* 1189 CottCh, (*in*) *hangere de Totenham* c. 1200 Clerkenwell, *la Hangre* 1350 Ipm, *le greate Haunger in Tottenham* 1547 FF. Cf. Hanger Hill *infra* 91.

MARKFIELD HO[4] is *Merkefeld* 1502 Ct. Cf. also *le Merk, Merkgrove, Merkmede* ib. The place was by the parish and Hundred boundary, *v.* mearc.

MITCHLEY MARSH[5] is *Michelhey* 1306 RecStBarts, *Mocheleye* 1327 BM, *Mochilley, Mochillefeld* 1502 Ct. The earliest form suggests that this name is a compound of OE micel, 'great, big' and (ge)hæg, 'enclosure.'

SEVEN SISTERS[6]. This spot took its name from seven elm trees which stood near Page Green, where the Seven Sisters Rd (made in 1831–3) joins the main Ermine St. They are marked as 7 *Sesters* 1754 R, *Seven Sisters* 1805 O.S. Cf. RobinsonT 44.

TOTTENHAM HALE is *le Hale* 1502 Ct, *the Hale* 1547 Deeds Enrolled, *Tottenham Hale* 1754 R, and was the home of Richard

---

[1] Surviving in CLENDISH RD. [2] Surviving in DUCKETTS RD.
[3] Now ST ANNES RD. [4] Surviving in MARKFIELD RD.
[5] Surviving in MITCHLEY RD.
[6] Surviving in SEVEN SISTERS RD.

atte Hale (1274 *Ass*). *v.* healh, 'angle, corner,' and cf. Hale *supra* 59.

TOTTENHAM HIGH CROSS is *le Hiecros* 1409 RobinsonT, *Hiecrosgrene* 1467 ib., *Totenham Hyghcrosse* 1551 FF. This was not one of the 'Queen Eleanor' crosses (cf. Charing Cross *infra* 167) but an ordinary wayside cross, the history of which is not known.

WEST GREEN is *le Westgrene* 1502 *Ct*. It lay on the west boundary of the parish.

WILDMARSH is *Wildemers* late 12th BM, *Wildemerssh* t. Ed 3 *Rental*, *Wildemerssh bregge* 1410 Cl, *Tottenham Wilde Marshe* 1571 Sess. *Wild* must here have the sense of 'waste, uncultivated,' etc. Cf. Wild Brooks (PN Sx 147).

WOOD GREEN[1] is *Wodegrene* 1502 *Ct*, *Woodgreene* 1611 PCC. It was a hamlet at the edge of Enfield Chase. Cf. also *Wodlee in Totenham* 13th AD ii, *Wodelegh* 1383 IpmR which may have been near by. *v.* leah.

ASPLYN FM[2] and PAGE GREEN[3] are to be associated with the families of Richard *Hasplyn* (1559 FF) and John *Page* (1558 ParReg).

BARNFIELD HO is *Barn Field* 1843 *TA*. Cf. *Bernestrete* 1408 RobinsonT, *Barn close* 1619 ib. BROAD MEAD is (*le*) *Brademade* 1197 FF, -*mede* 1294 *Ass*, 1306 RecStBarts. *v.* mæd. BROADWATER FM[4]. Cf. *Broad Waters* 1600 RobinsonT. BROOK HO[5]. Cf. *Brokesfen* c. 1480 ib. CARBUNCLE DITCH is *Garbol dich* 1408 RobinsonT, *Garbell Ditch* 1600 ib., *Carbuncle or Garbell Ditch* 1840 ib. The original name would seem to contain the word *garboil*, 'confusion, disturbance,' hitherto not recorded before 1548 (cf. NED *s.v.*) with a strange later corruption. The interpretation of the name is obscure. CROWSNEST FM is *Crawenest* 1317 BM. DOWNHILLS[6]. Cf. *le Downe* 1467 RobinsonT, 1502 *Ct*, *Down Hills* 1619 ib. ELM LODGE. Cf. *le grene elme* 1502 *Ct*. THE HERMITAGE[7] is (*le*) *Hermitage* 1465, 1569 RobinsonT.

---

[1] Now a separate borough.
[2] *Asplins* 1789 RobinsonT. Surviving in ASPLINS RD.
[3] *Pagisgrene* 1467 ib., 1502 *Ct*. Surviving in PAGE GREEN RD.
[4] Surviving in BROADWATER RD.   [5] Surviving in BROOK RD.
[6] Surviving in DOWNHILLS AVENUE.   [7] Surviving in HERMITAGE RD.

MOUNT PLEASANT[1] is so named in 1723 (DKR xli). *v. infra* 207.
NIGHTINGALE HALL is so named in 1754 (R). PARK[2]. Cf. *Parke-
feld* 1502 *Ct.* ST DUNSTANS WELL is *Dunstans Well* 1619
RobinsonT, 1843 *TA.* STONEBRIDGE HO[3]. Cf. *Stonebrigge* 1592
Ct. TOTTENHAM MARSH is *Tottenham Mershe* ib. WILLOUGHBY
FM[4]. Cf. *Wilbyes, Wilobiesholme* 1467 RobinsonT, *Manor of
Wylloughbyes* 1557 FF. Philip *Wylgheby* died in 1366 holding
land in Tottenham (RobinsonT 107).

VI. OSSULSTONE HUNDRED[5]

Osulvestan(e) 1086 DB, *Osolvistan* 1172 P, -*ves*- 1235 *Ass*
Osulfestan 1167, 1168 P
Osolvestone, Osulveston, Osolston 1274 *Ass*
Oselston 1290 Ipm, *Ossulston* 1610 Speed
lez Osilston Pyttes 1484 Gatty, *Osolston* 1614 ib.

'At the stone of *Oswulf*,' *v.* stan. This was probably a stone
marking the meeting-place of the Hundred (cf. Gatty i, 58). It
has been surmised that its site was near the present Marble
Arch, but in 1484 (cf. *supra*) there is mention of *Westmynster
lane* leading between Tyburn and *lez Osilston Pyttes*. *Westmynster lane* is the later Park Lane (*v. infra* 181) and in a Grosvenor Estate map of 1614 (Gatty, Plate 31, cf. i, 57) *Osolston* is
marked as a field-name about half way down Park Lane on the
east side just beyond the present South St (*infra* 183). No stone
is marked in that map and none survives at the present day.

The Borough of Acton

ACTON

Acton(e) 1181 StPauls DB (p), 1232 Cl *et passim*, (*juxta
Braynford*) 1294 *Ass*
Aketon 1211 Cur, 1213 Abbr, 1316 Ch

---

[1] Surviving in MOUNT PLEASANT RD.   [2] Surviving in PARK LANE.
[3] Surviving in STONEBRIDGE RD.   [4] Surviving in WILLOUGHBY RD.
[5] With the exception of Friern Barnet (an urban district), the names in
this Hundred have been grouped under the modern boroughs, the boundaries
of which, however, mainly coincide with the ancient parishes. The exceptions
are Finsbury and Holborn, neither of them at any time parish names. Poplar
includes three parishes and Stepney more, *v. infra* 136, 148.

Chirche Acton 1347 FF, (*Churche*) 1551 ib.
Aghton' 1398 Works

'Farm by the oak tree(s),' *v.* **ac**, **tun**. Distinguished as near Brentford. *Church* to distinguish from East Acton *infra*.

NOTE. BOLLO LANE is *Bolhollane* 1408 *Ct*, i.e. 'bull hollow.' CHURCH-FIELD RD. Cf. *Church Field* 1842 *TA*. EASTFIELD RD. Cf. *Estfeld* 1229–39 StPaulsCh, *East Field* 1842 *TA*. GREEN LANE is *Greene Layne* 1551 Lysons. HORN LANE is so named in 1754 (R). MILL HILL RD. Cf. *Mill Hill* 1819 G. NORTHFIELD RD. Cf. *Nordfeld* 1229–39 StPauls Ch. OLDFIELD RD. Cf. *Ye old ffeilde* 1650 Feret. SOUTHFIELD RD. Cf. *Southfeld* 1380 Cl, *South Field* 1842 *TA*. THE VALE is *Acton Vale* 1819 G. WARPLE WAY. Cf. *The Warple* 1717 HammSurv. *v.* **worple**.

ACTON WELLS is so named in 1754 (R). There was a spa here discovered in the early 18th century (Walford i, 16), at one time a popular resort.

BOLLO BRIDGE[1]. *Bolebregge* 1229–39 StPaulsCh, *Bolholbregge* c. 1470 *Ct*. Earlier 'bull bridge,' or 'bull hollow bridge,' cf. Bollo Lane *supra* and *v.* **holh**. The bridge was over Stamford Brook (*supra* 6), called *Boller Brook* (1826 Bridges).

EAST ACTON is *Estacton* 1294 *Ass*, 1412 FF, *Estactongrene* 1474 *Ct*. This was formerly a distinct hamlet.

FRIARS PLACE is *Fryers Place* 1680 S, representing the land in Acton granted to St Bartholomew's, Smithfield, in 1374 (*v.* Lysons ii, 4).

OLD OAK COMMON is *old oake lande, common called Old Oake* 1650 Feret. Possibly this is to be identified with the earlier wood called *Eldeholt* 1380 Cl, *Oldeholte* t. Hy 5 *Ct*. 'Old wood,' *v.* **holt** and Introd. xvii.

THE STEYNE[2] is so named in 1780 (Lysons). It was a small triangular green by the main Uxbridge Road. No earlier forms have been noted but we may compare *le, la Stene* 1365 *Ct*, t. Ric 2 *Rental* (Sunbury), *la Stene* 1485 *Ct*, *Worton Stene* 1498 ib., *furlong voc. Stene* 1498 *Rental* (Isleworth, near Worton), *via voc. le Stene in Drayton* 1455 *Ct* (Drayton in Ealing). These must all be from OE *stæne*, 'stony place,' discussed fully in PN Sx 292, *s.n.* Old Steine.

---

[1] Surviving in BOLLO BRIDGE RD.   [2] Surviving in STEYNE RD.

WALES FM[1] is *Wails Farm* 1819 G, *Whales* 1822 O.S. and is said to be a corruption of *Wells* Farm from Acton Wells *supra* 82 (Baker 154).

The Borough of Bethnal Green

BETHNAL GREEN[2]

Blithehale 13th AD i, *Blithenhale in Stebenhethe* 1341 AD ii, *Blythenhale* 1389 FF

Blethenalegrene 1443 Ct, *Blethenall Grene* 1550 Pat, 1565 PCC, *Blithnall Grene* 1563 SR, *Bletenhall grene* 1592, 1600 SR

Bednalgrene 1568 FF, *Blethenell Grene al. Bednall Grene* 1569 FF, *Bethnall al. Bednall grene* 1576 StPaulsMSS, *Bed(d)-nol(l)greene* 1600, 1602 Sess, *Bethnal Greene* 1657 ib., *Bethnoll Greene* 1664 ib., *Bednall Green* 1680, 1710 S

The second element is healh, 'angle, nook, corner,' etc. The first may be the OE *blīðe*, 'happy, blithe,' but more likely it is a personal name *Blīða*, a hypocoristic form of OE personal names in *Blīð-*, as *Blīðhelm*. Cf. also Blinsham (PN D 86).

BISHOPS HALL is *Bi(s)shops Hall* 1495 ECP, 1542 RobinsonH, 1592 PCC, *Bushopes Hall* 1535 VE, *Byshops Hall* 1703 Gascoyne, *Bonners Hall* 1745 R, *Bishop Bonners Hall* 1808 Cary, so named from an old house of the Bishops of London, lords of the manor of Stepney, which stood here till the mid 19th century. The site of the house is now partly within Victoria Park, and BONNER ROAD still preserves the memory of the 16th-century bishop under whose successor the manor passed into lay hands.

CAMBRIDGE HEATH is so named in 1596 (ShoreSurv) and is referred to as *(super) comm̄ pasture que vocatur Camprichthesheth*, *Camprichesheth* in 1275 (RH). It is clear that the first part of the name has nothing to do with Cambridge. It looks more like some personal name, to be compared with such names as OE *Centwine* (DB *Cantwin*), *Centweald, Centa* (LVD), *cæntinces treow* (692 BCS 81), with the common *a* for OE *e(æ)* before nasals (cf. Introd. xvii). *Campriht* might well be a ME descendant of OE **Centbeorht, *Cæntbeorht*. Cf. Alperton *supra* 52.

---

[1] Surviving in WALES FM RD.   [2] A hamlet of Stepney till 1743.

BETHNAL GREEN STREET-NAMES

AUSTIN ST is *Austin Street* 1703 Gascoyne, *Austins Street* 1746 R.
Cf. *Austin* family from 1615 (ParReg). BETHNAL GREEN RD is marked
in 1720 Strype (Map) and 1745 (R) and named before 1799
(Horwood). Part of its western end was formerly Church St *infra*:
the modern continuation beyond that includes the older *An(c)kor Street*
1682 Morgan, 1698 ParReg, *Anchor Street* 1703 Gascoyne, probably
so named from an inn sign. BOUNDARY ST, so called because it is on
the border between this parish and Shoreditch, was the northern part
of *Cock Lane* 1538 ShoreSurv, 1746 R. Presumably the Cock was the
sign of an inn. BRICK LANE. It is partly in Stepney, *v. infra* 155.
CAMBRIDGE RD (1868 LCCN). The south part was earlier *Dog
Row* 1662 ParReg, *The Dogg Row* 1729 ib. The northern part was
the original *Bethnal Green* 1703 Gascoyne, 1746 R. CHURCH ST, so
named in 1746 (R), originally led to the church from the part of the
parish first built up, as far as *Church Row* 1799 Horwood. The section
still remaining was earlier the southern part of *Cock Lane* 1703 Gascoyne, 1720 Strype (Map Bk IV). CLUB ROW is so named in 1703 (Gascoyne), *rue de Cloberout* 1700 ParRegFr. COLOMBIA RD (1875 LCCN)
was earlier *Crabtree Lane* 1703 Gascoyne, 1746 R, *Crabtree Row* 1799
Horwood. EBOR ST (1886 LCCN) was earlier *York Street* 1676 ParReg,
1746 R, *Old York Street* 1799 Horwood. The change was made in order
to distinguish it from other York Streets. GIBRALTAR WALK is *Gibraltar*
1746 R, perhaps a nickname for remoteness, since at that date it marked
the end of the built-up area. GLOBE RD is so named in 1808 (Cary),
earlier *Globe Lane* 1708 Hatton, still earlier *Theven lane* c. 1600
LMxAS vi, *Theeving Lane* 1703 Gascoyne. Cf. the same name in
Westminster *infra* 184. 'Thieves' lane.' The upper part was formerly
Back Lane ib., 1831 Elmes. GREEN ST, with its continuation Roman
Rd *infra*, was "the kings way leading from Bethnal Green to Old
Ford" 1550 Survey, *v.* Old Ford and Old St *infra* 136, 98. It was
so named in 1799 (Horwood) and was possibly so called because it led
to Bethnal Green. It is marked as a *Drift Way* in 1703 (Gascoyne) and
1746 (R), *v. infra* 205. HACKNEY RD is *The road to Hackney* 1703
Gascoyne. Its western end was once *Collyers Lane* 1550 Survey,
Colier Lane c. 1600 LMxAS vi. HARE ST is so named in 1682 (Morgan).
Just near was *Haresmershe* 1541 FF, *-marshe* 1542 RobinsonH, *Hare-
marsh(e)* 1579 Ipm, 1746 R. OLD FORD RD was *Old Ford Lane* 1703
Gascoyne, 1745 R. OLD NICHOL ST is *Nicholstreet, Nicholas Street*
1697 ParReg, *Nicolls Street* 1703 Gascoyne, *Old, New Nichol Street*
1746 R. Cf. *Nicholls* family from 1589 (ParReg). ROMAN RD, *v. supra*.
RUSSIA LANE is *Rushy Lane* 1703 Gascoyne, 1720 Strype. SATCH-
WELL ST. Cf. *Scachwells Rents, by Satchwells Garden* 1703 Gascoyne,
Satchells Rents 1746 R. Cf. Katheren *Satchwell* 1621 ParReg. SCLATER
ST is so named in 1732 (PC), 1746 (R), *Slaughter Street* 1799 Horwood,

perhaps from the family of Richard *Slater* (1659 ShoreSurv), but cf. *Slaughters Land* beside it in 1703 (Gascoyne). THREE COLTS LANE is *Three Colt Yard* 1746 R, from an inn sign. VIRGINIA RD was *Castle Street* 1703 Gascoyne, 1746 R. 200 yards to the east along Virginia Rd is MOUNT ST (map in Kelly's Directory, 1940), now SWANFIELD ST, a revival of *Swan Fields* 1746 R. One may assume that Castle St and Mount St alike take their names from the fort near Shoreditch Church erected by order of the Common Council in 1643, *v.* LnTopRec xiv, 6 and cf. Mount St in Stepney and in Westminster *infra* 157, 181. The extreme east part of Virginia Rd was already *Virginia Row* in 1703 (Gascoyne). It was possibly a nickname from its being then on the remote outskirts of London.

The Borough of Chelsea

CHELSEA

Caelichyth 799–802 BCS 201, *Celichyð* 816 (11th) ib. 358
Celchyth 789 (10th) ib. 255
(*æt*) *Cealchyþe* c. 900 ASC (*s.a.* 785 A)[1], *Cealchithe* 1071–5 Reg
Chilcheþe, Chilcheheþe 1042–66 (13th) *WAM, Chilc(he)hethe* 1270, 1315, 1324 FF, 1274 *Ass, Chilchenheth* ib.
Chelched[2] 1086 DB, *-hud* 1197 FF, *Chelchee* 1214 Cur, *Chelc(he)hethe* 1231 FF *et passim* to 1428 FA
Chulcheth(e), Chircheheth 1274 *Ass*
Chelchuthe 1300 Pap, *Chelch(e)huth(e)* 1316 FA, 1333, 1347 FF, 1341 NI, 1382 AD i, *Chelchuythe* 1524 *SR*
Chelch(e)hith 1309 FF, 1482 PCC, *Chilchith* 1319 Londin
Chels(e)hithe 1499 FF, 1539 *AD, Chelceheyth* 1519 FF
Chelcehith 1523 FF, *Chelshith* 1535 VE
Chelsey(e) 1523, 1528 FF, *Chelseghe* ib.
Chelsyth al. Chelsey 1556 FF, *Chelsey al. Chelchithe* 1583 Recov, *Chilcy* 1655 ParReg (Kensington), *Chelsea* 1754 R

Chelsea is a difficult name. The general assumption, on the basis of the forms in the Anglo-Saxon Chronicle, has been that it is a compound of cealc, 'chalk' and hyð, 'landing place' (cf. McClure 157 n., PNEW *s.n.*, DEPN *s.n.*), but even if we interpret the name as 'lime-port,' i.e. 'place where lime was landed,'

---

[1] So also in B, C, D, E and F texts.
[2] *Cercehede* written above in the MS.

there are serious difficulties about such an etymology. The form *Caelichyth*, from an early 9th-century original (confirmed by the form *Celichyð*, an 11th-century copy of a 9th-century charter), is older than the Chronicle form and is really inconsistent with it. The Chronicle form in its turn is inconsistent with the later forms; OE *cealc* should give later *chalke* and possibly *chelke* but not *chelche*, *chilche*. The Wiltshire *Chalke* (PN W 203–4) has a form *Chelche* in DB, but *ch* here represents a *k*-sound, and later we always have *Chelke*, *Chalke*. Further, it is only out of a form *Chelche* (pronounced [tʃeltʃə]) that we can possibly develop a later [tʃels], though even that development at so late a date is surprising. Probably *cealc* is an early example of folk-etymology. It was these problems which led Bradley (EHR xxxviii, 317) in his review of Gover's *Place-names of Middlesex* to suggest that the first element was OE *cælic*, *calic*, *cælc*, *celc*, 'cup,' rather than *cealc*, 'chalk,' though, as he himself noted, it does not seem very likely that this loan-word (from Lat. *calix*) would form part of an English place-name, even if we could allow that 'cup-shaped' harbour or landing place was a very likely early name for Chelsea. For loss of final *th* cf. Stepney *infra* 149.

LITTLE CHELSEA is *Little Chelcy* 1655 ParReg (Kensington), *Lickle*, *Leckle Celsey* 1659 ib., *Little Chilcy* 1661 ib., *Little Chelsey* 1663 Pepys' Diary. This was a former hamlet on the Fulham Road west of the north end of Church St, marked in early maps down to the time when the district was built over (c. 1840–50).

CHELSEA STREET-NAMES

ASHBURNHAM RD is so named from Ashburnham House which stood here till c. 1880, named from the second Earl of *Ashburnham* who lived here c. 1780 (Beaver 161). The road follows the course of the earlier *Hob Lane* (1620 FaulknerCh), i.e. 'goblin lane.' BEAUFORT ST, formerly *Beaufort Row* 1794 Horwood, was laid out in 1766 across the site of the great house bought by the first Duke of Beaufort in 1682 (Beaver 138–40). An earlier *Beaufort Street* (1741–5 R) was the western continuation of Cheyne Walk, between that house and the Thames. BLACKLANDS TERRACE (1857 LCCN) preserves the name of *Blacklands Lane* 1794 Horwood, 1815 FaulknerCh which became *Marlborough Road* from a tavern there shown by Horwood called *The Marlborough* before 1829 (ib. ii, 49). This was near the former *Blacklands House*

1717 MapCh, in an area called *Blacklande, Blakelandes* 1544 Survey.
CADOGAN SQUARE. Cf. *Cadogan Place* 1815 FaulknerCh. In 1753
Sir Hans Sloane (*v. infra* 88) died, leaving half his estate to his second
daughter who had married Charles, Lord *Cadogan* (FaulknerCh i, 373).
CARLYLE SQUARE (1872 LCCN), named after Thomas *Carlyle*, was
earlier *Oakley Square*. Cf. Oakley St *infra* 88. CHESHAM ST, *v. infra*.
CHEYNE ROW [tʃeini], formerly *Great Cheyne Row* 1708 Beaver,
1808 Cary, *Cheyne Row* 1815 FaulknerCh and CHEYNE WALK, so named
in 1794 (Horwood) (*v.* also Beaufort St *supra* 86) were named after
Charles *Cheyne* (d. 1698) and his son William, lords of the manor of
Chelsea from 1660 to 1712 (FaulknerCh i, 329, 338). Cf. *Lord Cheyne's
Lands* 1717 MapCh. CHURCH ST is *Church Lane* 1698 FaulknerCh.
The northern part, formerly *Upper Church Lane*, was *the Road to the
Cross Tree* 1717 MapCh, *v.* Queen's Elm *infra* 88. CREMORNE RD
(1878 LCCN) takes its name from the pleasure gardens here 1845–77
(Beaver 160), on the site of *Cremorne House*, bought by Lord Dartrey,
later Viscount *Cremorne*, in 1778 (FaulknerCh i, 65). DANVERS ST,
begun in 1696, was named after Sir John *Danvers* (d. 1655) who had
a large house near (FaulknerCh i, 172). FLOOD ST (1865 LCCN) was
so named from Mr L. T. Flood (d. 1860), a benefactor to the parish
(Beaver 320, 339). It was formerly *Queen Street* (ib.), earlier *Robinson's
Lane* 1794 Horwood, and before that *The Pound Lane* 1741–5 R. Cf.
le commun pound 1544 Survey. FRANKLIN'S ROW is so named in 1746
(R), probably from Thomas *Franklin*, mentioned in 1681 and 1693
(FaulknerCh i, 219, ii, 157). FULHAM RD is *highway leading to Fulham
Ferry* 1679 FaulknerCh. HANS TOWN, the area which includes Sloane
St, etc. (*v. infra* 88) and HANS PLACE (so named in 1794 Horwood),
were laid out c. 1777 (Beaver 347). KINGS RD is *The King's High Way
from Chelsea to London* 1620 FaulknerCh, *The King's Private Road* 1717
MapCh, 1808 Cary, *The King's Road* 1746 R, a road constructed to
give more direct approach from Whitehall to Hampton Court (Faulkner
Ch i, 43). LAWRENCE ST is so named in 1717 (Map) from a family
which resided in the old manor house there, bought by Sir Thomas
Lawrence from Henry VIII (FaulknerCh i, 263). LOTS RD crosses land
called *lez lotte* 1544 Survey, *le lottes* 1544 *Ct, quatuor parcell' prati voc.
lez Lottez* 1557 Pat, *The Lots* 1815 FaulknerCh, c. 1840 *TA*. It retains
in its name a memory of the 'lots' of ground "originally a part of the
manor over which the parishioners had Lammas rights" (Beaver 161).
LOWNDES SQUARE. In 1746 (R) the land here is marked *Lowndes Esq.*
John *Lowndes*, a descendant of the owner in 1746, built the square
1837–9 (W and C). The family seat was near Chesham (Bk), hence
Chesham St (ib.). MANOR ST is so named in 1794 (Horwood). It
crosses the site of the garden of the new manorhouse built by Henry VIII
(ChelseaSurv i, pl. 1). Cf. "footpath by the garden wall of the Lord
of the Manor" (1696 FaulknerCh). MILMAN'S ST is *Mil(l)man's Row*
1789 FaulknerCh, 1815 ib., from Sir William *Milman* (d. 1713)
(FaulknerCh i, 75). MULBERRY WALK is a relic of the attempt made
c. 1721 to use the park (cf. Park Walk *infra* 88) as a silkworm nursery

(FaulknerCh i, 149–50). OAKLEY ST was built c. 1830, commemorating
Lord Cadogan of *Oakley*. Cf. Cadogan Square *supra* 87. PARADISE
WALK was earlier *Bull Walk* 1799 Horwood, from an inn. PARK WALK
commemorates the former Chelsea *Park*, marked as *Lord Wharton's
Park* in 1717 MapCh. It was *Lovers Walk* ib. PAVILION RD is
Pavilion Street 1815 FaulknerCh, from a house called *The Pavilion*
which stood here 1777–1879 (Beaver 43). POND PLACE is *Pond Place*
1829 FaulknerCh, from a pool in the north-west corner of Chelsea
Common (Beaver 339). QUEEN'S ELM and ELM PARK GARDENS commemorate a tree called *Queens Tree* 1586 Beaver, *Queen Elm* 1687 ib.,
the Cross Tree 1717 MapCh, traditionally associated with Queen
Elizabeth, *v.* Church St *supra* 87. RANELAGH GROVE commemorates
the former pleasure gardens c. 1740–1802 (W and C), laid out on an
estate of the Earl of *Ranelagh*, now part of the grounds of Chelsea
Hospital. Cf. *the Earl of Ranelagh's House and Lands* 1717 MapCh.
RILEY ST was built c. 1790 (FaulknerCh i, 74). Cf. Stephen *Riley*
(1802 Poll). ROYAL HOSPITAL RD. The south-west part was earlier
Paradise Row 1717 MapCh, 1831 Elmes. *v. infra* 207. ST LEONARDS
TERRACE (1867 LCCN) was *Green's Row* 1794 Horwood, built 1765
and named after the then landowner (FaulknerCh ii, 216). SLOANE ST
and SQUARE are both so named ib., from Sir Hans *Sloane* (of British
Museum fame) who purchased the manor of Chelsea from the Cheyne
family in 1712 (FaulknerCh i, 338). The earlier name of the area was
Great Bloody Field (VCH ii, 320). Cf. *Bloody Gate* and *Bridge, infra*.
SMITH ST was begun to be built by Thomas *Smith* in 1794 (FaulknerCh
ii, 216). SWAN WALK is so named in 1794 (Horwood), from an old inn.
Cf. *the meadow next the Swan* 1681 FaulknerCh. TURK'S ROW is so
named in 1746 (R). WORLDS END is so named t. Charles II (FaulknerCh i, 63) and WORLDS END PASSAGE in 1815 (ib. i, 40). It is
Way between the Pales 1717 Map. It is at the western end of the
village, the name being descriptive of a remote situation, *v. infra* 206.

　Lost names include those of two bridges over the Westbourne,
Bloody Bridge 1719 FaulknerCh i, 43 (cf. *Bloody Gate* 1590 ib.) and
Chelsea Bridge 1746 ib., earlier *Stonybridge* 1544 Survey; also *Wilder-
ness Row* 1746 R, north-west of Ranelagh Gardens.

Chiswick[1]

CHISWICK [tʃizik]

(*of*) *Ceswican* c. 1000 (c. 1125) ASCharters
Chesewic 1181 StPaulsDB, t. John AD ii *et passim* to 1470
　FF, with variant spellings -*wyk*(*e*), -*wik*, *Chesewich* 1222
　StPaulsDB
Chisewich' 1229 StPaulsCh, *Chiswyk* 1537 FF, -*wick* 1754 R

[1] Now part of the Borough of Brentford and Chiswick.

Cheesewyke t. Eliz ChancP, *Cheeswick* 1638 ParReg (Brentford)
Cheswyke 1566 FF, *-weke* 1568 ib.

'Cheese farm,' *v.* wic. Cf. Chiswick (PN Ess 522). The
earliest form would seem to derive from a dat. pl. form.

NOTE. BARROWGATE RD. Cf. *Barrowgates* c. 1840 *TA*. BURLINGTON
RD. Richard Boyle, 4th Earl of Cork and 3rd Earl of *Burlington*,
inherited a house and land in Chiswick in 1731 (Draper 106).
CHISWICK HIGH RD. Cf. "at Chiswick at the highway there" 1613
Sess. A part of the Great West Road, *v. supra* 10. CORNEY RD.
Cf. *Corney House* 1602 Lysons, *Corney Lodge* 1865 O.S. DEVONSHIRE
RD and DUKE'S AVENUE and MEADOWS. The Duke of Devonshire is
a ground landlord here. From this association come also BOLTON RD,
HARTINGTON RD and PAXTON RD. HOGARTH LANE commemorates the
painter, who lived at HOGARTH HO (c. 1865 O.S.). THE MALL, like the
place of that name in Hammersmith *infra* 110, seems to be a copying
of the famous Westminster name *infra* 181, as denoting a fashionable
neighbourhood. MAWSON'S LANE takes its name from Dr *Mawson*
(ob. 1716) (Draper 99). POWELL'S WALK was earlier *Paul's Walk* (ib.
176). The manor of Chiswick belonged to the Dean and Chapter of
St Paul's.

BEDFORD PARK. This is a residential district built in the late
19th century, the name commemorating the residence in the
parish in the 17th century of the Russells, Dukes of Bedford
(Walford i, 8). Cf. Bedford Square *infra* 117.

CHISWICK AIT is *Ye Twigg Eight* 1650 Feret, 1741–5 R, *Chiswick
Ait* 1819 G. This is ME *eyte, ayte,* OE iggoð, 'islet.' Cf. Eel Pie
Island *supra* 30 and *Neat infra* 170. The original first element
is presumably the common word *twig*.

STRAND ON THE GREEN is *Stronde* 1353 FF, *Stronde in parochia
de Cheswyk* 1412 Cl, *Ye Strande* 1593 N, *Strand Green* 1710 S,
1754 R, *Strand under Green* 1760 Griffiths, *Strand on Green*
1795 Lysons. From OE *strand,* 'strand, shore, bank'; the hamlet
is so named because it lies along the north bank of the Thames.

SUTTON[1] is *Suthtona, Sutthona* 1181 StPaulsDB, *Suttone* 1222
FF, *Sutton Chesewyk* 1367 FF, (*by Chesewyk*) 1437 Pat, *Sutton
al. Bewregarde* 1456 Pat, (*al. Beauregard*) 1457 ib., *Sutton Court*
1597 PCC. 'South farm,' *v.* tun, probably with reference to

---

[1] Surviving in SUTTON COURT RD.

Acton to the north. The manor house of Sutton Court is now demolished. The French epithet appears only in the above Patent Roll records. It seems to mean 'fine view or prospect.' In early times there would have been a view from the manor house over the river towards the distant Surrey hills.

TURNHAM GREEN

(*campum de*) *Turneham* 1229–37, 1239 StPaulsCh
Turnham 1294 *Ass*, c. 1394 Works
Turnhamgrene 1396 Pat, 1429 *Ct, Turnehamgrene* 1470 ib.
Turnhamfeld 1437, 1456 *Ct, Turnham lane* t. Hy 6 ib.

This name should be compared with Turnham Hall (PN ERY 259–60) which is interpreted 'homestead by the river bend,' the first element being an unrecorded OE word **trun, *turn*, 'circular, circular place,' possibly by extension 'bend, bight.' Turnham Green was a hamlet on the Great West Road just below which the Thames makes a big sweep south between Chiswick and Kew Bridge. Possibly the name had reference to this bend and in that case it would be better to take the second element to be **hamm** rather than ham. Cf. Fulham *infra* 101.

GROVE HO is *the Grove* 1412 Cl and was the home of Robert de *Grava* (c. 1210 StPaulsCh) and Robert *atte Grove* (1353 FF). *v.* græfe *infra* 199.

The Borough of Ealing

EALING

Gillingas 693–704 (17th) StPaulsCh, *Gillinges* t. Hy 3 StPaulsMSS
Ilingis c. 1127 StPaulsMSS, *Yllinges* 1163–88 ib., 1236 Cl, *Illinges* t. John AD ii, *Yllingges* 1306 Londin
Illing' 1130 P, *Yllingg(e)* 1291 FF, 1308 Pat, 1309 StPauls MSS, *Chircheyllinge* 1274 *Ass, Illingg'* 1294 ib., *Cherche-ʒillyng* 1393 *Ct*
Gilling 1243 Pat, 1244–6 FF, *Gillingg'* 1274 *Ass,* -*ynge* 1314 Pat, *Gyllyngg(e)* 1294 *Ass,* 1327 Banco
Yilling(g) 1294 *Ass,* 1312 FF, 1316 FA, -*yng(ge)* 1307 Inq aqd, 1348, 1356 FF, 1399 Pat, *ʒillyng* 1393 *Ct,* -*ing* 1548 BM, *ʒillynggrene* 1393 *Ct*

Yellyng(e) 1307 Ch, 1341 NI, 1400 Pat, 1441, 1468 FF, 1535
  VE, *3ellingfelde* 1452 BM, *Yelyng* 1512 FF
Elyng 1553 FF, *Elyng al. Yelyng* 1566 ib.
Yelyng al. Illyng 1563 FF, (*al. Ealyng*) 1564 ib., *Eelinge* 1615
  Sess, *Ealing al. Yealing* 1622 BM

'The people of **Gilla*,' *v.* ingas, Ekwall, PN in *-ing* 52,
DEPN *s.n.* Church to distinguish from *Little* or *West* Ealing.

NOTE. BROOMFIELD RD. Cf. *Broom Field* c. 1840 *TA*. CLAYPONDS
LANE. Cf. *Clay Pond* 1819 G. CRAVEN RD was *Thieving Lane* 1741–5 R.
Cf. the same name *supra* 84. HANGER LANE is *Hanger Hill Lane* ib.,
v. Hanger Hill *infra*. POPES LANE is *Popelane* 1423 *Ct*, *Popes Lane*
c. 1840 *TA*. THE RIDINGS is *Reddings* c. 1840 *TA*, *v.* ryding. SOUTH
EALING RD was *Drum Lane* 1741–5 R. WINDMILL RD is *Windmill Lane*
ib. WOODFIELD RD. Cf. *Wood Fd* c. 1840 *TA*.

DRAYTON GREEN is *Drayton* 1387 Works, *Drayton in parochia
de 3illyng* 1393 *Ct*, *Dreyton* 1494 ib. *v.* West Drayton *supra* 33.
Drayton in Ealing lies near a large bend of the river Brent.

FORDHOOK HO is *Forthehoke* 1462 *Ct*, *Fordhook* 1754 Walford.
This name probably means 'the spur or hook of land in front,'
v. hoc and cf. Forty Hall *supra* 73.

GUNNERSBURY

  Gounyldebury 1334 Pat, *Gunnyldesbury* 1348, 1390 FF, *-bery*
    1377 IpmR, *Gonyldesbury* 1380 BM
  Gonelsbury 1487 Ipm, *Gonelbury otherwise Goneldisbury* 1531
    FF
  Gunnersbury 1593 N, *Gunsbury* 1651 Cai, *Gunnalsbury* 1682
    Morgan

'*Gunnhild*'s manor or fortified dwelling,' *v.* burh (manorial)
and Introd. xvi. The statement, often quoted in local histories,
that the place takes its name from *Gunhilda*, niece of King
Canute, seems to rest on unsupported opinion.

HANGER HILL is so named in 1710 (S) and marks the site of a
former wood referred to in *le Hangrewode* 1393 *Ct*, *Aungrewode*
t. Hy 5 ib., *Hangar wood* 1539 LP. *v.* hangra, '(wooded) slope.'

NORTHFIELDS is a new district name, preserving the old field-
names *Northfeld* 1455 *Ct*, *le Nether, le over north(e)feld* 1459 ib.

PITSHANGER PARK

> *Putleshangre* 1222 StPaulsDB, 1294 *Ass* (p), *Puttelleshangre*
> 1236 StPaulsCh (p), *Puttele-* 1274 *Ass* (p)
> *Pittleshangre* 1294 *GDR*, *Peteleshangre* 1408 *Ct*
> *Pytteshangre* 1493 *Ct*, *Pitch Hanger* 1819 G

The first element may be the OE *pyttel*, 'kind of hawk or kite,' a diminutive of *putta*, 'kite' (cf. Studies[2] 91), or we may have the bird-name used as a personal name as in Pittleworth (Ha), *Puteleorde* 1086 DB, *Puttelesword'* 1242 Fees. Cf. the nickname *Gorpittel* found in Devon (c. 1100) (Tengvik 362). The second element is hangra, '(wooded) slope.'

MASON'S GREEN is to be associated with the family of William *Mason* (1628 ParReg).

BRENTHAM is an artificial name (c. 1910) for a new district by the Brent. CASTLEBAR HILL is *Castlebeare* 1675 Ogilby, *Castle Beare* 1680 S. EALING DEAN is *3yllyngdeyn* 1456 *Ct. v.* denu. ELM GROVE was, according to Lysons (ii, 228), known as *Hickes upon the heath* in 1684. GROVE HO. Cf. *Ealing Grove* 1722 Lysons. LITTLE EALING is *Little Yelling* 1650 *FF*. LONDON STYLE is *London Stile* 1741–5 R. By the main London road. WEST EALING is *West(y)illing* 1234 StPaulsCh (p), 1287 FF, *West-yellyng* 1408 ib. Formerly a distinct hamlet.

The Borough of Finchley

FINCHLEY

> *Finchelee, -leya* c. 1208, 1213–16 StPaulsCh, *Finchel'* 1230
> FF (p), *-leye* 1258, 1272 FF, 1273 Pat, *-lee* 1274 *Ass*, *-ley*
> 1428 FA *et freq*, *Vynchelay* 1407 Pat
> *Finchesleg'* 1235 *Ass et passim* to 1483 FF, with variant
> spellings *Fynches-* and *-legh, -ley(e)*
> *Finchingeleye* 1260 FF, *Fynchingley al. Fynchley* 1581 *SR*
> *Fyncheley al. Frynchesley* 1547 FF

'Finch clearing or wood,' *v.* leah. Or the first element may be the OE *finc*, 'finch,' used as a personal name, as suggested by the genitival *s* in the majority of the early spellings. Cf. Godric *Finc* c. 1050 KCD 923 (Wo) (Tengvik 362), Finchingfield (PN Ess 425) and *finces stapol* (BCS 982, Meon, Ha).

NOTE. BALLARDS LANE is *Bal(l)ardeslane* t. Hy 5 *Ct*, 1524 AD vi. CHURCHFIELD RD. Cf. *Church Fd* 1683 MxNQ i. NETHER ST is *Netherstrete* 1448 Cl. 'Lower street,' *v.* neoðera.

GOLDERS HILL is *Godereshill* t. Hy 4 *Ct* and is probably to be associated with the family which gave name to the nearby Golders Green *supra* 58.

WOODSIDE is so named in 1686 (M). Cf. *Fyncheley Wode* 1468 Pat, *Woodsendfeld* 1548 FF. A part of the great Middlesex woodland area.

MOSS HALL[1] and TURNER'S WOOD are to be associated with the families of John *Mosse* (1474 *Ct*) and Roger *Turner* (1567 ParReg).

BUNKERS HILL is so named c. 1840 (*TA*). *v. infra* 205. CHURCH END is so named in 1683 (MxNQ i). COLDFALL WOOD is *place...called Colefall* 1599 Sess, 1666 HornseyCt. COLD-HARBOUR HO is *Coldharbour* 1675 Ogilby. *v. infra* 206. EAST END is *Estend* 1558 FF. FALLOW CORNER is *Follow Corner* 1680 S, 1686 M, (*Fallow*) 1710 S. NORTH END is so called in 1485 (MxNQ ii).

The Borough of Finsbury

NOTE. Finsbury was a prebendal manor of St Paul's which never became a parish. The present borough of Finsbury includes the parishes of St James and St John, Clerkenwell, St Luke, Old Street (separated from St Giles without Cripplegate in 1732), the extra parochial district of the Charterhouse, and the Liberty of Glasshouse Yard.

FINSBURY

> *Vinisbir'* 1231 FF, *Vinesbir'* 1235 *Ass*, -*bur'* 1275 RH, -*byri* 1288 StPaulsMSS, -*bury* 1397 IpmR, 1406 Pat, *Wynesbury* 1391 Pat
> *Finesbir'* 1235 *Ass et passim* to 1475 FF, with variant spellings *Fynes*- and -*bury*, -*bery*, *Soka de Fynisbyr'* 1274 *Ass*, *Fynesbury Soken* 1294 ib., *Fynesbury or Haliwelle* 1347 Pat
> *Fyn(n)ebyr'* 1253 FF, 1274 *Ass*
> *Halywell al. Vynesbury* 1406 Pat
> *Fynnesbury, Fenysbury* 1535 VE, *Fynnesburye feilde* 1564 Hust

---

[1] *Moss Hall* 1696 HornseyCt.

Finsbury, like Brondesbury, Barnsbury, etc., is no doubt a manorial *bury* rather than an ancient *burh* and the first element is more likely to be the Anglo-Scandinavian personal name *Fin* recorded several times in DB than the heroic *Finn*, in spite of the coincidence of the name of the ancient *Finnesburh*. For the later name cf. Feilitzen (251) where the name is recorded from Buckinghamshire, Essex, Lincolnshire, Suffolk. For *Vin-*, *v.* Introd. xvii. For *soka*, *v.* socn.

THE ARTILLERY GROUND, so named in 1746 (R), is *The New Artillery Garden* 1677 O and M, where the Honourable Artillery Company, then as now, drilled.

BUNHILL FIELDS BURIAL GROUND is *Bonhilles* 1544 LP, *Bonhil Field* 1567 Survey, *Bunne Hill* 1615 Sess, *Tindals Burying Ground* 1746 R (cf. W and C), *Bunhill Fields Burying Ground* 1799 Horwood. The ultimate history of the name is obscure. The name is associated with the story of the removal of the bones from St Paul's charnel house to Finsbury Field in 1549 (*v.* Stow i, 330), but it is clear that it was already in use a few years before that. The name is probably a compound of *bone* and *hill*, but it is difficult to fix the exact circumstances under which it arose.

CHARTERHOUSE is *le Charthous next Smythfeld* 1375 Hust, *Charterhous* 1385 ib. This is the Carthusian monastery founded by Walter de Manny in 1365. The two forms reflect corresponding variations in the French form from which they derive, viz. AFr *Chart(h)ous* and *Chartrous*, OFr *Charteus* and *Chartreus*.

CLERKENWELL [klɑ·kənwel]

(*juxta*) *fontem clericorum* (field) c. 1145 *Clerkenwell*, *Monasterium sanctimonialium Fontis Clericorum* 1145–50 BM *Clerkenewella* c. 1152 Hornsey, *Monialibus de fonte Clericorum* c. 1170 StPaulsCh, *Clerechenewella* c. 1175 BM, *villa de Clerkenewelle* 1190 Hornsey, *Clerkenewell'* 1198 Cur, 1211, 1236 FF, 1274 *Ass*, *Clerekenewelle* 1242 Fees, 1254, 1271 FF, 1274 *Ass*, *Clerconwell* 1399 Hust
Clarkynwell 1551 FF, *Clarkenwell* 1603 Stow

'Clerks' well or spring,' *v.* **wielle**. The explanation of the name is probably that suggested by FitzStephen's account, t. Hy 2 (LibCust i, 4) of the wells near London: "Inter quos Fons Sacer (*v.* Holywell *infra* 146), *Fons Clericorum*, Fons Sancti Clementis (*infra* 177), nominatiores habentur; et adeuntur celebriore accessu et majore frequentia scholarium, et urbanae juventutis in serotinis aestivis." The *clerici* after whom the well was named may have been these *scholars*, the students from the schools. They were not only schoolboys (whom FitzStephen calls (ib., 6) *pueri scholarum*); the schools of London at that period were of the same type as those which at Oxford developed into a university. The association with the Parish Clerks "who of old time were accustomed there yearely to assemble, and to play some large hystorie of holy Scripture" (Stow i, 15) is much later than the original name. In actual fact they seem to have played by Skinners Well *infra* rather than the 'Clerks' well.' Cf. Hassall's note in MLR xxxiii, 564.

FAGS WELL and SKINNERS WELL[1] (both lost) are so named by Stow in 1598 (ii, 86). They are *Fackeswell, Skinnereswell* 1197 FF, *Fageswelle* c. 1190 RecStBarts, *Scinn-, Skinnereswelle, Fageswelle* c. 1200 *Clerkenwell, Faggeswell* 1244 RecStBarts, *Skynnereswelle* 1385 LBk. These were the names of two wells or springs near Clerkenwell, covered over and lost since the 16th century; cf. LMxAS (N.S.) viii, 253–4. Both clearly derive from personal names. The second is the occupational name *skinner*, of Scandinavian origin. This example is some two hundred years earlier than the earliest example of that word in NED. Kingsford (Stow ii, 272) rightly rejects Stow's suggestion that it was so called because "the Skinneres of London held there certaine playes." The correct form and origin of the first name are uncertain.

HOCKLEY-IN-THE-HOLE (lost) is *Hockley Hole* 1654 PCC, *Hocklee in the Hole* 1667 Sess, *Hocley in the hole* 1667 ParReg, *Hocley the hole* 1674 ParReg, *Hockly i' th' Hole* 1722 ib. This name (changed

---

[1] Fogwell Houses, Court, Gardens, Ground and Pond (1530–44 LP) in Charterhouse Lane and near Long Lane preserved the name (LnTopRec x, 122). For the site *v.* Kingsford's note (Stow ii, 272) and LMxAS (N.S.) v, 82–3. *v.* Addenda xxxiii.

to *Ray Street* in 1774 and absorbed in Farringdon Rd since 1857)
was once applied to a street of ill-fame lying beside the Fleet,
often mentioned by 17th and 18th century writers. The name
may have been transferred from Hockliffe (Beds), called *Hockley
in the Hole* in 1675 (*v.* PN BedsHu 126–7), also at one time a
place of ill-repute.

MOUNT MILLS is (*The*) *Mount Mill* 1682 Morgan, 1700 Sess,
1720 ParReg. Stow (ii, 80), under a marginal heading *The Mount*,
explains that Queen Katherine of Aragon built a chapel here
on the site of a windmill which had been blown down and
"named it the Mount of Caluerie" and that the chapel was
afterwards destroyed and another windmill set up. Hence *Mount
Myllefeild* 1573 Sess. This is clearly the site of the fort ordered
to be erected "at the windmill in Islington way" in the Resolution of the Common Council for the fortification of London,
noted under Virginia Rd *supra* 85 and recorded by Lithgow in
1643 as *Mount Mil-Hill Fort*, cf. LnTopRec xiv, 6, 18, 34.

MOUNT PLEASANT is so named in 1732 (PC) and 1746 (R). It
probably was so called, as in other London examples, from a
heap of cinders or refuse which formerly occupied the site. Cf.
Dickens's reference in *Our Mutual Friend* to the mounds that
made the fortune of "The Golden Dustman." Cf. Laystall St
infra 118.

PENTONVILLE was named after Henry *Penton*, M.P. for Winchester, who had land here which he began to build over c. 1773
(Pinks 491).

SADLER'S WELLS belonged c. 1683 to one *Sadler*, who had a
'Music House' there and found a mineral spring in its garden.
In 1765 Rosoman, the then proprietor, replaced the Music
House by a theatre (Pinks 409, 419; W and C). Cf. *Sadlers Hall*
1698 ParReg (Clerkenwell).

SPA FIELDS PLAYGROUND and SPA GREEN preserve the name of
the area called *Spa Fields* t. George IV. In Rocque's map of
1746 the *London Spaw* is shown in the middle of it. Cf. *The Spaw*
1695 Sess, 1730 ParReg, *Ye Wells* 1699 ib., showing the common
18th century pronunciation of the word 'spa.' Cf. Pinks 151–2,
167–9.

FINSBURY STREET-NAMES

ALLEN ST is *Allen streete* 1681 ParReg, *Ellin street* 1731 ib. It is probably to be associated with the family of Walter *Allen* (1641 Sess). AYLESBURY ST is *Ailsbury street* 1716 ParReg. Near the site of a house of the Earl of *Aylesbury* (Pinks 276). BAKERS ROW is so named in 1729 (ParReg). BASTWICK ST was *Noble Street* 1732 PC, 1746 R. BATH ST is *Pesthouse Row* and *Ratcliff Row* 1746 R. BERKELEY ST was *Barkly Street* 1723 ParReg, on the site of a house here of Sir Maurice *Berkeley* in the 16th century (Pinks 279). BOWLING GREEN LANE. Two bowling greens are marked near the site in 1677 (O and M). BUNHILL ROW is so named in 1746 (R). *v. supra* 94. CENTRAL ST (1861 LCCN) was *Brick Lane* 1682 Morgan, 1746 R. CHARLES ST is so named in 1682 (Morgan), probably commemorating King Charles II. CHISWELL ST is *Chysel strate* 13th StPaulsMSS, *Cheselstrete* 1458 FF, *Chiswell Str* t. Eliz Agas, from OE *ceosol*, 'flint, pebble.' Cf. Chesil Bank (PN Do 165). CITY RD is so named in 1754 (R). It was formally opened in 1761 (W and C). Its southern end absorbed the already existing *Royal Row* 1746 R. COLD BATH SQUARE is so named ib. It is on the site of *Cold Bath Field* 1721 ParReg, so named from a spring discovered here in 1697 (Pinks 111). COMPTON ST is *Cumpton streete* 1695 ParReg, *Cumton streete* 1696 ib., from *Compton*, the family name of the Earl (now Marquess) of Northampton, the ground landlord. COPPICE ROW (now absorbed by Farringdon Rd) is *Codpeece Roe* 1669 ParReg, *Codpeese Roe* 1673 ib., *Codpece Roe* 1677 ib., *Codpiss Row* 1691 ib., *Cotpis Row* 1724 ib., *Coppice Row* 1726 ib. Cf. *Cod Piss Corner* 1800 Faden (in Edmonton). Probably so called as a haunt of women of ill-fame (cf. Sugden 124). CORPORATION ROW is *Corporation Lane* 1683 ParReg. Near here stood a Corporation Workhouse in the 17th century (Pinks 125–7). COWCROSS ST is *Cowcrosse strete* 1553 FF, from a cross referred to as *Kowecrosse* 1437 ib., *Cowe Crosse* 1438 ib. CYRUS ST was *King Street* 1723 ParReg, 1746 R. EXMOUTH ST (now MARKET) is so named c. 1838 *Oliver Twist*, ch. viii, taking its name from Admiral Lord *Exmouth*, t. George IV. FARRINGDON RD was constructed 1845–56, obliterating Coppice Row, Hockley-in-the-Hole, Townsend Lane and other minor courts and alleys. It is a continuation of Farringdon St in the City. FEATHERSTONE ST is so named in 1746 (R). GEE ST (1799 Horwood) was *The Rope Walk* 1732 PC, 1746 R. GLASSHOUSE YARD is so named in 1691 (Sess), probably from former glass works here, as in other cases. GOLDEN LANE is *Goldyng lane* t. Ed 1 StPaulsMSS, *Goldeslane* 1274 Ass, *Golden lane* 1317 Hust, *Goldenelane* 1320 Ass, *Goldynglane* 1324 Hust, 1342 Ass, 1358 Cl, *Goldynggeslane* 1361 Hust, *Goldelane* 1369 Pat. The first element is uncertain but it is probably the personal name *Golding*. GOSWELL RD is *Goswellestrete* 1393 LBk, from a former well or spring here, *Godewell(e)* 1197 FF, c. 1200 *Clerkenwell, Gosewell'* c. 1200 StPaulsCh, *aqua que vocatur Gosewell* 1320 Ass. Probably 'goose spring or stream.' HATFIELD ST is so named in 1709 (LCCDeeds). HELMET ROW is so named in 1721 (ParReg). IRONMONGER ROW is so named in 1746 (R). Cf. the same name in the City. LEVER ST (1861 LCCN). Part was *Ratclifs Layer* 1746 R. MIDDLE ROW (now CRESCENT ROW), perhaps the *Ratonsrowe* mentioned in 1373 (Hust), was *Retten* or *Rotten Rowe* 1537 LnIpm, *Rotten Row* 1677 O and M, 1799 Horwood, 1831 Elmes, *Ragged Row* 1746 R and in some maps to 1850 (*v.* LMxAS (N.S.) iv, 266). 'Rat-row,' from ME *ratoun*, a common nickname, often corrupted to *rotten*, *v. infra* 203. MITCHELL ST is so named in 1732 (PC). MYDDELTON SQUARE and ST, built c. 1820 (W and C) near the *New River Head*, commemorate the originator of that undertaking, *v.* New River *supra* 5. NEW ST is so named in 1732 (PC). NORTHAMPTON ST (now AGDON ST) is so named in 1799 (Horwood), cf. Compton St *supra* 97. Earlier known as *Wood Close* 1581 Sess, *Woodes Close* 1592 ParReg, 1682 Morgan. OLD ST is *Ealdestrate* c. 1200 *Clerkenwell*, *Eldestrete* 1275 RH, *-stret* 1291 Tax, *le Oldestrete* 1373 Hust, *Yealdestrete* 1535 VE, *Alderstreet* 1603 Stow. *v.* stræt and Introd. xvii. PEAR TREE COURT and ST. Cf. *Pear Tree Court* 1685 ParReg, *Paretree Court Lane* 1723 ib., *Pear Tree Street* 1732 PC. PEERLESS ST takes its name from "one other cleare water called *Perillous* pond, because diuerse youthes swimming therein haue been drowned" (Stow i, 16). The pond is called *Parlous Pond* in Middleton's *Roaring Girl* (1611), *Peerless Pool* in 1799 (Horwood). PENTON ST is *Penton Place* ib. For this and PENTONVILLE RD, cf. *supra* 96. PERCIVAL ST and SPENCER ST are so named in 1831 (Elmes) from *Spencer Percival*, Prime Minister 1809–12, a cousin of Lord Northampton, cf. Compton St *supra* 97. PETERS LANE is *Peeters street* 1687 ParReg. PLAYHOUSE YARD is so named in 1682 (Morgan) from the old *Fortune Theatre* here. RAY ST is so named in 1799 (Horwood). Part was earlier *Rag Street* 1746 R. RED LION ST is *Red Lyon Street* 1746 R, from an inn-sign. It was earlier *Garden Alley* 1677 O and M. ROSOMAN ST is so named after one *Rosoman*, its builder, proprietor of Sadlers Wells Theatre (Pinks 167). Earlier *Bridewell Walk* 1746 R; it led past the Clerkenwell *Bridewell*, a house of correction (Pinks 167). ST JAMES WALK (now Row) is so named in 1799 (Horwood). It was earlier *New Prison Walk* 1677 O and M, 1691 ParReg, 1746 R, from a prison formerly at its northern end. ST JOHNS ST is *Seint Jonestrete* 1376 AD ii, 1387 Pat, from the Priory of the Knights of *St John* of Jerusalem, Clerkenwell. SEKFORDE ST and WOODBRIDGE ST intersect an estate, most of the income from which was bequeathed by Thomas *Sekforde* (d. 1588) to endow an almshouse at Woodbridge (Sf). It was formerly *St Mary Close*, adjoining the nunnery (Pinks 176, 190; cf. LMxAS (N.S.) viii, 234). SEWARD ST takes its name from *Messrs Sewards Dye Ho* 1799 Horwood. SPA COTTAGES were built when the *Islington Spa* was pulled down in 1840. This was *Islington Wells* by 1685 or (alternatively) *New Tunbridge Wells* before 1690, *Islington Spa* by 1754 (Pinks 398–406). GREAT and LITTLE SUTTON ST are named from Thomas *Sutton*, the founder in 1611 of *Sutton's Hospital*, usually known as the Charterhouse and Charterhouse School (Pinks 337). The eastern part of Great Sutton St was earlier *Swan Alley* 1746 R. Cf. *Swan Alley al. Sutton Street* 1682 Morgan. TABERNACLE ST was *Windmill Hill* 1746 R; the north-east end had become *Tabernacle Walk* and *Tabernacle Place* by 1799 (Horwood), from one of Whitfield's tabernacles. For the windmills there, cf. Kingsford's note on Stow (ii, 370). TOWNS-END LANE (absorbed by Farringdon Rd) was *Towns End or Codpeice Row* 1677 O and M, *Towns End Lane* 1720 Strype (Map). It seems to have been an alternative name of Coppice Row *supra* 97. TURNMILL ST is *Trilmulle-* 1374 Hust, *Tryllemyl-* 1474 FF, *Tyrmyl-* c. 1493 ECP, *Turmel-* 1545 FF, *Tremel-* 1546 ib., *Tourmel-* 1553 ib., *Turnmelstrete* 1567 ib., *Turnemill streat* 1601 PCC, from a former mill referred to as *Trillemille* 1294 *Ass*, *Tryllemelle* 1353 Hust, on *Trynmylbroke* 1422 LnEng, river called *Turnemyll Broke* 1502 Pat, a name for the upper course of the Holborn R. (*supra* 4), used as a mill-stream (cf. LMxAS (N.S.) viii, 234, 236). There is an exact parallel in the name of a lost mill in Oxford, belonging to St Frideswide's, which is called *Trille*, *Trillemelle* c. 1180 St Frideswide's Cartulary, 1278 RH (p). The street, formerly a notorious slum area, is frequently spelt *Turnbull Street* by 17th and 18th century writers. Cf. Shakespeare, *Henry IV*, Act iii, Sc. 2. VINEYARD WALK is so named in 1799 (Horwood). A vineyard is shown there in a print of 1752. Cf. *tenement called le Vyne* 1306 Pinks. WARNER ST is so named in 1729 (ParReg) from a family which had property here in the 18th century (Pinks 636).

Lost street-names include *Cubreggestrete* 1300 RecStBarts and (all from ParReg) *The Causey* 1685, *Cut Throat Alley* 1727, *Frying Pan Alley* 1677, *The Hangman's Alley* 1681, *Mutton Lane* 1613 (probably a street of ill-fame), *Pissing Alley* 1683, *Three Pegions Alley* 1685 (doubtless from an inn sign). Note also *Copthall* 1594 (cf. *supra* 36), *The Cadge* 1608 (i.e. the cage or lock-up, cf. PN Nt 15), *The Buttes* 1618 (cf. *infra* 196) and *The Brickils* 1618, i.e. 'brick-kilns,' with common *kil(l)* for *kiln*, *Merlin's Cave* 1735, a famous place of amusement (Pinks 580).

Friern Barnet

FRIERN BARNET

la Bernet, la Barnate 1235 *Ass*, *Little Bernete* 1237 FF

Frerennebarnethe, Frerenbarnet, Fernebernete 1274 *Ass*, *Frerenebarnet* 1294 *GDR*, *Freresbarnet* 1336 Cl, *Freren Bernett, Friern Bñet* 1535 VE, *Fryernbarnet* 1550 FF, *Fryan Barnett* 1665 ParReg

Charneres Bernete 1294 *Ass*, *Sarner(e)sbarnet* 1316 FA, 1341 NI, *Sarnieres barnatt* 1322 *Cor*

Frerynbury 1428 FA

Fryeringe Barnet 1549 Pat, *Freering Barnet* 1551 Sess

'Place cleared by burning,' *v.* **bærnet**. The name originally included all the Barnets, but at an early date East and High Barnet were included in Hertfordshire because they were possessions of St Albans Abbey, cf. PN Herts 70–1. Friern Barnet remained in Middlesex because it belonged to the Knights of St John of Jerusalem, whence the later distinctive prefix, *freren* being a ME plural of *frere*, 'brother, *frater*,' cf. Fryerning (PN Ess 254). The 1428 reference is probably to the actual manor house, *v.* **burh** (manorial) and Introd. xvi.

COLNEY HATCH is *Colneha(t)che* 1492 *et freq StPauls*, 1575 Ipm, *Coanie hatch* 1593 N, *Cony Hatch* 1610 Speed, 1675 Ogilby. The *hatch* was a gate of Enfield Chase (*supra* 73). The forms are too late for any interpretation of the first element to be possible, but it would seem that the *l* is original, since it occurs in all the earliest spellings. One might compare Coleherne *infra* 128.

HALLIWICK[1]

> *Halewike* 1227 Ch, 1257 FF, *-wyke* 1252 Ch, 1402 IpmR, 1439 FF
>
> *Hallewyc* 1235 FF, *-wyk* 1547 ib.
>
> *Halwykstrete, Holwyklond* 1399 Works, *Halwikfeld* 1448 Cl, *Halywicke* 1549 FF, *Hallwyke al. Hallywycke* (sic) 1602 Ipm
>
> *Hollicke* 1593 N, *Hollick Wood* 1754 R

The absence of any spellings with a medial *i* shows that the first element can hardly be OE **halig**, 'holy,' and a compound of **halig** and **wic** would not in any case be a very likely one. This name must remain an unsolved problem.

OAKLEIGH PARK is a modern (late 19th century) name, suggested perhaps by the not far distant Oakhill in East Barnet (*v.* PN Herts 72).

WHETSTONE[2] is *Wheston* 1417 Cl, 1486–93 ECP, 1496 Pat, *Whetestonesstret* 1437 *Ct, Whetstone* 1492 ib., 1516 FF, 1535 VE, *Westone* 1535 FF, *Whetston Strete* 1571 *FF, Whetston al. Fryern* t. Eliz ChancP. 'At the whetstone,' from OE *hwetstān*. Cf.

---

[1] Surviving in HALLIWICK RD.   [2] Partly in Finchley.

Wheston (Db), *Whetston* 1271 FF, Whetstone (Lei), *Whetestan* t. Hy 2 (1318) Ch. Tradition holds that there was once a large stone here, on which the soldiers sharpened their weapons before the battle of Barnet in 1471.

FRIERN PARK is *Freren parke* 1507 *Ct.* WALLFIELD is *Walfeld* 1492 *StPauls*, *Wallefeld* 1494 ib., *Wallfelde* 1499 ib.

The Borough of Fulham

FULHAM [fuləm]

> *Fulanham* c. 705 (17th) StPaulsCh
> (*æt*), (*on*) *Fullanhamme* c. 895 ASC (*s.a.* 879, 880 Ā)[1], (*of*) *Fullanhamme* c. 1000 ASCharters, (*æt*) *Fullanhomme* 12th ASC (*s.a.* 880 E), (*at*) *Fullenham* t. Edw Conf (14th) ASWills
> (*æt*) *Fulanhamme* c. 1050 ASC (*s.a.* 879, 880 B)
> *Fuleham* 1086 DB *et freq* to 1316 FA
> *Foleham* c. 1127 StPaulsCh, 1232 FF, 1274 *Ass*, 1291 Tax
> *Fulleham* 1274 *Ass*, 1326 FF
> *Fulham* 1274 *Ass*, 1316 FF, *Fullam* 1533 PC

The second element in this name is clearly **hamm**, the name being descriptive of the position of Fulham in a low-lying bend of the river. The first is clearly *fullan* rather than *fulan*, so that the name cannot be derived from **ful**, 'dirty.' It would be difficult to give any sense to the adj. *full* as applied to **hamm**, and the probabilities are in favour of Ekwall's suggestion that we have here a personal name *Fulla* for which he notes a possible parallel in *Fullingadich* (BCS 34) in the bounds of Chertsey. Hence '*Fulla*'s **hamm**.'

COLEHILL LANE preserves the place-name *Colyshill* 1422 *Ct*, *Coleshill* 1438, 1445 ib., *Colhill* 1554 ib., and is *Collehillane* 1524 ib. It looks as if we may have here another example of the difficult Coleshill discussed in PN Sr 282, Wa 42. There is no stream here now, so the first element may be a personal name, though the forms are not sufficiently early to decide with any certainty whether this was of OE or ME origin.

---

[1] So also in MSS C, D and E except in E (*s.a.* 880).

COUNTERS BRIDGE[1] is *Countessesbrugge* c. 1350 Works, *Contesses-* 1421 *Ct*, *Contasse-* 1422 ib., *Cuntasse-* 1445 ib., *Countesbregge* 1475 ib., *Counters Bridge* 1612 ib. The reason for the name is not known with certainty; possibly it has reference to the *Countess* of Oxford (*v.* Earls Court *infra* 128), the bridge is on the boundary of the parishes of Fulham and Kensington. Cf. similarly *Counters Cross* for Countess Cross (PN Ess 380). *v.* Addenda xxxiii.

EEL BROOK COMMON is *Hillebrook* 1408, 1444 *Ct*, *-broke* 1459 ib., *Hellebrook* 1444, 1449 ib., *Helbroke* 1554 ib., *Eelbrook* 1820 FaulknerF. 'Hill brook,' with late folk-etymology. There is a very slight elevation here which would have been conspicuous owing to the dead level character of the surrounding country.

HURLINGHAM. The earliest reference for the present form is in 1626 (Feret). Earlier spellings from the Court Rolls include *Hurlyngholefeld* 1489, *Hurlynghamfyld*, *Furnynghamfeld* 1550, *Furnyngham-*, *Hurlynghamfeld* 1551, *Furningham ffeyld* 1567, *Furlingham feld* 1573. The forms are too late, corrupt and inconsistent to be explained. A similar interchange between initial *f* and *h* is found in Hinchingbrooke (PN BedsHu 261–2), Fremnells (PN Ess 154) and Filbert Haugh (PN NbDu 85).

MUNSTER HO[2] is *Muster House* 1745 R. Cf. *Mustow* 1397 *Ct*, 1680 S, *Great Mustowe* 1439 FF. The forms are too late for any certainty but it is tempting to take this as a compound of OE (*ge*)*mōt*, 'meeting place' and **stow**. Cf. Moustows (PN Sx 218) and *Mustoe Green* (PN Ess 439).

NORMAND HO[3]. Cf. *Noemansland* 1492 *Ct*, *Nomans Land House* 1710 S. 'No man's land,' i.e. 'land without ownership or in disputed ownership.' There is an earlier example of the name in *Nanesmaneslande* in 1086 (DB) in Ossulstone Hundred, in which King William, like King Edward, held twelve and a half acres. Other examples in the county include *Nonemanneslond* t. Hy 3 BM (Staines), *Nomanneslonde* 1390 Hust (near the Charterhouse). The second of these places is *No mans land beside*

---

[1] The old name for the bridge which carried the main road over Chelsea or *Counters* Creek at this point. Cf. *supra* 2.
[2] Surviving in MUNSTER RD *infra* 105.
[3] Surviving in NORMAND RD.

Smithfield (Stow ii, 81, 133). Kingsford (ib. 370) would identify the Domesday No man's land with this Charterhouse land. *v.* also *infra* 212.

PARR'S BRIDGE and DITCH (lost)

(*le*) *Perre* 1270, 1428 *Ct*, *Perrebrygg* 1386 ib., *Perredich* 1407 ib., *-bregge* t. Hy 5 ib., *Perbrigge* 1503 ib., *Perebrig* 1508 ib. *Pirybrigge* 1383 *Ct*
(*le*) *Pyrre* 1422, 1438 *Ct*, *Pirre* 1422 ib., *Pirrebrigge* 1435 ib. *Parrebrygge* 1476 *Ct*, *Parre* 1477 ib., *Pardyche* 1587 *Ct*
Pear 1673 *Ct*, *Parr's Bridge* 1838 FaulknerF

This was the name of the old ditch or watercourse which determined the boundary between Fulham and Hammersmith. The bridge was that which carried the present Fulham Palace Road (*infra* 104) over the stream. The early forms make it unlikely, though perhaps not impossible, that the first element is ME *perie, pirie* (OE *pirige*), 'pear tree,' as in Perry Oaks *supra* 39.

PARSONS GREEN

is *Personesgrene* 1391, 1437 *Ct*, *Personagegrene* 1457 ib., *Personnesgrene* 1534 ib. This was a hamlet which grew up round the parsonage house of Fulham (cf. Feret ii, 87).

SANDFORD HO, STAMFORD BRIDGE

Sandford 1236 StPaulsCh (p), 1272 FF, *Saunford* 1341 NI (p), *Saundfords* t. Eliz ChancP
Samfordesbregge 1444 *Ct*, *Sampfordbregge* 1449 ib., *Stamford-bregge* 1456 ib.

Sandford Ho (of which the shell remains) stood by Counters Creek *supra* 2. The 'sandy ford' here was later superseded by a bridge carrying the main road to Fulham (the present Kings Rd). The later corruption has a parallel in Stamford Hill in Hackney *infra* 107.

WALHAM GREEN [wɔləm]

Wendenegrene 1386 Works, *Whendengrene* 1437 *Ct*, *Wendengrene* 1444, 1459 *Ct*
Wendenesgrene 1397, 1393, 1429 *Ct*, *Wandenesgrene* t. Hy 5, 1457 ib.

Wanam Grene 1546 FF, *Wannam Grene* 1575 Sess, *Waneham Grene* 1584 *FF*, *Wandhams Grene* 1592 Sess, *Wanham Greene* 1668 *FF*

Wandon's Green t. Eliz ChancP, 1615 Sess, *Wandon Green* 1634 Feret

Wallam Green 1710 S, *Waltam Green* 1745 R, *Waltham Green* 1754 ib., *Walham Green* 1819 G

The *green* (*v.* grene) which grew up round the manor house of Wendon (*Wendon* 1448 Pat, 1481 IpmR). The name is probably of manorial origin, the family of (de) *Wenden(e)* or *Wanden(e)* being found as early as 1274 (*Ass*) in the parish. They probably came from Wendens (PN Ess 542). It is less likely that the place-name is of local origin, since there is no marked valley (**denu**) or hill (**dun**) in the parish.

BROOMFIELD HO. Cf. *Bromfeld* 1459 *Ct.* GROVE HO is *Grovehows* ib., *Grove House in Fulham* 1551 AD vi. NORTHEND is *Northend* 1459 *Ct.* Originally a hamlet at the north end of Fulham. SANDS END is called *atte Sonde* 1408 *Ct*, *Sand end in Fulham* 1655 ParReg (Kensington).

FULHAM STREET-NAMES

BAGLEYS LANE is so named from Robert *Bagley* and his son Charles, market gardeners here 1812–66 (Feret iii, 281–2). BROOMHOUSE LANE (now RD) is shown in 1741–5 (R). It takes its name from *The Broomhouses* 1454 *Ct* and intersects the area which gave name to Broomfield Ho *supra*. BURLINGTON RD (1882 LCCN) takes its name from a school here which belonged from 1807 to a Mr Roy of Old Burlington St, Piccadilly (Feret i, 123). Earlier known as *Sowgelders lane* 1578 *Ct*, *Sowgilders lane* 1674 ib., or *the backe lane* 1613 Feret. CHURCH ROW is *The Church Row* 1650 *Ct*. CRABTREE LANE. Cf. *Crabbetrehalfacre* 1449 *Ct*, *The Crabtre* 1492 ib., *Crabtree Feild* 1640 Feret, i.e. 'crab-apple tree.' DAISY LANE is said to have been earlier *Cut throat Lane* (Feret iii, 251). DAWES RD was earlier *Parys lane* 1437, 1449 *Ct*. It is called *Dawes lane* in 1555 (ib.), *Dawes Lane al. Parryes Lane* 1607 Feret. The earlier name derives from the family of Simon de *Parys* (t. Ed 3 ib.), the later name from the family of William *Dawe* (1294 *Ass*). FULHAM PALACE RD (1882 LCCN). Part was *Pyrrelane(ende)* 1437 *Ct*, *Perlane* 1487, 1552 ib., *Parrelane al. South lane* 1615 ib. *v.* Parr's Bridge *supra* 103. The road was *The church highway* 1571 ib., leading from the hamlet to Fulham church. FULHAM RD is *Fulham Lane*

1741–5 R. Earlier *London Lane* 1507 *Ct.* GREYHOUND RD is so named from an old inn here. Earlier *Muscal lane* 1552 *Ct*, *Mustallane* 1554 ib. HIGH ST was earlier *Burystrete* 1391 *Ct et freq* to 1552 ib., *Berestrete* 1391, 1404, 1422 ib., *Bearestreete* 1607 ib., *Barestreete* 1660 ib., i.e. 'street by the *bury* or manor house,' *v. infra* 196. HURLINGHAM RD, *v.* Hurlingham *supra* 102. It was *Back Lane* 1705 ib., 1848 Feret. KINGS RD. *v.* Kings Rd, Chelsea *supra* 87. LILLIE RD was earlier *Payneslane* 1419 *Ct*, from the family of Henry *Paine* (1386 ib.). The present name derives from Sir John *Lillie* (1790–1868) who lived here (Feret iii, 20). MARGRAVINE RD commemorates Lady Craven, wife of the *Margrave* of Brandenburgh who had a house here c. 1790 (Feret iii, 24) (German *Markgräfin*). MUNSTER RD is *Mustewlane* 1486 *Ct*, *Mustowlane* 1553 ib. *v.* Munster Ho *supra* 102. NORTH END RD is *Northstrete* 1488 *Ct*, *North End Lane* 1649 ib., so named because it was at the north end of the houses along the highway beyond Walham Green, cf. 1741–5 R and *v.* Northend *supra* 104. PARSONS GREEN LANE is *Parsons Greene Lane* 1650 *Ct.* PETERBOROUGH RD preserves the memory of Peterborough Ho (demolished 1895), so named in 1697 from Lord Mordaunt, third Earl of *Peterborough* (Feret ii, 129). The earlier name for the house was *Bryghtwelles tenement* 1386 *Ct*, *Bright-welles* 1395 ib., *Bryghtwelle* 1437 ib. PURSERS CROSS RD. Cf. *Pursers-crosse* 1553 *Ct.* Probably named from an ancestor of Richard *Purser*, living in the parish in 1625 (Feret ii, 201). SHORROLDS RD takes its name from the family of John *Sherewold* t. Hy 6 (Feret ii, 262). STAR RD is so named from the old Seven *Stars* Inn here. TALGARTH RD is so named from an estate of the Gunters, ground landlords, in Breconshire. So also GLIDDON, GLENDWR and TREVANION RDS near by, and EDITH RD, named from the wife of Robert Gunter (Feret ii, 278). TOWNMEAD RD. Cf. *Towne meads* 1647 ib. iii, 259, probably referring to the common meadows of the parish.

The Borough of Hackney

HACKNEY

> *Hakeneia* 1198 Cur, *-eye* 1236 Cl, 1242 Fees *et passim* to 1443
> *Ct*, with variant spellings *-ei(e)*, *-ey(e)*, *Hakne* 1231 FF
> *Hackeneye* 1253 Cl, *Hackney* 1535 VE, *Hacquenye* 1593 N
> *Hekeney* 1314 Pat
> '*Haca*'s well watered land or marsh,' *v.* eg.

CLAPTON is *Clopton* 1339 Pleas (p), 1380, 1391 Cl (p), 1509 *Ct*, 1550 Pat, 1556 FF, *Clapton* 1593 N. 'Farm on the hill.' The first element is probably an unrecorded OE *clop*, cognate with German dial. *klopf*, 'rock,' MDan *klop*, 'block, lump.' See further Ekwall DEPN *s.n.* Clapcot. Clapton is situated on high ground, descending steeply to the river Lea on its eastern side.

DALSTON is *Derleston* 1294 *Ass* (p), 1443 *Ct*, *Dorleston* 1388 FF
(p), 1581 Simpson, *Darleston*, *Darlston* ib., *Dalston* 1741–5 R.
Probably '*Dēorlāf*'s farm,' *v*. tun.

DE BEAUVOIR TOWN was named after the family, originally from
Guernsey, of the landowner who built it c. 1840 (RobinsonH
181). The estate (partly in the parish of Shoreditch) which they
had acquired in 1687 (ShoreSurv) was called *Bammes*, *Baumes*
or *Balmes*[1]. It is referred to as the manor of *Hoggeston al. Bams*
1509–10 ShoreSurv (cf. *Bammes gate* ib.), *Baumes* 1590 Robinson-
H, 1795 Lysons, *Balmes* 1593 ShoreSurv, *The Bames* 1604, 1662
RobinsonH, *Bames* 1634 ShoreSurv, *Balmes al. Baumes* 1696
RobinsonH. The name is pseudo-manorial in origin. We may
compare the personal name *Bamme* found among London citizens
in the 14th and early 15th century (ShoreSurv) and Henry
Bamme (1413 Williams, Holborn context).

HACKNEY WICK is *ferm of Wyk* 1299 Hust, *Wyke* 1399 IpmR,
Wick House 1741–5 R, and was the home of Robert de *la Wike*
(1231 Bracton) and (   ) *atte Wyk in Hakeney* (1294 *Ass*).
'Dairy farm,' *v*. wic.

HOMERTON is *Humburton* 1343 AD vi, *Homberton* 1355 Misc,
Humbertonfeld 1443 *Ct*, *Humberton* 1550 Pat, Survey, *Hum-
merton* 1581 Simpson, *Hamerton* 1680 S, 1724 Moll, *Humerton*
1741–5 R. 'Farm of (a woman named) *Hūnburh*,' *v*. tun.

KINGSLAND is *Kyngeslond* 1395 Hust, 1443 *Ct*, 1550 Pat. It may
have been a part of Hackney in the possession of the Crown
when the manor was held by the Bishop of London.

LONDON FIELDS is *London Field* 1540 Survey, *his great field of
land and pasture…commonly called London Felde…in the parish
of Hakney* 1547 Pat and may have been so named because it lay
near the London end of Hackney parish.

MARE STREET is *Merestret* 1443 *Ct*, *Gonneston strete al. Merestrete*
1550 Pat, *Merestret*, *Meerstreete* 1593 N, *Mayre street* 1605
RobinsonH, *Marestreete* 1621 Sess, *Meare street* 1741–5 R.
Mare St is now the chief street in the borough of Hackney, but

---

[1] See further *s.n.* WHITMORE ST *infra* 148.

as shown by early maps the name was originally applied to a small hamlet on the main road at the extreme south of the parish on the Bethnal Green (then Stepney) border. Cf. *supra* 83 n. The greater part of what is now Mare St was earlier Church St (*Church streete* 1605 RobinsonH, (*Street*) 1741–5 R) from the parish church just to the east of the main road. The first element of Mare St is probably ME *mere*, *meare*, 'boundary' (OE *gemære*) from the position of the hamlet on the parish boundary.

MILLFIELDS is *Mellefeld juxta Mellelane* 1443 *Ct*, *lee* (sic) *North*, *Southmyllefeld* 1547 Pat.

SHACKLEWELL is *Shekelwell* 1491 PCC, *Shakyl-* 1509 *Ct*, *Shakkel-* 1530 LP, *Shakel-* 1532 ib., *Shackewell* 1553 FF, *Shackerwell* 1680 S. The second element is wielle, 'spring, source.' The first is OE *sceacel*, 'shackle, fetter,' but its exact application in this and other *shackle*-names is uncertain. For a full discussion *v.* Shackleford (PN Sr 199–200).

STAMFORD HILL

> *Sanford* 1255 Misc, *Sa(u)ndfordhull* 1294 *GDR*, (*in villa de Hakeneye*) 1307 ib.
> *Saumforthill* 1382 Pat, *Sampfordehill* 1410 ib., *Samfordhell* 1433 *Ct*
> *Stamford Hill* 1675 Ogilby

Originally '(hill by) the sandy ford' with the same later corruption as in Stamford Bridge *supra* 103. The ford was over the Lea.

TEMPLE MILLS[1]

> *molendin' de Craggehege* 1274 *Ass*
> *Crachehegh* 1339 *StPauls*, *mill of Crachehegge* 1354 Pat, *Crathhegloke* (sic) 1355 Misc, *Cracchegge melle* 1394 *Cor*
> *Tempylmylle* 1461 Pat, *Temple Mill River* 1549 Ipm

For the old name we may compare Scrattage *supra* 25. The same element is found in *Cressemulles* 1362 Cl, *Crachemilles* 1374 ib., *les Cracchemulles* 1376 Pat, the name of some lost mills in

---

[1] The original mills were partly in Hackney, partly in Essex. Cf. Templars 172–3 and PN Ess 103.

East Smithfield. Temple Mills we may presume to have been
by a *cracche*-hedge. Professor Bruce Dickins interprets the
compound *cracchemilles* as 'timber-framed mills.'

HACKNEY DOWNS and HACKNEY MARSH. Here were the homes
of William *atte Doune* (1302 *Ass*) and John de *Mersshe* (1307
GDR). Cf. *lands of the lord called the Downe* 1550 Survey,
Hakenemersshe 1397 *Cor*.

HACKNEY STREET-NAMES

AMHURST RD (1866 LCCN) is so named from Lord *Amherst* of Hackney
whose family, the *Tyssens* (hence TYSSEN ST) had been lords of the
manor since 1697 (RobinsonH 304). BANBURY RD (1863 LCCN) was
named in commemoration of the grant which was made to John de
Banbury at the same time that the grant was made which ultimately
gave rise to Shore Rd *infra*. CAZENOVE RD. Cf. *Cazenoves Ho*
c. 1865 O.S. UPPER CLAPTON RD is called *Hackney Lane* 1741–5 R.
CLARENCE RD (1864 LCCN) was *Back Lane* ib. DE BEAUVOIR SQUARE,
etc. *v. supra* 106. HIGH ST, HOMERTON is *Humberton Street* 1652
Survey. LANSDOWNE RD (1862 LCCN) was *Mutton Lane* 1741–5 R.
Cf. *Mutton Field* 1652 Survey. LONDON LANE is so named in 1808
(Cary). MARE ST. *v. supra* 106. MAYFIELD RD preserves the old field-
name *Mayfeld* 1557 FF. MILLFIELDS RD is *Mellelane* 1443 *Ct*, *Millfeild
lane* 1652 Survey. *v. Millfields supra* 107. MORNING LANE is *Mourning
Lane* 1732 PC, *Money Lane* 1741–5 R. POND LANE. Cf. *Hakeneyponde*
1387 *MinAcct* and Reginald *atte Ponde* (1316 *Cor*). SHEEP LANE is
Ship Lane al. Galloes Lane 1550 Survey. SHORE RD is near the site of
Shore Place, earlier *Shoreditch Place* (Lysons ii, 458), where land was
granted to John de Banbury, John Blaunch and Nicholas *Shordych* in
1352. *Shorditch place* is so named by Stow (ii, 76) in 1598. He speaks
of it as a 'Kinges mannor.' WELL ST is so named in 1741–5 (R). Cf.
Welstretfeld 1443 *Ct* and Peter *atte Welle* (1294 *Ass*). There was an
ancient well here, called *Churchfield Well* (RobinsonH i, 8).

The Borough of Hammersmith

HAMMERSMITH[1]

> *Hamersmyth*' 1294 *GDR*, 1313, 1380 FF, 1322 Pat, 1349
>   Works, 1393 *Ct*, -*smytthe* 1307 *GDR*, 1388 FF
> *Hameresmithe*, -*smythe* 1312 Seld xxxiii
> *Hamyrsmyth in the parish of Fulham* 1535 FF
> *Hammersmith* 1675 Ogilby

[1] A hamlet of Fulham till 1834 (Feret i, 14).

This name is probably a compound of OE *hamor*, 'hammer' and *smyððe*, 'smithy,' as suggested by Bradley (EHR xxxviii, 317). Cf. Whitesmith (PN Sx 403).

BROOK GREEN is *Brookegreen* 1616 ParReg (Kensington). The brook here (now covered over) is referred to in *le Brooke, Brookbregge* t. Hy 5 *Ct, le Brookdyche, Brookstret* 1493 ib. Cf. also Adam *atte Brok* (1319 ib.).

RAVENSCOURT PARK *olim* **PADDERSWICK**

Palyngewyk 1270 FF (p), *Pallyngwyk* 1307 *GDR, Palengewyk* 1319, 1408, 1455 *Ct, Pallingwike* 1377 IpmR
Paningewik, -wyk 1274 *Ass*
Paleswyk juxta Fuleham 1294 *Ass*
Pallyngeswyk 1380 BM, Pat, *Palyngeswyke* 1487 Ipm
Palenswyke otherwise Padenswyke 1547 FF
Paddyngeswyke 1553 *Ct, Paddingwyke* 1593 N, *Padingwick* 1675 Ogilby
Ravenscourt formerly known by the name of Paddingswick 1765 HammSurv
Padderswick Green (hamlet), *Raven's Court* (house) 1819 G

The second element here is OE **wic**, 'dairy-farm.' The first is probably to be associated with the recorded OE personal name *Pælli* or the related but unrecorded *Palla*, the full form of the name having originally been either *Pællingawic*, '**wic** of *Pælli*'s people,' *Pællingwic*, '**wic** of *Pælli*' (*v.* ing) or possibly *Pællingeswic*, '**wic** of *Pælling*.' The forms with *n* show common confusion of *l* and *n*, those with *d* are due to confusion between the point-consonants *l* and *ḍ*. For other names containing *Pælli* cf. Palling (Nf) (PN in -*ing* 80) and possibly Pallingham (PN Sx 134). The history of the modern name is unknown.

SHEPHERDS BUSH is *Sheppards Bush Green* 1635 FaulknerF, *Shepperds Bush* 1675 Ogilby, *Shepards Bush* 1710 S, *Shepers Bush* 1745 R.

STARCH GREEN is *Storkesgrene* 1397, 1493 *Ct, Storkysgrene* 1459 ib. We find also in the Fulham Court Rolls *ten' de Storkes, Storkesgardyn, Storkispyghtell* t. Hy 5, *Storkesbregge* 1444,

Storkestwychene 1449. This last must have been at some cross-ways (OE *twicene*). It is likely that *Stork* was the name of some 13th or 14th century tenant. Cf. John *Stork* (1483 FF).

WORMHOLT FM and WORMWOOD SCRUBBS

Wormeholte 1189–99 StPaulsCh
Wermeholte, Wormhot (sic) 1198 Cur, *Wrmeholt* 1290 Ipm,
    Wermholt 1294 *Ass* (p), *Worm(e)holt(e)* 1375 Pat, 1397 *Ct*,
    1535 VE
Worm(h)oltwode 1437, 1444 *Ct*, *Wormholt Scrubbs* 1819 G
Wormall Felde 1550 Pat, *Wormolle wood* 1593 *AllSouls*
Wormewood 1654 DKR xl, *Wermer Wood Common* 1754 R,
    Wormwood Scrubbs c. 1865 O.S.

This is probably from OE *wyrma holt*, 'snake-infested **holt** or wood,' cf. Wormley (PN Herts 233). *Scrubbs* refers to low shrubs or brushwood, descriptive of the former open common here. *Wormholt* probably developed into [wəˑmət] and this was then wrongly taken to be a corruption of Wormwood [wəˑrməd].

HAMMERSMITH STREET-NAMES

BEAVOR LANE is *Beavor Street* 1813 FaulknerF, and should perhaps be associated with the family of Samuel *Bever* (mid 18th century Hamm Surv). BLYTH RD was *Blyndelane* 1554 *Ct*, *Blind Lane* 1741–5 R, *Blyth Lane* 1813 FaulknerF. In R it is shown as a lane ending 'blindly' in the fields. The present form may be simply a corruption of the older name. BRADMORE GROVE preserves an old place-name *Brademere, Bradmeredych, Mochilbradmere* t. Hy 5 *Ct*, i.e. 'wide mere or pool,' *v.* brad, mere. BRANDENBURGH RD. See Margravine Rd in Fulham *supra* 105. BROADWAY is so named in 1813 (FaulknerF). Originally merely a part of the main road where it is joined by the roads to Fulham and Shepherds Bush. COLET GARDENS (1893 LCCN) commemorates Dean *Colet*, founder of St Paul's School. Earlier *Red Cow Lane* (Feret ii, 278) from an inn so named. CREEK PLACE is *Creek Lane* 1813 FaulknerF, referring to an inlet of the Thames. GOLDHAWK RD is *Gould Hawk Lane* 1813 FaulknerF. Cf. *fossa vocata Goldhawkesdych* 1408 *Ct*, *Goldehawkes, le merssh de Goldhawkes* t. Hy 5 ib. The family of *Goldhawk(e)* occurs frequently in 15th century Court Rolls, and we find mention of one *Goldhauek* in Chiswick near by as early as 1222 (StPaulsDB). HAMMERSMITH RD is referred to as (*super*) *regiam viam* 1502 FaulknerF. See further *supra* 10. KING ST is so named in 1813 (FaulknerH). It was earlier *The Highway* 1624 LCCDeeds. A part of the Great West Road. THE MALL is so named in 1813 (FaulknerF),

perhaps a copying of Pall Mall, London (*infra* 181). PADDENSWICK RD,
v. Ravenscourt Park *supra* 109. RIVERSCOURT RD (1873 LCCN) was
earlier *Hog Lane* 1813 FaulknerF. ST PETERS RD was earlier *Warple
Way* ib. Cf. *le Worple* 1490, 1554 *Ct*, *le Worphill* 1494 ib. *v.* worple.
SHORTLANDS preserves an old field-name *Shortelond* t. Hy 5 *Ct*.
STANDISH RD was *Hope Lane* 1813 FaulknerF. WOOD LANE is *Wode-
lane* 1408 *Ct*, leading to Wormwood Scrubbs *supra* 110.

The Borough of Hampstead

HAMPSTEAD

> (*to medeman*) *Hemstede*, (*andlang*) *Hemstedes mearce* 959 (13th)
>   BCS 1351, *Hemestede* 1404 Pat
> (*æt*) *Hamstede* 978 (18th) BCS 1309
> (*in*) *Heamstede* 1066 (13th) KCD 824
> *Hamestede* 1086 DB
> *Hamsted*(*e*) 1230 Cl *et freq* to 1291 Tax
> *Hampsted*(*e*) 1258 FF *et passim*

'Farm-site,' *v.* hamstede. For the forms *hemstede* and *heam-
stede* (probably for *hæmstede*) cf. DEPN *s.v. hamstede*, where
Ekwall explains the forms as probably going back to OE *hǣm-
styde*.

NOTE. ABBEY RD is named from Kilburn Abbey (*rectius* Priory),
hence PRIORY RD. Cf. *Abbey Farm* 1795 Lysons. BELSIZE RD is *Belsize
Lane* 1741–5 R. *v. infra* 112. BRANCH HILL. Cf. *Branch Hill Lodge*
ib. BURGESS HILL (1903 LCCN) was named after the owners of the
estate ib. CHURCH ROW is *Church Lane* 1741–5 R. FLASK WALK is so
named from the flasks of chalybeate water sent to London (Barratt i,
177, 228). MILL LANE was *Shootup hill lane* 1741–5 R. *v. infra* 113.
PLATT'S LANE is to be associated with the family of Thomas *Platt* (c. 1840
TA). POND ST is *Pond Street* 1686 M, *Pound Street* 1741–5 R. ROSSLYN
HILL preserves the memory of *Rosslyn House*, built here by the Earl
of *Rosslyn* in 1793 (Barratt ii, 91–5). SPANIARDS RD leads to the old
Spaniards Inn, traditionally said to have been held by a Spaniard in the
16th century. Cf. *Spaniards Gate* 1741–5 R. WELL WALK is *Well
Street* 1686 M, *Well Walk* 1698 HCMag, from the Spa near by
(Barratt i, 180 ff.). WEST END LANE is so named in 1741–5 (R).
v. infra 113. *v.* Addenda xxxiv.

BARROW HILL. *Barrow* in this name would seem to be identical
in site with the *bæru*(*w*)*e* (dat. sg.) in the bounds of Hampstead
(959 BCS 1351) and is clearly a derivative of OE *bearu*, 'grove,
wood,' and has nothing to do with OE *beorg*, 'barrow, hill.' The
only other reference noted is in *pasture voc*' *Barrowes* 1539 *Rental*.

BELSIZE PARK is *Belassis, Belseys* 1317 *WAM, Belassize* 1360 ib., *Belces* 1500 *MinAcct, Belsis* 1535 VE, 1542 LP, *Belsuys* 1541 ib., *Belcys* 1542 Dugd ii, *Belsise* 1593 N. This is no doubt a French place-name, 'beautifully situated,' going back to OFr *bel assis*, cf. Belsize (PN Nth 232). Belsize Ho was on the slopes of Hampstead, facing south.

CHALK FARM is so named in 1819 (G) and is a corruption of the older name *Chaldecote* 1253 Cl, *Caldecote* c. 1400 Barratt, *Chalcotes, Chalcotts* 1531 LP, *Chalcot(e)* 1593 N, 1675 Ogilby, 1710 S, *Chacott (Lane)* 1594 SP, *Chalk* 1746 R. 'Cold cottages,' *v.* ceald, cot(e) and Introd. xvii. The soil here is clay.

FROGNAL is *Frognall* 1795 Lysons. The origin of the name is uncertain. It may be of manorial origin from the family of Thomas and Alexander *Frogenhall* (1542 FF). The family probably came from Frognall (K).

HAVERSTOCK HILL is so named in 1741–5 (R). The origin of the name is obscure. It may be that the place takes its name from a family which came from Stock in Essex (PN Ess 269), of which the 17th century form was *Haverstock*.

KILBURN[1]

> *Cuneburna* 1121–40 Dugd iii
> *Keneburna* 1121–40, 1130–60 Dugd iii, 12th *WAM*
> *Kyneburna* 1160–76 Dugd iii
> *Keleburne* 1181 StPaulsDB *et freq* to 1306 BM, *-birne* 1208 FF, *Kelburn* 1239 Lib, 1286 Pat, *Kelleb(o)urn* 1340, 1371 FF
> *Kelleburn* c. 1200 AD ii, 1370 FF
> *Kylleburne* 1229 Dugd iii, *Kileburn* 1272–91 Ipm, *Kylbourne* 1502 FF, (*or Keelebourne*) 1593 N
> *Kuleb(o)urn(e)* 1294 *Ass*, 1311 Pat
> *Gilborne* 1682 Morgan, 1724 Moll

If the earliest forms are to be trusted this would seem to go back to OE *cyne-burna*, 'royal stream,' or possibly *cȳna-burna*,

---

[1] The hamlet of Kilburn was partly in Willesden. The priory was in Hampstead parish.

'cows' stream.' If the *l*-forms are the correct ones, one must take the first element to be the personal name *Cylla*. For interchange of *n* and *l* cf. IPN 106.

PRIMROSE HILL is *Prymrose Hill* 1586 (W and C) and was probably descriptive of the wooded hill.

SHOOTUP HILL is *Shottuppe Hill* 1566 Ipm, *Shoteuphill* 1584 *AllSouls*, *Shotuphill* 1589 Ipm, *Shutt up Hill* 1594 ib., *Seutup Hill* 1710 S. Cf. *Shootuppfeild* 1593 *AllSouls*. The name is possibly to be interpreted literally, with reference to the sharp straight rise here on the main road (i.e. Watling Street).

FORTUNE GREEN is *Fortune Greene* 1646 Barratt. Cf. Fortune Gate *infra* 161. HAMPSTEAD HEATH is *Hampstede Heth* 1543 LP. HAMPSTEAD POND is *la ponde in villa de Hamstede* 1274 *Ass*. NORTH END is so named in 1741–5 (R). WEST END is (*le*) *Westende* 1535 VE, 1547 Pat. This name is preserved in *West End Lane*, at the south-west end of the village.

The Borough of Holborn

NOTE. The borough of Holborn includes, (i) the ancient parishes of St Andrew, Holborn and St George the Martyr, with the extra parochial areas of Grays Inn, Lincolns Inn, Staple Inn and the Liberty of Saffron Hill, (ii) those of St Giles in the Fields and St George, Bloomsbury.

HOLBORN [hŏubən]

(*on*) *Holeburne* 951–9 (13th) BCS 1351
Holeburne 1086 DB *et passim* to 1335 Ipm, with variant
    spelling -*bourn*(*e*), *pons de Holeburn* 1191 P
Holleburn 1235 FF, 1310 Orig, -*bourne* 1332–5 Ipm
Howeborne 1551 Pat, *Hautborne* 1703 ParRegFr
Holbourne by London 1567 Ipm
'Stream in the hollow,' *v.* holh, burna and *supra* 4. *v.* also
    infra 222.

ST ANDREW, HOLBORN. The church is first mentioned in BCS 1048 (cf. Appendix iii *infra* 222) in the phrase *to ðære ealde stoccene sancte Andreas cyricean*, i.e. the old wooden church of St Andrew. For *stoccene* cf. Stoke Newington *infra* 159. Later we have *parochia Sancte Andree de Holeburne* 1162 Templars.

BLOOMSBURY

(*in*) *Soca Blemund* 1242 Fees, *manerium de Blemund* 1274 *Ass*, *Soka Blemundi* 1286 Cl, *Soka Sancti Egidii et Blemond* 1316 FA

Blemondesberi 1291 AD i, -*bury* 1339 AD ii, 1376 Works, *Bloemundesbury* 1324 Cl, Ipm, *Blemundesbury* 1324, 1337 Ipm, 1336 AD ii, 1336 Pat, (*infra campum de*) 1376 Works *Blumbesbury* 1535 VE, *Blomesburye* 1567 FF, *Blumsberrie fieldes* 1603 Sess

The name is descriptive of the burh or manor of the *Blemund* family. William *Blemund* is mentioned in 1202 in a fine concerning part of *Totenhale* (*infra* 143). Elsewhere the family-name is spelt *Blemonte* or *Blemunt*. For a full history of the manor and for the history of the personal name reference should be made to Miss Jeffries Davis's article on The University Site, Bloomsbury, in LnTopRec xvii, 19 ff., including Appendix iii to that article. The family name is found also in *Blemundesdiche* (c. 1222), *Blemundesmed* (c. 1242), *Blemondispond* (1371) (ib. 117, 119, 121). For *soca*, *v. infra* 204. The parish of St George, Bloomsbury, was constituted in 1731 and consisted almost entirely of the Bloomsbury estate (ib. 73).

ELY PLACE is *Ely Place* t. Eliz Agas (cf. *Elie rentes* 1570 Williams, *Eelye Rentes* 1615 Sess), *Ely House* 1677 O and M. This marks the site of the London house of the Bishop of *Ely* till the 18th century. Cf. *The tenement of the Bishop of Ely* 1315 Williams, *land in Ely, London* 1335 Pat. The name is familiar through the reference in Shakespeare (*Richard III*, Act 3, Sc. iv). *Place* is here used of a residence, dwelling or house, the chief house of an estate. Cf. *Bathe place* and *the bysshop of Yorkes place*.

GRAYS INN, formerly the manor house of the St Paul's prebend of PORTPOOLE.

Purtepol(*e*) 1203 FF *et freq* to 1309 ib., (*Sokne*) 1294 QW, *Purpoole* 1586 PCC, *Perpoole* 1624 DKR xxxviii *Portepol*(*e*) 1240 StPaulsMSS *et freq* to 1535 VE, -*pul* 1249 AD ii, 1329 StPaulsMSS, *Portepulle* 1362 Cl, *Portpole juxta Holeborn* 1371 Ipm, *Portpulbrigg* 1380 Pat

Pourtepol t. Hy 3 AD ii (p), 1274 *Ass*, 1302 LBk, 1316 FA,
   1322 Pat, 1323 Ipm, 1340 Cor
Portpole maner vocat' Grays Inn in Holborne 1396 IpmR,
   Grayesin 1403 Williams, *Greys yn londes* 1413 StPaulsMSS,
   manor of Portpole commonly called Greyesynne 1506 Williams

The second element of the old name is OE *pol*, 'pool.' The
first element is obscure. It is identical with that found in
Purfleet (PN Ess 130) and *purtan ige* (BCS 1095) in Wiltshire.
For a discussion of this element *v.* PN Ess *loc. cit.* Ekwall
(DEPN) inclines to a personal name *Purta.*

The manor of *Purtepole* was held by Reginald de *Grey* at the
time of his death in 1308 (Ipm). For a full history of the later
manor and Inn of Court *v.* W. R. Douthwaite, *Gray's Inn* (1886)
and documents 646 ff. in Williams.

LINCOLNS INN is *Hospicium de Lincolsin* 1422 LiBlBk i, *Lyn-
colnesyn* 1427 ib., *Lyncollysyn* 1437 ib., *Lyncolnes Inne* 1488 Pat.
The records of the Society of that Inn show that by 1422 it was
in possession of an inn (*hospicium*) on its present site that
belonged to the Bishop of Chichester (hence CHICHESTER RENTS),
of which it obtained the freehold in 1580. There is an ancient
tradition that it had once been under the patronage of Henry
de Lacy, Earl of *Lincoln* (d. 1311), whose arms it began to use
as early as 1518, and possibly it took its name of Lincolns Inn
from his house in Shoe Lane which may have been thus called;
when it settled into its own inn down Chancery Lane that
naturally came to be called by its name. See C. L. Kingsford
in LnTopRec xi, 33–5 (cf. x, 136) for a summary of the relevant
facts, collected by W. P. Baildon (LiBlBk iv, 263–97). An
alternative suggestion (ignoring de Lacy), for which see Williams
1080–4 (cf. LnTopRec xi, 42–4), is that the Society was originally
established in quite a different house from the Earl's, but also
in Holborn (near Staple Inn), which in the middle of the 14th
century belonged to a certain Thomas de *Lincoln*, and that
it took its name from this house, which in 1369 became the
property of the Abbot of Malmesbury but was still called
Lincolnesynne in 1399 (Williams 1155), *Lyncolnesynne* 1417 (ib.
688, 1080).

8-2

St Giles-in-the-Fields

> *hospitali Sancti Egidii extra Londonium* 1100–35 (1330) Ch,
> *infirmi de Sancto Egidio* 1185 Templars, *Ecclesia S. Egidii
> infirmorum* t. Ric 1 BM, *S. Egid. Leprosorum extra London*
> 1239 ib.
> *Socka Sci Egidii, in paroch' Hospital' de Sco Egidio extra
> London* 1274 *Ass, in paroch' Sancti Egidii extra barr' veteris
> Templi* 1370 IpmR
> *Seintgilespitel* 1374 Hust, *agrum Divi Egidii* 1417 Memorials
> of Hy V, (*in*) *rure Egidii* c. 1446 Capgrave
> *Seynt Gyles in the ffield* 1563 SR, *St Gyles nere London* 1584
> PCC, *St Giles in the Feildes* 1615 Sess

The parish was so named from the dedication of the hospital
to St *Egidius*, of which the popular form, through Old French,
was *Giles*. This, with the parish church, similarly dedicated, and
the village near it, was originally isolated in the fields to the
west of London. For *socka* cf. *infra* 204.

Seven Dials is (*les*) *Seven Dials* 1707 ParRegFr, 1746 R. It is
mentioned in Evelyn's Diary (5th October, 1694), "I went to
see the building near St Giles where seven streets make a star
from a Doric pillar placed in the middle of a circular area." The
site was a close called *Marshland* 1537, later *Cock and Pye Fields*
(1682 Morgan to 1732 PC), from the *Cock and Pye Inn* which
adjoined it in 1650 (StGilesSurv i, 112–13).

Staple Inn is *Stapelhyne in Holbourne* 1436 Cl, *Staple Inne*
c. 1440 ECP, 1583 PCC. It would seem to be identical with the
earlier *le Stapledhalle* (in the parish of Holborn) 1333 Hust,
le Stapelhalle 1407 Williams. If so, the hall was so named from
its *staples* or pillars. We have similar reference to pillared halls
in William *atte Stapledehalle* in 1292, probably with reference
to a Stapled Hall in All Hallows, Barking. There was a Stapled
Hall in St Botolph Bishopsgate in 1330 and a Staple Hall in
Austin Friars in the 16th century (cf. Kingsford, *Notes on
Medieval London Houses* in LnTopRec xii, 31–2).

HOLBORN STREET-NAMES

BAINBRIDGE ST is *Banbridge Street* 1746 R and takes its name from Henry *Bainbridge*, a parishioner in 1649 (StGilesSurv). BALDWIN'S GARDENS is so named in 1677 (O and M) and is said to have been named after Richard *Baldwin*, one of Queen Elizabeth's gardeners, who built houses there in 1589 (W and C). BEDFORD ROW is so named in 1732 (PC). It is on the estate bequeathed by Sir William Harper (hence HARPUR ST), Lord Mayor 1561–2, for a school, etc. at Bedford (W and C). It was *Le Pyttes next Greyesyn* 1430 Williams, *Gravell Pittes* 1500 ib. (Williams 1668). BEDFORD SQUARE is so named from the Duke of *Bedford*, the ground landlord. It was laid out c. 1775 (StGilesSurv ii, 150). BETTERTON ST was earlier *Brownlow Street* 1682 Morgan, from Sir John *Brownlow* of St Giles, t. Charles 2 (StGilesSurv). The present name (given in 1877) commemorates the actor Betterton (1635–1710). BLOOMSBURY SQUARE is so named in 1684 (Sess). One of the earliest of the squares, it is mentioned by Evelyn in 1665. It was at first called *Southampton Square* after the Earl of *Southampton* (d. 1667) who built it, in front of his town house (LnTopRec xvii, 54–6) and the name persisted till after 1720 (Strype). BLOOMSBURY ST (1894 LCCN) was *Charlotte Street* 1799 Horwood, so named from the queen of George III. The southern end was *Plumptre Street* 1746 R from Henry *Plumbtree*, a citizen of *Nottingham* (Parton 365), who built *Nottingham Street* 1746 R. BROAD ST and HIGH ST probably correspond to *Strata Sci Egidij* t. Hy 3 Parton. Later *la rue St Giles* 1706 ParRegFr, *St Giles Broad St* 1708 Hatton, *Broad Street* (*St Giles*) 1732 PC, 1746 R. BROOKE ST is so named in 1682 (Morgan) and marks the site of the London house of Fulk Greville, first Lord *Brooke* (d. 1628). Hence Greville St *infra* 118. BUCKRIDGE ST takes its name from Edmund *Buckeridge*, a parishioner in 1676 (StGilesSurv). CHURCH ST, ST GILES is *Church Street* 1682 Morgan. Possibly it is *le Kirkewaye* of 1373 (Works). CLERKENWELL RD (1878 LCCN) absorbed the earlier *Liquor Pond Street* 1682 Morgan, (*Liquer*) 1746 R, 1749 ParReg (Clerkenwell). Cf. *Liquor Pond Feild* 1651 Sess. COPTIC ST (1895 LCCN) was earlier *Duke Street* 1682 Morgan. CORAM ST (1900 LCCN) is *Great Coram Street* 1810 Lockie and takes its name from Captain *Coram*, founder of the Foundling Hospital. COSMO PLACE was *Fox Court* 1746 R. DENMARK ST is *Dannemark Street* 1703 ParRegFr, *Denmark Street* 1720 Strype, probably commemorating Prince George of Denmark, husband of Queen Anne (K 34). DANE ST is *Dean Street* 1746 R. DEVONSHIRE ST is so named in 1682 (Morgan), taking its name from a house designed for one of the sons of the Duke of *Devonshire* (LnTopRec x, 5). DORRINGTON ST is *Dodington Street* 1746 R and commemorates Thomas *Dorrington*, citizen of London (Pinks 141). DYOTT ST is *Diot Street* 1704 ParRegFr, *Dyot Street* 1732 PC, from Simon *Dyott*, parishioner in 1676 (St GilesSurv). EAGLE ST is so named in 1708 (Hatton). EARLHAM ST is *Earl Street* 1691 StGilesSurv, *Erle Street* 1706 ParRegFr,

Great and *Little Earl Street* 1746 R. EMERALD ST (1885 LCCN) was *Grange Street* 1746 R, *Green Street* 1799 Horwood. ENDELL ST (1846 LCCN) corresponds to earlier *Bowl Yard* 1746 R (built by 1680 on the site of a messuage called *the Bowl* (StGilesSurv ii, 111)), *Old* and *New Belton Street* 1732 PC, 1746 R (from the Lincolnshire seat of Sir John Brownlow who leased the site for building in 1683 (StGilesSurv ii, 105)), *Hannover Street* 1746 R, 1831 Elmes. It was renamed in 1846 after the Rev. James *Endell* Tyler, rector of St Giles. EYRE ST (HILL) is *Ayre Street* 1746 R. FALCONBERG MEWS takes its name from *Fauconberg House*, the residence of the Earl of *Fauconberg* who married Mary, third daughter of Oliver Cromwell (K 71). FEATHERSTONE BUILDINGS take their name from Sir Heneage *Fetherstone* t. Chas 2 (Parton 154). FIELD LANE (absorbed by Farringdon Rd since 1857) is *Field(e) Lane* 1605 Sess, 1682 Morgan, and was perhaps so named because it led out into the fields beyond the City. GATE ST is *Yeates Street* 1746 R. GILBERT ST is so named in 1682 (Morgan). OLD GLOUCESTER ST (1873 LCCN) is *Gloucester Street* in 1746 (R), probably from the Duke of *Gloucester*, son of Queen Anne. GOLDSMITH ST (1883 LCCN) was earlier *The Coal Yard* where Nell Gwynn was said to have been born (W and C) (*The Cole Yard* 1648 Parton). GRAYS INN RD is *Purtepolestrate* 1234 AD ii, 1252–60 Williams, *street of Pourtepole* 1299 ib., *Grayes Inne Lane* 1419 ib., *Greys Inn Lane otherwise Portpole Lane* 1551 FF, (*al. Purpoole Lane*) 1599 AD vi, *v.* Grays Inn *supra* 114. The present Portpool Lane (*infra* 119) is a small lane leading out of Grays Inn Rd, but in old times the name Portpool Lane was applied to the main road itself (Williams 580). GREVILLE ST is *Grevil Street* 1682 Morgan, *v.* Brooke St *supra* 117. HART ST is so named in 1720 (Strype), probably from an inn sign. HATTON GARDEN takes its name from *the dwelling house called Hatton House* 1605 Sess. It is *Hatton streete* 1665 ib. Named from Sir Christopher *Hatton* t. Eliz (cf. DNB). HATTON WALL is so named in 1682 (Morgan). It included the north wall of the Garden. HIGH HOLBORN is *Highe Holborne* 1548 FF. It was earlier *Holeburne Strat(e)* c. 1183 Williams, 1251 StPaulsMSS, *Holeburnstrete* 1251 Williams. GT JAMES ST is so named in 1732 (PC). JOCKEY'S FIELDS is *Jockey Fields* ib. KEPPEL ST is *New Store Street* 1795 Map, but before 1800 had been re-named *Keppel Street* from the Marchioness of Tavistock, mother of the fifth and sixth dukes of Bedford, who was a daughter of William *Keppel*, Earl of Albemarle. Cf. LnTopRec xvii, 89. KIRBY ST is *Kerby Street* 1677 O and M, *Kirkby Street* 1682 Morgan, commemorating John de *Kirkeby*, Bishop of Ely in 1286 (LnTopRec x, 111), cf. Ely Place *supra* 114, or more probably the country home, Kirby Ho, Northants, of the Hatton family (ib. 113), cf. Hatton Garden *supra*. LAMBS CONDUIT ST preserves the name of the former *Lambs Conduit Fields* 1746 R. Cf. *The Condute Feld* 1550 Pat, *Lambs Conduit* 1682 Morgan, from William *Lamb*, citizen of London, who made a new conduit here in 1577 (Stow ii, 34). LAYSTALL ST, so named in 1799 (Horwood), was earlier *Leicester Street* 1720 Strype, 1746 R. A *laystall* was a place where refuse was laid (NED) and the street led to such a mound, *v. supra* 96. LEATHER LANE is *Le Vrunelane* 1233 AD ii, *Louerone lane* 1306 Hust, *Leueronelane* 1306 Williams, *Lyveroneslane, Liveronelane* 1331 Hust, *Leverounelane* 1353 Williams, 1354 Hust, *Lyvyrlane* 1411 AD vi, *Lyverlane* 1452 ib., *Loueronlane* 1457 Williams, *Lither lane al. Liver lane* 1604 Harben, *Leather Lane* 1682 Morgan. Probably 'Lēofrūn's lane,' the first element being an OE feminine personal name. LINCOLNS INN FIELDS is *Lincolnes Inne Feildes* 1598 Sess. *v.* Lincolns Inn *supra* 115. MACKLIN ST was so named in 1878, commemorating the actor. It was earlier *Lewkners lane* 1633 StGilesSurv, *Lutenors Lane* 1682 Morgan, 1746 R, *Lukeners Lane* 1700 Sess, from Sir Lewis *Lewknor* (1633 StGilesSurv). MALET ST (1907 LCCN) is on the site of Keppel Mews North (cf. Keppel St *supra* 118) and was named after Sir Edward *Malet* (1837–1908), diplomatist, who married a sister of the Duke of Bedford (LnTopRec xvii, 104–5). MIDDLE ROW PLACE preserves the name of *Middle Row* 1732 PC, 1746 R which, till 1867, stood in Holborn, blocking the roadway opposite the bottom of Grays Inn Road (W and C). MONMOUTH ST is so named from the Duke of *Monmouth*, natural son of Charles II, who had a grant of land in the neighbourhood, *v.* Soho *infra* 172. MONTAGUE PLACE is so named in 1810 (Lockie) and preserves the memory of *Montagu House* 1682 Morgan, on the site of the British Museum, built by Ralph *Montagu*, brother-in-law of Rachel Lady Russell (LnTopRec xvii, 59–62). It was earlier *New Bedford Street* 1795 ib., 89. MUSEUM ST is in the line of *Bow Street* and *Queen Street* 1746 R. NEAL ST corresponds to earlier *King Street* and *Cross Lane* 1746 R. The LCC renamed it from Thomas *Neale*, who in 1693 planned the streets on the Cock and Pye Fields (StGilesSurv ii, 112–13). Cf. Seven Dials *supra* 116. NEW SQUARE was *Little Lincolns Inn Fields* 1682 Morgan, *Lincolns Inn New Court* 1720 Strype, *Lincolns Inn New Square* 1746 R. NEWTON ST is *Newton Streete* 1650 ParlSurv, from William *Newton* the builder (1629 StGilesSurv). GT ORMOND ST is *A new street called Ormond Street* 1706 Sess. PARKER ST was *Parkers Lane* 1682 Morgan from Philip *Parker* (1625 StGilesSurv). PARTON ST, which in 1905 absorbed *Orange St* 1746 R, was named after the author of *Some Account of St Giles in the Fields*, published 1822 (LCCN 390, 641). PHOENIX ST is so named in 1732 PC, 1746 R. PORTPOOL LANE is *Perpool Lane* 1682 Morgan, *Purple Lane* 1732 PC. *v.* Grays Inn Rd *supra* 118. POWIS PLACE is on the site of *Powis House* built by the second Marquis of *Powis* c. 1700 (LnTopRec x, 14–15). PRINCETON ST is *Prince street* 1621 Aliens, *Princes streete* 1650 ParlSurv. QUEEN SQUARE is so named in 1708 (Hatton) from Queen Anne (LnTopRec x, 5). GT QUEEN ST is *Queenestreete* 1621 Aliens, *Queenes street* 1628 Sess. *Great* in contrast to the former *Little Queen St*, now absorbed in Kingsway. RED LION SQUARE is *Red Lyon Square* 1691 Sess, on the site of the former *Red Lion Fields* 1682 Morgan. So named from a former tavern here. RUSSELL SQUARE is so named in 1800 in the Act of Parliament relating to it (LnTopRec xvii, 84), from the family name of the Dukes of Bedford. GT RUSSELL ST is so named in 1682 (Morgan).

SAFFRON HILL is so named in 1602 (Sess), 1604 (PCC). It is *Suffering Hill* 1750 ParReg (Clerkenwell). It was originally a garden where saffron was grown, a part of the grounds of Ely Ho (*supra* 114). ST ANDREW ST is *St Andre St* 1706 ParRegFr. SANDLAND ST was *Bedford Street* in 1746 (R). It leads out of Bedford Row *supra* 117. SARDINIA ST takes its name from the *Sardinian* Chapel here, attached to the Sardinian embassy from 1721 till 1798 (LnTopRec viii, 103). It was *Duke Streete* in 1690 and until 1878 (St GilesSurv ii, 100). SHORT'S GARDENS is *Shorts Garden* 1682 Morgan, from the family of William *Short* (1632 StGilesSurv) who acquired land here c. 1590 (K 35). SILVER ST is so named in 1682 (Morgan). SOUTHAMPTON BUILDINGS is so named in 1657 (PCC) and marks the site of the town house of the Wriothesleys, Earls of *Southampton* t. Edward 6 to Charles 1 (W and C). They afterwards moved to one facing Bloomsbury Square (*v. supra* 117) near which the last Earl built SOUTHAMPTON ST (so named in 1682 Morgan) and Row (so named in 1732 PC). SOUTHAMPTON ROW was widened in 1905, absorbing the former *King Street, Kingsgate Street* 1746 R, home of Mrs Gamp. This was so named from a gate here, used by the King when travelling on his 'private road' from Whitehall to Theobalds (*v. infra* and LnTopRec viii, 6). It is referred to as *the newe gate neere Drewry lane* 1620 StGilesSurv, *passage between the two gates in Holborn* 1631 ib., *Kings Gate* 1650 ParlSurv. TENNIS COURT is so named in 1746 (R). THEOBALDS ROW (now ROAD) is named in 1732 (PC). It was so named because it was the way along which James I rode when journeying between Whitehall and Theobalds, Herts. The east part is *Kings Way* 1682 Morgan. This is not the present Kingsway, cf. *infra* 180. TICHBORNE CT is *Titchburn Court* 1732 PC, *Stitchbone Court* 1746 R. Cf. Scrattage *supra* 25. TOTTENHAM COURT RD (partly in St Pancras) is *Tottenham Court Row* 1708 Hatton. It led from St Giles to Tottenham Court. Cf. *infra* 143. GT TURNSTILE is *Turne style lane* 1639 StGilesSurv, *Turne stile* 1657 ib., *the Turneing stile* 1650 ParlSurv, *Great Turnstile* 1691 Sess. Earlier names appear to have been *Turngatlane* 1522 StGilesSurv, *Turnpik lane* 1531 ib., *Turngayte lane, Turnpikelane* 1544 LP. VERNON PLACE is *Vernon Row* 1682 Morgan. VINE ST is *Wine streete* 1680 ParReg (Clerkenwell), *Vine Street* 1685 ib., *Wine street* 1746 R. WEST ST is *Oueste street* 1704 ParRegFr. WHETSTONE PARK is *Whetstons Park* 1682 Morgan, *Whetstones Park* 1692 StGilesSurv, from William *Whetstone* who erected houses here in 1636 (StGilesSurv). WHITE LION ST is *La Rue du Lion Blanc* 1703 ParRegFr, *Wait Lion Street* 1706 ib. WOBURN SQUARE dates from c. 1830 and is so named from Woburn Abbey, the Duke of Bedford's seat in Bedfordshire.

The Borough of Hornsey

Hornsey

Haringeie, -a 1201, 1213 Cur, 1201 FF (p)[1] *et passim* to 1428
  FA, with variant spellings *-yng-* and *-ey(e)*, *Harryngey* 1428
  EEW

Harengheye 1232 FF, *Haringheye* 1243 Pat

Heringeye 1241 Cl, 1279 QW, *-yng-* 1294 *Ass*, *Heringheie*,
  -eng- 1274 ib.

Haringesheye 1243 Cl, *Haringeseye* 1274 *Ass*, *-yng-* 1321 *Cor*,
  1369, 1377 FF, 1417 Pat

Harengee 1244 Pat (p), 1274 *Ass*, *-eye* 1316 FA, 1341 NI

Harngey(e) 1346 FF, 1431 AD vi

Harynsey 1401 *SR*, *Harnyssay* 1498 FF

Haryngeay 1465 FF

Harnyngey 1488 FF, *Harnyngsey* 1551 Sess

Harnesey 1524 LP, 1543 FF, *Haryngey otherwise Harnesey*
  1557 ib., *Haringsaye al. Harnesey* 1568 Sess

Haringaye, Heringay 1535 VE

Hornsey 1564 FF, *Haringay al. Hornesey* t. Eliz ChancP

Herneseye 1576 PCC

This is a difficult name and its early forms have been
exhaustively dealt with by Dr S. J. Madge in *The Origin of
the name of Hornsey* (1936). The second element in the name
is OE (ge)hæg, 'woodland enclosure,' with reference to a
part of the old Middlesex woodland. The first is OE *Hæring*,
a personal name which is found sometimes in the regular
gen. sg. form *Haringes*, but more often in the uninflected form
Haring. *Haringeseye* developed quite regularly to *Harnsey*,
Hornsey, but side by side with this there developed from
Haringeye a form *Har(r)ingay*, which in modern times has
been revived and come to be used of a district which is
largely in Hornsey.

Alternatively, we might perhaps take the original form to be
Hæringa(ge)hæg, 'enclosure of *Hær*'s people,' with occasional
development of inorganic *-es-* under the influence of names of

---

[1] The form in FF is printed *Haringue* but has been corrected from the
MS by Dr Madge who has also identified an earlier form *Harengh'* c. 1195
in an unpublished *AD*.

gen. sg. form. It is unfortunate that none of the forms are earlier
than the 13th century, for clearly by that time the real meaning
of the name had long since been forgotten.

NOTE. CAMPSBOURNE RD. Cf. Moselle R. *supra* 4. COLERAINE RD.
Cf. *the Lord of Coleraynes wood* 1653 ECP. FRIEZE LANE is *Fretheslane*
1504 AD vi, *Frithes Lane* 1607 HornseyCt, *Freeslane* 1617 ib., *Freeze-
land(s)* 1627 ib., and is to be associated with the family of John *atte
Fryth* (1406 *StPauls*). HIGHGATE HILL is *Highegate Hill* 1565 Sess.
HORNSEY LANE is *Haryngeylane* 1399 AD vi, *Hornesey Lane* 1603
HornseyCt. LODGE HILL is *Lodghill* 1593 N. A former residence of
the Bishop of London. SOUTHWOOD RD. Cf. *Southe Woddlane* 1607
HornseyCt. TOPSFIELD RD preserves the name of Topsfield Manor,
manor of Toppesfeldes 1375 AD iii, *Toppesfeld in Harengey* 1467 Cl,
Toppesfeld Hall 1483 AD vi, taking its name from the family of Thomas
de *Toppesfeld* (1343 FF) which must have come from Toppesfield
(PN Ess 463).

BISHOPSWOOD[1] is *Byssehopeswode* c. 1387 Knighton. It formed
part of the Bishop of London's manor in Hornsey from the
earliest times. The wood is already mentioned in 1241 (Cl) as
boscus de Heringaye.

BROWNS WOOD[2] (lost)

> *Brandeswode* c. 1250 *StPauls, Brondes-* 1254 Val
>
> *Brouneswod(e)* 1291 Tax, 1325, 1344 Pat, 1329 Londin, (*al.
> Brounesbury*) 1348 Pat
>
> *Broundeswode* 1450, 1461 Pat, *Brawndes-, Broundeswood* 1535
> VE
>
> *Broweneswood* 1482 ECP, *Browns Wood* 1745 R

This seems to be '*Brand*'s wood,' possibly the same man who
gave name to Brondesbury in Willesden *infra* 161. The places
are rather far apart, but both were St Paul's manors.

CROUCH END is *Crouchend* 1465 AD vi, *Crowchende* 1480 ib.,
the Crouche ende 1482 ib., *Crutche Ende* 1553 Sess and was by
the home of Stephen *atte Cruche of Haryngeye* (1352 AD ii) and
Geoffrey *atte Crouche* (1400 ib. vi). This is the *end* or quarter of
Hornsey where stood some ancient cross at the crossing of the
ways here, the first element being ME **crouche**, 'cross.' See
further HornseyRec 59.

[1] Surviving in BISHOPSWOOD RD.
[2] Later *Hornsey Wood* (*infra* 123). BROWNSWOOD RD, just outside
the borough, in Stoke Newington, is an antiquarian revival of the name
(HornseyRec 51).

DANE BOTTOM (lost) is *Danebotme* c. 1154, c. 1180 *Clerkenwell*, *Denebotme* ib., *Danbotme* c. 1580 *Add* 32100. It was the name given to low-lying land at the end of Stroud Green Lane, before the road rises towards Highbury (Lloyd 18). 'Valley-bottom,' *v.* denu, with the common south-eastern dialect form *dane* for *dene*. It has nothing to do with the Danes.

FINSBURY PARK. This name dates from 1857 when it was so named by Act, the park, on the site of the earlier *Hornsey Wood* (1741–5 R, etc.), being opened in 1869. It was so named because within the old Parliamentary borough of Finsbury, created in 1832, whose inhabitants initiated a movement for its acquisition (see J. J. Sexby, *The Municipal Parks of London*). The name now seems a curious misnomer, since it is far from the present Finsbury borough.

FORTIS GREEN is *Fortessegreene* 1613 HornseyCt, *Forte Greene*, *Fortesgreene* 1619 ib., *Fordesgreene* 1629 ib., *Fortes Greene* 1638 ib., *Fortres*(*s*) *Greene* 1681–93 ib., *Forty Green* 1754 R, *Fortis Green* 1813 EnclA. The O.S. map of 1864 records also Fortis Cottage and Fortismere. Cf. *Fortescroft* 1387 *Walden* (Edmonton). The origin of the name is obscure.

HARRINGAY. As the name of a district this name is quite modern (after 1880). It takes its name from the former *Harringay Ho* which shows an artificial restoration of the original spelling of Hornsey. See Hornsey *supra* 121 and, more fully, Madge, *Early Records of Hornsey* 60 ff.

HIGHGATE is *Le He*(*i*)*ghgate* 1354, 1359 Pat, *Heghegate* 1377 ib., *Heygate* 1391 FF (p), *Highgate* 1440 AD ii, 1529 FF, *Hyegat* 1543 ib. In old days before the construction of the New North Road by the Archway, the main Great North Road passed by here and a toll gate was, according to Lysons (iii, 59–60), set up at this spot by the Bishop of London, lord of the manor of Hornsey. It is one of the highest spots in the county (426 ft.).

MUSWELL HILL [mʌzəl], [mʌzwəl] takes its name from *Mosewell*(*a*) 1152–60 BM, 1294 *Ass* (p), 1320 Cl, *-welle* c. 1200 *Clerkenwell*, *Moswelcros* 1399 Works, *Muswell* 1535 VE, *Mussell Hill* 1631

HornseyCt, *Muzzle* 1641 ib., *Muscle Hill* 1746 R. 'Mossy spring,' *v.* meos, wielle. These names referred to an ancient spring or well here. The old name for the actual *hill* seems to have been *Pinnesknol, Pynnesknoll* 1288, 1294 *Ass, Pinsenall Hill* 1593 N, *Pinnesnoll Hill al. Muswell Hill, Pynesnoll Hill* 1610 HornseyCt, *Muswell Hill al. Pinchnoll Hill* 1617 ib. The second element of this name is cnoll, 'hill.' The first is probably the personal name found in Pinner *supra* 63.

STROUD GREEN is *land at Strode near Hyghebury* 1407 Hust[1], *Strode* 1432 ECP, *Strowde Grene* 1546 PCC, 1568 Sess, *Strode-grene* 1562 FF. *v.* strod, 'marshy land overgrown with brushwood.' The land here lies comparatively low.

COPPETTS FM is *Copits Farm* 1754 R, *Coppice Farm* 1819 G and is possibly to be associated with the farm lands on the outskirts of Bishop's Wood. GROVE HO. Cf. *the Grove or Bushe Close* 1630 HornseyCt. HORNSEY PARK is *(in) parco de Haringeye* 1241 Cl, *Haryngeseyepark* 1320 *Ass, Hornesey park* 1539 LP. SOUTH-WOOD HO. Cf. *Southwodd* 1465 HornseyCt, *Sow(e)wood* 1648, 1653 ib.

The Borough of Islington

ISLINGTON

> (*of*) *Gislandune* c. 1000 ASCharters
> *Iseldon(e)* 1086 DB *et passim* to 1554 FF, *-dun* 1176 RecStBarts, *Isildon* 1271, 1439 FF, 1398 Pat, *Isledon* 1320 FF, *Issildon* 1404 Pat, *Iselton* c. 1475 ECP, *Iseleton* 1525 PCC
> *Isendone* 1086 DB, *Ysendon* 1220 FF, *Isendon* 1235 *Ass*
> *Isoldona* 1163–81 StPaulsCh
> *Islyngton* 1464 AD vi, 1490 Pat, *Iselyngton* 1512 FF, *Isselyng-* 1545 PCC, 1552 FF
> *Iseldon otherwise Islyngton, Islyngdon* 1554 FF

'*Gisla*'s hill or down,' *v.* dun. *Gisla* would be a pet-form of OE personal names in *Gisl-*. Cf. Isleworth *supra* 27 and Isleham (PN C 22). The OE form explains the variant spellings with *n*.

---

[1] There is a place *Strode* mentioned in 1374 (Hust) but there is no clue as to where it is.

BARNSBURY

villa de Iseldon Berners, Iseldon Berneris 1274 *Ass*
maner' of Iseldon otherwise Bernersbury 1406 FF, *Berner(e)s-*
bury 1418 IpmR, 1436 FF, *Bernardysbury* c. 1475 ECP,
Barnersbury 1492 FF
Berners maner in Islesdon (sic) 1422 IpmR
Bernersbury otherwise Iseldon Berners otherwise Barnardesbury
1541 FF
Barnesbury 1543 ib.

This is a manorial *bury* name, *v.* burh and Introd. xvi.
William de *Berners* held land here in 1235 (*Ass*) and Radulfus
de *Berners* in 1242 (Fees). Cf. Alton Barnes (PN W 317).

CANONBURY [*olim* kæmbəri]

Canonesbury 1373 Misc, 1433 Pat
Canbury 1544 DKR xxv, 1798 Stockdale, *Canonbury* 1535
VE, (*al. Canbury*) 1552 Pat, *Canonbury al. Canbury* 1570
FF, *Cambury* 1593 N, 1686 M, 1710 S

This is another manorial *bury*-name, *v.* Introd. xvi. The
canons of St Bartholomew's, Smithfield, were granted land in
Islington t. Hy I (Dugdale vi, 297). Cf. Canons Park *supra* 67.
v. Addenda xxxiv.

COPENHAGEN HO and FIELDS is *Coopen Hagen* 1680 S, 1686 M,
Copenhagen 1735 Tomlins and generally to c. 1850 when the
house was demolished and the land built over. According to
Tomlins (24 ff.) it was so named because it was occupied by the
Danish ambassador in 1665. The name remains in *Copenhagen*
Tunnel on the L.N.E.R. which passes beneath the site.

HIGHBURY

Neweton Barrewe, Berewe 1274 *Ass, Newenton Barwe* 1294 ib.
Newton Berners 1274 *Ass*
Heybury 1349–96 Gesta, *Heyghbury* 1407 Hust, *Highbury*
1535 VE
Newenton al. Newyngton Barough al. Newington Barowe al. the
manor of Highbury 1548 Pat

This must at one time have been a part of the neighbouring
Stoke Newington parish (*infra* 159). *Bar(r)ewe, Berewe* is a

manorial addition, Thomas de *Barewe* having held land in Islington in 1271 (FF). This manor (*v.* **burh** (manorial)) stood on higher ground than either Canonbury or Barnsbury, hence the epithet *high.*

HOLLOWAY is *le Holeweye in Iseldon* 1307 GDR, *Holway* 1473 Pat, 1535 VE, *Holewey* 1487 Ipm, *Holwey* 1489 Pat, (*Islynton*) 1541 FF, *Halway* c. 1493 ECP, *Holowey* 1543 FF, *Holowaye al. Netherholowaye* 1553 ib., *Hollowaye* 1554 ib., *Halliwaye* 1593 PCC, *Holway the upper, the lower* 1593 N, 1741–5 R. 'Way in the hollow,' *v.* **holh, weg.** A common English road-name. The road-name later became a district-name. The hamlets of Upper and Lower Holloway were situated in a comparatively low-lying area between Highgate on the north-west and Islington to the south-east.

TOLLINGTON[1]

> (*of*) *Tollandune* c. 1000 ASCharters
> *Tolentone* 1086 DB, *Tolinton* 1274 *Ass, Tolyngton* 1468 FF, *Tollington* 1680 S
> *Tolendune* c. 1150 Round, *Commune of London*
> *Tolesdon, -dune* c. 1154 *Clerkenwell*
> *Tolindon* 1274 *Ass, -ing-* 1306 RecStBarts, *-lyn-* 1392 FF
> *Talington* 1336 Inq aqd, *Tallington Green* 1682 Morgan

'*Tolla*'s hill or hill pasture,' *v.* **dun.** Cf. *tollan dene* BCS 689 (Meon, Ha) and Tollesbury and Tolleshunt (PN Ess 304, 306).

ISLINGTON STREET-NAMES

BALLS POND RD is so named in 1841 (Lewis) and is probably to be associated with "John *Ball* at the Boarded House neere Newington Green" (17th Lewis 306). There was a large pond here until the early 19th century (ib.). BARNSBURY ST was earlier *Cut Throat Lane* ib. 166. Cf. *supra* 99. CALEDONIAN RD (1861 LCCN) is referred to as "the New Road from Battle Bridge to Holloway" in 1841 (ib. 46). It was constructed c. 1826 and named after the *Caledonian Asylum* for Scottish children, established in 1815 in Copenhagen Fields (W and C). It was earlier *Chalk Road* (LnTopRec viii, 58). CHURCH LANE is so named in 1735 (Tomlins). COMPTON RD (as also MARQUESS RD and NORTHAMPTON

---

[1] Preserved in TOLLINGTON PARK, PLACE and ROAD. The old manor covered the north part of the present borough.

PARK) were named after the Marquess of Northampton, lord of the manor of Canonbury (W and C). CROSS ST is so named in 1735 (Tomlins), perhaps because running across from Upper St to Essex Rd. DANBURY ST was *Brick Lane* 1808 Cary. ESSEX RD (1864 LCCN) was *The Lower Street* 1735 Tomlins, *Lower Street* and *Newington Green Lane* 1741–5 R, *Lower Street* and *Road* 1817 Wilkinson, in contrast to Upper St *infra*. HIGH ST (1817 Wilkinson) was *The Broad Way* 1808 Cary. Perhaps referred to as *The Strete* in 1540 (Tomlins 77). HOLLOWAY RD. *v.* Holloway *supra* 126. It was *Highgate Road* 1817 Wilkinson, the old name for it, probably never disused altogether, being afterwards resumed. HORNSEY RD was earlier *Tallingdone Lane* 1593 N, *Tallington Lane* 1841 Lewis, *v.* Tollington *supra* 126. An alternative name was (*The*) *Devils Lane* 1611 Survey, 1732 PC, 1741–5 R. HYDE RD preserves an ancient field-name, *the Hyde* 1540 Tomlins. *v.* Hyde Park *infra* 168. LIVERPOOL RD (1831 Elmes) was earlier *Islington Back Lane* 1741–5 R, running behind the High St. MILDMAY PARK and RD were named after the family of Sir Henry *Mildmay* which had held an estate here from the 17th century (Lysons iii, 136). NEW NORTH RD was constructed in 1812 (Lewis 404). PARK LANE was *Kettle Lane* 1735 Tomlins. POPHAM RD (1872 LCCN) was earlier *Frog(g) lane* 1692, 1735 Tomlins, 1741–5 R, where it is shown leading to buildings called *Frog Hall*, *v. infra* 205. POPLAR ST was *The Alder Walk* 1732 PC, *Elder Walk* 1811 Nelson. PROVENCE ST marks the site of *Provence Field* 1735 Tomlins. RANDELL'S RD may possibly be near the old field *Randulffesfeld* (1306 RecStBarts), containing the OGer personal name *Randolph*. ST PAULS RD (*a.* 1848 (mogg), cf. Tomlins 23) was earlier *Hopping Lane* 1735 Tomlins, 1841 Map (in Lewis), preserving the field-name *Hoppingefeild* 1540 Tomlins, *Hoppinges* 1609 Hust, *The Hoppinge* 1611 Survey. Possibly 'place where hops were grown,' cf. Hoppinghill (PN Nt 128). SHERRINGTON RD was earlier *Hagbush Lane* 1735 Tomlins. STONEFIELD ST is on the site of a field so named in 1735 (Tomlins 12). TUFNELL PARK preserves the memory of William *Tufnell* who held the manor of Barnsbury in 1753 (Tomlins 106). UPPER ST is so named in 1735 (ib.), 1741–5 (R), in contrast to Lower St, now Essex Rd (*supra*). WHITE CONDUIT ST is *White Conduit Lane* 1735 Tomlins. Cf. *Cundicke Feld al. Hill Feld* 1540 ib., *Condyte feld* 1553 Pat, *Condett felde* 1556 Tomlins, from an old *conduit* or water channel. WINGFIELD ST was (*The*) *Black Lane* 1746 R, 1811 Nelson. YORK RD (1881 LCCN) was earlier *Mede Lane* 1553 FF, *Mayden Lane* 1649 StPancSurv, *Maid Lane or Maiden Lane* 1735 Tomlins, *Maiden Lane* till the middle of the 19th century (maps). This was an ancient way from Grays Inn Lane to Highgate (LnTopRec viii, 17). An earlier name may have been *Shereway* (t. Ric 2 Gatty), since it formed the boundary between Islington and St Pancras parishes. Cf. *Shere Lane infra* 183.

Lost names include *Heame Lane, Cream Hall, Mount Pleasant, Pierpoints Row, Boarded River Lane* (all 1735 Tomlins). The last was near the New River (*supra* 5). For Mount Pleasant, *v. supra* 96.

The Royal Borough of Kensington

KENSINGTON

    Chenesiĩ 1086 DB
    Kinsentona, -tun, Kinsnetuna t. Hy 1 Abingdon, *Cinsentuna*
        1154–89 ib., *Chinsentun* 1189 ib., *Kinsingtoun* 1595 PCC
    Chensnetune t. Hy 1 Abingdon, *Kunsentun* ib.
    Kensinton(e) 1221 FF *et freq* to 1316 FA, with variant spelling
        -yn-, Kensenton 1264, 1270 Ipm
    Kensington 1235 *Ass et passim*, with variant spelling *-yng-*,
        Keynsington 1230, 1287 FF, *Kenesingeton* 1274 *Ass*

    '*Cynesige*'s farm,' *v.* ingtun.

BROMPTON is *Brompton* 1294 *Ass* (p), 1481 IpmR, *Bromton* 1309 FF, *Brumpton* 1380 Cl, 1596 ParReg, *Brompton greene* 1607 *Ct*, *Brumetone* 1610 ParReg. 'Broom farm,' *v.* tun.

COLEHERNE HO[1] is *Colneherne* 1430 *Ct*, *Colhyrne* 1433 ib., *Colehearne* 1653 ParReg, *Coolehearne* 1656 ib., *Cooldhearne* 1661 ib. The forms are too late for any interpretation of the first element to be offered. The second element is clearly OE hyrne, 'corner, angle.'

CROMWELL RD preserves the memory of the former *Cromwell House* (demolished c. 1850). This was *Hale House* 1606 etc. ParReg, *Hale House commonly called Cromwell House* 1820 FaulknerKe, so named from a tradition that Henry Cromwell, son of the Protector, once lived here. He was married in Kensington (1653 ParReg). The older name is to be associated with the place called *le Hale* 1400 *Ct*, *Halefeild* 1617 ib., *v.* healh, 'corner, angle.' Cf. Tottenham Hale *supra* 79.

EARLS COURT is *Earles Court* 1593 *Ct*, 1614 *FF*, *Erls Cort* 1654 ParReg. This hamlet grew up round the court-house of the de Veres, Earls of Oxford, lords of the manor of Kensington from DB to the 16th century. The manor house of Earls Court was not demolished until 1886. It covered the site of the present Barkston and Bramham Gardens.

    [1] Demolished in 1900. The name is preserved in COLEHERNE COURT.

HOLLAND HO takes its name from Henry Rich, Earl of *Holland* whose wife inherited it in 1621 (Earl of Ilchester, *Home of the Hollands* 9–10). Cf. *The Earle of Hollands House* 1658 ParReg, *Holland House* 1664 ib.

KENSINGTON PALACE is *The Park House* 1664 FaulknerKe, *Nottingham House* 1690 ib. The estate was bought by William III from the Second Earl of Nottingham in 1690 (ib. 452).

NORLANDS[1] is *Northlandes* 1428, 1433 Ct, *Norlandesgate* 1438 ib., *Norlands* 1607 ib. The name was originally applied to the open lands of the north part of the parish.

NOTTING HILL and BARNS[2]

Knottynghull' 1356 Works, 1361, 1374 Pat
Knottyngwode 1376 Cl, 1430 *Ct, -ing-* 1382 Cor
Knottyngesbernys 1462 Pat, *Knottyngbernes* 1475 ib., *Knottinge Bernes* 1476 IpmR
Notingbarns 1519 FF, *Nuttyngbarnes* 1543 LP, 1550 Pat, *Notynghyll* 1550 Sess, *Nuttyng Woode* 1550 Pat, *Noten barns* 1675 Ogilby, *Noding Hill* 1680 S

The element *knottyng* in Notting Hill presents a problem. The only other place in southern England which presents a parallel is Knotting (PN BedsHu 15). Knotting stands on a definite hill, and before the growth of London, Notting Hill and Campden Hill, appeared from the west, as shown in old views, as low, rounded eminences rising from the Middlesex plain. It is tempting therefore to adopt the suggestion put forward by Zachrisson, and by Ekwall (DEPN) that the first element in these names is a lost OE word **cnott* denoting a 'hill,' in which case Knotting (Beds) would derive from *Cnottingas* and have to be interpreted as 'place of the dwellers on the hill,' while Notting Hill might perhaps be interpreted as containing an element *cnotting* denoting a hill. The difficulty about such an interpretation is that, apart from these two names, no other example is known in southern or midland England of a place-name containing the element **cnott*, and it would be

---

[1] Surviving in NORLANDS SQUARE.
[2] Surviving in NOTTING BARNS TAVERN in Silchester Rd.

rather a remarkable coincidence if it were found only in these two *-ing* compounds. Alternatively, the Bedfordshire place-name has been interpreted by Ekwall as containing a nickname *Cnotta*, derived from OE *cnotta*, 'knot,' the whole name meaning '*Cnotta*'s people,' and Notting Hill and Notting Barns as containing a family name *Knotting* borne perhaps by some unknown holder of land here who came from Bedfordshire. The forms given above carry Notting Hill and Notting Barns some 120 years further back than the forms known to Ekwall, but they do not make such an interpretation impossible. No certain solution is yet possible.

Notting Hill-Gate takes its name from a turnpike gate which formerly stood here at the junction of Church St with the main road (Gladstone 57). The district was earlier known as The Gravel Pits (*the Gravilpits, the Gravill pits* 1654 ParReg, *Kinsington grauill Pittes* 1675 Ogilby). For mention of 'gravel pits' in other Middlesex parishes *v. infra* 203.

KENSINGTON STREET-NAMES

Abingdon Rd recalls the grant of the church of St Mary (hence *Abbots*) to the abbot of Abingdon, Berks. Cf. Dugd i, 406. Addison Rd recalls the essayist who in 1716 married Charlotte, Countess of Warwick, of Holland House (FaulknerKe 111). Allen St. Cf. "East of Earls Court Lane Mr Allen is now (i.e. 1820) building two large rows of houses" (FaulknerKe 603). Barkston and Bramham Gardens and Wetherby Rd are on or near the site of Earls Court House (*supra* 128), and were named by the builder after places near his home in the West Riding of Yorkshire. The Boltons. Possibly so named from former fields here associated with the tenancy of William *Bolton* (1533–8 ECP). Brompton Rd is *Bromtonlane* 1430 Ct. *v. supra* 128. The stretch of Brompton Rd from the Oratory eastwards to Yeoman's Row was formerly known as *Bell Lane* (1793 Cary), from an inn called *The Bell and Horns*. Campden Hill. Named from *Campden House* (burned down 1862), *The Lord Cambdens house* 1656 ParReg, *Cambdune House* 1659 ib., *Cambden House* 1663 ib. The house was built c. 1612 by Sir Baptist Hicks, created Lord *Campden* in 1628 (FaulknerKe 418). Cheniston Gardens. The name was suggested by the DB spelling of Kensington (*v. supra* 128), in which, however, the *Ch-* was pronounced *K-*. Chepstow Villas, Ledbury Rd, Pembridge Square. The land here was sold by the Ladbrokes to Mr Jenkins of Hereford, who named the streets after places in or near his native county (Gladstone 167).

CHURCH ST is *Church Lane* 1658 FaulknerKe, 1808 Cary. CLARENDON RD (*a.* 1861 LCCN) was earlier *Green's Lane* 1741–5 R. John *Greene* held land here in 1656 (Gladstone 39). COURTFIELD GARDENS preserves the field-name *Courtefeld* 1642 *Ct*, with reference to the near-by manor-house of Earls Court (*supra* 128). CRANLEY GARDENS is so named from Viscount *Cranley*, the title of the eldest son of the Earl of Onslow (from Cranleigh, Sr). *v.* Onslow Square *infra.* CROMWELL RD. *v. supra* 128. EARLS COURT RD is *Earles Court Lane* 1612 *Ct. v. supra* 128. EDWARDES SQUARE (built c. 1804) is so named from William *Edwardes* of Haverfordwest, who possessed this part of the manor of Kensington through marriage with the sister of the third Earl of Holland (Faulkner Ke 88). LONGRIDGE RD, MARLOES RD, NEVERN SQUARE, PEMBROKE SQUARE, PENYWERN RD, PHILBEACH GARDENS, TEMPLETON PLACE and TREBOVIR RD are named from places in Pembrokeshire where the Edwardes family had property. FULHAM RD. *v. supra* 104. GLOUCESTER RD was *Hog moor(e) lane* 1612 *Ct*, and as late as 1858 (Daw), probably descriptive of a muddy tract. Re-named after Maria, Duchess of *Gloucester* who had a house here c. 1800 (W and C). HARRINGTON GARDENS. The Earl of *Harrington* had land in Kensington (c. 1840 *TA*). See also FaulknerKe 611. HIGH ST is (*The*) *High Street* 1630, 1645 FaulknerKe. HOLLAND PARK AVENUE is part of the main Oxford road, *v. supra* 10. It is referred to in Kensington documents as *the great road to Acton* 1652 ib., *Uxbridge Way* 1664 ib. HOLLAND ST is so named in 1658 ib. HOLLAND WALK is *Lord Holland's Lane* 1772 ib. *v.* Holland Ho *supra* 129. IFIELD RD (1870 LCCN) and FINBOROUGH RD were earlier *Honye lane* 1612 *Ct*, *Honey Lane* 1741–5 R, probably descriptive of a muddy road, *v. infra* 205. KENSINGTON SQUARE is *a new street called the Square* 1690 Sess. LADBROKE GROVE. Richard *Ladbrooke* owned the land here in 1624 (LCCDeeds) and the family sold it for building purposes in 1845. MELBURY RD is so called after the Dorset seat of Lord Ilchester of Holland House. NORLAND SQUARE. *v.* Norlands *supra* 127. ONSLOW SQUARE was built on land belonging to the Earl of *Onslow*. PHILLIMORE GARDENS &c. are named after the landowners. Building began in 1787 (FaulknerKe 437). PITT ST is *Pitt Buildings* 1820 ib., from the family of George *Pitt* (1693 ib.) and Stephen *Pitt* (1814 ib.). PORTOBELLO RD is shown in 1820 ib., leading to *Porto Bello Farm* (demolished c. 1870), probably named from the victory of Admiral Vernon at *Porto Bello* in 1739. The farm was older than this date, but its earlier name is not known. QUEENS GATE follows roughly the line of the earlier *Gore Lane* 1665, 1820 FaulknerKe. *v.* Kensington Gore *infra* 169 and cf. ALBERT GATE. REDCLIFFE GARDENS was earlier *Walnut Tree Walk* 1746 R, 1820 FaulknerKe. SCARSDALE VILLAS named from *Scarsdale House*, which may have been built by the fourth Earl of *Scarsdale* t. Anne (ib. 440). SELWOOD TERRACE is *Sallad Lane* 1741–5 R, 1808 Cary. The later name derives from 'Mr Selwood's nursery,' which is mentioned in 1712 by Narcissus Luttrell. SHEFFIELD TERRACE. On the site of *Sheffield House*, referred to as "Mr James Sheffield's house" in 1663 (FaulknerKe).

STANHOPE GARDENS takes its name from Earl *Stanhope*, landowner here c. 1840 (*TA*). It is on the site of the old pleasure resort *Florida Gardens* (1793 Cary). STRATFORD RD. William *Stratford* had land in Kensington c. 1840 *TA*. THISTLE GROVE is *Thistle Grove Lane* in 1820 (FaulknerKe 406). DE VERE GARDENS commemorates Aubrey *de Vere*, the holder of the manor of Kensington in DB. Hence also AUBREY RD. VICTORIA RD (north end) with LAUNCESTON PLACE follow the track of *Love Lane* 1657 Sess, 1741–5 R. WARWICK RD. Robert, 2nd Earl of Holland, succeeded to the title of Earl of *Warwick* in 1673 (FaulknerKe 88). WRIGHTS LANE is so named in 1820 ib. It was built by Gregory *Wright* c. 1774 (ib. 439). YEOMANS ROW is so named in 1794 (Horwood). YOUNG ST is so named in 1808 (Cary), deriving from the family of Robert *Yong* (1502 FaulknerKe), Thomas *Younge* (1630 ib.).

The Borough of Paddington

PADDINGTON

> (*in*) *Padintune* 959 (13th) BCS 1050, t. Hy 3 BM, 1222 Westlake, *Padinton(e)* c. 1110 Crispin, 1168 P (p), 1185 Templars, 1224 FF, 1291 Tax, *Padynton* 1316 FA
>
> *Paddingtone* 998 (13th) Thorpe, *-ton* 1493 FF
>
> *Padington* 1042–66 (13th) *WAM*, 1274 *Ass*, 1321 FF, *-yng-* 1294 *Ass*, 1353, 1422 FF
>
> *Patintone* c. 1110 Crispin, *Patyngton* 1398, 1493 Pat
>
> '*Pad(d)a*'s farm,' *v.* ingtun. Cf. Padbury (PN Bk 55).

NOTE. BISHOP'S RD is so called because from 1550 until the 19th century the Bishop of London was lord of the manor of Paddington (W and C). CRAVEN HILL is so named in 1795 (Lysons) from Lord *Craven* who had an estate here (ib. iii, 331). EDGWARE RD, *v.* Watling St *supra* 9. It is referred to in a Paddington document of 1549 (Robins) as *highway called Watlyng Street*. HARROW RD is so named in 1741–5 (R). It is called *The Green Lane* in 1555 (Robins). MOSCOW RD and ST PETERSBURGH PLACE were built c. 1818 (FaulknerKe 585), possibly commemorating the visit of the Czar Alexander I in 1814. ORME SQUARE was built c. 1820 by a Mr *Orme* of Bond St (Robins 52). PRAED ST is so named from William *Praed*, one of the first directors of the near-by Grand Junction Canal (Robins 112). QUEENS RD (now QUEENS WAY) was *Wesborn Green Lane* 1746 R, leading to Westbourne Green (*v. infra* 133). *Black Lion Lane* 1838 Cruchley, from an inn.

BAYSWATER is *place called Bayards Watering* 1652 FaulknerKe, *Bayards Watering Place* 1654 ParReg (Kensington), *Bayeswater* 1659 PCC, *Beards Watering Place* 1680 S, *Bayards Watering Place or Bayswater* 1752 LCCDeeds. This was originally the name of the place where the Westbourne stream crossed the main Oxford Road and as late as the end of the 18th century there were only a few houses at this spot. Tanner (*Notitia Monastica*, Middlesex xii) gives an earlier form from a Westminster document of 1380, viz. *aqua vocata Bayards Watering Place*. Besant (*London North of the Thames* 139–40) quotes this wrongly with the form *Baynards* and tries to associate the place with the *Baignard* who held land in the demesne of the Church of St Peter of Westminster, but there is really no evidence in support of this.

MAIDA VALE, mentioned in 1868 (LCCN), was so named in distinction from *Maida Hill* (preserved in *Maida Hill West*) which is marked in 1817 (Mogg). It probably took its name from the battle of *Maida* in Italy (1806). In popular parlance it is used as if it were the name of a district. It is really a street-name.

WESTBOURNE is *Westeburn(e)* 1222 Westlake, 1259 FF, 1319 Pat, *Westbo(u)rn(e)* 1294 *Ass*, 1302 *GDR*, 1316 FA, *Westborne Grene* 1548 Pat, *Washborne Green* 1680 S, *Wesborn Green* 1754 R. The earliest forms with medial *e* suggest that this name does not mean 'west stream' (*v.* **burna**) but goes back to OE (*bī*) *westan burnan*, '(place) west of the stream.' The hamlet lay just west of the stream as shown in earlier maps. Cf. PN D xxxvii. The name remains in Westbourne Grove and Park.

The Borough of Poplar

NOTE. The metropolitan borough of Poplar is composed of the parishes of Poplar (a hamlet of Stepney till 1817), St Leonard's Bromley and St Mary Stratford Bow (a chapelry of Stepney till 1719).

POPLAR

    Popler 1327 Banco, *Le Popler* 1351 Cl, *Poplar* 1486 FF
    Popeler 1340, 1341 FF, (*in Stebbenheth*) 1350 Ipm, *Populer* 1346 *Ct*, 1547 FF, *le Popelere* 1355 BPR, *le Popeler* 1443 *Ct*, *Poppeller* 1535 VE
    Popiller 1358 BPR, *Popiler* 1362 Cl, *Popellier* 1399 FF
    Popley 1542 FF

'(At) the poplar tree.' The NED does not record the word *poplar* before 1382, but it may well have entered the English language at a much earlier date.

Bow *olim* STRATFORD (AT) BOW

> *Stratford* 1177 P, 1199 Cur, 1244 Fees, 1247 Ch, 1273 BM,
> *Strafford* 1203 Cur
> *Stretford* 1265 FF (p), 1314 Cl, 1593 N, *Stret(t)ford atte*
> *Bowe* 1349 Orig, 1407 Pat, (*at*) 1522 FF
> *Stratford atte Bowe* 1279 FF, 1316 Pat, c. 1400 Chaucer,
> *Prologue*, (*next Stebenhuth*) 1325 FF, (*ate Boghe*) 1303 Pat,
> (*atte Bough*) 1323 ib., (*juxta Redhope*) 1346 Works, (*at Bowe*)
> 1445 Pat, (*of the Bowe*) 1449 ib., (*at the Bowe*) 1494 FF,
> (*at Bowe*) 1535 VE, (*the Bowe*) 1543 PCC, (*le Bow(e)*) c. 1560
> ChancP, 1805 O.S., (*on the Bow*) 1593 N
> *Stratford bowe* 1547 PCC, 1606 ParReg, *Bow(e)* 1594, 1597 ib.

The ford was that where the Roman road to Colchester crossed the various branches of the Lea, one of which forms the county boundary, *v.* stræt, ford and cf. Stratford on Avon (PN Wa 236). The bridge is said to have been built t. Hy 1 and was presumably so named from its arched shape. Cf. Bow (PN D 360) and Bow St *infra* 176. Lysons (iii, 490), on the authority of an inquisition taken before the King's justices in 1303, tells the story of its building by Good Queen Maud. She heard that the ford at Old Ford was dangerous and diverted the highway to where it now runs, namely between Stratford and West Ham, causing bridges to be built to span the Lea[1]. Local tradition has it that she ordered the bridge to be built in the shape of her bow when floods held her up while hunting. Stratford was formerly the name of a district partly in Middlesex, partly in Essex (cf. PN Ess 96). BOW BRIDGE is referred to in (*ultra*) *pontem de Stretford* 1294 Ass, (*iuxta*) *pontem de Stratford* 1346 Works, *Bowebrigge* 1461 Pat, *the stone bridge called Bowe-*

---

[1] The Deputy Keeper of the Records has very kindly traced this document, which is calendared as *Miscellaneous Chancery Inquisitions* i, 521, and checked Lysons' rendering of the full document as preserved in the PRO. The most important variation is that the passage which speaks of "an iron railing upon a certain bridge, called Lockbridge" should have been rendered "a barrier with locks upon," etc.

brydge 1541 LP. Bow Creek (the mouth of the Lea) is *Bow Creek* 1754 R and is earlier referred to as *Luymudhe* 13th AD iv, *Leymoth* 1547 FF, *v.* Lea R. *supra* 4.

Bromley

> (*of*) *Bræmbelege* c. 1000 ASCharters
> *Brambeley* c. 1128 AD i *et passim* to 1536 FF, with variant
>   spellings *-legh(e), -ley(e), -le(e), Brambelestrate* 12th AD ii
> *Brembellee* 12th AD ii, *Brembeleg'* 1226 FF, *Brembelley* 1282
>   AD ii, *et freq* to 1354 ib., with variant spellings *-ley(e), -le,*
>   *Brembeleye strate* 1282 AD ii, *Bremlegh* 1346 Works, *Bremley*
>   1467 Pat
> *Brameley* 1135–54 AD ii, *Bramleia* 1201 FF, *-legh* 1346
>   Works, 1371 FF, *-ley(e)* 1394, 1523 ib., 1598 Stow
> *Brombelleg'* 1251 FF, *Brombele* 1274 *Ass*
> *Bromlegh* 1274, 1542, 1564 FF, *Bromeley St Mary* 1532 ib.,
>   *Bromley* 1541 ib., *Bromley-by-Bow* 1786 LibReg
> *Brumlegh* 1351 AD i

'Clearing overgrown with brambles,' *v.* leah. Later the first element was confused with 'broom' from OE *brom*. For *strete, strate*, in the lost *Bromleystreet, v. infra* 204.

Blackwall is *Blakewale* 1377 Walford, *the wall called Blakwall* 1480 Pat, *Blakwall* 1483 ib., *Blackewall* 1561 Sess. An earlier reference to the wall may be found in *Walemers* 1288 *AD, Walmerssh* 1430 Pat. *v.* mersc, 'marsh.' The *wall* was no doubt an artificial bank constructed to keep out the river. Cf. Millwall (*infra* 136), Rotherhithe Wall, Narrow Wall and Broadwall, also on the banks of the Thames.

Cubitt Town. This district was laid out by William *Cubitt*, the Victorian builder and planner of Belgravia, c. 1850 (Walford i, 546). For other names of this type cf. Somers Town *infra* 142, Canning Town (PN Ess 97) and Summerstown (PN Sr 37).

Isle of Dogs is *Isle of doges ferm* 1593 N, *Poplar Marshes or Isle of Dogs* 1799 Horwood. The origin of this name has never been satisfactorily explained. Cf. W and C *s.n.*

Probably it is a nickname of contempt. The district was earlier known as Stepney Marsh. Cf. (*in*) *landmarisco de Stebeh'* 13th AD iv, *marsh of Stebenhithe* 1365 ib. i, *Stepheneth mershe* 1432 IpmR.

MILLWALL now the name of the western part of the Isle of Dogs (*supra* 135) was originally that of the river wall called *Marsh Wall* (1754 R). Its later name is due to several mills which stood on the wall in the 18th century. (See Gascoyne, R 1741–5 and Seale.)

OLD FORD is *Eldefordmelne* 1230 Bracton, *Eldeford in Stubenheth* 1268 Pat, (*le*) *Eldeford*(*e*) 1311 Londin, 1323 AD i, 1374 Cl, *Oldeford*(*e*) 1313 Abbr, 1383 IpmR, 1388 FF, *-forthe* 1384 ib., *Aldeforde juxta London* 1381 WI. 'Old ford,' perhaps in distinction from Stratford lower down the river Lea. This area was at one time part of Stepney. For the phonology *v.* Introd. xvii.

PONTEFRACT or POUNTFREIT (lost)

(*apud*) *Pontem Fractum* 1230 P, (*manor of*) *Pontefracto* 1303 FF, (*de*) *Ponteffracto super Tamisiam* 1334 ib.
Pountfreit in com' Midd' 1307 GDR, (*in Stepheneth Mershe*) 1432 IpmR, *Pountfreyt* 1430 Wollaton
Ponfrayt upon Thames 1323 Ipm, *Pountfreyt* 1358, 1458 FF, *Pomfreyth* 1363 Ipm, *Pomfret* 1366 Orig

This is a French name identical with Pontefract (PN WRY 148), the forms, as in that name, being often latinised in old documents. The site of the 'broken bridge' is not known, but the 1432 reference suggests that it was in or near the present Isle of Dogs *supra* 135.

POPLAR STREET-NAMES

BOW LANE is so named in 1703 (Gascoyne), leading to Bow *supra* 134. COLD HARBOUR is *Coleharbor* 1617 Allgood, 1643 ParReg, *Cold-* 1639 ib., *v. infra* 206. It is on the north-east corner of the Isle of Dogs, facing eastwards. COBORN and TREDEGAR RDS. In 1703 (Gascoyne) these streets formed one thoroughfare with a right-angled bend marked *Bare Binder Lane* and *Beer Binder Lane*. It is *Barebinder Lane* in 1617 (Allgood). Cf. the old name for George St in the City. It may be that the name is to be associated with *bearbind*, an old name for convolvulus. DEVONS RD was *Bromley Lane* 1741–5 R, leading from Limehouse to

Bromley. EAST INDIA DOCK RD. The dock is near the site of a dock constructed in 1614 by the East India Company (cf. W and C). HIGH ST POPLAR is *Poplar Street* 1669 ChancP. MANCHESTER RD (1884 LCCN) was *Arrow Lane* 1741-5 R. NORTH ST is *Popler northstrete* 1617 ParReg. OLD FORD RD is *Old Ford Lane* 1703 Gascoyne. See Old Ford *supra* 136. ORCHARD PLACE. There is an orchard near here in Gascoyne's map (1703). PENNYFIELDS is *Penny feild* 1663 ParReg, *Peny Feild* 1703 Gascoyne, probably so called from the one-time rent. *v.* feld. ROBIN HOOD LANE is *Robin Hood's Lane* ib. ST LEONARD'S ST was *Foure Milstrett* 1551 Pat, *Four Mill Street* 1741-5 R, from four mills which stood by the Lea. Cf. *Fouremullelok* 1345 Works.

The Borough of St Marylebone

MARYLEBONE[1] (*olim* TYBURN) [*olim* mæribən]

> *Tiburne* 1086 DB, 1235 *Ass*, 1277 Abbr, -*bourn* 1291 Tax, -*bern* 1316 FA
>
> *Teyborn(e)* 1312 Fine, 1598 Stow
>
> *Maryburne* 1453 LBk, 1505 *AD*, -*bourne* 1492, 1509 FF, *Mariborne* 1535 VE
>
> *Tyborne otherwise called Maryborne* 1490, 1504 FF
>
> *Marybon* 1542 LMxAS iv, *Marribon* 1612 Sess, *Maribone* 1623 BM, *Marrowbon* 1625 ParReg (Kensington)
>
> *Marylebone* 1626 PCC, *Mary le Bone* 1746 R

Originally Tyburn, from the river (*supra* 6). Later known as *Marybourne* from the dedication of the new church erected in the 15th century. The substitution of the Saint's name was perhaps due to the odium attaching to the name Tyburn itself from its association with the famous gallows. For *bone*, *v. infra* 196. The introduction of the *le* is of later date. Popular etymology has suggested that this stood for *Mary the good*—this is obviously impossible. More probably the *le* was introduced on the analogy of St Mary le Bow, the *le* in that name having that loose connective sense which it commonly has in place-names of that type. The name *Tyburn* survived in *Tyburn Tree*, the well-known place of execution near the site of the present Marble Arch, until the end of the 18th century.

[1] For early forms and an interesting discussion of the name *v.* the article on the name Marylebone by the late Mr Arthur Bonner in LMxAS (N.S.) iv, 75-84.

Lisson[1]

> *Lilestone* 1086 DB, *Lislestone* t. Hy 1 (1373) Pat
> *Lilleston* 1198 FF, 1244 Fees *et passim* to 1561 FF, with variant spelling *Lylles-*
> *Lylleston Grene* 1547 PCC, *Lising Green* 1610 Speed, *Lissett Greene* 1649 Madge, *Lisson Green* 1795 Lysons

'*Lille*'s farm,' *v.* tun. Cf. Lillesdon (So), *Lillesdon* 1225 Ass and *lilles ham* (BCS 479).

Oxford St (for earlier names *v. supra* 10) is *The Road to Oxford* 1682 Morgan, 1707 Chiswell (*New Map of London*), 1720 Overton (*New Plan of London*), *Oxford Road* 1720 Senex (*Plan of London prefixed to Strype*), and as late as 6th May 1770 and 26th April 1771, Horace Walpole writes in his letters of *The Oxford Road* and *Oxford Road*. But a stone still *in situ* at the corner of Rathbone Place, near the eastern end of the street, is inscribed *Rathbones Place in Oxford Street*, 1718. Both *Oxford St* and *The Road to Oxford* occur on J. Smith's *Plan of London* (1724); there used to be a stone inscribed *Oxford Street* 1725 on No. 1 (at the eastern end), and according to Lysons (iii, 257), *Oxford Street* was used from 1729 (see W and C). In Rocque's map of 1746 the part of the road west of the stream is still *Tiburn Road*, that eastward is *Oxford Street*; in the map of 1754 all is *Oxford St*. It would appear that the word *street* spread gradually westward as the northern side of the road was built, and the preponderance of *Oxford* over other places, e.g. Uxbridge (*v. supra* 10), after which the road was once named and which persisted west of Edgware Rd (cf. Horwood) may perhaps have been partly due to the development of the Holles estate by the second Earl of *Oxford* (*v.* Cavendish Square *infra* 139). Tyburn, as in the case of Park Lane *infra* 181 would be dropped because of the association of that name with the place of execution.

Regents Park is *The Regents Park* 1817 Mogg and takes its name from the Prince *Regent*, afterwards George IV. See Regent St *infra* 182. Its area corresponds roughly to that of the Marylebone Park of Tudor times (*park of Maryborne* 1558 Pat, *Marybone Park* 1574 PCC, *Marrowbone Park* 1649 Madge).

---

[1] Surviving in Lisson Grove and Street. The old manor included the north-west part of Marylebone parish.

St Johns Wood is (*juxta*) *boscum prioris Sci Johannis* 1294
GDR, *Seynt Johns Woode* 1524 VCH ii, 1547 Pat, *Grete St Johns
Wood* 1558 Pat. The wood was granted to the Knights Templars
but passed into the possession of the Hospitallers with their other
property (LMxAS (N.S.) iv, 73–4). Its former wild condition
may be realised from the statement (1545 LP ii, 346), "As well
seek to clear England of foxes by killing those in St John's
Wood."

ST MARYLEBONE STREET-NAMES

Baker St is so named in 1794 (Horwood) from Sir Edward *Baker* of
Ranston, Dorset, a friend of Mr Portman (W and C). *v.* Portman
Square *infra*. Bell St is so named in 1799 (Horwood), from an
inn sign. Berners St is so named in 1746 (R) from William *Berners* of
Woolverstone Hall, Suffolk, who held land here (W and C). Cavendish
Square was planned in 1715 (Lysons). In 1710 the manor of Marylebone
was bought by John *Holles*, Duke of Newcastle, who was given that
title after his marriage with a daughter and heiress of Henry *Cavendish*,
second Duke of Newcastle, a relative of the Earl of Devonshire. His
daughter and heiress, Henrietta, married in 1713 Edward *Harley* who
in 1724 succeeded his father as Earl of Oxford, Earl *Mortimer* and Baron
Harley of Wigmore Castle and who had property at Wimpole, Cambs.
The estate passed to William Bentinck, second Duke of *Portland* (whose
seat was at Welbeck and who had property at Carburton and Clipstone,
also in Notts) through his marriage in 1734 with Lady Margaret
Cavendish Harley, daughter of the above. Their eldest daughter married
the second Viscount *Weymouth*. Hence also Henrietta St, Holles
St, Margaret St, Mortimer St, (Great) Portland St (northern
part formerly *Portland Rd* 1793 Horwood), Welbeck St, all in 1746 R,
and Market Place (*Oxford Market* 1746 R), Wigmore St (*Wigmore
Row* ib., (*St*) 1792 Horwood) and Wimpole St (*Wimple St* 1746 R,
Wimpole St 1792 Horwood). Later came Bentinck St, Carburton
St, Clipstone St, Devonshire St and Place, Harley St, Weymouth St, all shown by Horwood, 1792–3, as is Portland Place,
built c. 1778. See W and C and Lysons iii, 257. Langham Place is so
named from Sir James *Langham* of Cottesbrook (Nth) (W and C).
Manchester Square, built c. 1776–88, was named after the fourth
Duke of *Manchester*, whose house forms the north side (Smith 199).
Marylebone Lane is *Marybone lane* 1649 Madge, 1708 Hatton. It
was earlier *Lustie Lane al. Long Lane* 1589 Sess. Marylebone Rd
is part of the *New Road from Paddington to Islington*, made under an
Act of 1756, *v. infra* 144. Oxford St, *v. supra* 138. Portman Square
was begun c. 1764 by William Henry *Portman* (d. 1796) of Orchard
Portman, Somerset. His grandmother belonged to the *Seymour* family,
the head of which was the Duke of *Somerset*, hence Orchard St,
Seymour St, Somerset St. Later, the chief seat of the Portman

family was at Bryanston near Blandford, Dorset. Hence BLANDFORD
ST, DORSET ST (and later the Squares so named). All these are shown
by Horwood, 1794 (see W and C). RATHBONE PLACE is so named in
1718 (HCMag vi) and takes its name from its builder, Captain Rathbone (ib. 73). ST JOHNS WOOD RD coincides in part with *St Johns
Wood Lane* 1741–5 R, 1794 Survey. *v. supra* 139. STRATFORD PLACE was
begun c. 1774 by the second Earl of Aldborough whose family name
was *Stratford* (Smith 225).

The Borough of St Pancras

ST PANCRAS [*olim* pæŋkridʒ]

> (*ad*) *Sanctum Pancratiū* 1086 DB, *eccl. S. Pancratii* c. 1183
> BM, *ecclesia Sancti Pancracii* 1428 FA
>
> *Parochia S. Pancratii extra Lond'* 1291 Tax, 1294 *Ass, parochia
> Sancti Pancrassi* 1353 FA, *Pancras chirche* c. 1387 Works,
> *St Pancras in the Fields* 1531 FF, *St Pancrace* 1558 PCC
> *Pancrich* 1575 Saxton, *Pankeridge al. St Pancras* 1588 *Recov,
> Pancras* 1593 N, *Pankridge church* 1613 ParReg (Clerken-
> well), *Pankeridge* 1616 *FF, Pancrass* 1754 R

The old village and parish took their names from the church,
dedicated to St Pancras. *Pancratius* was a martyr in the time of
Diocletian. Cf. Pancrasweek (PN D 156).

BATTLEBRIDGE (now KINGS CROSS)

> *Bradeford* 1207 FF, *Bradforth* 1454 AD vi
>
> *Bradefordebrigge* c. 1387 Works, *Bradfordbrege* 1492 Williams,
> *Bradfordbrige in the parish of St Pancras* 1532 FF
>
> *Battyl brydge* 1559 Hust, *Battle Bridge al. Batford Bridge*
> 1625 Sess

Originally 'broad or wide ford' (over the Holborn), *v.* **brad,
ford**. The later name seems to be a mere corruption of the old
one through folk etymology. The name Battlebridge survived
as that of a district well into the 19th century and the place is
occasionally referred to by novelists of that period (cf. *Oliver
Twist*, ch. xlii). Later, however, the area came to be known as
Kings Cross, from a statue of George IV which stood from 1830
to 1845 at the cross-roads there, and the name was perpetuated
when the Great Northern Railway(now L. and N.E.) adopted it for
its terminus, built 1852 (W and C), Battlebridge surviving now
only in BATTLE BRIDGE RD, a small, out-of-the-way thoroughfare.

THE BRILL (lost) was the name of an earthwork now covered by the L.M.S. Railway, once part of Somers Town (*v. infra* 142) (Lysons iii, 343). It is *The Bruel* 1741–5 R, *the Bruil* 1788 Faden. Cf. *Brill Terrace* 1827 G. This is the word *bruil, broil*, a forest term denoting a park or wood stocked with beasts of the chase, cf. Broyle (PN Sx 70–1) and Brail (PN W 332).

CAMDEN TOWN is so named in 1795 (Lysons iii, 366) from Charles *Pratt*, Earl *Camden* of Camden Place, Kent, whose seat was Bayham Abbey, Sussex, d. 1794 (DNB). He married the daughter of Nicholas *Jeffreys* of Brecknock Priory, through whom he obtained possession of the manor of Kentish Town (*v. infra*), this part of which he began to let for building in 1791 (*v.* letter from Horace Walpole quoted in W and C). Hence BAYHAM ST and PLACE, JEFFREYS ST and PLACE and PRATT ST.

CANTELOWES[1] was a name of the former prebendal manor of *Cantlers* or *Cantlows* (*Cantelous* c. 1480 ECP, *Cantlers al. Kentyshetowne* 1535 VE, *Cantlers* 1686 M, *Cantlowes oth. Cantlers oth. Kentish Town* 1793 LCCDeeds). This probably takes its name from Roger de *Cantilupo*, a canon of St Paul's (1242–9 StPancSurv 26). Cf. *Cantlowbury* (PN Herts 159).

GOSPEL OAK. The oak is mentioned in 1761 (StPancSurv) and 1819 (G) but has since been cut down, the name remaining only as that of a district. It was on the Hampstead-St Pancras boundary. The name is not an uncommon one with reference to a place where a halt was made and the gospel read during the Rogation week ceremony of beating the bounds.

KENTISH TOWN

> *Kentisston* 1208 FF *et passim* to 1348 Ipm, with variant spellings *Kentis(s)h-* and *-tun(e)*, *-toun*, (*La*) 1257 FF, *Lakentistone* t. Hy 3 AD ii, *Le Kentesseton* 1278 *Ass*, *Kenteshton, La Kentishton* 1294 ib.
> *Kantistun* c. 1220 AD ii, *Cantisseton* c. 1235 ib., *Cantish Towne* 1650 HornseyCt
> *Kentisshtown* 1488 FF, *Cantlers al. Kentyshe Towne* 1535 VE

---

[1] Surviving in CANTELOWES RD.

This would seem to be 'Kentish farm' or 'farm held by someone nicknamed *le Kentiss(h)*,' *v.* tun, but the history of the name is unknown.

KEN WOOD is *Canewood, Canewoodlane, Canewoodfeldes* 1543, 1546 LP, *Cane Wood* 1558–79 ECP, *Caen Wood* 1640, 1642 *ParReg* (Hornsey), 1661, 1689 ib. (St Pancras), 1822 O.S., *Cane Wood* 1603–25 ib., 1686 M, 1750 Seale, *Ken Wood* 1741–5 R, 1779 Belv. KEN WOOD Ho is called *Caen Wood House* c. 1750 in Lady Mary Wortley Montagu's letters. Side by side with the wood we have also *Cane Feilde* c. 1539 *Harl* 3739 and *Canelond* 1540 *MinAcct* in J. H. Lloyd's paper reprinted in the *Hampstead Express*, 15th October 1921. The origin of the name is uncertain. It has been suggested that it derives from Reginald *Kentewode*, a dean of St Paul's, mentioned in 1434 (FF), but the 16th-century forms do not favour this. In later times the name is frequently spelled *Caen* Wood by association with the French place-name, this spelling persisting till the 19th century.

PARLIAMENT HILL. The origin of the name is entirely obscure. Lloyd (291) records a good many speculations with regard to it.

RUG MOOR (lost; a prebendal manor of St Paul's)

> *Rugemere* 1086 DB, 1206 Cur, 1291 Tax, *-mare* 1206 Abbr
> *Ruggemere* 1207 Cur, c. 1250 *StPauls*, 1361, 1373, 1374 Pat
> *Bouggemere* (sic) 1219 FF
> *Roggemere* 13th *StPauls*, *Rogemere* 1370 Londin
> *Rugmere* 1322, 1436 Pat, *-mer* 1535 VE, 1539 *Rental*
> *Reggemere* (sic) 1341 NI
> *Rug Moor Field* 1755 LMxAS vi

The first element of this and other place-names in *Rug-* has been taken by Ekwall (*Studies*[2] 88 ff.) to be an OE **hrucge*, 'woodcock.' The second element is *mere*, 'pool.' Rug Moor Field was in the extreme north-west corner of the parish adjoining Marylebone, just east of the present Zoological Gardens (LMxAS (N.S.) iv 65, HCMag iv).

SOMERS TOWN is *Sommers Town* 1795 Lysons, 1799 Horwood. Lysons speaks of Lord Somers's estate at the Brill (*supra* 141) and says that a part of Sommers Town, which was begun to be built about 1786, was built on the site of the Brill (Lysons iii, 343, 346, 366). It is *Somers Town* in 1819 (G). This seems to be the earliest place-name instance of the London use of *Town* to denote an urban unit regularly laid out, usually on a part of an estate hitherto not built over. Cf. the remark of Evelyn in his Diary (9th February, 1664–5) that Lord Southampton was building "a little Town" in Bloomsbury, to which, however, the name was not applied.

TOTTENHAM COURT[1]

  (*of*) *þottanheale* c. 1000 ASCharters, *Thottenhal* 1235 *Ass*, *Thote-* 1241 Cl, *Thotenhale* 1274 *Ass*
  (*in*) *berwika quod Tottenheale appellatur* 1042–66 (13th) *WDB* *Totenhala* 1083 (15th) *WDB*, *Totenhal(e)* 1184 StPaulsCh, 1202 FF *et freq* to 1341 NI, *-hall* 1349 Cl
  Totehele 1086 DB, *-hale* t. Ric 1 BM, *Tottehal* 1247 FF
  Totnalfeld 1411 AD ii, *Totnalcourt* 1411 Cl, 1422 *AD*, *Totenhalecourt* 1487 Williams, *Tottonhall Court* 1518–29 ECP, *Totenhall Courte* 1545 LP, *Tottenhall Courte* 1588 *Recov* *Totten Court* 1593 N, *Tottenham Court* 1741–5 R

Probably '*Totta*'s angle or corner of land,' *v.* healh. Cf. Tottenham *supra* 78 which evidently influenced the later development of the name. The forms with initial þ and *th* are a little disturbing, but no name *þotta* is known and it should be noted that for Tottenham itself we have at least one 13th-century form with initial *Th-*. *Court* is here used in the sense 'manor-house.'

ST PANCRAS STREET-NAMES

ALBANY ST follows roughly the line of *The Green Lane* 1746 R, perhaps identical with *le Greneweye* t. Hy 3 AD iv, *Grenestret* t. Ed 6 Sess. AMPTHILL SQUARE is so named from the seat in Bedfordshire of a branch of the Russell family. The Duke of Bedford had an estate in

---

[1] Preserved in TOTTENHAM COURT RD *supra* 120. Miss Jeffries Davis, in her monograph on Bloomsbury (LnTopRec xvii, 22 ff.), holds that the name *Totenhale* covered not only the manor attached to the prebendal stall of *Totenhale* in St Paul's, but also the 11th-century *berewic* of Westminster Abbey bearing the same name. The name of this *berewic* became extinct in the 13th century and the forms given above refer for the most part to the St Paul's manor.

this area till 1833 (LnTopRec xvii, 47), hence also the following, from places on his property elsewhere: in Bedfordshire, CARDINGTON ST, GOLDINGTON CRESCENT and ST, HOUGHTON PLACE, OAKLEY SQUARE; in Northamptonshire, HARRINGTON SQUARE and ST, and from a farm near Tavistock (*v. infra* 145) CROWNDALE RD (1863 LCCN). This was formerly *Fyggeslane juxta Pancraschirche* 1388 Works, *Fyggeslane* 1405 StPancSurv, *Fig Lane* 1741-5 R, 1848 Mogg, probably from a family name. Later it was *Gloucester Place*, cf. LCCN. BAYHAM ST, *v. supra* 141. CARTWRIGHT GARDENS (1908 LCCN) was formerly *Burton Crescent* 1831 Elmes, named after James *Burton* (hence BURTON ST) who built it on land formerly known as *the Sandhills* (1795 Map), left to the Skinners' Company by Sir Andrew *Judd*, Lord Mayor 1551-2, to maintain almshouses in London and a school at Tonbridge (Stow i, 113). Hence JUDD ST and TONBRIDGE ST, both so named in 1831 (Elmes). CHARLOTTE ST is so named in 1770 (Bowles) from the wife of George III. DARTMOUTH PARK is named from William Heneage, Earl of *Dartmouth*, a governor of Highgate School 1876-1900 (StPancSurv 143). ELM ST is *Elmn Street* 1746 R. ENDSLEIGH ST, *v.* Tavistock Square *infra* 145. EUSTON RD is a part of the long thoroughfare originally called *The New Road from Paddington to Islington*, laid out under an Act of 1756 (LnTopRec xvii, 67-9). It crossed an estate, formerly the demesne of the manor of Tottenham Court, then held by the second Duke of *Grafton*, whose seat was at Euston Hall, Suffolk, and who was descended from the Duchess of *Cleveland*, mistress of Charles II. This afterwards passed to his grandson, Charles *Fitzroy*, created Baron Southampton in 1780, who married a daughter of Sir Peter *Warren* (DNB). He began FITZROY SQUARE in 1793 (W and C), and after his death in 1797 his widow continued to develop the estate. Hence CLEVELAND ST, GRAFTON ST, WARREN ST (all so named in 1799 (Horwood)) and, later, EUSTON SQUARE, from which the station was named c. 1840. GOLDINGTON CRESCENT, *v.* Ampthill Square *supra* 143. GOODGE ST (mentioned in 1777 (W and C) and shown by Horwood (1799)), is named from William *Goodge* who owned the site in 1776 (LnTopRec xiv, 20 n.). GORDON SQUARE is so named in 1831 (Elmes) from the Duke of *Gordon*, father of the second wife of the sixth Duke of Bedford (LnTopRec xvii, 91). GOWER ST, begun c. 1780 (StGilesSurv) (northern parts formerly *Upper Gower St* 1799 Horwood, 1831 Elmes and *Gower St North* to 1864, beyond these *George St* 1810 Lockie, 1831 Elmes to 1937, LCCN and Supplt.) was named after the first Earl *Gower*, father of the second wife of the fourth Duke of Bedford (LnTopRec xvii, 77). The southern part, in Holborn, was laid out at the same time as Bedford Square (*v. supra* 117). GRAFTON ST, *v.* Euston Rd *supra*. HAMPSTEAD RD is *Road to Highgate* 1746 R. HARRINGTON SQUARE and HOUGHTON PLACE, *v.* Ampthill Square *supra* 143. HOWLAND ST, which intersects an area belonging to the Duke of Bedford, was so named before 1795 (Map) from the family of the wife of the second Duke, cf. PN Sr 29. JEFFREYS ST, *v. supra* 141. JUDD ST, *v.* Cartwright Gardens *supra*. KINGS CROSS RD (1863 LCCN), *v. supra* 140. The part along the Fleet valley is called *Black Mary's Hole* in 1732 (PC) and 1746 (R), and later *Bagnigge Wells Road* (W and C). MILLFIELDS LANE. Cf. *Myllefeyldes, -feldes* 1535 StPancSurv. OAKLEY SQUARE, *v.* Ampthill Square *supra* 143–4. OSSULSTON ST is so named in 1799 (Horwood), when the southern part was *Willsted St.* The reason for the name is uncertain; it was not the site of the Hundred meeting-place (*v. supra* 81). PARK ST was earlier *Slipshoe Lane* 1716 StPancSurv. PRATT ST, *v. supra* 141. STORE ST is *Great Store Street* 1770 Bowles. SWAIN'S LANE is *Swayneslane* 1492 StPancSurv, *Swayns lane* 1609 ib., *Swines lane* 1631 ib. TAVISTOCK SQUARE (laid out before 1803 (LnTopRec xvii, 85)). The Duke of Bedford owns the manor of Tavistock (Devon). So also ENDSLEIGH ST and TAVITON ST from places on his property there (cf. PN D 217, 222). TONBRIDGE ST, *v.* Cartwright Gardens *supra* 144. TORRINGTON PLACE and SQUARE take their names from Viscount *Torrington*, father of the first wife of the sixth Duke of Bedford (LnTopRec xvii, 90). TOTTENHAM COURT RD. See under Holborn street-names. WARREN ST, *v.* Euston Rd *supra* 144. WATERLOW PARK was named in 1889 when Sir Sidney *Waterlow*, Lord Mayor in 1872, presented this part of his estate to the London County Council for the use of the public (StPancSurv i, 9).

The Borough of Shoreditch

SHOREDITCH

Soredich c. 1148, c. 1160 ShoreSurv[1], *Schoredich* 1236 FF, 1291 Tax

Soresdic 1183 StPaulsCh, *-dich* 1242 Fees, 1248 FF, 1250 HMC iv, 1346 Cl, *-dych* 1275 RH, *S(c)horesdich(e)* 1214 Cur (p), 1221, 1238 FF, 1274, 1294 *Ass*, 1288 *AD*, *Syoresdich* 1252 FF, *Schoresdig(h)* 1274 *Ass*, *Shorisdich* 1300 Mayors

Sordige t. John StPaulsMSS, *Sordich* 1357 FF, *Sordissh* 1491 PCC

Shordige 1274 *Ass*, *Shordyk* 1323 Londin, *-dich* 1457 FF, *Shoredich al. Shoredick* 1650 Madge

Sorsdich 1255 StPaulsMSS

Sewersditch 1598 Stow

Chardesse 1704 ParRegFr

As the City of London lay between this place and the Thames, Ekwall's interpretation (DEPN) "ditch leading to the shore (of the Thames)" cannot be accepted. The persistent genitival *s* in

---

[1] Quoted from Ancient Deeds A 13848 (PRO).

most of the ME forms suggests comparison rather with Shores-worth (PN NbDu 179), but the interpretation of that name is exceedingly doubtful.

HAGGERSTON

Hergotestane 1086 DB

Hergotestune c. 1220 *Add*, -*ston* 1274 *Ass*, Cl

Heregodeston 1221–30 Fees, *Hergodeston* 1274 *Ass*

Haregodeston 1242 Fees, *Hargodestone* 1250 StPaulsMSS, 1303 FF, *Hargarston* 1593 ShoreSurv

Argeston c. 1470 ECP, (*al. Hurleston*) 1566 LnIpm, *Argarston* 1549 FF, *Hargolston* 1553 ib.

Agerston 1561 FF, *Hagerstone* 1798 Stockdale

Haggiston 1680 S, *Agoston* 1797 Stockdale

'At the stone of *Hærgod*,' *v.* stan, if the DB form is genuine. If not, the second element is tun, 'farm.'

HOLYWELL PRIORY

fons qui dicitur Haliwelle c. 1100 (1337) Dugd iv, *Haliwell(e)* 1179 P, late 12th BM *et freq* to 1388 Pap, *Halewell* 1274 *Ass*, 1295 LBk, 1314 Ipm, *Halywell al. Vynesbury* 1393 Pat, *Halywell* 1426 EEW, 1428 FA, *Hallywell near London* 1568 FF, *Holywell* 1510 PCC, *Holliwell* 1576 ib.

'Holy well or spring,' *v.* halig, wielle. The name is preserved in Holywell Lane *infra* 148.

HOXTON

Hochestone 1086 DB, *Hockeston* 1545 FF, *Hockesdon* 1593 N

Hocston 1221 FF, *Hoxton(e)* c. 1250 *StPauls*, 1291 Tax, 1322 Pat, 1362 Londin *et passim*

Hogeston 1370 FF, 1371 Cl, *Hogeston al. Hocston* 1504 Pat, *Hogesdon* 1528 FF, *Hogesdon al. Hoxton* 1625 PCC

Hoggeston 1352 Cl, 1443 FF, 1500 ECP, *Hoggesdon* 1501 ChancP, *Hoggeston al. Hoggesdon* 1553 FF

Hoggston 1503 ECP, *Hogston, Hogsdon* 1546 LnIpm, *Hogsden* 1593 N

Hodgson 1610 Ben Jonson, *Alchemist*

Haxton 1745 R

'*Hōc*'s farm,' or possibly *Hogg*'s, *v.* tun. Hoggeston (PN Bk 67) is certainly a compound of *Hogg* and shows a DB form *Hochestone*.

NORTON FOLGATE[1] is *Terra Nortune* t. Hy 1 StPaulsCh, *Norton-folyot* 1433 FF, *Norton Folyet* 1456 Pat, *Nortonfoly* 1458 FF, *Norton Folyot* 1478 ib., *Norton Folgate* 1556 ib., (*otherwise Norton Folyott*) 1568 ib., *Norton Fallgate* 1697 ParReg (Stepney), and may have been the home of Robert de *Norton* (1324 FF). 'North farm,' *v.* tun. It was just north of the City boundary. This was anciently a manor of St Paul's, so *Foliot* may be from Richard *Foliot*, a canon of St Paul's in 1241 (StPaulsMSS). Cf. Brondesbury and Mapesbury *infra* 161, 162. Final *yot*, *yet* was confused with dial. *yet*, 'gate,' and later replaced by StEng *gate*.

WENLOCKS BARN[2]

> *Wenlakesbir'* c. 1250 *StPauls*
> *Wenlokesbern*, -*bur'*, -*beri*, *Wellokesberne*, *Welkesberne* 1274 Ass, -*beri* 1291 Tax, *Wenlokes Barne* 1535 VE, *Wenlockes Barne* 1557 FF, *Wenlocke Barn* 1817 Wilkinson
> *Wallokesbern*(*e*) 1294 *Ass*, 1318 Pat, 1341 NI, *Wal*(*l*)*okes Berne* 1337 Cl, 1558 Sess, *Wainelocks Barn* 1592 Moulton

The earliest forms show confusion between burh (manorial) and bern. The former was perhaps the original second element. A Robert de *Weneloc* is witness to a charter of St Paul's (13th StPaulsMSS). He is probably to be associated with this place. His family must have come from Wenlock (Sa).

SHOREDITCH STREET-NAMES

BOWLING GREEN WALK. The Bowling Green is marked in 1746 (R). BRITANNIA ST is named from the old theatre near-by. Cf. *The Britania Gardens* 1794 ShoreSurv. CHARLES SQUARE is so named in 1685, probably after Charles II (ShoreSurv 75 n., 151). Part of the neighbouring CORONET ST was formerly *Queen Street* ib. CURTAIN RD is *The Curtain Road* 1682 Morgan, 1677 O and M, *The Curtain* ib., from the old Curtain

---

[1] Surviving as a street-name. Most of the Liberty is now in Stepney.

[2] A lost prebendal manor of St Paul's. The name is preserved in WENLOCK RD and ST.

Theatre (*The Curtayne playhouse* 1603 SP). Earlier references to the site include *close called the Curteyn* 1544 ShoreSurv, *house called the Curtayne* 1586 ib. The origin of the name is obscure. Part of GREAT EASTERN ST was *Willow Walk* 1745 ib. HABERDASHER ST crosses the site of *Haberdashers Hospital* 1746 R. HACKNEY RD is *the common waie leadynge towards Hackney* 1585 ShoreSurv. HAGGERSTON RD is *Hargarston lane* 1593 ib., *v. supra* 146. HOLYWELL LANE is *Haliwellelane* 1382 Cor, *v. supra* 146. The earlier *Haliwellestret*, etc. is Shoreditch High St (*infra*). HOXTON SQUARE is so named in 1732 (PC). HOXTON ST is *Hoxton strete* 1467 AD vi, *Hoxdon way* 1545 LP. HYDE RD was *Hyde Lane* 1558 ShoreSurv. Cf. *la Hide inter Hakeneye et London* 1294 *Ass*. KINGSLAND RD is part of Ermine St *supra* 8. It is *The North Road* 1682 Morgan, *Kingsland Road* 1720 ShoreSurv, leading to Kingsland *supra* 106. MILL ROW. Cf. *Mill Feild* 1627 ib. MYRTLE ST is so named in 1794 ib. NEW INN RD. Cf. *New Inn Yard* 1682 Morgan, 1746 R. NICHOLS ST. Cf. *Saynt Nicholas Felde* 1545 LP, *Nichollfeld* 1550 FF. NUTTALL ST (1878 LCCN) was *Dirty Lane* 1745 ShoreSurv, earlier *Webbes lane al. White Hart lane* 1589 ib. John *Webb* was living in the parish t. Charles 1 (Ellis 268). PIMLICO WALK. Cf. *Pimlyco* 1609 ShoreSurv, *Pimlico Gardens* 1799 Horwood, *v.* Pimlico in Westminster *infra* 171. PITFIELD ST is *Petfield Street* 1720 Strype, 1746 R, *Pitfield Street* 1732 PC and is so named from *Pyttefeld* 1556 Tomlins, *field called Pitfield* 1625 ShoreSurv. SHOREDITCH HIGH ST is *Shoredyche strete* 1550 FF. Earlier known as *Haliwellestrete* 1294 *Ass*, 1313 FF, *Holywelle streete* 1601 Ellis. *v.* Holywell Priory *supra* 146. UNION ST is on the site of *Copt Hall Yard* 1676 ShoreSurv. Cf. also *Copt Hall, close called Copt Hall* 1502 ib., taking their name from some house or hall with a peaked roof here. Cf. Copthall *supra* 36. WHITMORE RD (so named from Sir George *Whitmore*, owner of the estate in the 17th century) was earlier *Bammes lane* leading to *Balmes* in Hackney *supra* 106. WORSHIP ST is so named from John *Worsop*, merchant tailor, who held land beside it in the 16th century (1567 Surv). It is *Hog(g) Lane* 1660 Porter, 1677 O and M. After 1732 part of it became *Worship St* (1745 ShoreSurv).

Lost names include *Land of Promise, Small Beer Alley* 1732 PC.

The Borough of Stepney

NOTE. The Metropolitan Borough[1] has three components: (*a*) The greater part of the medieval parish of Stepney. This included the hamlets which later became the separate parishes of Shadwell (1669),

---

[1] The Domesday vill of Stepney seems to have included Hackney, and the border areas were once, probably before they became exempt from the jurisdiction of the City, in the Portsoken, a ward without, except the western part of the Tower and most of Tower Hill which were originally within the Wall of the City itself. See further Madge, *Early Records of Hornsey* 31–45.

St George-in-the-East, formerly the hamlet of Wapping (1727), Christ Church Spitalfields (1729), St Anne Limehouse, with part of the hamlet of Ratcliff (1730), and also those of Bethnal Green and Poplar, and the chapelry of Bow, now in other boroughs; while what remained was divided into the civil parishes of Mile End Old Town (in which the church was situated and which kept the rest of Ratcliff). (b) White-chapel, separated from Stepney in the 14th century, and its daughter parish, St John's Wapping. (c) Some areas bordering on the City, including the Tower, with Tower Hill, the little remaining of the precinct of St Katharine's, the Liberty of East Smithfield and the civil parish of Holy Trinity Minories[1].

STEPNEY

(of) *Stybbanhyþe* c. 1000 ASCharters

Stibenhed(e) 1086 DB, *-heth(e)* 1274, 1294 *Ass*, 1275 Pat, *Stybeney* 1232 Bracton, *Stibenhythe* 1294 *Ass*, *Stybenhithe* 1337 Ipm

Stebbenheda early 12th StPaulsMSS, *Stebenee* 1198 FF, *Stebehee* 1199, 1218 ib., *Steben(h)eth(e)* 1242 Fees, 1274 *Ass*, 1291 Tax, 1353 FA, *-heithe* 1274 *Ass*, *-eyth* 1358 FF, *-hithe* 1291 Ch, 1288, 1315 AD i, 1349 Orig, *-huth(e)* 1294 *Ass*, 1316 FA, 1319 AD i

Stubbehid(a) 1172, 1174 P, *-huda* 1177 ib., *Stubbenheth(e)* 1289 AD ii, 1362 Orig

Stubehed(a) 1173 P, *-heða* 1175 ib., *Stubenhee* 1199 Cur, *-heth(e)* 1268 Pat, 1294 *Ass*, *-huth* ib.

Stibbehed(e) 1178 P, 1219 FF, *-heye* 1222, 1224 Bracton, *Stibbenhith* 1243 Cl, *-hethe* 1299 LBk

Stebbehey 1230 Bracton, *-huth* 1235 *Ass*, *Stebbenheth* 1291 Tax, *Stebbunhuth* 1323 AD i, *Stebunheth* 1535 VE, (al. *Stepneie*) 1591 PCC

Stibbeneie al. Stebenuthe 1274 Ipm, *Stebbintheth* (sic) 1277 FF, *Stybenhithe* 1300 LBk

Stepenhithe 1370 FF, *-heth* 1399 Pat, 1452 FF, *Stepynhithe* 1400 Pat, *Stepneth(e)* 1429 ChronStAlb, *Steppeneygh* 1499 FF, *Stepneyhyth* 1516 ib.

Stebenheth al. Stepney 1466 IpmR, *Stepneth* 1491 Pat, 1543 FF, 1552 PCC, *Stebnheth al. Stepney* 1542 FF

Stevenhyth 1525 FF

[1] Now ecclesiastically in the parish of St Botolph Aldgate, to which East Smithfield has always belonged.

'*Stybba*'s landing place,' *v.* hyð. For the personal name cf. Stebbing (PN Ess 457) and *to stybban snade* BCS 1054 (Bishopstoke, Ha). For the phonetic development cf. Chelsea *supra* 85.

STEPNEY GREEN was the home of John *atte Grene* (1367 FF). It is so named in 1682 (Morgan).

KNOCKFERGUS (lost) is *Knockfergus* 1597 *et freq* ParReg, 1613 Sess, *-vergus* 1613, 1661 ParReg, *-verges* 1624 ib., *Cable Street heretofor called Knockfergus* 1695 Sess, *Knock Fergus* 1793 Cary. This name appears first in the ParReg in 1597 and then frequently to the end of the 17th century. A possibility is that this is a transferred name, brought by some Elizabethan soldier from Ireland. It would seem to have been applied to a hamlet or settlement on the lines of the present Cable St *infra* 155. The Irish place-name means '*Fergus*'s hillock.'

LIMEHOUSE

> *le Lymhostes* 1367 *Cor*, 1370 Works, (*les*) 1380 AD i, *le Lymhostes juxta le Redeclyf* 1382 *Cor*, *Les Lymehostes near London* 1387 Pat
> *le Lymost by Stebynheth* 1421 Pat, *Lymost* 1496 FF, 1504 PCC
> *Lymehurst(e)* 1535 VE, (*al. Lymehoste*) 1547 LP
> *Lymehouse* 1547 FF, *Lymouses* 1550 Pat, *Limehouse Buttes* 1566 Sess

'Lime oasts or kilns.' The second element is OE *āst*, 'oast, kiln.' In 1380 (AD i, C. 364) Peter atte Hacche, *limeburner*, was granted a cottage and garden here. LIMEHOUSE REACH (a stretch of the river here) is *Limehouse Reache* 1588 Walford.

MILE END

> *La Mile ende* 1288 Ipm, *Milehende* 1298 Mayors, *le Milende* 1307 GDR, *la Milende* 1383 Pat, *Milhende* 1412 AD vi, *Mylle end gren* 1554 Machyn, *Mileindgrene* 1605 ParReg
> *Mylesende* 1395 Works, *Mileshende in the parish of Stebenheth* 1404 Pat, *Le Milesinde* 1405 ib., *the Miles ende* 1603 Stow

Self-explanatory. The hamlet was so named because of its position on the old London-Colchester road at a distance of about one mile from Aldgate. *v.* Addenda xxxiv.

PRUSON[1] ISLAND (lost) is *Sprusons Iland* 1628, 1629 ParReg, *Prusens Iland* 1635 ib. *et freq*, *Sprusonds Iland* 1647 ib., *Sprusande Iland* 1649 ib., *Sprusens Island* 1654, 1656 PCC, *Sprusands Island* 1671 ParReg, *Pruson Island* 1698 ib. This seems to have been the name of a small island or elevated tract of land in Wapping Marsh. The history of the name is obscure but it may possibly be associated with the family of Frances *Prusands* (1667 ParReg). For the addition of inorganic *s* cf. the note on Scrattage *supra* 25.

RATCLIFF

> *la Rede clive* 1294 GDR, *la Redeclyve juxta Stubenheth* 1307 ib., *la Redeclyf* 1380, 1438 Pat
> *Radeclyve* 1305 Pat, *Radclif, -clyf* 1422, 1430 FF (p), *-clyffe* 1550 Pat, *la Radeclyff* 1502 ib.
> *Redclyve* 1363 Pat, *Redclyf'* p. 1394 Works, (*in the parish of Stebunhith*) 1414 Hust
> *le Reedclyff* 1442 Pat
> *Ratclyff(e)* 1524 LP, 1562 FF, *Ra(c)klif* 1555, 1592 PCC, *Ratlif* 1596 ParReg

'Red slope,' *v.* clif. The name must have been given to the slight rise up from the Thames bank to the level ground above. The reason for the epithet *red* is not clear.

SHADWELL

> *S(c)hadewell(e)* 1222 Bracton, 1223 FF, 1235, 1294 *Ass*, 1314 Pat
> *Scaldewell* 1314 Cl (p), *Shaldewell* 1316 Ch

Probably 'shallow well or spring,' *v.* sceald, wielle. Cf. Scaldwell (PN Nth 131). Cf. *Schadfliet(e)* 1204 P, *Schadflet* 1218 AD ii, which was also in Stepney parish but the exact site is unknown. *v.* fleot.

SPITALFIELDS (*olim* LOLSWORTH)

> *Field called Lollesworthe in the parish of Stepney* 1278 StPaulsMSS, *Lollesworth* 1540 LP
> *Spittellond* 1399 StPaulsMSS

[1] Surviving in PRUSOM ST *infra* 157.

The Spitel Fyeld t. Eliz Agas, *Spyttlefeildes* 1561 Sess,
   Spittell Feild 1588 ib., *Spitrefils* 1708 ParRegFr
*Spittle Heape otherwise Lollisworth, Spittle Fields al. Lolsworth
   Fields in the parish of Stebunheath* t. Eliz ChancP, *Spittle
   Hope* c. 1650 ib.

These were originally fields belonging to the priory of St Mary
Spital founded in 1197 (Dugdale vi, 623). Cf. *Seintmariespitel
in Shordich* 1394 *Cor, Seyntmaryspithill* 1429 PCC, *St Mary
Spetyll* 1474 ib., the actual site of the house being in Shoreditch
parish. The older alternative name appears to mean '*Lull*'s
enclosure,' *v.* **worþ**. Cf. Lulsley (PN Wo 59). See also **hop**,
'(marsh) enclosure.'

WAPPING

molendina de Wapping' 1218–26 StPaulsCh, *mill called Wap-
   ping in Stebbehey* 1231 FF, *Wappyng* 1436 Pat
Wappinges 1231 Bracton, 1272 Pat
Wappingge atte Wose 1345 AD ii, *-yngge* 1346 ib., 1372 *Cor,
   Wapping in the Woose* 1504–15 ECP, (*Woze*) 1598 Stow
Wallemarshe al. Wapping Marshe 1562 Sess
Woppin 1650 Sess

No certainty is possible with regard to this name. Probabilities are that we have to do with a personal name *Wæppa*,
noted already under *Wappingthorne* (PN Sx 237), Wappenham
(PN Nth 62) and Wappenbury (PN Wa 148). Such a name
might readily be used as a pet form for *Wǣrbeald, Wǣrbeorht*
or *Wǣrburh*. If that is the case the name denotes '*Wæppa*'s
people.' The early loss of final *-es* would not be surprising (cf.
the forms for Ealing, Yeading (*supra* 90, 40).

Professor Ekwall (PN in *-ing* 52 and DEPN *s.n.*) would prefer
to take the word as a singular *ing*-derivative of a lost OE word
related to OE *wapol*, 'froth,' OFris *wapel, wepel*, 'pool, mire,'
but there is not much evidence for such a word. It has been
suggested that it lies behind Wapley (Gl), DB *Wapelie*, but as
this lies near the top of a hill some 400 ft. up, topographical
reasons do not make such a derivative very likely. The additional
atte Wose is from OE *wāse*, 'mud, ooze' (cf. Ouse, PN Sx 6, PN
Nth xlvi), and it has been suggested that 'mire at mud' would go
well together. It might, however, be also regarded as pleonastic.

WHITECHAPEL

> *St Mary de Mattefelon* 1282 Hust, *Church of St Mary Matre-*
> *felun* ib., *St Mary Matefelun* 1320 StPaulsMSS, 1323 Cl,
> (*Maderfelon*) 1352 FF, *parish of the Blessed Mary Matfelon*
> *of White Chapell* 1452 ib., *parish of St Mary Matefelon*
> *al. Whitechappel* 1566 Sess
> *New Chapel without Aldgate* 1295 Misc
> *Whitechapele by Algate* 1340 Pat, *la White Chapel* 1344 Pleas,
> *Whitechapele* 1348 FF, *-elle* 1359 ib., (*in Algatestrete*) 1363 ib.
> (*apud*) *Albam Capellam extra Algate* 1342 *Ass*
> *la Whitechapele without Algate* 1370 AD ii
> *Witschaepel* 1550 Aliens, *Woitechapel* 1708 ParRegFr

Originally a 13th-century chapel of ease of Stepney, the
name may, like the numerous Whitchurch names, have had
reference to the colour of the stone, or perhaps, as suggested in
PN D *s.n.* Whitchurch, may actually have referred to a stone
building at a time when most small churches were still built of
wood. The additional *Matefelun* is probably a man's name added
to distinguish this church from other London churches dedicated to St Mary such as St Mary Abchurch, St Mary Woolnoth
containing similar additions. The name would probably be that
of a founder or prominent benefactor. The French surname
Matefelun, 'kill-felon,' is found as the name of a wine-merchant
(Richard *Matefelun*) in 1230 (P); he had business in Middlesex,
Norfolk and Lincolnshire.

The Minories

THE MINORIES [minəriz]. This parish takes its name from the
Abbey of St Mary of the Minoresses of the Order of St Clare,
founded here in 1293 (Tomlinson ii). Cf. *The Minoresses without*
Alegate 1341 Hust, *The Minoress Sisters* 1342 ib., *The Minoresses*
of St Clare without Aldgate 1368 ib., *house called le Menoresse*
1412 ib., *le Myneris* 1548 Tomlinson, *le Mynery House, the late*
monastery called le Mynoresse 1553 Pat, *The Mineris* 1571 Aliens.
The inmates were popularly known as 'The Poor Sisters of
St Clare,' whence the name (Latin *Sorores minores*). After the
Dissolution the Abbey house was granted to the Bishop of Bath

and Wells in exchange for his residence near Temple Bar and became known as *Bathe Place*. Bishop Barlow in 1548 agreed to the recession to the Crown of the messuage called *Bathe Place*, formerly called *le myneryes* and ultimately the whole property formerly included within the precincts of the monastery passed in the time of Queen Elizabeth into the possession of the Crown (Tomlinson 80–6, 109–19). Much of the site was used for the purposes of the Ordnance Department (cf. Artillery Lane and Haydon St *infra* 155–6). About the same time we first hear of the parish of "the church of the Minories" (ib. 161), corresponding to the old precincts. The street-name known as MINORIES is called *Minorie street* in 1624 (Aliens). Most of it is within the City of London.

The Liberty of East Smithfield

EAST SMITHFIELD is *Estsmethefeld juxta Turrim* 1229 Cl, *Est Smythefeld* 1272 FF, *Est Smethefeld* 1274 *Ass*, 1275 RH, *-feud* 1297 Ipm. 'Smooth open space,' *v.* smeðe, feld. *East* in distinction from *West* Smithfield on the other side of the City.

The Liberty of the Tower

The Liberty of the Tower takes its name from *His Majesty's Tower*, commonly known as *The Tower*, the name given to the entire fortress surrounding the original *White Tower* of William Rufus. The earliest use of the name in its native form is found in ASC (E) *s.a.* 1097, where we hear of the wall which was being built round þone tur, while in the same document (*s.a.* 1101) we read of Ranulf Flambard escaping from þam ture. The name of the nucleus of the fortress has clearly been transferred to the whole fortress or stronghold. For the term *liberty* used of a district with certain special privileges cf. *Ye Liberty of ye Tower of London which Liberty is also called ye Royalty of ye Tower and ye Manor of ye Tower* (Tomlinson 184).

TOWER HILL is *Tourhulle* 1343 AD ii, *le Tourhill* 1348 Hust, *la Tourhulle* 1399 Cor, *Toerhil'* 1550 Aliens, from the Tower of London *supra*.

STEPNEY STREET-NAMES

ADLER ST (1913 LCCN) was *Union St* 1799 Horwood. It was re-named after Dr Adler, the Chief Rabbi, d. 1912. ALIE ST is *Ayloffe Street* 1617 Allgood, 1691, 1702 Sess, *Ayliff Street* 1746 R, of unknown origin. ARTICHOKE HILL is *Artichoak Hill* ib. and takes its name from an inn. ARTILLERY LANE is *Artyllerye lane* 1600 Aliens and takes its name from *Artillerieyeard* 1603 Stow, *Artillery Ground* 1682 Morgan, otherwise *The Kings Tower Ground*, "whereunto the Gunners of the Tower doe weekely repaire" (Stow i, 166). Earlier *Tasell close* (1603 Stow) from "*the Tasels* (i.e. teasles) planted for the use of Clothworkers" (ib.). BACK CHURCH LANE is *Church Lane* 1682 Morgan. This lane and Church Lane *infra* were one before the construction of Commercial Rd. BELL LANE is so named in 1677 (O and M), probably from an inn sign. BEN JONSON RD (1872 LCCN) was *Cow Lane* 1799 Horwood, 1855 Map, leading to *Worlds End* 1746 R, which was then at the end of the built-up area. BETTS ST is *Bettstreet* 1696 ParReg from the family of Thomas *Bett* (1620 ib.). BLACK EAGLE ST is so named in 1698 (Sess). It is *Blacaigle street* 1717 ParRegFr, probably from an inn sign. BLOSSOM ST is so named in 1746 (R). BOSTOCK ST is *Bostwick Street* ib. from the family of Thomas *Bostock* (1613 ParReg), John *Bostweeke* (1639 ib.). BOW COMMON LANE was earlier *Pesthouse Lane* 1703 Gascoyne, 1720 Strype. It is partly within Poplar borough. BREEZER'S HILL is *Breze Hill* 1746 R. BREWHOUSE LANE is so named ib. BRICK LANE is (*The*) *Brick Lane* 1542 Robin-sonH, 1619 ParReg, *Brickkill lane* 1622 ib., i.e. brickkiln lane. Cf. *place called the Brickhills* 1588 Sess and Brickhill St Fm (PN Wa 43). BROAD BRIDGE is so named in 1746 (R). BROAD ST is so named in 1696 (ParReg). BROOK ST is *Brokstrete* 1405 StPauls, *Brokestrate* 1409 AD i, *-strete* 1453 Pat. BURDETT RD (1862 LCCN) is so named from Baroness *Burdett*-Coutts, donor of the Colombia Market (W and C). BURR ST is so named in 1746 (R). Robert *Burre* was living in the parish in 1605 (ParReg). BUTCHER ROW is so named in 1703 (Gascoyne). BUX-TON ST (1883 LCCN) takes its name from Truman, Hanbury, *Buxton* and Co., Brewers (cf. Hanbury St *infra* 156). It was earlier *Spicers street* 1697 ParReg, *Spicer Street* 1746 R, perhaps from the family of *Spicer*, found in the ParReg from 1582. CABLE ST is so called in 1703 (Gas-coyne). See *Knockfergus supra* 150. Mary *Cable* was living in the parish in 1629 (ParReg). In 1703 (Gascoyne) the east part is marked *Swan Street*, probably from an inn. Another name for the street was *Bluegate Street* 1692 Sess. Cf. also *Blewgatefeild* 1663 ParReg. CANNON ST is *Cannon street* 1697 ib., *la rue du Canon* 1701 Aliens. OLD CASTLE ST is *Castle Street* 1682 Morgan, 1697 ParReg. CHIGWELL HILL is so named in 1746 (R). Henry Bayley of *Chigwell* (Essex) was married in the parish in 1648 (ParReg). CHURCH LANE is so named in 1636 ib., from White-chapel Church. CINNAMON ST is so named in 1694 (Sess), perhaps from the sale of that spice here. CLEVELAND ST (1865 LCCN, now CLEVELAND WAY) was earlier *Red Cow Lane* 1746 R, 1808 Cary. The

present name commemorates the Earl of *Cleveland*, lord of the manor
t. Chas 1. CODE ST was earlier *George Street* 1682 Morgan, 1746 R. COL-
CHESTER ST is so named in 1746 (R). COMMERCIAL RD is *New Commercial
Road* 1808 Cary. It traverses part of the former *Sermon Lane* 1703 Gas-
coyne, 1746 R. COMMERCIAL ST is a new street, following part of the
course of the original Grey Eagle St *infra*. COUTTS RD. Cf. Burdett Rd
supra 155. CRISPIN ST is *C(h)rispin Street* 1677 O and M, 1682 Morgan,
(*Crispian*) 1696 ParReg, from the family of Adam *Crispin* (1629 ib.).
DENMARK ST is so named in 1698 (Sess), probably commemorating
Prince George of Denmark, husband of Queen Anne. DOCK ST (1876
LCCN) was *Salt Peter Bank* 1708 Hatton, *Salt Petre Bank* 1746 R.
DORSET ST is *Dorcetstreet* 1697 ParReg, *Darsé Street* 1708 ParRegFr.
The family of *Dorset* appears in the ParReg from 1634. ELBOW LANE
is so named in 1682 Morgan from its shape at that date. ELDER ST
is so named ib. FASHION ST is *Fashion Street* 1676 ParReg, 1682
Morgan, *Fash(i)ons street* 1697 ParReg, of unknown origin. FIELDGATE
ST is *Whitechapel Field Gate* 1746 R. Cf. *Whyte Chappell Feldes* 1551
Sess. FLEUR-DE-LIS ST is *Flower de Luce Alley* 1685 ParReg, *Flowerdelis
Street* and *Alley* 1746 R. FLOWER AND DEAN ST is *Dean and Flower
Street* 1677 O and M, 1682 Morgan, *Dean and Flowers Street* 1697
ParReg, *Deane and Floers Street* 1698 ib., *Flower and Deane street* 1700
ib., *Floordin Street* 1702 Aliens. Perhaps from the families of *De(a)n(e)*
and John *Flower* 1578, 1617 *et freq* ParReg. FOLGATE ST is *White Lyon
Yard* 1746 R. FORT ST is so named ib. Cf. *King Davids Fort* 1697
ParReg. Possibly from one of the forts erected during the Civil War,
cf. Mount St *infra* 157. FOURNIER ST (1893 LCCN) was *Church Street*
1746 R. FOX LANE (now GLAMIS ST) is *Foxes lane* 1636 *et freq* ParReg,
Fox Lane 1682 Morgan, from the family of Thomas *Fox* (1573 ParReg).
GLASSHOUSE FIELDS. Cf. *The Glas House* 1594 Aliens, *Glashousefeilds*
1698 ParReg and Glasshouse Yard *supra* 97. GOODMAN'S FIELDS and
YARD. Cf. *Goodmans Yard* 1656 PCC, *Goodmans Fields* 1682 Morgan.
Stow (i, 126) speaks of a farm adjoining the Abbey of the Minoresses of
which one *Goodman* was the farmer. Doubtless his family gave name
to the Fields and Yard. Cf. John *Goodman* (1604 ParReg). OLD (now
WAPPING LANE) and NEW GRAVEL LANE are *Gravell lane* 1619 ib., (*Old*)
1625 ib., (*New*) 1628 ib. GREEN BANK is *The Greenebanke* 1641 ib.
GREY EAGLE ST was so named in 1697 (ib.) and 1746 (R). It is *Gre Aygle
Stret* 1705 ParRegFr. Cf. Black Eagle St *supra* 155. GROVE ST is
le Grove strete 1376 AD ii. GUN ST is *Gun Lane* 1703 Gascoyne.
HANBURY ST. *v*. Buxton St *supra* 155. The old name was *Brounes Lane*
1697 ParReg, from the family of Ralph *Browne* (1568 ib.). HARRIS
TERRACE is *Harris's Court* 1746 R. HAYDON ST and SQUARE take their
name from Sir William *Heydon*, Master of the Ordnance in the 17th
century, when the Ordnance Department was in the Minories. GREAT
HERMITAGE ST is so named in 1746 (R), from a former house
Hermitage 1592 PCC, *Armitage* 1642 ParReg, 1682 Morgan. Cf. "The
Hermitage, so called of a Hermite sometime being there" (1598 Stow ii,
72). *v*. Addenda xxxiv. HIGH ST, SHADWELL is *Upper Shadwell* 1682

Morgan. HUNTON ST is *Hunt Street* 1703 Gascoyne, 1720 Strype, probably from the family of *Hunt(e)* found in the ParReg from 1585. KING DAVID LANE is *King David's Lane* 1746 R. LAMB ST is *Lam Street* 1697 ParReg, (*Lamb*) 1746 R. LAMBETH ST is *Lambert Street* 1702 Sess, 1746 R, from the family of *Lambert* found in the ParReg from 1576. Cf. Lambeth Hill in the City, of similar origin. LEMAN ST is *Lemmon Street* 1692 Sess, (*Leman*) 1694 ib., (*Lemon*) 1746 R, from the family of John *Lemman* (1627 ParReg). LIMEHOUSE CAUSEWAY is *Limehouse Casey* 1680 ib. LOVE LANE was *Cutthroat Lane* 1746 R. LOWDEN ST is named from the family of Jane *Loweden* (1676 ParReg). MANSELL ST is so named in 1702 (Sess), from the family of Edward *Mansell* (1585 ParReg). MARKET ST is *Shadwell Market* 1746 R. MEDLAND ST (1866 LCCN) was *Queen Street* 1703 Gascoyne, 1746 R. MILE END RD is referred to as *Oldestrete* 1383 Works, *v. supra* 150. MILK YARD is *Milke Yard* 1658 PCC. OLD MONTAGUE ST is *Monntague Street* 1698 Sess, *Montegue Strit* 1704 Aliens. MOUNT ST (now MOUNT TERRACE) is to be associated with *place called the Mount* 1691 Sess, one of the Parliamentary forts of 1643 which lay to the west of the present London Hospital. In the original resolution of the Court of Common Council it is described as "a hornworke with two flankers at Whitechapel windmills." For the site *v.* LnTopRec xiv, 6, 27–8. NARROW ST is so named in 1746 (R). NIGHTINGALE LANE (now THOMAS MORE ST) is *Nightingale Lane* 1543 LP, 1658 PCC, *Nechtingal leane* 1624 Aliens. NORTHEY ST (1876 LCCN) was *The Rope Walk* 1746 R. OCEAN ST is so named in 1682 (Morgan). PEARL ST is *Pearle Street* 1676 ParReg, of obscure origin. PELHAM ST (now WOODSEER ST) is *Pellam Street* 1697 ParReg, *Pelemme Street* 1705 ParRegFr, from the family of *Pelham*, first found in the ParReg in 1643. PENANG ST (1912 LCCN) was *Silver Street* 1703 Gascoyne, 1746 R. PENNINGTON ST is *Pennington Street*, (-*tons*) 1697 ParReg, from the family of Henry *Penington* (1607 ib.). PRESCOT ST is so named in 1702 (Sess), from the family of Philip *Prescot* (1627 ParReg). PRINCELET ST is *Princes Street* 1746 R. PRINCES SQUARE is so named ib. PRUSOM ST (1872 LCCN). *v.* Pruson Island *supra* 151. The street is earlier *King street* 1653 ParReg, 1746 R, *Kingstreete* 1660 PCC. QUAKER ST is *Quaker Street* 1691 Sess, (*Quoakre*) 1698 ParRegFr, (*Coacre*) 1704 ib., (*Couaquer*) 1707 ib. RATCLIFFE ORCHARD. Cf. *The Orchard* 1746 R. REDMANS RD is *Redmans Row* 1808 Cary, from the family of Hinrie (sic) *Redman* (1615 ParReg). It was earlier *Mile End Green Lane* 1746 R. REDMEAD LANE is *Redmade lane* 1669 ParReg, (-*mayd*) 1674 ib., (-*maid*) 1703 Gascoyne, 1708 Hatton, 1746 R. RHODESWELL RD. Cf. *Rogues Well Lane* 1703 Gascoyne, 1720 Strype, from an old well here, *Rogues Well* 1651 StepneyMem, 1703 Gascoyne, 1720 Strype, *Rhode's Well* 1746 R. ROPEMAKERS FIELDS is *Ropemaker(s) Feild* 1640 ParReg, 1703 Gascoyne. ROSE LANE is so named in 1641 (ParReg). ROYAL MINT ST is so named from the Mint established here in 1811. First known as *Heggestrete* (sic) t. Ed 3 AD ii, *Hogge-* 1321 Cor, 1366 Cl, *Hoglane* 1544 LP, presumably from the pigs which frequented it. Later it was *Rosemary Lane* t. Jas 1 ECP, 1608

ParReg *et freq* to 1811, *Hoglane al. Rosemarylane* 1633 *Recov.* A more popular name was *Rag Fair* from the second-hand clothes shops here. ST ANNES RD is *St Annes laine* 1651 ParReg. ST GEORGE ST was formerly *The highway at Ratclyf* 1561 Sess, *Ratcliffe high way* 1641 Hust. *v.* Ratcliff *supra* 151. ST KATHERINE'S WAY and DOCK. Cf. *Katerines Dokke* 1422 Pat, *Saint Katerines Wharf* 1446 ib., *S. Catheryns laen* (sic) 1550 Aliens, *St Catrins Docke* 1594 ib., from the former hospital of St Katherine here, founded in 1148 (Dugdale vi, 694). SALMON LANE is so named in 1703 (Gascoyne), probably from the family of Robert *Salmon* (1623 StepneyMem). It is *Sermon Lane* 1746 R. SCHOOLHOUSE LANE is *Sch(o)ol(e) House Lane* 1628 ParReg, 1682 Morgan, and is so called from the Coopers' Company's School. SHEPPY PLACE is *Shepherds Gardens* 1746 R. SHIP ST is so named ib., probably from an inn sign. SPITAL ST is *Spitelstrete* 1235 FF, *Spittlestreet* 1697 ParReg, from the priory of St Mary *Spital. v.* Spitalfields *supra* 151. SPRING GARDENS PLACE was *Bull Lane* 1746 R. STEPNEY CAUSEWAY is *la Cauce* 1382 *Cor, Stepney Causeway* 1703 Gascoyne. Cf. *supra* 68. STEWARD ST is so named in 1746 (R). SWAN ST (now PORTSOKEN ST) is *Swan Alley* ib. TENCH ST is so named in 1720 (Strype), probably from the family of *Tench*, found in the ParReg from 1634. TENTER GROUND is so named in 1746 (R). Cf. *The Tenter yardes* 1589 ParReg, *Tenter feild* 1682 Morgan and *v. infra* 206. THRAWL ST is *Thrale Streete* 1665 ParReg, (*Throll*) 1677 O and M, 1682 Morgan, (*Thrall*) 1697 ParReg, from the family of Gregory *Thrawl* (1626 ib.). THREE COLT ST is *Threecolt street* 1638 ib., from an inn sign. TOWER BRIDGE APPROACH was *The Iron Gate* 1708 Hatton, *Iron Gate* 1746 R. VALLANCE RD (1863 LCCN) was *Virginia Row* 1703 Gascoyne, 1746 R. Like Virginia Rd *supra* 85, it lay in the 18th century on the edge of the built-up area of London. VIRGINIA ST is so named in 1746 (R). It lay then by open country. WAPPING HIGH ST is *Wapping St* 1703 Gascoyne. WAPPING OLD STAIRS is *Wappin old stayres* 1658 ParReg. WAPPING WALL is *Wappinge Walle* 1611 ib. Cf. *Wallemarshe al. Wapping Marshe* 1562 Sess. WEAVER ST is *Weaver's Alley* 1746 R. WELLCLOSE SQUARE. Cf. *le Well close* 1546 *AD, field called Welfelde* 1593 Sess, *Welclose* 1608 ParReg. WELL ST is so named in 1697 ib. WENTWORTH ST is *Wentworthstreete* 1619 ib. Edward VI granted the manor of Stepney to Thomas *Wentworth*, Lord Chancellor in 1550 (Pat). WHELER ST is *Wheelerstreete* 1660 ParReg, *Whiler Street* 1708 Aliens, from the family of Thomas *Wheler* (1589 ParReg). WHITE-CHAPEL RD is *Whitechappell strete* 1568 AD iv, a part of the main road (*v. supra* 9). WHITE HORSE LANE is so named in 1703 (Gascoyne). WHITE HORSE ST is *Clyvestre* (sic) 1371 Works, *Whitehorsstreete* 1595 ParReg, *Clyff strete* c. 1600 LMxAS vi, *Cleave Street al. White Horse Street* 1617 Allgood. The 'cliff' is that at Ratcliff *supra* 151. The later name is from an inn. WHITE'S ROW is *White Row* 1696 ParReg, 1746 R. WHITE'S YARD was *Glasshouse Street* ib. WILKES ST (1893 LCCN) was *Munmouth Street* 1677 ParReg, (*Monmouth*) 1703 Gascoyne, 1746 R, probably so named from the Duke. WORCESTER ST is so named ib., from the Earl of Worcester's Estate in Stepney (1646 Lords Journals). (S.J.M.)

Some lost street-names, now covered by the Docks, include *Smack Alley* 1677 O and M, *Smock Alley* 1695 ParReg, *Hartichoke lane* ib., *Artichoak lane, Meeting House Alley, The Match Walk, Labour in vain street, Cats Hole, Worlds End, Shakespear Walk* 1746 R. Other unidentified names are *Chapelstrate* 1317 AD vi, possibly identical with Whitechapel Rd *supra* 158, *Hacchestrete juxta Est Smethefeld* 1276 RH (the context suggests St Katherine's Lane *supra* 158), *Milhill* 1641 ParReg, *Frying Pan Alley* 1643 ib., *Maidenhead lane* 1639 ib.

The Borough of Stoke Newington

STOKE NEWINGTON

> *Neutone* 1086 DB, *-tona* 1152–60 BM, *Neweton* 1197 FF, *Newtun* 1245 Ch, (*Canonicorum*) 1254 Val, 1322 Pat, (*juxta Clerekennewelle*) 1274 FF
>
> *Newinthon* 1255 Misc, *Newenton* 1274 Ass, *Newynton* 1286 Ch, 1387 Pat
>
> *Neweton Stocking, Stoken* 1274 Ass
>
> *Stokneweton* 1274 Ass, *Stokene Neuton, Stoke Newenton* 1294 ib., *Stokneuton* 1316 FA, *Stokeneweton* 1391 Pat, *Stokenewnton* 1459 BM
>
> *Stokenewington* 1535 VE, *Newington* 1549 FF

'New farm,' *v.* tun. The additional prefix is OE *stoccen*, 'of stumps,' with occasional confusion with *stocking*, 'place of stumps,' perhaps added to distinguish from Newington Barrow, now Highbury *supra* 125. *Canonicorum* from the canons of St Paul's who held the manor in DB.

NOTE. ABNEY PARK. Sir Thomas *Abney* (ob. 1721) held the manor of Stoke Newington t. Anne (RobinsonSN 36 ff.). Cf. *Lady Abneys land* 1734 ib. BROWNSWOOD RD preserves the name of the old prebendal manor (just over the Hornsey border). *v. supra* 122. CHURCH ST is so named in 1734 ib. CLISSOLD PARK is so named from Augustus *Clissold* who married the heiress of the Crawshay family, which had long held the estate formerly called Crawshay Fm. It was opened in 1889 (Sexby, *Municipal Parks*, 320 ff.). LORDSHIP RD is *The Lordship lane* 1734 RobinsonSN, referring to land belonging to or under the jurisdiction of the lord of the manor, *v.* NED. QUEEN ELIZABETH'S WALK is so named in 1734 (RobinsonSN).

NEWINGTON GREEN is *Newyngtongrene* 1480 Pat.

The Borough of Willesden

WILLESDEN [wilzdən]

> *Wellesdune* 939 (14th) BCS 737, *Wellesdone* 1086 DB, 1274
> *Ass*, *Welesdone* 1298 AD iv
> *Willesdone* 939 (14th) BCS 737, *-don(a)* 1181 StPaulsDB *et
> passim* to 1535 VE, with variant spelling *Wylles-*, *Willesden*
> 1290 FF, 1535 VE
> *Wilesdune* 1185 BM, 1229–41 StPaulsMSS, *Wyles-* 13th AD v,
> 1294 *Ass*
> *Wullesdon* 1248 FF, *Woolsdon* 1724 ParReg
> *Wyllendon* 1274 *Ass*
> *Wylsdon* 1563 FF, *Willesdon al. Wilsdon* 1658 *Recov*, *Wilsdon*
> 1675 Ogilby and generally to c. 1840

Perhaps 'hill of the spring' (*v.* wiell, dun), though this is a
very difficult type of genitival compound. Cf. Tengstrand lv,
lvi, and note *Wellesmoregate*, *Wyllesmore* 1548 MxRec, close
at hand. The usual 17th, 18th and early 19th century spelling
was *Wilsdon*, the form Willesden being adopted c. 1840 by the
London and Birmingham railway.

TWYFORD[1]

> *Tueverde* 1086 DB, *Twiferde* 1183 StPaulsCh, *-ferd*, *-fierd*
> 1219 FF, *-verd* 1222 StPaulsDB (p), *-ferd* c. 1250 *StPauls*
> *Twiford* 1199 Cur *et freq*, with variant spelling *Twy-*, *Twyford*
> *al. Twyforth* 1402 Pap
> *Westwyford* 1274 *Ass*, *Est Twyford next Wylesdon* 1294 FF
> *Twyver* 1562 FF

'Double ford,' *v.* twi, fyrde. There were two fords near
together over the Brent here until recent times. West Twyford
was a small parish of 300 acres, East Twyford was a hamlet of
Willesden. TWYFORD ABBEY is a modern 'abbey,' built early in
the 19th century.

[1] The parish of West Twyford was transferred to the Borough of Ealing
in 1926; part of this area was transferred to the Borough of Willesden in 1934
and a part of this transferred area was re-transferred to the Borough of
Ealing in 1937 (*ex inf.* the Town Clerk of the Borough of Ealing).

BRONDESBURY is *Bronnesburie* 1254 Val, *Brondesbury* 1291 Tax, 1366 Londin, *-biri* 1328 Pap, *Brounesbury* 1322, 1468 Pat, *prebende de Braundes* 1341 NI, *Bromeswode al. Bromesbury* 1346 Pap, *Brundesbury* 1535 VE, *Broomsbury* 1638 Lysons. This is probably a manorial *bury* name (*v.* burh and Introd. xvi), perhaps deriving from *Brand* (*Braund, Brando*), a canon of St Paul's, mentioned in deeds 1180–1216 (StPaulsMSS 8, 16, 17, 42). *Brand* is an Anglo-Scandinavian personal name. *v.* Addenda xxxiv.

CHAMBERLAINS WOOD[1] is *Cha(u)mberleyneswod* 1254 Val, 1291 Tax, *Chaumberleyne Wode* 1322 Pat, *p'bende de Chaumbres* 1341 NI. Probably part of the estate in Twyford annexed to the *camera* of St Paul's Cathedral (StPaulsCh xxxvii).

DOLLIS HILL is *Daleson* (sic) *Hill* 1593 N, *Dalleys Hill* 1612 *All Souls, Dalleyes Hill* 1619 ib., *Dallis* 1710 S, *Dollys* 1754 R, *Dolleys Hill* 1819 G. The origin of this name is not known. It is doubtful whether there is any connection between it and Dollis in Hendon *supra* 58. Were it not for the first form (possibly corrupt) we might perhaps take it to be manorial in origin, from some family coming from Dawley *supra* 37.

DUDDEN HILL is *Dodynghill* 1544 DeedsEnrolled, *Doddinge Hill* 1549 Pat. In 1475 (StPaulsMSS 59) there is mention of a "water called *Doddysforde*" in Willesden, which may have been near-by. Perhaps both ford and hill take their name from one *Dodd* or *Dodda*, ing being loosely connective.

FORTUNE GATE[2] is *Fortune Gate* 1680 S, cf. *Forton(e) feld* 1300, 1416 *All Souls, Fortune feild* 1593 ib. This piece of land may have been so called because it was *foran-tune*, i.e. in front of the *tun* of Harlesden (cf. *infra* 162). Cf. the similar use of *forebury* in Essex and Hertfordshire (PN Ess 596, PN Herts 262). It is difficult to say whether The Fortune, Temple Fortune, Fortune Green *supra* 51, 59, 113 have any similar origin.

[1] Preserved in CHAMBERLAYNE RD.
[2] Surviving in FORTUNE GATE RD.

HARLESDEN

> *Herulvestune* 1086 DB
> *Herleston* 1195 StPaulsCh, 1197 StPaulsMSS, 1241 Londin
> *et freq* to 1330 FF, with variant spelling *-lis-*, *Herlesdon* 1291
> Tax
> *Harleston* 1365 FF *et freq* to 1795 Lysons, *-don* 1564 FF, *-den*
> 1606 BM
> *Holsdon greene* 1650 Feret
> '*Heoruwulf*'s or *Herewulf*'s farm,' *v.* tun.

KENSAL GREEN

> *Kingisholte* 1253 FF, *Kingesholt* 1290 Ipm, *Kynges-* 1367 Cl
> *Kynsale Grene* 1550 Pat, *Kensoll grene* 1557 ib., 1593 *All Souls*,
> *Kensell Grene* 1658 ParReg (Kensington)
> *Canselgreene* 1653 ParReg (Kensington), *Cancelgrene* 1654 ib.

'The king's wood,' *v.* **holt.** Cf. Wormholt *supra* 110, near-by.
The exact royal owner is unknown.

MAPESBURY HO[1] is *Mapesberi* c. 1250 *StPauls*, *Mapesbury* 1254
Val, 1291 Tax, *Mappesber'* ib., *Mapesbury* 1309 Londin, 1341
NI, 1391 Pat, *-bery* 1322 ib. This is a manorial *bury*, *v.* burh
and Introd. xvi. Walter *Map* was a prebendary of St Paul's
c. 1180 and is mentioned at that date in connection with
Willesden (BM).

NEASDEN

> (*ad*) *Neasdune* 939 (14th) BCS 737
> (*of*) *Neosdune* c. 1000 ASCharters
> *Niesdon* 1194 P (p), *Nisedon* 1194 CR (p), *Nesdone* 1254 Val,
> 1291 Tax, 1322 Pat, 1322 AD iv
> *Nesedon* 1320 AD v, *-dem* (sic) 1507 Pat
> *Nisdon* 1326 Pat, *Neesdon* 1535 VE, *Needsden* 1750 Seale

Obviously 'nose-shaped hill,' the shape of the hill here being
particularly well marked, but the history of the early forms is
obscure. The form *Neasdune* is late and of no authority, but
Neosdune is from a 12th-century document containing good
11th-century forms. There may have been some confusion

---

[1] Surviving in MAPESBURY RD. Cf. *Mapes Hearn* c. 1840 *TA*.

between OE *næss* and *nōs(e)*, related words denoting 'nose, promontory' (cf. Hackness, PN NRY 112), but this does not in any way explain the development to [ni·zdən] rather than [nezdən].

OXGATE FM[1] is *Oxegate* c. 1250 *StPauls*, 13th AD v, 1248 Cl, 1254 Val, 1291 Tax, 1298 AD iv (p), 1322 Pat. Self-explanatory. It may have been a gate to prevent cattle straying out on to Watling Street.

PARK ROYAL. This is a fancy name given to a piece of land where an unsuccessful attempt was made to establish a fixed ground for the holding of the annual show of the Royal Agricultural Society. Later (c. 1910) the land was gradually built over and the name became that of a district now partly outside Twyford parish.

SHERRICK GREEN[2]

(grove of) Sirewic 1226 AD v
(brook called) Scyrewyk 1306 AD v, *Shirwykbrigg, Shirwyk-
    strete* 1425 AD iv
Scher(e)wykfeld 1306 AD iv, v, *Sherewick lane* 1556 St
    PancSurv
Shirrewykfeldes 1449 AD iv
Sherricke 1593 *All Souls, Sherrick Wood* 1650 *ParlSurv,
    Shirick Green* 1754 R, *Sherrick Green* c. 1815 EnclA.

The second element is wic, 'dairy farm.' The first element is scir, but the sense is uncertain. The stream in the second reference rose by Watling St (Edgware Rd) and flowed west to the Brent. To the north of the stream were the prebendal manors of Neasden and Oxgate, so the stream was a boundary one and we may have scir in the sense 'district.'

WILLESDEN GREEN is *Willesdone Grene* 1254 Val, 1322 Pat, *Wilsdon grene* 1584 *All Souls*. This was formerly a distinct hamlet.

CHURCH END is *the Churchend* 1593 *All Souls*. GREENHILL FM is *Green Hill* 1822 O.S. LONGCROFT is *Long(e)croft(e)* 1593 *All*

---

[1] Surviving in OXGATE LANE and GARDENS.
[2] Surviving in SHERRICK GREEN RD.

Souls. Roundwood Park was formerly *Hunger Hill* (Potter). This is *Hunger Hill* 1416, 1593 *All Souls*. Cf. *infra* 207. Stonebridge Fm. Cf. *The Stone Bridge* 1741–5 R (over the Brent).

WILLESDEN STREET-NAMES

Aberdeen Rd is named from the Earl of *Aberdeen* who had an estate on Dollis Hill. Cf. Gladstone Park *infra*. All Souls Avenue and College Rd. All Souls College, Oxford, holds land in the parish. Brentfield Rd. Cf. *Breyntfeild* 1593 *All Souls*. It leads to the Brent. Brook Rd marks the course of a former stream which joined the Brent. Near-by were Brooksbank Cottages (old 6″). Cf. also *Brokefe(i)ld* 1584, 1593 *All Souls*. Chambers Lane is so named ib. Chichele Rd commemorates Archbishop *Chichele*, through whose counsel Henry VI granted land here to All Souls (Potter 115). Church Rd. Cf. *Churchend lane* 1593 *All Souls*. Dog Lane is so named in 1741–5 (R). Dollis Hill Lane. *v.* Dollis Hill *supra* 161. It was earlier Bowers Lane (Potter 118), *Bourelane* 1415 ib. Dudden Hill Lane is *Duddinghill lane* 1593 *All Souls*. *v.* Dudden Hill *supra* 161. Fortune Gate Rd. *v.* Fortune Gate *supra* 161. Gladstone Park recalls the fact that Gladstone was a frequent visitor to the Earl and Countess of Aberdeen at Dollis Hill. Glynfield Rd. Cf. *Glynfield House* (old 6″). Grange Rd. Cf. *The Grange* ib. Greenhill Park Rd. Cf. *Green Hill* 1822 O.S. Harrow Rd is *Harrowe way* 1593 *All Souls*. The part of the road near Kensal Green is marked as *Honeypot Hill* 1741–5 R, 1825 O.S. Cf. the same name in Stanmore *supra* 66. Haycroft Gardens. Cf. *Haycroft* 1840 Potter. Kilburn Lane is *Kilbournelane* 1593 *All Souls*, leading to Kilburn *supra* 112. Mount Pleasant Rd. Cf. *Mount Pleasant* (old 6″) and *v. infra* 207. Neasden Lane is *Nisdon Lane* 1741–5 R and is referred to as *the lane that ledith from Neasdon to Willesdon grene* 1593 *All Souls*. Oaklands Rd. Cf. *Oakland Ho* (old 6″). Pound Lane was earlier *Petticote Stile Lane* (Potter 116). It is just possible that this is a corruption of *Perycrofte lane* 1593 *All Souls*, i.e. 'pear croft.' *Croft* often develops to *croat, crote, cote* in late forms, especially in field-names, *v. infra* 197. Sellon's Avenue preserves the name of Sellon's Farm (old 6″), deriving from John *Sellon* who held it in 1815 (Potter 132). Walm Lane is *Warme lane* 1593 *All Souls*, *Warne Lane* 1595 Sess, *Walm Lane* 1741–5 R, *Wealm lane* 1819 G. Willesden Lane was earlier *Mapes lane* 1352 Potter, 1741–5 R, *Maplislane* (sic) 1383 Works, deriving from the same man who gave name to Mapesbury *supra* 162. The *l* in the Works form may be a clerical or transcription error for *p*. Lost names include *Crokeslane, Loverdeslane* 1306 AD iv, *Grene lane, Wood lane, a warple way* (*v.* **worple**), *the Higheway* (probably Edgware Rd) 1593 *All Souls*.

VII. CITY OF WESTMINSTER

Westminster

WESTMINSTER. By tradition the site of the abbey was earliest known as *Torneia* 785 (13th) BCS 245, *Torneie* 969 (c. 1100) Crawford, (*in*) *loco terribili quæ ab incolis Thorney nuncupatur* 969 BCS 1290. The meaning was 'thorn island,' cf. Thorney (PN C 56), and referred to an island formed by two branches of the Tyburn at its outfall into the Thames[1]. Early spellings of Westminster include *Westmunster* 785 (13th) BCS 245, *Westminster* 959 (c. 1100) ib. 1050 (both from untrustworthy documents), *Westmynster* 972–8 ib. 1290, *Westm'* 993 KCD 684, (*into*) *Westminstre* 1066 (13th) ib. 824 and (*æt, to, on*) *Westmynstre* from the ASC *s.a.* 1039, 1049, 1066. Westminster is not mentioned by name in DB but is referred to as "villa ubi sedet æcclesia Sancti Petri." The name means 'west mynster,' this word having here the sense of 'monastery,' and it was so named because it lay to the west of London.

NOTE. Of Westminster parish churches dating from medieval times we may note: ST CLEMENT DANES, *par. Scī Clementis ecclesie Dacorum* 1100–35 (1330) Ch, *ecclesia Sancti Clementis que dicitur Dacorum* 1185, 1189 Templars, *gara Sancti Clementis* (*Dacorum*) 1187, 1194, 1197 P, *parochia Sancti Clementis* 1204 Cur, *Denscheman parosch* 1266 FF, *parochia Sci Clementis le Daneys extra Lond'* 1274 Ass, (*extra barram Novi Templi*) 1294 ib., *Seynt Clement Danes* 1500 AD v. Stow says it was "so called because Harolde a Danish king and other Danes were buried there" (ii, 96), but the reason for the name is really unknown. For *Dacorum* cf. PN Herts 25. The *gara* or 'gore' of land may be the point of land at this end of Westminster with the river on the south, London to the east and the old parishes of St Andrew Holborn and St Giles in the Fields to the north. Cf. Kensington Gore *infra* 169.

ST MARGARET, *ecclesia Sancte Margarete in nostro cymiterio stante* c. 1130 Dugd i, *parochia Scē Margarete atte Chering* 1250 FF, *ecclesie Beate Margarete* 1255 Cl, *ecclesia Sancte Margarete apud Westmonasterium* 1428 FA, *Seynt Margates* 1552 Machyn, *St Margett* 1559 PCC. *v.* Charing Cross *infra* 167.

ST MARTIN IN THE FIELDS, *eccl. Sci Martini* 1254 Val, *parochia Sci Martini in Camp'* 1291 Tax, *St Martin by les Mewes* 1406 Pat, *St Mart(e)yn in lez Fe(i)ldes* 1493 PCC, 1567 Sess, *St Martyns near Charyng*

---

[1] Commemorated in THORNEY ST, a street dating from 1931.

Crosse 1597 PCC. The church originally stood in the fields by the royal mews, cf. St Giles in the Fields *supra* 116.

ST MARY LE STRAND, *parochia Ste Marie de Stronde* 1274 *Ass*, (*de la Strand*) 1291 Tax, (*atte stronde*) 1305 Pat, *Our Lady at Stronde* 1489 BM. *v.* Strand *infra* 173. *le* is used here in the common loosely connective fashion. It was earlier *parochia de Innocentibus in villa Westm* c. 1220 BM, *eccl. Sanctorum Innocentium* 1241 Cl.

ALBANY. Frederick, Duke of York and *Albany* disposed of his house here in 1804 when it was converted into chambers known as *Albany* (W and C).

ALDWYCH

> *Vetus vicus* 1199 Cur, *Aldewich, -y-* 1211 Cur, 1219, 1233,
>   1258 FF, (*extra la Temple Barre*) 1405 StPaulsMSS
> *Aldewic* 1211 Cur, 1236 FF, *Aldewyk* 1294 *Ass*
> *Oldewiche* 1393 Cl, *Oldwich close* 1613 Sess
> *Foscewe Lane al. Adwych* (sic) *Lane* 1551 Pat

'The old dairy farm,' *v.* wic. Originally it was just outside the City. Aldwych Lane survived as the later Wych St *infra* 185. The name Aldwych was given by the LCC in 1903 to the new street of which the eastern arm passes near the site of the old Wych St.

THE AMBRY or ALMORY (lost) is *the Aumorie* 1494 Westlake, *Little Almoury* 1500 WmCharities, *Almerie strete, the Amners* 1542 LP, *The Almery* 1544 Aliens, *le Almery* 1556 Pat, *the Amnerie* 1593 N, *Greate Ambre* 1659 PCC, *Great Almerie* 1682 Morgan, *Almonry* 1831 Elmes. "*The Elemosinary or Almory* now corruptly the Ambry, for that the Almes of the Abbey were there distributed to the poore" (Stow ii, 123). It was demolished when Victoria Street was made c. 1850. Cf. Armoury Fm (PN Ess 360).

BUCKINGHAM PALACE is on the site of *Buckingham House* 1708 Hatton, and is named from John Sheffield, Duke of *Buckingham*, who bought the house (since twice rebuilt) in 1702. It was purchased by George III in 1762 (W and C). The site was earlier known as *Mulbury Garden feild* 1614 Gatty, *Ye Mulberry Garden feild* 1665–70 Map, *The Mulberry garden* 1668 Pepys, the garden having been planted by James I in the hope of introducing the silk industry into London. The first house on this site was Goring House, mentioned by Evelyn as destroyed by fire in 1674. It was rebuilt and renamed Arlington House by the Earl of *Arlington* (cf. *infra* 175) and afterwards sold to John Sheffield (LnTopRec v, 128).

CHARING CROSS

> (*to*) *cyrringe* 979–1016 (13th) Crispin
>
> (*la*) *Cherring'* 1198 Cur (p), 1232 Ch, *la Cheryng(g)e* 1243 FF, 1294 *Ass*, *La Cherryng in Westminster* 1258 Pat
>
> *La Charryng* 1263 Pat, *la Charring* 1274 *Ass*, *in vico de la Charing* 1303 Orig
>
> *The stone cross of Cherryngge* 1334 Ipm, *La Charryngcros* 1360 Pat, *Charryngcrouch(e)* 1364 Cl, 1378 Pat, *Cherryng Cross* 1368 Cl, *Cherryngescrouche* 1383 Works, *Charryngcrouch* 1413 Pat, *Char(r)yngcrosse* 1443 FF

This is OE *cierring*, 'turning, turn,' from *cierran*, 'to turn,' with reference either to the bend in the river here, or more probably to the fact that *Akemannestrete* (*supra* 10) made a well-marked bend at this point, near the site of the present Trafalgar Square. Cf. *Charynghegge* c. 1470 Ct (Fulham). See further Appendix iii. For the interchange of *cross* and *crouche* in the 14th and 15th century records cf. *infra* 173. The old forms show that the traditional association of the name with Fr *chère reine*, with reference to Queen Eleanor, has no justification.

COVENT GARDEN. This was originally a garden or walled enclosure belonging to the monks of Westminster Abbey (K 40–1), the earliest reference to it (dating from 1222) probably being in the phrase *secundum divisionem gardinorum Tholy et Monachorum Westmonasteriensium* in the bounds of St Margaret's, Westminster (Westlake 231). It is *Covent Gardyn* 1491 LBk, *le Convent Garden* 1537 LP, *le Covent Garden of Westminster* 1544 ib.

EBURY[1]

> *Eia* 1086 DB, *Eye* 1087–97 Crispin *et freq* to 1406 AD ii, with variant spelling *Eie*, (*island of*) 1236 FF, (*juxta pontem de*) 1294 *Ass*
>
> *Eubery* (sic) 1300 Ipm, *Eyghebury, Eyebury* 1323, 1344 Ipm, *Eiburye* 1325 Inq aqd, *Eybury, Eybery, Ebery* 1535 VE, *Highbury al. Eyberie* 1596 ChancP

----

[1] Preserved in EBURY BRIDGE, SQUARE and STREET.

'Island, well-watered land,' *v.* **eg**, with later addition of manorial *bury*, *v.* **burh**. The name referred to an island in the former marshy land here, now covered by the streets of Pimlico. The old manor of Ebury (*Eia*) was the west part of the present City of Westminster, including Hyde Park, and was excluded from the bounds, as given in BCS 1048 (*v. infra* 222).

ENDIFF (lost) is *Anedehea* 13th StMargSurv, *Enedehuthe* t. Hy 3 ib., *Enedhuthe* c. 1270 ib., *Enedehyeth* 1296 ib., *Hevedehuth* (sic) 1307 Ipm, *lane of Henedehuthe* 1355 StMargSurv, *street called Enedehuthe* t. Hy 6 StMargSurv, *Endyve* 1461 ib., *lane called le Endif* 1499 ib., *le Endiff lane* 1523 ib., *Endyve lane* 1532 LP. 'Landing place or wharf frequented by ducks,' from OE *ened*, 'duck' and hyð, *v.* Chelsea *supra* 85. Cf. *Redriff* for Rotherhithe (PN Sr 28) and *Eriffe* for Erith (K), 1685 ParReg (Stepney). The place was on the river between Charing Cross and Westminster Abbey and the lane was one which led eastwards from King St (*infra* 180), now covered by the Embankment and Government buildings.

HAY HILL FM[1] is *Ey Hille* t. Hy 6 Gatty, *Ayehille* 1531 ib., *Eye Hille* 1531 LP, *Eyhill* 1549 Pat, *Aye Hill* 1553 Sess, *Hay hyll besyd Hyd Parke* 1554 Machyn, *Hayhill Farm* 1742 LCCDeeds. Cf. *Eyfeld*, *Eymore* 1481 AD i. The first element seems to be ME *eye* from OE *eg*, 'island, well-watered land,' etc., probably with reference to land by the Tyburn which flowed just by. Cf. Tyburn *supra* 6.

HYDE PARK

> *Hida* 1204 FF, *la Hyde* 1257 ib., 1274 *Ass* (p), *la Hyde by the town of Westminster* 1353 Pat
> *Hide Park* 1543 LP, (*le*) *Hyd*(*e*) *Parke Corner* 1553 Machyn, 1555 Sess

Hyde was originally a part of the manor of Ebury and must in the first place have consisted of only one *hide* (*v.* hid) or about 100–120 acres of that manor. Later, in the 13th century, it became a sub-manor and its area was no doubt extended. The

---

[1] Surviving in HAY HILL (street), a steep hill between Berkeley and Dover Streets.

present *park* was created by Henry VIII after the dissolution and was originally a royal preserve, not open to the people until a much later date. The *Corner* is at the present day a somewhat vague term, but in 1555 the reference was clearly to the spot where Park Lane joined the main road to the west (now Piccadilly).

KENSINGTON GORE (now a street-name) is (*in*) *loco qui Gara appellatur* 1121–40 Dugd iii, *Kyngesgore* 1270 Misc, *the Gore* 1646 ParReg, *the Kings Gore* 1657 ib. This is OE **gara**, 'gore, wedge, triangular-shaped piece of land,' etc., referring no doubt to the long narrow wedge of which Queen's Gate forms the base and the point of which lies at the junction of Brompton Rd and Knightsbridge. Cf. Gore Hundred *supra* 49–50. It is not known what king is referred to.

KNIGHTSBRIDGE

(*in*) *Cnihtebricge* 1042–66 (13th) *WDB*
Cnithtebruga 1121–40 Dugd iv
Knichtebrig' 1235 *Ass*, *Cnichtebrugge* t. Hy 3 BM *et passim* to 1383 IpmR, with variant spellings *Knighte-*, *Knyghte-*, *Kniste-*, and *-bregge, -brigge, -brygge*
Knyghtesbrugg 1364 FF

'Bridge of the young men,' *v.* **cniht**. Cf. *cnihtabryge* BCS 216 in Oxfordshire. The bridge was over the Westbourne stream (*supra* 8) which was crossed by the main Great West Road at this spot.

LONGDITCH (lost) is *Langedich* 1198 FF, 1379 AD i, (*street of*) 1253 Pat, *Launditch* 1504 *Rental*, *Londitch* 1626 ECP, *Long Ditch* 1682 Morgan, 1720 Strype, 1746 R. This was the name of a ditch, an old boundary of Westminster Abbey precincts. It ran roughly up the present Princes St and then along the east side of St James's Park behind the present Government buildings (cf. Smith 72).

MARLBOROUGH Ho was built by Wren for the Duke of *Marlborough* in 1709 (W and C).

MAYFAIR. This was open land until towards the end of the 17th century. A fair was held in Brook Field (cf. *infra* 176) in the first week in May during the reign of Charles II. Cf. "a fair held in the parish of St Martin in the Fielde, commonly called May Fair" (1702 Sess). It was suppressed in 1709, but soon revived, though building had begun in the area by 1704 (W and C).

NEAT (lost)

> *la Neyte* 1320 Fine, 1325 *MinAcct*, (*by Westminster*) 1325 Pat,
> *la Neite* 1360 BPR
> *la Nayte* 1324 Orig, 1344 Ipm
> *le Neate* 1556 FF, *Neat Houses* 1710 S, 1746 R, *Neat House Gardens* 1819 G

This name represents a ME *atten eyte*, 'at the islet,' *v.* **iggoð**, with the common misdivision as in names like Nash, cf. also PN Herts xxv. The site was near the river in the present Pimlico district and the land may have been so named in distinction from Ebury *supra* 167, a larger island of marsh.

PETTY FRANCE is *Petefraunce* 1494 Westlake, *Pety Fraunce* 1518 ib., *Petty Fraunce* 1576 Sess, 1597 AD v, 1746 R. It was a small district of Westminster at the west end of Tothill St. Already in 1682 (Morgan) it was the name of a lane leading to the old *St James St* (*infra* 176). The name was changed to *York Street* towards the end of the 18th century, but the old name was restored in 1920 through the influence of Sir Lawrence Gomme, Clerk of the LCC. It is now a continuation of Tothill St. There was also a *Petye Caleys* in 1531 (LP). It lay on the east side of King St (Parliament St) leading to the river. According to Widmore this was where the wool-staplers from Calais resided while other French merchants lived in Petty France (Walcott 289).

PICCADILLY. The earliest reference for the name would seem to be in *Pickadilly Hall in St Martin in the Fields* 1623 Sess. Other 17th century spellings quoted in K are *Pickadillie*, *Pecadily* 1627, *Pickadilla* 1633, *Piquidillo* 1662, *Peckadillie* 1665. We may add *Peckadilly* 1637 SP. In the earliest reference the name is applied "to a range of houses extending up the east side of Windmill Street, whence it came to be applied generally to the neighbouring district and more particularly to the gaming house and ordinary at Shaver's Hall. In none of these uses did it apply to any part of the street now called Piccadilly" (K 97). The origin of the name has been much discussed. As far back as 1656, Blount in his *Glossographia* mentions two possible derivations, based on the supposition that the word is to be associated with *piccadil* used in the 17th century of "a border of cut work inserted on the edge of an article of dress, especially on a collar or ruff, later transferred to the collar itself." He suggested that the ordinary called *Pickadilly* might have been so called because it was then the "outmost or *skirt* house of the suburbs that way" or from the fact that a certain tailor who built it "got much of his estate by Pickadillies which in the last age were much worn in England." Such nickname origin is quite possible and the nickname character of the name is confirmed by a passage in SP (1636), "Simone Austbiston's (i.e. Osbaldeston) house is newly christened. It is called Shaver's Hall as other neighbouring places thereabout are nicknamed Tart Hall, *Pickadel Hall*." The name of the hall was soon applied first to the district and next to the street. In the 1633 reference above there is a note on "the small wild buglosse which grows upon the drie ditch banks about *Pickadilla*," showing that the name was already applied to a district. See more fully K 71–4, 92, 97–8.

PIMLICO is *Pimplico* 1630, 1664 Gatty, *the king highway at Pimplico* 1681 ib. (referring to the road to Chelsea), *Pimlico* 1741–5 R. There was a similar place-name in Hoxton, preserved in Pimlico Walk (*supra* 148). The earliest references to the Hoxton one, according to ShoreSurv, are *Pimlyco or Runne Redcap* 1609, *Pimlico House* 1742, *house called Pimlicoe* 1745. It is also referred to as *Pimlico* by Ben Jonson in *The Alchemist* (Act v, Sc. 2). A clue to the origin of the name is suggested by a quotation by E. F. Rimbault in MxNQ (First Series i, 474) from a rare tract, *Newes From Hogsdon* (1598), "Have at thee then, my merrie boyes, and hey for old Ben Pimlico's nut browne." It would seem that "Ben Pimlico" was a Hoxton innkeeper of fame whose name was later transferred to his house. The Westminster name (given to a district almost uninhabited before the 19th century) was presumably copied from the Hoxton one, though there appears to be no actual proof of this. See further Sugden 412.

ST JAMES'S PARK is *Seynt James Newe Parke* 1555 Sess and is on the site of an ancient hospital dedicated to St James (VCH London 542 ff.). Cf. *hospital' leprosis puellis de Scī Jacobi extra London justa* (sic) *Westm̃* 1204 ChR, *Hospital' Sci Jacobi extra London* 1274 BM, *Hospital of St James by Charyng* 1386 Pat, *the hospital called Saynt James in the Feld* 1531 LP. See also St James's Square and St *infra* 182.

THE SAVOY. This name is to be traced to Peter of *Savoy*, uncle by marriage to Henry III, who was granted land in *la Straunde* (1246 Ch) on which he built a palace, the head of the later Savoy manor. Cf. *a messuage called le Sauveye* 1324 Pat, *manor of Savoie* 1348 ib., *Sauvaye* 1351 Cl, *Savoy* 1476 FF, *Savoystrete* 1501 AD iv, *the Savoy Steyres* 1563 Sess. The *stairs* were the steps leading down to the river at this point.

SCOTLAND YARD[1]. This area is referred to as *a parcel of land late of the King of Scotts* 1440 Pat, *Kyng of Scottis ground* 1462 ib., *p'cellam terr' voc' le Scotland ground* t. Hy 8 *MinAcct*, *Scotland Yard* 1656 SP. Cf. also "a parcel of land, formerly belonging to the King of Scotland, in Co. Midd. lying between a hospice of the Archbishop of York on the south" (1519 LP vol. iii, Pt. i, 176). This last document is endorsed "For the ground called Scotland by York's Place." *v.* Whitehall *infra* 174. Cf. also "a large plotte of ground inclosed with bricke and is called Scotland, where great buildings hath beene for receipt of the Kings of Scotland" (Stow ii, 101).

SOHO. The earliest references are *So Ho* 1632 K, *place called So Howe* 1634 ib., *Sohoe* 1636 ib., *Soe-Hoe in St Martins in the Fields* 1681 Sess, *Soe Hoe feildes* 1684 Sess. The origin of this name has been discussed by Kingsford (K 66–9) and others. The theory that it is an old hunting cry is supported by the fact that the name seems to have been given in the first place to certain fields, later built over. We know that hunting took place here in 1562 (Machyn 162). The old legend that the name was taken from the Duke of Monmouth's battle-cry at Sedgemoor (1685) is incorrect, as the forms quoted above show that the

---

[1] The original site is that of Great Scotland Yard (not New Scotland Yard) between Northumberland Avenue and Whitehall Place.

name was in use many years earlier. Rather, it was the house of
the Duke of Monmouth which stood here till 1773 (LnTopRec
v, 130), which suggested his battle-cry at Sedgemoor (K 69).

SOMERSET HO is so named in 1593 (N) and takes its name from
the former palace here, built by the Protector *Somerset*, t. Ed 6.
Cf. *Somerset Place* 1555 Pat, *Denmark House al. Somerset House
al. Stronde House* 1672 DKR xx. James I gave it to his Queen,
Anne of Denmark.

STONE CROSS (lost). There was a stone cross "without the bar
of the New Temple" traditionally supposed to have been erected
by William Rufus "in devotion to the Holy Cross and for the
health of the souls of himself and his mother, Queen Maud"
(Misc ii, 26). It was in the Strand, possibly on the site of the
present church of St Mary. It is referred to as *crucem lap'* 1274
RH, *la Croisse de Piere* 1293 Chroniques p. 23, *la Brokenecrouche
in the suburb of London* 1323 Ipm, (*atte*) *Stonecrouch* 1337 Cl,
crucem fractam 1342 Ipm, *Brokyncros* c. 1419 LibAlb. Thomas
le Barber is described alternatively as being T. le B. *atte Stonecrouch* (1337 Cl) and T. le B. *atte Brokencrouche* (1339 Pat).
Pleas of the county of Middlesex were frequently summoned to
be at the *Stone Cross of la Straund* (1242 Pat). The stone is
described as headless by Stow in 1598 (Stow ii, 91).

THE STRAND

> *Stronde* 1185 Templars, (*la*) 1294 *Ass, Stranda* 1219 FF, (*la*)
> 1220 ib., *in vico Strand'* 1222 ib., *street called la Straunde*
> 1246 Ch

This is OE *strand*, 'strand, bank, shore.' The name was given
in the first place to the Thames bank as in the phrase *andlang
stremes be lande and be strande on merfleote* (BCS 1048) in the
bounds of Westminster, where the reference is clearly to the
whole length of the river bank from the mouth of the Fleet to
the Chelsea boundary (see further Appendix i). Part of the
street (near St Clement Danes) was known as *vicus Dacorum*
1222 FF, (or *Densemanestret*) 1233 ib., *vicus Sancti Clementis*
1230 ib., *Densyemannestrete* 1246 ib. (cf. *supra* 165), while the
part near St Mary le Strand (cf. *supra* 166) was known as *vicus
Innocentium* 1219 ib.

TOTHILL

Tothulle, -hill, -hell late 12th BM, *Totehull* 1294 *Ass*
Tuthulle late 12th BM, *Touthull* 1256 Ch, (*street towards*)
    Thothull 1257 Pat
Tootehyll fylde 1550 StMargSurv, *Tuttlefields* 1675 Ogilby

'Look-out hill,' from ME *tote*, cf. PN Sx 31. There can never
have been a natural hill here, but the name may have referred
to some artificial mound or barrow, perhaps that referred to in
the phrase (*of*) *þan hlawe* 979–1016 Crispin, *v.* hlaw. See
further Appendix i. Tothill Fields were built over in the 19th
century, but the name survives in Tothill St *infra* 184. *Tothill*
was possibly the mound shown in 1746 (R), south-west of
Horseferry Road (Walcott 281).

WHITEHALL (PALACE) is *mansion' domini Regis voc. Whytehale al.*
Yorke place 1530 StMargSurv, *Yorke Place which is called White*
Hall 1533 ib., *Whytthalle at Westminster that sometime was the*
bysshope of Yorkes place ib., *Whight Halle* 1536 LP. York Place
was the London residence of the Archbishops of York; it was
taken by Henry VIII after the fall of Wolsey[1]. The new name
may well have arisen from the new stone building which had
been started by the Cardinal and was completed by Henry VIII.
This Whitehall should not be confused with the 'White Hall'
within the Palace of Westminster which is referred to as *The*
White Hall at Westminster 1394, 1421 Cl, *The White Hall within*
the king's palace at Westminster 1506 Pat.

WESTMINSTER STREET-NAMES

ABINGDON ST is so named in 1746 (R) and took its name from a mansion
of the Earls of *Abingdon* which formerly stood here (Westlake 397). It
was earlier *Durty Lane* 1650 *ParlSurv, Lindseys Lane or Dirty Lane* 1732
PC. ADELPHI. Cf. *Adelphi Wharfs* 1799 Horwood. The streets round
here were built by the Adam *brothers* (Greek ἀδελφοί) c. 1770. AIR ST
is *Ayre Street* 1671 W and C, of unknown origin. See K 112. ALBE-

---

[1] Cf. *Henry VIII*, Act iv, Sc. 1, ll. 94–7:

    3*rd Gent.* To York-place, where the feast is held.
    1*st Gent.*   Sir,
                You must no more call it York-place, that's past,
                For since the cardinal fell, that one's lost:
                'Tis now the king's and call it Whitehall.

MARLE ST is so named in 1708 (Sess), on the site of *Albemarle House* (1682 Morgan) belonging to the second Duke of *Albemarle*, son of General Monk (K 108). ALDFORD ST (1886 LCCN) was earlier *Chapel Street* 1746 R, from Grosvenor *Chapel*. APPLE TREE YARD is so named in 1746 (R). ARCHER ST is *Arch St* 1675 K, 1682 Morgan, *Orchard street* 1720 Strype, *Archer Street* 1746 R, 1799 Horwood. ARGYLL ST is *Argyll Street* 1746 R, and owes its name to a house here of the Dukes of *Argyll* (K 124). ARLINGTON ST is so named in 1746 (R) from the Earl of *Arlington*, one of the Cabal ministry (K 95). Here was *Arlington House* 1682 Morgan. ARNE ST was earlier *Dirty Lane* 1746 R. Addenda xxxiv. ARTILLERY ROW from the old *Artillery Ground* ib. where there were shooting butts (Walcott 324). ARUNDEL ST is so named in 1682 (Morgan). It was on the site of *Arundel Place* 1554 Pat, a house of the Earls of Arundel, ancestors of the Dukes of Norfolk. Cf. Norfolk St and Surrey St *infra* 181, 183. GREAT AUDLEY ST is so named in 1746 (R), from Hugh *Audley* who owned land here t. Chas 2 (W and C). AXE YARD (lost) is so named in 1647 (Sess). Cf. "tenement or brewhouse called *the Axe*" 1523 AD i. It is frequently mentioned in Pepys's Diary, since he lived in the street. It is now covered by government buildings. BABMAES ST is *Bab Mays Mewes* 1732 PC, 1746 R and is so named from *Baptist May*, Keeper of the Privy Purse to Charles II (W and C). BARTON ST is so named in 1746 (R) from *Barton* Booth the actor (Walcott 318). See further Cowley St *infra* 177. BATEMAN ST is on the site of Monmouth House, the property of William, first Lord *Bateman* (c. 1700) (K 69–70). Earlier *Queen Street* (1682 Morgan). BEAK ST is so named in 1691 (Sess) from Thomas *Beake*, a builder (1685 ib.). See K 123. BEAR ST is *Bear Lane* 1682 Morgan, from an inn-sign (W and C). BEDFORDBURY, on the site of a house of that name, is so named in 1682 (Morgan), apparently a late use of *bury*, *v. infra* 192. This house was erected by the Earls of Bedford in 1601 and took the place of Russell or Bedford House, earlier the Bishop of Carlisle's Inn, on the south side of the Strand (Stow ii, 95). On their marriage into the Southampton family the home of the Bedfords was again moved to Bloomsbury. BEDFORD ST is so named in 1682 (Morgan) from the Earl of *Bedford*, the ground landlord. BELGRAVE SQUARE and the derivative BELGRAVIA take their names from Belgrave (Ch) where the Duke of Westminster has property. BELL YARD is so named in 1657 (PCC), taking its name from a tenement called *le Belle* in 1545 (LP). BENNETT ST is so named in 1692 (Sess) from Henry *Bennett*, Earl of Arlington (*v. supra*). BERKELEY ST and SQUARE are *Berkeley Street* 1708 Hatton, (*Square*) 1746 R. They are named from the house of John, Lord *Berkeley* of Stratton (ob. 1678) (K 110). *Berkley House* is marked in 1682 (Morgan). BERWICK ST is *Berwick Street* 1689 K, 1708 Hatton, *Bar-* 1720 Strype. BIRDCAGE WALK is *The Birdcage Walk* 1808 Cary. Cf. "The *Bird Cage* in St James Park" 1683 SP, the name of the king's aviary there. BOLTON ST is so named in 1708 (Hatton) and is perhaps so called from the family of Raphe *Boulton* (1603 ChwAcct). OLD and

New Bond St are *Bond Street* 1708 Hatton, *New Bond Street* 1732 PC, *Old Bond Street* 1754 R. They are named from Sir Thomas *Bond*, comptroller of the Household to Queen Henrietta Maria (K 108). Bourchier St is *Milk Alley* 1746 R. Bow St is so named in 1682 (Morgan), from its curved course (Strype ii, 93). Boyle St is *Noel Street* 1746 R. For the present name cf. Cork St *infra* 177. Brewer St is so named in 1692 (Sess). Brick St is so named in 1732 (PC). Bridge St is so named in 1746 (R). It was made at the time of the building of Westminster Bridge (1739–50). It covered the site of the earlier *Woolstaple* or wool-market, cf. *Wolstable, le Rounde Wolstable* 1544 FF, *The Woolstaple* 1545 WmCharities, *Longwolstable* 1549 Pat, *le Roundewolstaple* 1650 ib., *Round* and *Long Woolstaple* 1665 Westlake. Already in 1353 (Pat) there is mention of the staple (i.e. market) of wool to be held at Westminster. See further Stow ii, 103, 375. Bridle Lane is *Bridle Lane, Brydall Lane* 1692 Sess and is to be associated with the family of John *Brydell* (t. Jas 1) (K 26). Broad St (now Broadwick St) is so named in 1704 (K 117). Broadway is *The Broadway* 1662 WmCharities. It was originally a wide space where Petty France and Tothill St met and was later extended to a new street. Broken Cross (lost), *Broken Cross* 1682 Morgan. The site is now covered by Princes St. Brook St is so named in 1746 (R). Cf. *Greate, Little Brooke feilde* 1650 ParlSurv. The Tyburn flowed just near. Bruton St is so named in 1746 (R) from Lord Berkeley's estate in Somerset (K 134). Buckingham Gate (1861 LCCN) was earlier *St James Street* 1682 Morgan, *James Street* 1746 R. Buckingham St. George Villiers, Duke of *Buckingham* was granted land here in 1621 on which he built a house (StMartSurv iii, 54). Hence also Duke St, George St, Villiers St *infra* 178–9, 184. Bulinga St is named from the *bulunga fenn* of the Westminster Charter (BCS 1048). Burleigh St is so named in 1708 (Hatton). Cf. Exeter St *infra* 178. Burlington Ho is so named in 1746 (R). The original house was built by the first Earl of *Burlington* in 1665 (K 104 ff.). Bury St is *Berry Street* 1682 Morgan from one *Berry*, ground landlord t. Chas 2 (W and C). Butcher Row (lost) is so named in 1657 (PCC), 1746 (R). It was demolished early in the 19th century. Cannon Row is *Chanon Aley* 1482 Westlake, *Canon row* 1534, 1537 LP, (*le*) *Chanon Rowe* 1547 Pat, t. Eliz Agas, *Chanell Rowe* 1556 Machyn, *Channon Rowe* 1620 Sess, *Cannon row vulg. Channel Row* 1732 PC. "Chanon Row, so called for that the same belonged to the Deane and Chanons (*sic*) of St Stephens chappell who were there lodged" (Stow ii, 102). Carey St is *Cary Street* 1708 Hatton, from Nicholas *Carey* (1676 Worsley). Carlisle St is so named in 1746 (R) from *Carlisle House* built here in 1692 by the Earl of *Carlisle* (K 70). Carlos Place (1866 LCCN) was earlier *Charles Street* 1746 R. Carlton House Terrace preserves the name of Carlton Ho (*Charlton House* 1746 R, *Carlton* 1819 G) built by Hugh Boyle, Lord *Carleton* t. Anne (W and C). Carnaby St is *Karnaby Street* 1703 ParRegFr. Carteret St is so named in 1708 (Hatton) and takes its name from Sir Edward de

Carteret who was granted a lease here in 1680 (StMargSurv i, 80).
CARTING LANE was earlier *Dirty Lane* 1746 R. CASTLE LANE is so
named ib. It was earlier *Cabidge Lane* 1664 Bayne, *Cabbage Lane* 1720
Strype. Cf. *le Calbege* 1550 Pat. CASTLE ST (lost) is so named in 1682
(Morgan) from an inn-sign (MxNQ iii, 19). It is now the lower part
of Charing Cross Rd. CATHERINE ST is *Catharine Street* 1682 Morgan
from *Catherine* of Braganza, wife of Charles II. CAXTON ST (1883
LCCN) is a modern street-name commemorating the printer, who
worked in Westminster. Earlier *Little Chapel Street* 1667 WmCharities.
CECIL COURT takes its name from certain holdings of the Earl of
Salisbury in St Martin's Lane dating from the 17th century (K 47).
CHANDOS ST (now CHANDOS PLACE) is *Shandois Street* 1682 Morgan,
Shandes 1692 Sess, from Lord *Chandos* (ob. 1654) (W and C). Pepys
speaks of his house in the phrase "my simple Lord *Chandois*." GREAT
CHAPEL ST is *Chappeil Streete* 1656 HCMag vi from the chapel of
St Margaret's church burial ground, formerly on this spot. CHARING
CROSS RD was constructed c. 1880. The north part occupies the site of
the old CROWN ST (*Hog lane* 1585 Map, 1650 *ParlSurv, Crown Street
al. Hog Lane* 1700 K 65). CHARLES ST (Covent Garden) is *Charles
streete* 1658 PCC, (St James Sq) *Charles Street* 1682 Morgan, (Berkeley
Sq) *Charles Street* 1746 R. The first is named from Charles I (W and C),
the second from Charles II (K 96), the third from Charles, Earl of
Falmouth, brother of Lord Berkeley (ib.). CHESTER SQUARE. The
name was suggested by the Duke of Westminster's manor of Eaton
Hall which is near Chester. CHURCH ST is so named in 1682 (Morgan),
from the church of St Anne, Soho. CLARE MARKET is so named in 1690
(Sess). It was earlier *New Market* 1593 N, 1602 ParReg. It was founded
by John Holles, Earl of *Clare*, t. Chas 1 (W and C). CLARGES ST is so
named in 1746 (R), from Sir Walter *Clarges*, brother-in-law of Monk
(K 105). See Albemarle St *supra* 174–5. CLEMENTS LANE is *St Clements
Lane* 1677 O and M, from the church (*supra* 165). Near here was
St Clements Well, v. supra 95. CLEVELAND SQUARE. Cf. *Cleveland
Street* 1746 R from *Cleveland House* (1682 Morgan) belonging to
Barbara, Duchess of *Cleveland* (K 128). CLIFFORD ST is so named in
1746 (R), from Thomas, Lord *Clifford*, one of the Cabal (K 128). Cf
Arlington St *supra* 175. COCKSPUR ST is *cock spurr street* 1753 StMart
Surv, probably because cocks' spurs were sold here (ib. iii, 151). (GREAT)
COLLEGE ST is *College Street* 1746 R. Earlier *The Dead Wall* 1682
Morgan. It ran behind the south wall of Westminster School. OLD and
NEW COMPTON ST are *Compton Street* 1682 Morgan, from Sir Francis
Compton (K 68). CONDUIT ST takes its name from the old conduit or
water channel here. Cf. *Kyngesconduteesheved* 1366 AD i, *Condet mede*
1536 LMxAS ii, *Cunditt meadowe* 1585 Map. See further K 130 ff.
CONSTITUTION HILL is so named in 1746 (R). CORK ST is so named ib.,
from Richard Boyle, Earl of *Cork* (K 128). COVENTRY ST is so named
in 1682 (Morgan), from Henry *Coventry*, Secretary of State, who had
a house here in 1673 (K 85). COWLEY ST is so named in 1746 (R),
from Cowley (*supra* 32), the home of Barton Booth (Smith 401)

(*v. supra* 175). CRAIG COURT is *Craggs Court* 1746 R, from Joseph *Craig*, who erected buildings here in 1693 (StMargSurv i, 218). CRANBOURN ST is so named in 1682 (Morgan) from Viscount *Cranborne*, son of the Earl of Salisbury (K 47). CRAVEN ST is so named from William, Baron *Craven*, who acquired land here in 1687 (StMartSurv iii, 29). Earlier *Spurre Alley* 1617 ib., perhaps so called from the selling of spurs here. CURZON ST is so named c. 1710 (Clinch) from George Augustus *Curzon*, Earl Howe (W and C). It is *Cousens St* 1754 R, probably a colloquial form. In Curzon St, Calne (PN W 256), earlier *Cusinestrete, Cosenstrete*, we have a similar corruption the other way round. DACRE ST is *Dacres Street* 1682 Morgan. Cf. Strutton Ground *infra* 183. D'ARBLAY ST (1909 LCCN), earlier *Portland Street* 1746 R, was re-named after Madame *d'Arblay* whose father (Dr Burney) lived in Poland St near by (K 135). DARTMOUTH ST is so named in 1708 (Hatton) from the Earls of *Dartmouth* (Walcott 73). DAVIES ST is named from Mary *Davies* who married Thomas Grosvenor in 1676 (K 134). Cf. Grosvenor Rd *infra* 179. DEAN ST is *Deane Street* 1678 K. DEANERY ST (1886 LCCN) was earlier *Dean St* 1746 R. DEAN FARRAR ST (1904 LCCN) was earlier *New Tothill Street* 1746 R, *v. infra* 184. DEAN'S YARD is *Deanes Yard* 1658 Faithorne, where live the Deans of Westminster. DENMAN ST was earlier *Queen St* 1678 K. DEVEREUX COURT is so named in 1676 (Worsley). See Essex St *infra*. DOVER ST is so named in 1708 (Hatton) from Henry Jermyn, Baron *Dover* and Earl of St Albans (K 108). Cf. Jermyn St *infra* 180. DOWN ST is *Downe Street* c. 1710 Clinch. Perhaps so named from the family of William and Edward *Downes* found in the locality in 1585 and later (K 33). DOWNING ST is so named by Pepys (1660) from the house built here by Sir George *Downing* (1623–84) (StMargSurv 91, 109). DRURY LANE is *Drury lane* 1598 Stow, *Drewrie lane* 1607 StGilesSurv, *Drury lane nere Lincolnes Inne Feildes* 1617 Sess, from *Drurye house* 1567 StGilesSurv, the home of Richard *Drewrye* (1554 Sess). It was the western and northern end of the old *Aldwych lane, v. Wych St infra* 185. DUCK LANE (lost) is so named in 1682 (Morgan), 1746 (R), probably a muddy way. It was demolished for Victoria St c. 1850. DUKE ST is so named in 1682 (Morgan), *v.* Buckingham St *supra* 176. DUNCANNON ST was built in 1837 and named from Lord *Duncannon*, Chief Commissioner of Woods and Forests at the time (Acres 115). DURHAM HILL and DURHAM HOUSE ST preserve the memory of *Durham House*, the former town house of the Bishops of *Durham* (LnTopRec x, 110). EATON SQUARE is named from *Eaton Hall*, the Cheshire seat of the Duke of Westminster. EBURY ST, *v. supra* 167. ECCLESTON SQUARE is named from Eccleston, a village by Eaton Hall (Ch). EDWARD ST is so named in 1686 (K) from Sir *Edward* Wardour (cf. Wardour St *infra* 184). ESSEX ST is so named in 1682 (Morgan). Robert Devereux, Earl of *Essex* (t. Eliz), had a house here named *Essex House* (1601 SP). "Essex House of the Earle of Essex lodging there" (Stow ii, 92). EXETER ST is so named in 1682 (Morgan) from a house here belonging to Thomas Cecil, son of Lord Burleigh, created

Earl of *Exeter* in 1605 (W and C). FARM ST is so named in 1799 (Horwood) and preserves the memory of Hay Hill Fm, *v. supra* 168. FRITH ST is *Frith Street* 1682 Morgan, *Frif Street* 1706 ParRegFr, *Thrift Street* 1746 R, from Richard *Fryth* "a great (and rich) builder" (K 68). GEORGE ST is so named in 1682 (Morgan). *v.* Buckingham St *supra* 176. GEORGE ST (Hanover Square) is *Great George Street* 1746 R, probably named from George 2. GERRARD ST is so named in 1682 (Morgan), from Charles *Gerard*, first Earl of Macclesfield (ob. 1694), who owned land here (K 61). GLASSHOUSE ST is so named in 1682 (Morgan). GOLDEN SQUARE is *Golden Square* 1688 K, (*Golding*) 1708 Hatton, (*Golden*) 1733 ParReg, "from the first builder thereof" (Hatton). GRAFTON ST is so named in 1708 (ib.) from the Dukes of *Grafton* who owned land here; they had a house in Bond St (K 109). GREEK ST is so named in 1682 (Morgan) from the church for Greek refugees which stood here (K 67). GREEN PARK is so named in 1746 (R), formerly a part of St James's Park. GREEN ST (now IRVING ST) is so named ib. and takes its name from the Green Mews (K 51). Cf. Trafalgar Square *infra* 184. GREYCOAT PLACE is so named from the school, founded 1698 (Smith 396). GROSVENOR RD, SQUARE, ST are named from the family name of the Dukes of Westminster. The Square is marked in 1746 (R). GROSVENOR GATE is so named c. 1724 (Lysons). HALF MOON ST is so named c. 1710 (Clinch) from a former inn-sign. HAMILTON PLACE is *Hamilton Street* 1732 PC, from Col. James *Hamilton*, Ranger of Hyde Park t. Chas 2 (W and C). HANOVER SQUARE is so named in 1720 (Strype) from the reigning family. HART ST (FLORAL ST 1895 LCCN) is so named in 1682 (Morgan) from an inn which stood here, *The White Hart* (W and C). HAY HILL, *v. supra* 168. HAYMARKET is *Hay Market* t. Eliz Agas, *the waye to Charing Cross from Colbroke* (i.e. Colnbrook) 1585 Map, *The Haymarket neer Peccadilly* 1661 K. First a market and then a street-name. HENRIETTA ST is so named in 1682 (Morgan) from the queen of Charles I. HOLLAND ST is *Hollen Street* 1746 R, 1799 Horwood. HOLYWELL ST (lost) is *viam regiam que vocatur Holewey* 1373 Works, *street called Holwey* 1398 Cl, *Holewlane* 1414 Williams, *Holliwell Street* 1677 O and M, *Hollowell Street* 1682 Morgan. 'Hollow way,' cf. Holloway *supra* 126, with later corruption. Demolished for Aldwych c. 1901. HORSEFERRY RD (1865 LCCN) was earlier *Market Street* 1682 Morgan, 1746 R. So named because it led to the old horse ferry over the Thames to Lambeth (*le Horsefery* 1536 LP). HOUGHTON ST is *Haughton Street* 1682 Morgan, 1746 R, from Sir John Holles of *Haughton*, Notts (W and C). HOWARD ST is so named in 1746 (R). It is on the site of Arundel Ho (*v. supra* 175). HUNGERFORD BRIDGE took its name from Hungerford Inn, *Hungerford Inne, late of Robert Hungerford, knight, Lord Hungerford* 1472 Pat, *Hungerfordes Inne next Charynge Crosse* 1530 FF, when it was in the possession of Walter *Hungerford*. IVY LANE is so named in 1732 (PC). It took its name from the lost *Eyvy Bridge* 1543 ChwAcct, *Ivye Bridge* 1594 ib., *Iuie Bridge* 1598 Stow, presumably self-explanatory, cf. Ivybridge (PN D 278). An earlier name of the bridge, which crossed a small tributary of the Thames and divided the parish of St Clement Danes from that of St Mary le Strand, was *Ulebrigg* (1222 Westlake), i.e. 'owl's bridge.' Ivy Lane was destroyed when the Hotel Cecil was built, now replaced by Shell Mex House. JERMYN ST is *Jermin Street* 1682 Morgan, (*Jerman*) 1692 Sess, (*German*) 1720 Strype. Cf. Dover St *supra* 178. KING ST (now WHITEHALL) is *strata regia* 1222 Westlake, *regie strete* 1368 Orig, *Kyngestrete* 1376 AD i, *the kings highway from Charyngcrosse to Westminster* 1440 Pat, *le Kyngestrete* 1457 ib., *Kinges streete* t. Eliz Agas, *Kings Streete called Strandway* 1649 ParlSurv. Before the construction of Whitehall (street) this was the road leading from Charing Cross to Westminster. It was largely superseded by Parliament St *infra* 181 and completely disappeared when that street was widened in the 19th century. KING ST (Covent Garden) is so named in 1682 (Morgan) from Charles II. KINGLY ST (1906 LCCN), near Golden Square, was earlier *King Street* 1746 R. KINGSWAY is a new thoroughfare constructed 1902–5. The name was chosen by the LCC. It is not to be confused with the old *Kingsway supra* 120. LEICESTER SQUARE. Robert Sidney, second Earl of *Leicester*, was granted land here in 1630, *Leicester Ho* was erected here in 1631 and demolished in 1791. *Leicester Square* is first marked in Hatton (1708), earlier *Leicester Fields* 1682 Morgan, *Lestrefils* 1703 ParRegFr (cf. K 52 ff.). LEWISHAM ST (1888 LCCN) is named from Viscount *Lewisham*, the title of the heir of the Earl of Dartmouth. Cf. Dartmouth St *supra* 178. It was earlier *St John Street* 1746 R, 1799 Horwood. LEXINGTON ST was earlier *Little Windmill Street* (K 113). LISLE ST is so named in 1708 (Hatton). It takes its name from the second title of the Earls of Leicester (K 56) whose house was close at hand. *v.* Leicester Square *supra*. LONG ACRE. Cf. *pasture called Longeacre* 1547 Pat, *The Long Acurs, the baksyde of Charing Cross* 1556 Machyn. Originally a field-name, *v. infra* 195. LUPUS ST commemorates Hugh *Lupus*, Norman earl of Chester, an ancestor of the Dukes of Westminster (Clinch 121). MACCLESFIELD ST is so named in 1746 (R). *Macclesfield House* stood here till 1888 (K 62). Cf. Gerrard St *supra* 179. MADDOX ST is so named in 1731 (LCCDeeds) from Thomas *Madockes* (1690 ib.) who owned land here (K 132–3). MAIDEN LANE is *Mayden Lane* 1657 PCC. MANETTE ST (1895 LCCN) was earlier *Rose Street* 1746 R. GREAT MARLBOROUGH ST is *Marlborough Street* c. 1710 Map, probably in honour of the Duke (K 122–3). Note BLENHEIM ST near-by. MARSHAM ST is *Marsham Street* 1692 Sess, (*Masham*) 1720 Strype, from John *Marsham*, t. Chas I (Walcott 132). MATTHEW PARKER ST was earlier *Bennet Street* 1746 R. The present name commemorates Archbishop *Parker* (Walcott 73). MEARD ST is *Meards Court* 1746 R. MERCER ST is so named in 1682 (Morgan). The Mercers' Company owned land here (K 2). MILFORD LANE is *Mylforth lane* t. Eliz Agas, *Mylford stayres* 1593 N, *Milford Lane* 1619 PCC. Stow (ii, 92) says "why so called I have not read as yet." MILLBANK. Cf. *land called the Mill Bank* 1546 LP from the mills belonging to Westminster Abbey. MILL ST is so named c. 1713 (K). SOUTH MOLTON ST is so named in 1732 (PC),

(*Row*) 1746 R. MOOR ST is so named in 1700 (K). MOUNT ST is so named 1746 R, from *Oliver's Mount*, part of the earthworks thrown up here in 1643 (*v.* LnTopRec xiv, 34). NEW INN PASSAGE preserves the memory of New Inn (*The New In of the Stronde* 1397 Cl), demolished in 1903. NEWPORT ST is so named in 1654 (K) and in 1692 (Sess), from Lord *Newport* who had a house here (K 62), marked *Newport House* in 1682 (Morgan). NEW ST is so named ib. NOEL ST is *Newel Street* 1746 R. NORFOLK ST is so named in 1682 (Morgan). It is on the site of Arundel Ho *supra* 175. NORTH ROW is so named in 1746 (R). It is at the extreme north-west corner of Mayfair. NORTHUMBERLAND AVENUE was constructed in 1875 on the site of the demolished *Northumberland Ho*, the town house of the Dukes of *Northumberland*. ORANGE ST is *Orang* (sic) *Court* 1720 Strype. ORCHARD ST[1] is so named in 1655 (PCC). It is on the site of the Abbey Orchard. OXENDON ST is so named in 1682 (Morgan) from Sir Henry *Oxendon* (c. 1670) who had a house here (K 77). PALACE YARD is *Ye Greate, Newe Pallace Yard* 1650 *ParlSurv*. It was an open space in front of Westminster Palace. Stow (ii, 121) notes "the sayd pallace before the entrie thereunto hath a large court" and (ib. 120) speaks of it as *The Pallace Court*. PALL MALL was originally *Spittelstrete* 1222 Westlake, *vicus hospitalis Sancti Jacobi* 1243 FF, *way called Spitel strete* 1327 Parton, because it led to St James's Hospital. The present name is found as *Pall Mall Walk* in 1650 (cf. NED *s.v.*), *Pall Mall* 1658 Faithorne, *Pell Mell* 1659 PCC, so called from the game of *paille maille* or *pelmel*, first played here in the reign of Charles I (cf. NED *s.v.*). PALMER ST is so named from *Palmers alms houses* (Hatton 1708), the gift of Mr John *Palmer* (ib.). PANTON ST is so named in 1682 (Morgan) from Col. Thomas *Panton* who owned land here in 1664 and later developed it (K 84, 113). PARK LANE is *Westmynster Lane* 1484 Gatty, so called because it led from Watling St to Westminster. It was later *Tyborne lane* 1721 LMxAS ii (cf. *supra* 137), *Hide Park Lane* 1733 LCCDeeds, *Park Lane* 1796 Lysons. PARLIAMENT ST (1746 R) was constructed as part of the approach to the new bridge (*supra* 176). GREAT PETER ST is *Sant Peterstreet* 1624 HCMag vi, *St Peter streete* 1659 PCC, *Peter Street* 1682 Morgan, from the saint to whom the Abbey is dedicated. PETER ST (Soho) is so named in 1675 (K 116). PETTY FRANCE, *v. supra* 170. PICCADILLY, *v. supra* 170. The street was first known as *Portugal Street* 1692 Sess, 1746 R, cf. Portugal St *infra* 182. It is *Piccadilly Street* 1673 K, *Piccadilly Street al. Portugal Street* 1685 ib., *Pickadilly* 1763 R. PICCADILLY CIRCUS. By a strange chance this covers the site of a house and garden belonging to Lady Hutton, of which the garden lay by a field known as *The Round Ringill* 1585 Map and elsewhere as *The Round Rundell* 1650 K. Cf. K 100. *rundell* is used of a circular enclosure or field (cf. *rundle* 2.d. in NED), while *ringill* must be the word *rengell*, *ringell* used of a small ring and here applied to a circular field (cf. *ringle* sb.[1] in NED). PIMLICO RD, *v.* Pimlico *supra* 171. It is *Strumbelo* 1746 R, south-eastwards of the earlier *Rombelowe Feilds* (1614 Gatty)

---

[1] Now ABBEY ORCHARD ST.

v. Addenda xxxiv. POLAND ST is so named in 1708 (Hatton). PORTUGAL
ST is so named ib., from Catherine of Braganza, queen of Charles II
(W and C). PRINCES ST was constructed c. 1765 (Walcott). It traverses
the site of the old *Broken Cross* (*supra* 173) and in part *Longditch*
(*supra* 169). GREAT PULTENEY ST is *Poulteney Street* 1682 Morgan,
from land which Sir William *Pulteney* laid out for building c. 1670
(K 114). LITTLE PULTENEY ST was earlier *Knaves Acre* 1732 PC, so
called from a field here (K 115 ff.). The old name is a common term
of reproach, cf. *infra* 207. OLD PYE ST is *Pye Street* 1682 Morgan,
from Sir Robert *Pye*, resident in this part of Westminster (Walcott
285). QUEEN ANNE'S GATE was earlier *Park Street* 1746 R. It was a
continuation of Queen St *infra*. OLD QUEEN ST is *The Quenez strete*
1553–8 ECP. It is *new street called Queen Street* 1698 StMargSurv,
earlier *Long More Banke* 1555 ib. Cf. *Langmere* 1222 Westlake, *Longe-*
more 1536 LP. REGENT ST was constructed c. 1820 as part of the plan-
ning scheme which included Regents Park *supra* 138, absorbing the
greater part of Swallow St (*infra* 183) as also *Shug Lane* (*infra* 183).
ROCHESTER ROW is so named in 1746 (R), from the fact that many of
the later Deans of Westminster were also Bishops of Rochester (W
and C). ROMNEY ST takes its name from property belonging to Charles
Marsham, Earl of *Romney* (Smith 396). Cf. Marsham St *supra* 180.
It was earlier *Vine Street* 1682 Morgan, 1720 Strype. Cf. also *the Vyene*
garden 1537 Walcott, perhaps from the abbey vineyard. ROTTEN ROW
is so named in 1781 (Clinch). The origin of this name is not certain.
It is not likely to be the *rotten row* so often found in street-names, which
is a corruption of *ratonrowe*, 'rats' row,' a term of contempt for a poor
row of houses. Cf. PN Nt 16. As it is a very late name it may really
be 'rotten row' with reference to the dry loose soil here. RUPERT ST
is so named in 1682 (Morgan) from Prince Rupert (K 113). RUSSELL ST
is so named in 1665 (Sess). It was on an estate of the Dukes of
Bedford (1795 Map). Cf. Russell Square *supra* 119. SACKVILLE ST
is so named in 1679 (K) from one Captain *Sackville* who was
living here in 1676 (ib. 103). Alternatively known as *Chip Street*
1675 ib., *Ship Yard* 1682 Morgan, perhaps so named from Allen *Chip*
who lived in *Portugal Street* (i.e. Piccadilly) in 1673 (K 103 n. 2).
(GREAT) ST ANNES ST is *St Anns* 1656 PCC. Cf. *Sainte Anns Chappell*
1576 Westlake. ST ERMINS HILL is so named in 1732 (PC); it is earlier
St Armyneshill 1584 Smith. Stow in 1598 calls it *St Hermits Hill*.
Later corruptions are *Torments Hill* 1720 Strype, *Torment Hill* 1746 R,
1799 Horwood. ST JAMES'S SQUARE is so named in 1682 (Morgan).
ST JAMES'S ST is so named in 1624 (PCC) from the old palace and
hospital, *v. supra* 172. ST MARTIN'S LANE is so named in 1585 (Map),
from the church. Earlier *The Churche Lane* 1542 ChwAcct. BROAD and
LITTLE SANCTUARY are *The Seyntwary* t. Hy 6 Walcott, *The Sanctuary*
1519 LP, *Brode Sentwarye* 1581 PCC. It was a precinct of the abbey
in which refugees might be protected from the civil power (Walcott
80–1). SAVILLE ROW is *Savill Row* 1746 R, taking its name from
Dorothy *Savile*, heiress of William, Marquis of Halifax, wife of the

Earl of Burlington. Built in 1733 (K 128). Cf. Burlington Ho *supra*
176. SAVOY ST is *Savoystrete* 1501 AD iv. *v.* The Savoy *supra* 172.
SERLE ST is *Searl Street* 1708 Hatton, taking its name from Sir Henry
Serle (ob. 1690) who held land here (W and C). SHAFTESBURY AVENUE
was constructed c. 1880 and in 1886 was named after the seventh Earl
of *Shaftesbury*, the well-known philanthropist. SHEFFIELD ST is so
named in 1682 (Morgan). SHEPHERDS MARKET is so named in 1746 (R).
Its owner was Edward *Shepherd*, an architect, who formed it c. 1735
(W and C). There is also a John *Shepherd* mentioned in 1726 in
connection with this part (LCCDeeds). SHERE LANE (lost) was *Shire-
lane* 1544 LP, *Sheare lane* 1607 PCC, *Sheere lane* 1657 ib., *Sheer Lane*
1708 Hatton. It was on the Westminster-City boundary, *v.* scir,
'boundary.' It was destroyed for the new Law Courts c. 1870.
SHERWOOD ST is *Sherwood Street* 1679 K, 1746 R, *Sheriff Street* 1682
Morgan, *Sherard Street* 1708 Hatton, 1720 Strype. It is said to be so
called from one Squire *Sherwood* who was resident in Pulteney St in
1683 (K 125). SH(R)UG LANE (lost) is *Suggen lane* 1391 K, *Suggene-* 1405
Cl, *Sug-* 1491 LBk, *Shug-* 1682 Morgan, 1746 R and later. This may be
'hedge sparrows' lane' (OE *sucgena lane*) from *sucga*, 'hedge sparrow.'
The lane was absorbed by Regent St during its construction (c. 1820).
SIDNEY PLACE, earlier *Sidney Alley*, is like Lisle St *supra* 180, to be
associated with the family of the Earls of Leicester. Cf. Leicester
Square *supra* 180. SILVER ST is *Little Silver Street* 1704 K. Perhaps
from silversmiths there, cf. Stow i, 299 for Silver St in the City.
Now Beak St *supra* 175. GREAT SMITH ST is *Smith Street* 1708 Hatton,
1746 R, from Sir James *Smith*, the ground landlord (Hatton i, 76).
SOHO SQUARE is *Kings Square al. Soho Square* 1700 K, *v.* Soho *supra*
172. From Gregory *King* the Herald who first projected the Square
(c. 1680) (K69). SOUTH ST is so named in 1746 (R). SOUTHAMPTON ST
is so named ib. See Southampton Row *supra* 120 and cf. Bedfordbury
and Russell St *supra* 175, 182. SPRING GARDENS is *The Springe Garden*
1580 StMartSurv iii, *Spring Garden* 1682 Morgan. THE STRAND. *v.* The
Strand *supra* 173. STRAND LANE is *Stronde lane* 1593 N. STRATTON ST is
so named in 1720 (Strype) from John, Lord Berkeley of *Stratton* (K 110).
Cf. Berkeley Square *supra* 175. STRUTTON GROUND is *Sturton Ground*
1633 Sess, 1656 PCC, *Stretton Ground* 1682 Morgan, from *Stourton
House* 1593 N which stood here, belonging to Lord Dacres (Walcott
282). SUFFOLK ST is so named in 1682 (Morgan) from the town house
of the Earls of *Suffolk* which stood here (K 88–9). SURREY ST is so
named in 1682 (Morgan). It is on the site of Arundel Ho (*v.* Arundel St
supra 175) and is named from one of the titles of the Dukes of
Norfolk. SUTTON ST is so named in 1700 (K 65) from Sutton Court,
Chiswick (*supra* 89), the then home of the Fauconbergs, landowners
here. Close by is FALCONBERG COURT which is *Falconbridge Court*
1746 R. SWALLOW ST is to be associated with the family of Thomas
Swallowe (1536 LP). Cf. *Swallow close* 1650 ParlSurv. TAVISTOCK ST
is so named in 1746 (R) and took its name from one of the titles
of the Dukes of Bedford, the ground landlords. Cf. Tavistock

Square *supra* 145. TENTERDEN ST is *Tenderdown Street* 1746 R. THIEVING LANE (lost) is *Thevynlane* 1424 Westlake, *Thevynglane* 1542 LP, *Thevinglane* 1556 Pat, *Thieving Lane or Bow Street* 1732 PC. Stow (ii, 104) says it was so called "for that theeves were led that way to the Gate House, while the sanctuary continued in force." More probably it was simply a nickname of reproach for a neighbourhood of ill-repute (cf. *supra* 84). As shown in maps the lane had a marked *bow* or bend in the middle. It was destroyed for Victoria St c. 1850. THORNEY ST is a modern street, the name commemorating the old name for the site of the Abbey, *v. supra* 165. TOTHILL ST is *vicus versus Tothill* late 12th BM, *Tothull street* 1372 AD i, *Tuthilstrete* 1437 IpmR, *Totehilstrete* 1480 FF, *Tuttle Street* 1691 Sess. This last is the usual form in the 17th and 18th century records. See Tothill *supra* 174. TRAFALGAR SQUARE was constructed 1829–41, the name commemorating the battle. It covers the site of THE MEWS, cf. *les Muwes* 1294 *Ass*, *The Muwes* 1405 Cl, *le Mewehous at Charryng* 1460 Pat, *le Muse next Charinge Crosse* 1557 Pat, *The Mewes* 1585 Map, *the great Mewes* 1720 Strype, where was the royal falconry (cf. *mews* in NED). TUFTON ST is so named in 1682 (Morgan) from Sir Richard *Tufton* (ob. 1631) who built it (Walcott 322). An earlier name for the northern end was *Bowling(e) All(e)y* 1650 ParlSurv, 1746 R. VAUXHALL BRIDGE RD is called *New Road* in 1817 (Mogg). VICTORIA ST was constructed c. 1850 when *The Ambry, Duck Lane, Thieving Lane* (*supra* 166, 178) and other slum areas were demolished. VIGO ST is *Vigo Lane* 1746 R, commemorating the battle of 1702. VILLIERS ST is *Villers Street* 1682 Morgan, *v.* Buckingham St *supra* 176. VINCENT SQUARE is named from William *Vincent*, Dean of Westminster (ob. 1816). It was a part of the former Tothill Fields *supra* 174 (Walcott 329). WARDOUR ST is named *Old Soho, otherwise Wardour Street* in 1691 (Sess), from Sir Edward *Wardour* t. Chas 2, who had a leasehold interest here (K 115). WARWICK SQUARE and ST (Pimlico). The Duke of Westminster owns property at Tachbrook (hence TACHBROOK ST) and other places near Warwick. Warwick St follows the course of the old *Willow Walk*, so named 1720 (Strype), 1746 (R), a lane leading past the osier beds of Neat House Gardens. WARWICK ST (Soho) is so named in 1682 (Morgan). Sir Philip *Warwick* had a house here t. Chas 2 (K 115). WATER LANE is so named t. Eliz Agas, leading from the Strand to the river. WELLINGTON ST, of which the name commemorates the Duke, was constructed c. 1830 to give approach to *Waterloo* Bridge, opened in 1817. WHITCOMB ST is *Whitcombe Street* 1682 Morgan, of obscure origin. The south part was earlier *Hedge Lane* ib., 1696 Sess, shortened from the earlier *Colman Hedge Lane* 1585 K. Cf. *Colmanhegg* 1390 Pat, *-hegge* 1405 Cl, and cf. further Colman St in the City, *colman* being probably a charcoal man. The 'hedge' was the western boundary of the 'fields' of St Martin and St Giles (K 2). WHITEHALL. The street was extended during the 18th century, obliterating the north end of the old King St (*supra* 180). It was named from Whitehall *supra* 174. WHITEHORSE ST is so named in 1746 (R) from a former inn here.

GREAT WILD ST is *Weld Street(e)* 1679 Sess, (*Wild*) 1691 ib. It is named from Humphrey *Weld* who had a house here in 1639 (StGiles Surv). For the sound development cf. Introd. xvii. GREAT WINDMILL ST is *Windmill Street* 1671 K, from the former *Windmill Feild* 1585 Map, perhaps identical in site with *Wynmulleshull* 1366 AD i. The windmill was still here in 1650 (K 98). WOOD ST is so named in 1656 PCC, 1682 Morgan. WOODSTOCK ST is so named in 1732 (PC). WYCH ST (lost) is *Oldewiche lane* 1393 Cl, *street called Aldewyche* 1398 ib., *Wiche Street* 1677 O and M, (*Wich*) 1682 Morgan, preserving in an abbreviated form the old place-name Aldwych (*supra* 166). Originally it was the name of the whole thoroughfare from the Strand to St Giles, the upper part being later named Drury Lane (*v. supra* 178). It was destroyed for the construction of Aldwych and Kingsway c. 1902–3. YORK ST (Covent Garden) is *Yorke streete* 1653 PCC. YORK ST (St James's Square) (now DUKE OF YORK ST) is so named in 1682 (Morgan).

Lost or unidentified names include *le Blakehalle* 1222 Westlake, *le Blakestole* 1550 Pat, *Cheynygates* ib. (cf. PN Nt 16), *Green Alley* 1583 PCC, *Codpeice Court* 1732 PC (cf. Coppice Row *supra* 97), *Hoppyndehalle* 1377 StMargSurv, *Hoppyngehalle* 1475 ib.

The Temple (within the City of London, but extra-parochial)

THE TEMPLE. The house of the Knights Templars in London was first located in Holborn. Later (c. 1160) their house was moved to its present site and became known as the New Temple (*Novum Templum* 1162, 1185, etc. Templars), the original site being referred to as the Old Temple (cf. *juxta vetus Templum extra barram de Holeburne* 1204 FF and the map by Miss Honeybourne in *Norman London*). After the downfall of the Templars the site passed into the gradual possession of the Knights of St John at Clerkenwell (*v. supra* 98), who obtained the whole by a royal grant in 1338 and about ten years later let it to a body of lawyers (VCH, London i, 489). The Inner Temple is mentioned by name in 1440 (Paston) and in 1447 (ib.) it is referred to as *The Inner In in the Temple att London.* The Middle Temple is mentioned by name in 1404 (Williamson) and in 1451 (Paston) is called *The Mydill Inne.* Old Courts and Lanes within the Temple precincts include BRICK COURT, *the Bricke Court* 1619 MTRec, said to be so named because it was the first structure in brick in the Temple. THE CLOISTERS are mentioned in 1517 (ITRec) and 1612 (MTRec). CROWN OFFICE ROW (1730 ITRec iv, 225; cf. Hatton ii, 646) is so called because the Clerk of the Crown in the King's Bench, who had his office in the Inner Temple from t. Hy VII till 1882 (ITRec i, xxviii *et passim*, cf. *Crown Ct* 1632 MTRec) was there during that period. ELM COURT is *Elme Court* 1620 MTRec. ESSEX COURT is so named in 1631 (MTRec) from the fact that it was adjacent to Essex House (*v.* Essex St *supra* 178). FIG TREE COURT is *The Figtree Courte* 1574 ITRec. In 1516 (ib.) there is mention of *the chamber next the fig tree*. FOUNTAIN COURT was earlier *The Hall Court* 1646 MTRec, from the fact that it is adjacent to Middle Temple Hall. It is *Hall or Fountain Court* 1732 Worsley from the fountain here, erected in 1681 (MTRec). GARDEN COURT is so named in 1676 (Worsley) from the garden (*Myddell Temple Gardeyne* 1544 LP). HARE COURT is *Mr Hare's Court* 1587 ITRec, *Hare Court* 1677 O and M, named from Master Nicholas *Hare*, Treasurer in 1584 (ITRec). INNER TEMPLE LANE is so named in 1608 (MTRec). KINGS BENCH WALK is so named in 1677 (O and M). It is *The Kings Bench Walks* 1732 Worsley. Cf. *for gravel for the new walks before the Kings Bench office* 1623 ITRec. It is named from the Kings Bench Office, burnt down in 1666 and again in 1677 when it was rebuilt lower down (Williamson 511, 517–8). MIDDLE TEMPLE LANE is so named in 1568 (ITRec) and is called simply *The Lane* 1608 and later (MTRec). It is probably referred to in *a common passage through the middle of the court of the new Temple to the Thames* 1329 Cl. NEW COURT is so named in 1676 (Worsley). The ground on which it is built was earlier a part of Essex House (*v. supra* 178). PLOWDEN'S BUILDINGS are named from Master *Plowden*, Treasurer in 1561 (Williamson). PUMP COURT is so named in 1620 (MTRec). TANFIELD COURT is so named in 1732 (Worsley) from Master Robert *Tanfield*, Treasurer in 1631 (MTRec). It was earlier known as VINE COURT (1620 ib.). Cf. Fig Tree Court *supra*.

THE ELEMENTS, APART FROM PERSONAL NAMES, FOUND IN MIDDLESEX PLACE-NAMES

This list includes all elements used in uncompounded place-names or in the second part of compounded place-names. Most words found as the first elements of place-names are also included if they are of historical, cultural or linguistic interest. Under each element the examples are arranged in three categories, (*a*) uncompounded elements and those in which the first element is a significant word and not a personal name, (*b*) those in which the first element is a personal name, (*c*) those in which the character of the first element is uncertain. Where no statement is made it may be assumed that the examples belong to type (*a*). Elements which are not included in the *Chief Elements used in English Place-Names* are distinguished by an (n) after them. The list is confined with few exceptions to names for which there is evidence before 1500.

ac Acton, Coal Oak. **ætsteall** (n) Astlam (?).
bærnet Barnet. ME **barre** (n) Potters Bar.
bearu Barrow Hill. **beonet** Bentley.
beorg Barrowfield, Roxborough, Smallbury, (c) Wemborough.
bern Grove Barns, (c) Notting Barns, Wenlocks Barn.
bot (n) Botwell (?). ME **bowe, boghe** (n) Bow.
bræmbel Bromley.
broc Brook (4), Brook Green, Eel Brook, Walbrook.
brom Brompton, Broomhill.
brycg *Battle Bridge*, Bollo, Bow, Brentford, Cannon, Counters and Cranford Bridge, Knightsbridge, Maidens Bridge, *Parr's Bridge*, Queen's, Silk, Staines and Stamford Bridge, Stonebridge, Uxbridge.
burh Bury, Bury Field, Bury Street (2), Canon-, E-bury, Edgware Bury, High-, Kings-, Old-bury, *Stadbury*, Sudbury, (b) Barns-, Blooms-, Brondes-, Fins-, Gunners-, Mapes-, Sun-bury.
burna Bourne (2), *Fishbourne*, Holborn, Tyburn, Westbourne, (b) Marylebone, (c) Kilburn.
*byde (n) Bedfont, Bedwell (?).
cætt (n) Cattlegate. ME **cauce** (n) Stepney Causeway.
cealc Chalkhill. **ceald** Chalk Farm.

ceosol Chiswell Street.   ME chase Enfield Chase.

cierring (n) Charing.   ciese Chiswick.   cirice Whitchurch.

clæg Clay Hill.   clæne Clendish.

late OE clerc (n) Clerkenwell.   clif Ratcliff.

*clop (n) Clapton.   cniht Knightsbridge.

cnoll Knowle Green, *Pinchnoll.*   coppede Copthall (2).

cot(e) Chalk Farm, Eastcote, *Northcott*, Sheepcote, *Shipcotes*, *Southcote*, Southcott.

ME court (n) Earls, Hampton and Tottenham Court.

ME cracche, crecche (n) Scrattage, *Cracchegge.*

cran Cranford.   croft Westcroft.

ME crosse Bulls, Charing, Cow, Pursers and Tottenham High Cross, *Stone Cross.*

ME crouche Crouch End and Charing Cross.

cyne (n) Kilburn (?).

cyning (n) Kensal Green (?), Kingsbury, Kingsland.

dal Dawley (?).   denu Ealing Dean, (b) Mogden.

dic Clendish, Grim's Ditch, (c) Shoreditch.

dierne Durnsford.   docce (n) Dog Ait.   dræg Drayton (2).

dun Downs, Down's, Downage, Down Barns, Downhills, Hackney Downs, Hendon, Neasden, *Stickleton*, Uxendon, (b) Hilling-, Horsen-don, Isling-, Tolling-ton, (c) Brimsdown, Willesden.

ean (n) Enfield (?).

eg Ebury, *Ray*, Cowey (?), Forty (2), Rammey, *Thorney*, (b) Hackney, Yeoveney, (c) Pentonhook.

ende Crouch, East, Field, Hatch, Hayes, Mile, North (2), West (2) and Wood End (2), (b) Kings, Kitts and Ponders End.

ened *Endiff.*   eowestre Osterley.

falod Old Fold.

feld Feltham (?), Field End, Broad-, Broom- (3), Church-, East-, Hare-, High-, Link-field, London Fields, Mark-, Mill-, North-, Old- (2), Park-, Ravens-field (2), South-, Spital-fields, Wall-, Wood-field, (c) En-, Hounds-field, Poors Field.

*felte (n) Feltham (?).   finc (n) Finchley (?).   fleot Fleet.

ford Ford, Battle Bridge, Brent-, Cran-, Durns-ford, Green-, Halli-, Long-ford, Old Ford, Sand-, Stam- (2), Strat-ford (2), (b) Hodford, (c) Ashford.

forð (n) Fordhook, Forty (2).

ME frere (n) Friern Barnet, Fryant Fm.

full (n) Fulham (?).   funta (a) Bedfont.   fyrhðe Frith.

gærstun Gaston.   gamen (n) Ganwick (?).

gara Gore, Kensington Gore.

geat Cattle-, High-gate, Manygates, Ox-, South-gate, (b) *Grins-gate.*

gos Goswell.   **græfe** Grove (4).   **græfe or grafa** Grove (3).

ME grene Bethnal, Brook, Cony, Greenford, Kingsbury, Newington, Parsons, Stepney, Stroud, Turnham, Walham, West, Willesden and Wood Green, (b) Bounds, Golders, Goulds, Page, Palmers and Starch Green, (c) Fortis, Fortune and Roe Green.

hæcc Hatch End, (c) Colney Hatch.

(ge)hæg Longhedge, Mitchley.

hæþ Heath (2), Heathrow, Hatton, Hampstead, Hanwell, Hillingdon, Hounslow and Pield Heath, (b) Cambridge Heath.

halig Halliford, Holywell.

ham or **hamm** Astlam, Felt-, Lale-ham, (b) *Blechenham*, Icken-, Totten-ham, (c) Turnham.

hamm Ham, Hampton, (b) Colham, (c) Ful-, Twicken-ham.

hamstede Hampstead.   **hana** (n) Hanwell (?), Hanworth (?).

hangra Hanger (2), *Hangerwood*, (c) Pitshanger.

heah Hendon, Highbury, Highfield, Highgate.

healh Hale (2), *Hale*, Cattlegate, Northolt, Southall, (b) Totten-ham Court, (c) Bethnal.

heall Copthall (2), Cowley and Mimms Hall, Moor-, White-hall, Wood Hall.

hearg Harrow.

hecg (n) Headstone (?), *Cracchegge*, Downage, Gutteridge, Scrattage.

here Harefield.   **hese** Hayes, Heston.

hid *Hide*, Hyde (3), North Hyde.   **hlaw** (b) Hounslow.

hlinc Lynch.   **hlyp(e)** Ruislip.   **hoc** Ford-, Penton-hook.

hoh Hoe (?).   **holh** Holborn, Holloway.

holt Kensal Green, Old Oak (?), Wormwood.   **hop** Hope.

hroc Roxborough, Roxeth.   ***hrucge** (n) *Rug Moor*.

hrycg Plumridge.   **hus** Cowhouse, Grove House.

hwit Whitchurch, Whitton.

hyll Hill (3), Hillend, Hillhouse, Bush Hill, Chalk-, Clay-hill, Eel Brook, Felthamhill, *Hanger Hill*, Mill Hill, Royal, Stamford Hill, Tothill, Windmill Hill, (b) Childs, Golders and Winchmore Hill, (c) Colehill, Dudden, Marble and Notting Hill.

hyrne (c) Coleherne.   **hyrst** (b) Bayhurst.

hyð Chelsea, *Endiff*, (b) Stepney.

iggoð Chiswick and Dog Ait, *Gose Eyte*, Isleworth Ait, *Neat*.

ing Wapping (?).

ingas (b) Ealing, Yeading, (c) Wapping (?).

ingtun (b) Alper-, Charl-, Edmon- (?), Harling-, Kemp-, Kensing-, Ken-, Oaking-, Padding-, Tedding-ton.

inn (n) New and Staple Inn, (b) Gray's Inn, Lincoln's Inn.

læge Leylands. læl (n) Laleham. læs Cowleaze.

lamb Lampton.

land Broadlands, Kingsland, Ley-, Nor-lands, Normand, Shoe-land, Short-, Wood-lands.

lanu Holywell, *Thieving* (2), Moor and Wood Lane, (b) Ballards, Leather, Popes and Swain's Lane, (c) Golden Lane.

leah Bent-, Brom-, Daw-, Oster-ley, (b) Cowley, *Lotheresley*, Wembley, (c) Finchley, Waxlow, Yiewsley.

loc Enfield Lock. ME logge (n) Lodge.

mæd Broadmead. (ge)mæne (n) Manygates.

(ge)mære (b) Winchmore (?), Mare Street.

mearc Markfield. meos Muswell.

mere Bradmore, *Rug Moor*, Stanmore.

mersc Marsh (4), Marsh Lane, Hackney and South Marsh, Wildmarsh.

micel Mitchley.

mor Moor, Moorfields, Moorhall, Moor Lane, Harefield Moor, Stanwellmoor.

myln Turnmill. myncen Minchenden.

mynster Westminster.

ora Nower, (b) Pinner. ME ost (n) Limehouse.

ME parke Park (9), Old Park. pinn (n) Pinner (?).

pirige Perry, Perivale. pol (c) Portpool.

ME ponde (n) Hampstead Pond. ME popler (n) Poplar.

preost Preston. pyttel (n) Pitshanger (?).

ræw Heathrow. read Ratcliff. ryding Woodridings.

ryge Royal. rysc Ruislip.

sand Sands End, Sandford, Stamford (2).

sceacol (n) Shacklewell. sceald Shadwell.

sceaphierde (n) Shepperton. sceolh Shoeland (?).

scir Sherrick. seað (c) Roxeth. slæd Fennyslade.

smeðe Smithfield (2). smyððe (n) Hammersmith.

spell Spelthorne. ME sperte (n) Spirt.

ME spitel (n) Spittlefields. stæne (n) Steyne.

stan Staines, Stanmore, Stanwell, Whetstone, (b) Haggerston, Ossulstone.

sticol *Stickleton*. stig Mistletoe. stigel (b) Betstile.

stoccen Stoke Newington. stocking Stockingswater.

stow Munster (?).

stræt Stratford (2), Brent, Brook, Bury (2), Cheney, Chiswell, Green, Grove, Mare, Nether, Old, St Johns, Spital and Well Street, (b) Page Street, (c) Turkey Street.

strand Strand (2). strod Stroud Green. sulh (n) Silk.

teo (n) Tyburn.

þorn Spelthorne, (b) Elthorne.

*trun, *turn (n) Turnham.

tun *Tunworth*, Ac-, Bromp-, Clap-, Dray- (2), Hamp-, Hat-, Hes-ton, Kentish Town, Lamp-, Little-, Nor-, Pres-, Shepper-ton, Stoke Newington, Sut- (2), Whit-, Wor-ton, (b) Bos-, Dals-, Edmon-ton, Harlesden, Homer-, Hox-ton, Lisson, Sipson.

twi Twyford.   twicce (n) Twickenham (?).

ME vale (n) Perivale.

weala Walbrook.   weald Weald.   weall Blackwall.

weg Holloway.   wer (b) Edgware.

*werpels (n) Warple, *Warple*.

wic Wyke, Aldwych, Chiswick, Hackney and Hampton Wick, Halliwick, Sherrick, (b) *Padderswick*.

wielle Bed-, Clerken-, Ful-, Gos-, Han-, Holy-, Mus-, Penny-, Shackle-, Shad-, Stan-well, (b) Dormers Well, Waxwell, (c) Bot-, Mas-, Pink-well.

wild Wildmarsh.

worþ (b) *Baber*, Harmonds-, Isle-worth, *Lulls*-, *Rids*-, *Tunworth*, (c) Hanworth.

wudu Wood End (2), Woodfield, Wood Green, Wood Hall, Woodside, Bishops and Chamberlains Wood, Crickle-, Highwood, St Johns Wood, North-, Nor-, Short-wood, (b) Brownswood, (c) Ken and Pear Wood.

wyrm (n) Wormwood Scrubbs.   wyrt Worton.

CELTIC NAMES

The river-names Brent, Colne, Lea and Thames.

FRENCH NAMES

Belsize, Poplar, *Pountfreit*.

NOTES ON THE DISTRIBUTION OF THESE ELEMENTS

A few notes on the distribution of certain place-name elements may be given. The significance of this distribution depends to a considerable extent upon a comparison with the distribution in other counties, more especially in neighbouring and adjacent counties. For the distribution in neighbouring counties cf. PN Ess 565–70, PN Herts 243–7, PN Bk 251, PN Sr 350–2. The distribution in Kent has not been fully analysed but the material is fairly full in PN K.

broc, burna. The examples are about equal in number, but no examples of **broc** are found in the names of important places.

burh. Only two of these, Kingsbury and Sunbury, are ancient parishes, and they are probably the only two that go back to OE times. The others are of later manorial origin and there is only one example, viz. Edgware Bury, where the element is added to the parish name. It is worth noting that most of the medieval examples are in Ossulstone Hundred near London. There are three examples in Islington parish alone and two in Willesden.

cot(e). In proportion to the size of the county this element is slightly more frequent than in Surrey, Essex, Hertfordshire and Buckinghamshire. Three of the examples are now lost. Most of them are in Elthorne Hundred.

denu is very rare but this is probably due to the general lie of the land.

dun. This element is fairly common. Seven examples are parishes or old manors.

eg. The examples occur, as one would expect, near the Thames or Lea.

feld. The distribution agrees roughly with that for the neighbouring counties, but except for Enfield, Harefield and the two Smithfields, the examples refer to small and unimportant places.

grene is common, the examples, as in the adjacent counties, being mainly late.

ham, hamm. Colham, Fulham and Twickenham are certain examples of **hamm** as shown by the early forms. Of the seven other names, Feltham, Ickenham, Laleham and Tottenham are DB manors and are probably **ham**-names. Astlam and Turnham appear later and are uncertain.

heall. This element is more common than in Hertfordshire and Surrey, but less frequent than in Essex.

hyrst. This element is very rare, as in Hertfordshire. It is more common in field-names.

ingtun. In proportion to the size of the county, this element is much more frequent than in the adjacent counties. Seven of the ten examples are either DB manors or parishes or both.

leah. This element is less common than in the adjacent counties. Only two of the nine examples are DB manors.

tun. The proportion of tun-names is about equal to that of Buckinghamshire and is much higher than that for Essex, Hertfordshire and Surrey. Only eight of the twenty-seven examples are DB manors. Only two, Edmonton and Preston, are in the north of the county, and the element is also rare in the southwest (Spelthorne Hundred). There are a good many in the neighbourhood of Hounslow, viz. Hatton, Heston, Lampton, Sipson, Sutton, Whitton, Worton. North-east of London we have Clapton, Dalston, Homerton, Hoxton, Norton and (Stoke) Newington, all near one another. Most of the other examples lie a little to the west of London, viz. Acton, Drayton in Ealing, Kentish Town, Sutton in Chiswick, Boston, Harlesden, Lisson, Brompton. (West) Drayton is an isolated example on the Buckinghamshire border.

wic. The proportion agrees with that for the neighbouring counties. Chiswick is a parish name but none is a DB manor.

worþ. There are seven examples, two of which are now lost. Three of the others are parishes and DB manors. All except the lost *Lolsworth* in Stepney are in the west of the county.

PERSONAL NAMES COMPOUNDED IN MIDDLESEX PLACE-NAMES

Names not found in independent use are marked with a single asterisk if they can be inferred from evidence other than that of the place-name in question. Such names may be regarded as hardly less certain than those which have no asterisk. Those for which no such evidence can be found are marked with a double asterisk.

(a) OLD ENGLISH

Babba (Baber), *Bǣga (Bayhurst), *Betti* (m), *Bettu* (f) (Betstile), *Blæcca* (*Blechenham*), *Blīða (Bethnal (?)), *Bord* (Boston), *Bōt* (f) (Botwell (?)), *Cæntbeorht (Cambridge Heath), *Cēolrēd* (Charlton), *Cǣna* (Kempton, Kenton), *Cofa (Cowley), *Cola* (Colham), *Cylla (Kilburn (?)), *Cynesige* (Kensington), *Dēorlāf* (Dalston), *Dēormōd* (Dormers Well), *Ēadhelm* (Edmonton), *Ealhbeorht* (Alperton), *Ēana (Enfield (?)), *Eccel (Ashford (?)), *Ecgi* (Edgware), *Ella* (Elthorne), *Fin* (Finsbury), *Finc* (Finchley (?)), *Fulla (Fulham (?)), *Geddi* (Yeading), *Geofa* (Yeoveney), *Giella (Ealing), *Gīsla (Islington), *Gīslhere* (Isleworth), *Haca (Hackney), *Hærgod* (Haggerston), *Hana* (Hanwell, Hanworth (?)), *Heremōd* (Harmondsworth), *Herewulf* (Harlesden), *Hilda (Hillingdon), *Hlōþhere* (*Lothersley*), *Hōc (Hoxton (?)), *Hodda (Hodford), *Hogg (Hoxton (?)), *Horsa* (Horsendon), *Hrōc (Roxborough (?), Roxeth (?)), *Hūnburh* (f), *Hūnbeorht* (m) (Homerton), *Hund (Hounslow), *Hygerēd* (Harlington), *Lēofrūn* (f) (Leather Lane), *Lil* (Lisson), *Lull* (*Lullsworth*), *Mocca* (Mogden), *Ōswulf* (Ossulstone), *Pad(d)a* (Paddington), *Pælli*,

*Palla (*Padderswick*), *Pin*, *Pinna (*Pinchnoll*, Pinner), **Purta (*Portpool*), *Pyttel (Pitshanger (?)), *Sibwine* (Sipson), *Stybba (Stepney), *Sunna (Sunbury), *Ticca* (Ickenham), *Toca* (Oakington), *Tolla (Tollington), *Totta* (Tottenham (2)), *Tuda* (Teddington), **Twicca (Twickenham (?)), *Wæc (Waxwell), *Wæmba (Wembley), *Wæppa (Wapping (?)), *Wife (Yiewsley (?)), *Wulfwīg (Wolves Lane), *Wynsige* (Winchmore Hill (?)).

(b) Old Scandinavian

Gunnhild (f) (Gunnersbury).

FEUDAL AND MANORIAL NAMES

There are very few examples of the addition of the manorial owner's name in order to distinguish one manor from another, but we may note Friern Barnet, Cowley Peachey, Newington Barrow and Norton Folgate. The addition of any distinctive epithet is equally uncommon but we may note *Cold Kennington*, the old name for Kempton Park, and Stoke Newington.

There are a number of examples of **bury** in compounds with the personal names of the holders of the manor, many of whom have been identified. Such are Barnsbury, Bloomsbury, Brondesbury, Finsbury, Gunnersbury, Mapesbury, or, compounded with other elements, Canonbury, Ebury, Highbury, Sudbury, *Norbury*, *Oldbury*.

Genitival compounds deriving from personal names are fairly common, as in Aylwards, Balmes, Bounds, Bowes, Bruce (Castle), Cantelowes, Ducketts, Durrants, Fawnes, Flambards, Pates. Sometimes the personal names themselves are ultimately of territorial origin as in Clutterhouse, Mockings, Swakeleys.

Sometimes the territorial name itself appears in unchanged form as the name of the manor, as in Poyle, Savoy, Weir Hall, and in Brackenbury, Clavering and Knightscote (Fms), Dyrham (Park), Walham (Green), or a personal name may so appear as in Breakspear.

FIELD AND MINOR NAMES

(a) *Field and minor names arranged under the forms of their elements, mainly as recorded in EPN. For* (n), *v. supra* 187.

ac, 'oak.' Interesting compounds are *Goblin oake* (1680), *Seynt Thomas oke* (c. 1600). *Esterache* (13th) is probably '(at the) east oak,' while *Chaldokfeld* (1316), *Cheldokefeld* (1321) is perhaps a compound denoting 'cold oak.' *v.* Introd. xvii.

æcer is common. We have reference to (a) size, as in *Lytel-halfacre* (1377), *Onaker* (1250), *Twayacres* (1685), *Threnacres* (1464), *Foureacres* (1448), *Vifaker, Sovenhacres* (t. Hy 3), *Eytacres* (1308), *Nineacre* (1315), *les noefacres, les disacres* (1347), *Tyenacre* (1377), (b) shape, as in *Langacre* (1237), *Roundeacre* (1544), *Sharpacre, le Pykedacre* (1485) (*v.* piked), (c) situation, as in *Merkakere* (1270) (*v.* mearc), *Lampetacre* (1444) (i.e. loam-pit acre), *le Foracre* (1332), (d) creatures feeding there, as in *Ganderacre* (1467), *Coweacre* (1411), (e) owner or occupier, as in *Bernardesacre* (1427), *Goldbeteresacre* (1411), *Munchin four acres* (1409) (i.e. 'nuns'' (*v.* Minchendon *supra* 69)). Descriptive epithets are added in *Geldeneakre* (1380), 'golden acre' (cf. *infra* 213) and *Blackacre* (1574).

æpse is found in *wogan æpsan* (959), '(at the) crooked aspen.'

æsc is found in *Sareseyneshe* (1551), 'Saracen ash,' why so called we do not know.

alor, 'alder,' is found in *Fridesaldre* (1201), apuldor, 'apple-tree,' in *apoldre* (959), *le Brodeappeldore* (1434), *Horeapuldore* (1376), 'grey appletree.'

bedd (n) is twice found in *Wythebed* (1380), *Whetheybed* (1458).

beorg, 'hill, barrow,' is found in *þone clofenan* (i.e. 'cloven') *beorh* (962), *le Berwe* (t. Ric 2), *le Northborowe* (1302), *Tichelberch* (1252), i.e. 'tile-hill.' The first two are found in Sunbury and must have reference to barrows as there are no natural hills here. *Skarborowe* (1443) in Kensington is curious, for one can hardly have a Scandinavian *scarth* here. The name may be manorial or family and derive from Scarborough (NRY).

botm is found in *le Botme* (1302).

bræc, 'land newly taken into cultivation,' is found in *Brache* (1207 and 1380), *le Brach, Westbrech* (t. Ric 2). It survives in modern field-names in the form *breach*.

broc is common as in *Broca* (1208), *Padebrok* (1274) ('toad-brook'), *Smalbrok* (1485) or, compounded with a personal name, *Baillesbrok* (1420) and *Densshesbroke* (1404).

brocc-hol is found in *Brockehole* (1312) in Hampstead.

brom is found in *Edenbrom* (t. Ric 2).

brycg is found in various compounds. It is associated with animals in *Horsbrige* (1302), *Bolebregge* (1229), with neighbouring buildings in *Shepecotebrigge* (1353), with a vehicle in *Cartebrugge* 1371. In *Wythynbrigge* (1445), *Russenbrygge* (1495) we may have reference to causeways of withies or rushes on marshy ground, cf. Roy's Bridge (PN Nt 95–6), Risebridge (PN Ess 119), and further references given under those names. *Nunnebreg* (1365) belonged to the nuns of Merton Abbey. *Loundresbregge* (1443) in Kensington was presumably on the road to London (Anglo-French *Loundres*).

burh is fairly common. *Erthbery* (13th) in Stepney was clearly an old earthwork. *Eldebury* (1312) in Hampstead and (1387) in Hackney might be either earthworks or manor-houses. *Alfrichesburi* (1240) is probably a manor-house. *Buryfield* is common and probably denotes one near a manor-house.

burna is used fairly commonly. It is often reduced colloquially to *bone*, as in *Bone* Mead, Maryle*bone*. Cf. PN Bk 98, PN Herts 71.

busc, 'bush.' *Quabbebussh* and *Welbussh* (1413) have reference to the site (*v.* quabbe), *Burymannesbushe* (1365) to the owner.

ME **butte** (n) is fairly common, often in the plural, and has reference to strips of ground abutting on a boundary, often at right angles to other ridges in the field. We may note *lez Buttes* (1313) and two examples of *Whit(e)buttes* (1436, 1438). Some of the *buttes* may have reference to archery-butts.

bytme, 'bottom,' is found in *le Bitme* (1456) and *Holebytymhill* (1426), 'hollow bottom.' It survives in the modern *Bittoms*.

ME **close** (n) is common but late; common are references to things growing there as in *Bromeclose* (1537), *Busshie close* (1558), *Fernyclose* (1557), *Fyrsenclose* (1540), *Rose Close* (1612), *Saffron Close*. We may note also *Chequerclose* (1624), *Dovehouse* and *Cundit Close* (1549), *Shiphouse Close* (1537) and *The Diall Close* (1644).

cnæpp, 'knot, hill,' has been noted once in *Knappe hilles* (1475) and **cnoll** in *Meaden knowles* (1556).

ME **coninger** (n), 'rabbit-warren,' is not so common as usual. We may note *Conningarfeld* (1542) and *Connygree* (1619).

cote, 'cottages,' is fairly common as in *Aldecote* (1252), *le Shepecote* (1556), and, with personal names, *Piperescote* (1272) and *Wlfrichescot* (1229).

croft, 'small enclosure,' is one of the commonest elements. It is compounded with (*a*) plant-names in *Ban-, Bene-croft* (1436), *Farncroft* (1197), *Fernicroft* (13th), *le Ferncroft* (1492), *Otecroft*

(t. Hy 6), *Peasecroft* (1625), *Perycroft* (1448), *Piricroft* (1321), *le Rushcroft* (1436), *Thyselcroft* (1434), *Whatecroft* (1434), *Whetecroft* (1564), (*b*) animal and bird names in *Chalfcroft* (1277), *Calf-*, *Chelfe-croft* (1312), *Fauconcroft* (t. Ed 3), *Gosecroft* (1388), *Horscroft* (1346), *Tadicroft* (1302) (i.e. toad), (*c*) a descriptive epithet in *Bradecroft* (1274), *Brodecroft* (1252), *Littelcroft* (1252), *le Neucroft* (1380), *Scharpecroft* (1391), *Threherned* (1403) (i.e. 'three-cornered'). Other compounds are *Homecroft* (1252), *Kitchencroft* (1754). Compounds with personal names are numerous as in *Vitaliscroft* (1267), *Wlfrichescroft* (1229), *Thomelines croft* (t. Hy 3), *Walterescroft* (1325), *Wattescroft* (1387). The *Menecroft* (1401) was probably held in common (*v.* (ge)mæne). *Seintmaricroft* (1301) and *Spyttal croft* (1443) were probably parts of religious endowments. *Croft* is sometimes reduced to *cot*, *cut* in modern field-names.

cros. Note *Tyledecros* (1383), presumably with some covering.

ME **crouche**, 'cross,' is found compounded with personal names in *Donkescrouche* (1372), *Sawyngescrouche* (1448).

cumb, 'valley,' has been noted in *le Combe* (1431) and *Lotcombe* (1547).

dal, 'share in the common field,' is occasionally found as in *Langedole* (1329), *Harpdole* (1685).

dell, so common in Hertfordshire, is late and rare in Middlesex, as in *Dellshott* (1636), *Dell Field* (1754) and *Taper dell* (1475). The only parish in which it is common is South Mimms on the Hertfordshire border. For the full significance of this name in that county *v.* PN Herts 253.

denu, 'valley,' is occasionally found. In ME it takes the form *le Dene* (t. Ric 2) or *le Dane* (13th) (*v.* Introd. xvii). It is found in the compound *hwæte dene* (962) in the parish of Sunbury, though the ground here is dead level. Note also *Danefeld* (1329).

dic, 'ditch, dyke,' is common, as one might expect in this well-watered county. *Mearcdic* (962) and *le Meredych* (1485) were probably boundaries, *v.* mearc, (ge)mære. Descriptive compounds are *le Eldedich* (1394) (i.e. 'old'), *Depedych* (1458), perhaps also *Blanchediche* (1228).

dun is occasionally found as in *Cartdoune* (1387), *Couldedowne* (1636) or, with a personal name, *Lefsiesdon* (13th) from OE *Lēofsige*.

dyncge, 'manure heap,' is found in *le Denge* (1502), *Dinge* (1574).

eg, 'marsh land,' is fairly common as in *Ludwardeseye* (1436). It often survives in the form *Ray* from ME *at ther eye* > *at the reye*.

elm has been noted in *Sprendelme* (sic) (1387) for 'spread elm,' *Brendelme* (1642), i.e. 'burned elm,' *le Hygh Helmes* (1545) and, with a personal name in *Simondesselme* (1448).

ende, 'end, quarter, district,' is occasionally found as in Bk, Herts, Ess.

ersc, 'stubble-field,' has been noted in *Whetersshe* (1365).

ett (n), a collective suffix, commonly found with tree and plant names, is probably found in *Withett* (1647).

fal(o)d has been noted in *Pondfald* (1450), i.e. 'pinfold.'

feld, 'open land,' is very common. Only in some of the later examples has it the sense 'enclosed space' which we now associate with the word *field*. We have a descriptive first element in *Brodefeld* (1228), *Eldefeld* (1337), *Longefeld* (13th), *Netherfeld* (1302), *Stonifeld* (1205), *Witefeld* (1256), *lez Wowefeldes* (14th) (from OE *wōh*, 'crooked'), reference to what grows there in *Grasfeld* (1277), *Hethfeld* (1467), *Otfeld* (1339), to trees in *Byrchfeld* (1470), *Pirifeld* (1339), to its fallow condition in *le Fallowfeld* (1537), *Leifeld* (13th) (from OE *lǣge*, 'fallow'), to the site in *Danefeld* (1329) (*v.* denu), *Mersshfeld* (1383), to birds and livestock in *Fugelefeld*, *Wrenfeld* (13th) and *Drakefeld* (1519). *Hunifeld* (t. Hy 3) was probably a sticky or muddy field (cf. *infra* 205). *Bellfield* (1538), *Churchfeld* (1552), *Mynchyngfeld* (1553) (*v.* Minchendon *supra* 69) and *Spettellfeld* (1541) were probably religious endowments. We have reference to the common field and its divisions in *Estfeld* and *Westfeld* (1202) and *le comonfeld* (1592). For *Homfeld* (1274) and *Homefeld* (1441) *v.* ham. Very common are compounds with personal names as in *Berneresfeld* (1316), *Sagorsfeld* (1321) (OE *Sǣgār*), *Palmeresfeld* (c. 1200), *Brihteuefeld* (13th) (OE *Beorhtgiefu* (f)).

fenn, 'marsh,' is found in *bulunga fenn*, *lundene fenn* (959), *le Fen* (1272), *le Fanne* (t. Ric 2), *Langefen*, *Schortfanne* (1201). For *fan(ne)*, *v.* Introd. xvii.

feorðung, 'fourth part,' '*farthing*,' has given rise to some field-names containing the element *farthing*. Sometimes it may denote a measure of land, sometimes it may represent the monetary valuation.

fleot, 'small stream.' A few examples are found in parishes with marshland such as *Barbeflete* (1306) in Enfield, *Holflete* (1252) and *Melflet* (1245) (*v.* myln) in Edmonton, *Schadflet* (1218) (i.e. 'shallow' (*v.* sceald)) in Stepney.

furh, 'furrow,' is occasionally found as in *Roughfourwe* (1473) and *Waterfurrows* (1754).

furlang is common and generally has reference to one of the strips of the common field. We have reference to its size in compounds with *le Longe* (1307), *le Schert* (1302), *le Short*

(1403), to situation in compounds with *Broc* (t. Ric 2), *Dane* (1365) (*v.* denu), *Dych* (1436), *Crouch* (1380), *Lane* (1436), *Strat* (1598), to crops in *Bamfurlong* (1445), *Ryefurlong* (1457). Very rarely is mention made of the owner as in *Pilcheresfurlong* (1373). Note also *Namelesfurlong* (1380) (i.e. 'nameless').

fyrhŏe, 'woodland,' is occasionally found in the form *frith* as in *wood called Frith* (1203).

gærstun, 'paddock,' is occasionally found as in *le Garston* (1329), *Gasson* (1665).

gara, 'gore,' is found in such names as *Gara Lamberti* (t. Hy 3), *le Gore* (1235), *le Goren* (pl.) (t. Ric 2), *The Goore* (1438).

ME garden is fairly common. The earliest examples are *Southgardyn* (1316) and *Pirygardyn* (1376) from pirige, 'pear-tree.' Note also *Revysgarden* (1450), *Beegardyn* (1457), *Edwynesgardyn* (1450) and *Cokkowesgardyn* (1401). *Hop Garden* is occasionally found.

geard, 'yard, enclosure,' is found in *Wingeard* (1201) (i.e. 'vineyard') in Stepney and, compounded with a personal name, in *Ordmaresgerd* (1227).

geat, 'gate, gap,' is fairly common as in *sandgeat* (959), *Stonygate* (1316), *Courtegate* (1436).

græfe, graf(a), 'grove, thicket,' are common but difficult to differentiate and were often confused. Richard de *la Grave* and Richard *atte Grove* in Kingsbury (*supra* 63) seem to be the same person. See also under Grove Barns *supra* 19. *la Graue* seems to refer to a place now called The Grove *supra* 66 and there is similar confusion under Grove House in Chiswick *supra* 90. Compounds with personal names are frequent as in *Algaresgrave* (1321), *Scottesgraf* (13th).

ME grene is common as in *Hartgreene* (1650), *Hasylgrene* (1448), *Stylgrene* (1445). Compounds with personal names are frequent, such as *Adgoresgrene* (1297), *Gubbesgrene* (1439), *Herewoldysgrene* (1428).

(ge)hæg, 'enclosure.' We may note *Longa Haia* (1198), *Horshey* (1445). It is found occasionally in the modern form *hay(s)*.

hæcc, 'hatch, gate,' is fairly common in woodland areas.

haga, 'enclosure, tenement,' is very common. Compounds with a personal name are specially frequent, such as *Arnoldeshawe* (1321), *Cowperehawe* (1436), *Gunnildeshawe* (1321), *Johanhawe* (1380), *Symondeshawe* (1421). Other compounds are *le Grenehawe* (1351), *Eldehawe* (1426), *le Scepenhawe* (1331) (i.e. '(by the) shippon'), *Esthawe* (1302), *Caponhawe* (1451).

ham appears as a first element in a number of field-names in the form *hom(e)* and is descriptive of a field which is in the immediate neighbourhood of an estate or mansion. Early examples are *Homfeld* (1274) and *Homefeld* (1441).

hamm, 'bend in river, enclosure,' is found in *le Hamme* (1426), *Southamme* (t. Hy 6), *Barnhamme* (1250).

hamsteall, 'farm steading,' is found several times as in *le Hamstalle* (1392), *Hamstalemede* (1424).

ME **hanginde** (n), 'hanging,' used of sloping ground, not necessarily particularly steep, is occasionally found. This is the southern dialect form of the present participle. In modern names it survives in the form *Hanging*.

hangra, 'wooded slope,' is found in *fox hangran* (974), *Clehangre* (1256) (from **clæg**).

heafod, 'headland of ploughed land,' is found in *Longehedes* (1338).

healh, 'nook, corner,' is common as in *le Hale* (t. Ric 2), *Southehale* (1302), *le Foulehale* (1411), *Shortehale* (1318).

heall, 'hall,' is found in *Coldhall* (1377), *Coppydhall* (1502) (i.e. 'peaked hall'), *Elmehalle* (1538), *Tylehall* (t. Ed 3), *Wodehalle* (1431).

hecg, 'hedge,' is common as in *Brodhegge* (1277), *Langehegge* (1467), *Sharpehegge* (1413), *le Cuttydhegge* (1401), *Foxholehegge* (1483). *le Merehegge* (1375) was probably a boundary hedge, *v.* (ge)**mære.**

hid is found occasionally as in *le Hyde* (1289), *le Halfhyde* (1480), *Taloweshyde* (1439).

hielde, 'slope,' is found in *Stanmereheld* (1289).

hlaw, 'hill, barrow,' is found in *eadbryhtes hlaw* (962).

hlinc, 'slope,' is found in *le Lynche* (1441), *Waterlynch* (1329).

hoc, 'hook, corner,' is fairly common as in *la Hoke* (1302), *Pikeshoc* (12th), *Horsmanhok* (1436), *Quabhoke* (1538) (from **quabbe,** 'marsh').

hoh, 'hill-spur,' has only been noted in *Samsonesho* (1228).

ME **holm,** 'water-meadow,' is occasionally found as in *Southolm* (1318), *Roweholme* (1467), *Spitelholme* (1467).

hop, 'enclosure (especially in marshland),' is found in *Redhope, Trendlehope* (1345) in Stepney (from **tryndel,** 'circle'), and with a personal name in *Kenewardesshop* (13th).

hyll is common. We have reference to what grows there in *Benehill* (1578), *Bromehil* (1598), *Farnhull* (1302). *Vernehille* (1480) (*v.* Introd. xvii), *Rihille* (1434), *Shrobbenhill* (1450), *Thornhyll* (1483). *Clophill* (1455) contains the same first element as Clapton *supra* 105.

hyrne, 'corner,' is fairly common as in *Stenelytleherne* (1450), *Clerkesherne* (1444), *Hogmanherne* (1575). It survives as *hearne*.

hyrst, 'wooded hill,' is fairly common as in *Brokeherst* (1490), *Foxhurst* (1446), *Mapeldereherst* (1277), i.e. 'maple-tree', *Note-*

hirst (1312) (i.e. 'nut'), *Stonyherst* (1306), *Tymberhurst* (1312), *Wydehurst* (1450), *Wolfherst* (1574). The first element in *Bemerherste* (13th) in Hampstead is OE *bīemere*, 'trumpeter' (cf. Bemerton PN W, 225). Occasionally we have compounds with personal names such as *Cotteshyrst* (962), *Doddeshurst* (1512).

hyð, 'landing place,' is found occasionally. Its modern form is *hithe* or *hythe*.

iggoð, 'islet, small piece of marshland,' is found in *The Eighte* (1636) and (with affixed *n*) in *le Neate* (1547). Cf. *Neat supra* 170. It survives in the forms *Ait*, *Eyot*, *Aight*, *Eight*, and is commonly used of islets in the Thames.

innam (n), 'piece of land taken into cultivation,' is found in *Innome* (1329). Cf. PN Sx 29–30, PN Sr 272, 362, PN Ess 583.

lacu, 'small stream,' is found in *Quethelake* (sic) for *Quechelake* (1326) (from ME *queche*, 'thicket'), *Hartelake* (1542), *Swift Lake* (1636).

læs, 'pasture,' is fairly common. We may note *Bromlese* (1443), *Busshelese* (1467), *Chalvelese* (1367), *Horselease* (1574), *Oxlese* (1439), *Somerlese* (1312) (i.e. 'summer pasture'), *Shepelease* (1557), *Stonelase* (1467), *Swanne leace* (1557). Compounds with personal names are rare, as in *Admerslese* (1441) (from OE *Éadmǣr*). It appears in modern field-names in the form *leaze*, *leys*.

land is very common. Doubtless we often have reference to the *lands* or strips in the common field. Descriptive compounds are found in *Blakelond* (1428), *Goldenelond* (1380), *Grenelond* (1229), *Smalelond* (1365), *Longelond* (1321), *Sortelond* (1227), *Eldlond* (t. Ric 2), *Newelond* (1329), *Rowlond* (t. Ric 2), *Scherpelond* (1338), *Stonylond, Stranglond* (1380), *Stinkindelond* (c.1250). We have reference to things growing in *Appelond* (13th), *Bandland* (1490) (from bean), *Bromlond* (1302), *Flexlond* (1438), *Napeland* (13th) (from *nǣp*, 'neap, turnip'), *Sedlond* (1343), to creatures feeding there in *Goselond* (t. Ric 2), *le Mouslond* (1490), *Schiplond* (1439), to shape in *Bowestrenglond* (1321). *Onesmons* (t. Ed 3) is 'one man's.' *le Revelond* (1401) is associated with the reeve, *Knyghtlond* (1376) with the cniht or young serving man; *Boiland* (13th) in Stepney seems to contain the common boy (cf. PN Ess 426). Occasionally we have compounds with a personal name as in *Bernardeslond* (1321), *Herefreðinglond* (825), *Levegareslond* (13th), *Payneslond* (1494), *Tolleslond* (1277). *Poors Land* was a charitable endowment.

ME launde, 'woodland opening,' is found in *Olde Lawne* (1656) and survives in modern fields called *the Lawn*.

leah, 'wood, clearing,' is found in a few additional early names. It is compounded with tree and plant names in *risc leage* (972),

Pirilegh (1312), *Bromleye* (1537), and with ME *spōn*, 'wood-shaving,' in *Sponlee* (t. Hy 6).

mæd, 'meadow,' is very common. It is often compounded with words having reference to water as in *Flodmede, Mormede* (1319), *Spertemed* (1380) (cf. Spirt Lane *supra* 26), *le Welmede* (1485), *le Wermede* (1380). We may note descriptive compounds such as *Holmede* (1357), *Hullymede* (1337) (i.e. 'hilly'), *Lange-mede* (1290), compounds with plant and tree names such as *Linmede* (t. Hy 6) (from *līn*, 'flax'), *Rissemad* (1250) (i.e. 'rush'). *Dolmede* (1332) and *Lotmede* (1547) were portioned out, *Trendel-mede* (1312) was circular, *Lady meade* (1537) and *Prostmade* (12th) were probably religious endowments (*v.* preost), *Gospel-mede* (1459) was probably on the parish boundary, the gospel being read there in the beating of the bounds. *Dourymede* (1460) is presumably self-explanatory. Occasionally we have personal names as the first element as in *Edrichesmad* (1201), *Duddemede* (1444). *Costowemede* (13th), *Cottemede* (1302) were associated with cottages, *Hamstalmede* (1424) with a farm steading (*v.* hamsteall), while *Tounemede* (1443) was near a village or hamlet (*v.* tun).

(ge)mæne, 'common,' is found in such names as *menecroft* (1401). It is often used of land on the boundary of two parishes.

mearc, 'boundary,' is found in a few names such as *Markstakes* (1483).

mere, 'pool,' is common, but when the site cannot be identified it is difficult to distinguish it from OE **(ge)mære**, 'boundary.' We clearly have **mere** in *riscmere* (962), 'rush-pool.' *Warge-mere* (1189) in Fulham is a compound of OE **wearg**, 'felon, criminal,' possibly the pool was one in which criminals were drowned.

mersc and **mor** are fairly common. **mor** has the common south country sense 'marshland' and none of the associations of the North Country 'moors.'

ord, 'point,' has been noted in *le Ord* (1302).

pæð. *Dosserespathe* (13th) and *Pedderespath* (1294) were paths used by pedlars (ME *dossere, peddere*).

ME **pightel**, 'small enclosure,' is very common and is found earlier than usual. Early examples are *Fullerespictel* (c. 1200), *Deringespictel, Nicholes Picthtel* (1252), *Gresputhel* (13th) (i.e. 'grass'), *Stonipiktell* (c. 1237). Other examples are *Chalfes-pyghtell* (1441) (*v.* cealf, 'calf'), *Edwardespyghtell* (1392), *Strode-pyghtell* (1448) (*v.* strod), *Welpightil* (1467) and *Pightilcroft* (1443). The nasalised form **pingle** is found occasionally as in *one little close called the Pingle* (1572) and *Walnutt Tree Pingwell* (sic) (1602). It survives in the forms *pightle, pickle.*

ME piked (n), 'with *pikes* or corners,' is occasionally found as a descriptive element. It appears in modern field-names in the form picket.

ME pleyne (n), 'plain,' is found in *Sibilespleyne* (1441) in Enfield.

plegstow, 'play-piece,' has been noted once in *Pleyestowe* (1250) in Edmonton.

ME plott, platt is occasionally found as in *la Plottes* (1275), *la Plotte* (1443), *Stokyngplatte* (1441) (*v.* stocking).

pol and ME ponde (n) are occasionally found as in *le Horspole* (1373), *Flodyate pole* (1441), *Sommerpoole* (1636), *Frithpond* (t. Ed 3) (*v.* fyrhðe), *Duddingespond* (1428), *Rothulvespond* (1345) and *Sweynespond* (t. Ed 3).

pund (n), 'enclosure, pound,' survives in the modern *pound*.

pytt is common. We have *Cheselputtes* (1275) for gravel (OE *ceosol*), *Cleypytt* (1539), *Colpytt* (1332) for charcoal,' *le gravel- pytte* (1450), *Lamput* (1321) and *le Lomepytt* (1351) for loam (OE *lām*), *Marlepet* (1490). It appears later in the forms *pit, pet*.

ME quabbe (n), 'marsh,' is occasionally found as in *le Quabbe* (1339) in Hackney.

ME queche (n), 'thicket,' is found in *Quache* (t. Hy 6), *Bushfield queche* (1593) and *Quethelake* (sic) *supra* 201.

ræw, 'row,' has been noted twice in the compound *Raton(e)- rowe*, 'rat-row,' a common nickname for a squalid row of houses, once in Tottenham and once in Fulham in the 15th century.

rið, riðig, 'small stream,' is occasionally found as in *holan riðe* (972), *Fullerith* (1434), *Wellreadye* (1619).

ryding, 'clearing,' is common as in *Ruding* (1275), *Riddinges* (1284), *la Rudynge* (1302), *Redynges* (1394), *Reddinge* (1574), *Little Readinge* (1601), *Woderiding* (1413), *Woderedyng* (1472) and, with a personal name, *Savoriesrudinge* (1252). In modern field-names it appears in the forms *ridding, reeding, reading*.

sceat, 'corner of land, *shot*,' is very common. Commonest are compounds descriptive of its situation in relation to some other feature of the landscape, such as *Brokeshot* (1450), *Cunduytshote* (1373) (by some *conduit*), *Dellshott* (1636), *Hangershot* (1472) (*v.* hangra), *Hyndeheggeshot* (1440), *Medshot* (1552), *Stoniputte- schot* (1289), *Stretshot* (1470). Descriptive compounds are *Longshott* (1316), *Netherschote* (1410), *Middleshott* (1539), *Upp- shott* (1625). Other compounds are *Crowshotte* (1289) and *Ryschote* (1312). Occasionally it is compounded with a personal name as in *Balardesschottes* (1443). It is often found in modern field-names in the form *shot(t)*.

slæd, 'shallow valley,' is occasionally found as in *Appleslad* (1546), *Deepeslade* (1658), *Larckeslade* (t. Ric 2), *Haneworthslade*

(1357), *Merslade* (1431), probably a compound of (ge)mære, 'boundary.' It survives in the form *slade*.

ME **slipe** (n), 'narrow strip, *slip*,' is found very commonly as in *le Slype* (1492), *the Slipe* (1574). It survives in the modern field-name *the Slip*.

sloh (n), 'slough,' is found occasionally as in *Fouleslo* (t. Ric 2) and, with a personal name, *Samsonesloghe* (t. Hy 3).

OE **socn**, ME **soke** (Lat *soca*) denotes primarily 'right of jurisdiction' and then the district over which that right is exercised. More particularly it is applied to an area withdrawn from the jurisdiction of the ordinary courts for the benefit of its lord (cf. LnTopRec xvii, 27).

stapol, 'post, pillar,' is occasionally found as in the lost DB manor of *Stanestaple* (1086), *Staples* (1680) and, with a personal name, *Warynstaple* (1448).

stocc, 'stump,' is found in (ðam) *gemearcedan stocce* (959), 'the marked stump,' *le Polledestok* (1294), 'the pollarded stump' and *Calewestok* (1305) from OE **calu**, 'bare.'

ME **stocking**, 'stump-clearing,' is fairly common.

OE **stræt**, ME **strete** in this area is commonly used of a settlement along a road as in Brent Street, Bury Street, Grim Street, Mare Street, Turkey Street, *Brembeleystrete*.

strod, 'marsh,' is fairly common as in *Strode* (1189), *Smythe-strode* (1484), *Strodepyghtel* (1448). It commonly survives in the form *Stroud*.

þorn is fairly common as in *le Coppetthorn* (1332), 'pollarded thorn' (*v.* **coppede**), *Smalthorne* (1436) and *Thikthorne* (1446) and *Fairthorne* (1656).

tun, 'farm, hamlet, settlement,' is common in such modern names as *Town Meadow*, descriptive of pasture close to a village or hamlet. So also *Townsend*.

weg is common. We may note *le Greneweye* (t. Ric 2), *Twyseleweye* (1380) (from OE **twisla**, 'fork'), *Rodwey* (1250).

wic. A few additional unidentified examples have been noted, including *Boterwyk* (1316), i.e. 'butter-farm,' *Deyewyke* (1450), i.e. 'dairy-maid farm' (from ME **deye**), and compounds with personal names such as *Dermodeswican* (980) and *Pernelwyk* (1306).

wiell(e), 'spring, stream,' is very common. We may note *mearcwille* (962) which must have been on the boundary, *Puk-welle* (1436) which was goblin-haunted, *Cressewelle* (1426), *Melkwelesfeld* (1315) where the water must have been milky, and several compounds with personal or occupational names, such as *Billyngeswelle* (1377).

ME **worple**, **warple** (n), 'bridle-way.' See more fully under

Worplesdon (PN Sr 162) and EDD *s.v. wapple*. It survives as *warple*, *worple*.

worþ, 'enclosure,' is occasionally found in unidentified minor names as in *Eldewurthe* (1445). Such compounds as *Petitewurth* and *Granwurth* (i.e. *Grandwurth*) (1201) in Stepney suggest that the word was still a living element after the Norman Conquest.

wudu is common. *Inwood* denotes a wood in the demesne land. An early Middlesex example of *inwudu* is noted under Kingsbury *supra* 62.

(b) *Some of the more common elements in field and minor names either not found or of very rare occurrence in records earlier than the 16th century*.

bell is found occasionally in field-names; sometimes it is due to a neighbouring inn sign, sometimes the field is so called because it had been given for the upkeep of the church bells.

brick-kiln very commonly appears in the colloquial forms *Brickill*, *Brickell* or (with popular etymology) *Brickhill*.

bunkers-hill is a common field and farm name in this county and elsewhere. Its history is fully discussed in PNHerts 76–7. It may occasionally contain the recorded personal name *Bunker* but the frequency of the combination *bunker* and *hill* suggests that the name of the 18th century American battle must for some reason have become popular as a place-nickname.

coldharbour is a nickname of reproach for an exposed place and has no special archaeological significance (cf. PN Sr 406–10).

coneyborough, variant of *conyburrow*, 'rabbit-burrow.'

culver, 'dove, wood-pigeon,' is common as in *Culverwell*, *Culverhaw*, *Culvers Close*.

dial is occasionally found as in *the Diall Close*, *Dyall Field*. Its meaning is obscure. Cf. PN Sr 368.

drift-way is used of a cattle-path or lane, along which they are driven.

flash, 'shallow pool,' from ME *flasshe*, *flosshe*, is occasionally found.

frog is found in such names as *Frog Hall*, *Frog Lane*. This probably has reference to a wet or damp district.

gall, 'barren spot, spongy ground,' is occasionally found as in *White Gall*. Cf. PN Nth 263.

harp is common in field-names where the fields resemble that instrument in shape as in *Harp Shot*, *Little Harp*.

honey is common in field and minor names and generally has reference to the sticky or muddy nature of the ground.

hoppet, hoppit, 'small enclosure,' is frequently found (cf. PN Ess 582).

intake, 'land taken into cultivation,' is rarely used.

kitchen is common in such names as *Kitchen Fd* to denote fields cultivated for domestic purposes.

lammas is occasionally found in field-names and has reference to lands under particular cultivation till harvest which reverted to common pasturage at Lammastide (August 1st) and remained as such till the following spring.

laystall is a place where refuse or dung is laid. It is common in names in the old inhabited areas.

roundabout is common for a field which is circular or has a clump of trees in the middle (cf. PN Wa 336).

sainfoin commonly appears in field-names in the form *Saint-foin* (*Saint Foyne*) as if for 'holy hay,' a well-established bit of folk-etymology.

tenter-yard is very common in the 17th and 18th century London suburbs, as used for a ground for stretching and drying cloth (cf. NED).

(c) *Miscellaneous field and minor names.*

Among early names of a miscellaneous character we may note *Bigbag*(*g*)*e* (1574, 1695), *Byhindethehawes* (1345), cf. haga, *le Crumbe* (1302), *apud Deedcherle* (1436), i.e. 'by (the) dead churl,' with reference perhaps to the discovery of a dead body or possibly with reference to an ancient barrow (cf. similar names in PN Herts 261), *Goldhord* (1219), probably so named from treasure-trove, *innome* (1329), i.e. land taken into cultivation (cf. PN Ess 583), *la Newrente* (1299), *the rounde aboute felde* (1574), *terra vocat' Scratching* (1690), *le Stappe* (1302), i.e. 'the step,' *le Swellowe* (1564), 'deep hole, cavity,' *la Treangle* (1457), i.e. 'the triangle.'

Nicknames figure very largely among field and minor names. They have reference to

(a) Remoteness, as in Botany Bay, Great Virginia, Virginia Row, Nova Scotia, Worlds End, New England, No Man's Land (specially common where two or three parishes meet).

(b) Infertility, as in Starvehall Fm, Bare Bones, Hunger Hill and Lands, Thirst Close.

Other terms of reproach are Coldharbour (cf. PN Sr 406–10 where it is shown that the term is of no particular archaeological significance), Folly (cf. PN Wa 382–5) where it is shown that the term properly has reference to some form of human extravagance, stupidity or the like. For names containing the element *honey* cf. *supra* 205. Friday Field is doubtless a term of reproach from the proverbial ill luck attaching to that day (cf. PN Sr

410–11). For Frog Hall, etc., *v. supra* 205. Nicknames of contempt or reproach are Poor Rachel, All Stones, Knaves Acre, Whim Wham, Halfpenny Bottom, Handkerchief Field, Thieving Lane, Rotten Row. Hundred Acres may be ironical and, at least in one case, is used of a field of less than two roods.

Less common are nicknames of praise such as Butter Field, Nicelands, Fortune's Close, Paradise, Thriving land, Widows Cruise, Land of Promise. Paradise in street-names may be ironical. Shoulder of Mutton is common with reference to the shape of a field. Mount Pleasant is ambiguous. It may be a nickname of praise; in the town it may be used ironically (cf. *supra* 96).

(*d*) *Field-names of which the history can for the most part be traced, arranged under hundreds and parishes. The basis is in each case the Tithe Award for the parish, where such exists. For many parishes, especially for those now within the county of London, no Tithe Award is in existence, but, for some of these, selections of 18th or early 19th century field-names have been taken from local histories. The names in the Award, or in the other sources just mentioned, are given first. These are followed by those names for which we have no early spellings but which can be explained by reference to the glossary of elements found in the field and minor names (supra 195–206).*

Spelthorne Hundred

ASHFORD. Brook Meadow (cf. *le Brok* t. Ric 2 *Rental*). For Home Meadow, Broad Leaze, *v.* ham, læs.

BEDFONT. Broom Hills (*Bromehilfeilde* 1598 *Rental*). Mead Furlong (*Meedfurlonge* 1438 Cl, *v.* furlang). Old Fd (*Eldefelde* ib., *v.* Introd. xvii). Witherly (cf. *Whytherley grove* 1557 Pat). For Breach, Culverwell, Hanging Lands, Long Shot, Road Shott, the Slade, *v.* bræc, culver, hanging, sceat, slæd. For Shoulder of Mutton *v. supra*.

HAMPTON. For Home Fd *v.* ham. Great Stews, i.e. 'fish-ponds.'

HANWORTH. From the EnclA (1801) we have Ray Close (*v.* eg) and Town Mead (*v.* tun).

LALEHAM. Great Ayte (cf. *la Neite* 1329 *MinAcct* and *v. Neat supra* 170). Cherry Croft (id. 1690 *Ct*). Long Dole (*Langedole* 1329 *MinAcct*, *v.* dal). Oatcrofts (cf. *Otlond* ib.). For Home Fd, Hernes Close, Gravel Pightle, Pound Close, the Slip, *v.* ham, hyrne, pightel, pund, slipe.

LITTLETON. Culver Haw, *v.* **culver, haga.** Many Kings is possibly a complimentary nickname, *v. supra* 207.

SHEPPERTON. East Fd (*Estfeld* c. 1380 *HarlCh*). Ferris (*Wester-neuerrye* ib.). Inner Haggle (cf. *Hoggehell* ib., i.e. 'hog-hill'). Lammasses (cf. *Lammas Lands* 1633 Madge and *supra* 206). Newlands (*Newelond* 1329 *MinAcct*). West Fd (*Westfeld* t. Ric 2 *Rental*). For Home Fd, Great, Little and Coombes Ayte, Mill Eyot, Nichols Pickle, *v.* **ham, iggoð, pightel.** For Poor Rachael *v. supra* 207.

STAINES. The Dean Meadow (*le Dene* t. Ric 2 *Rental*, *v.* **denu**). Hale Mill (cf. *le Hale* ib., *Halemyllende* 1485 *WAM*, *v.* **healh**). Mill Mead (cf. *Melneforlong* t. Ric 2 *Rental*, *v.* **furlang**). Newses Mead (cf. *Newes bridge* 1589 BM). Penny Croft (*Pennecroft* 1275 *WAM*, *v.* **croft**). Thick Thorns (*Thikthorne* 1446 ib.). Withy Gate Fd is so named in 1754 (R) (cf. *Wytheneende* t. Ric 2 *Rental*, probably containing unrecorded OE **wiðegn*, 'withy'). For Church and Hythe Eyot, Church Lammas, Roundabout, Thames Shott, *v.* **iggoð, lammas, roundabout, sceat.** For Devils Bush Fd and Shoulder of Mutton, *v. supra* 207.

STANWELL. Bean Closes (*Beneclose* 1546 *Rental*. Cf. *Benecroft* 1367 Cl). Blacken Grove (*Blakinggrave* 1337 *Rental*, *Blakyngrave* 1404 AD iii, *v.* **græfe**). Borrough Hills (cf. *Borowfelde* 1546 *Rental*). Bushy Close (cf. *Busshye leasse* ib.). Court Leys (*Court Ley* ib.). Home Fd (cf. *Homcrofte* 1252 AD iii and **ham**). Mark Furlong (*Markforlang* 1367 Cl, *v.* **mearc, furlang**). Middle Furlong (*Middelforlang* ib.). Oat Close (cf. *Otecroft* 1450 *Rental*). The Warren (id. 1546 ib.). For the Driftway, Fan Close, Waterfurrow Ditch, Lords Hays, Broad and Court Leys, the Lawn, the Pightle, Winding Shott, *v.* **drift-way, fenn, furh, (ge)hæg, læs, launde, pightel, sceat.** For Bare Bones *v. supra* 207.

Isleworth Hundred

ISLEWORTH. Wheatcroft (*Wetecroft* 1375 Cl). For Pound Fd and Copthorne *v.* **pund, þorn.** For Butter Fd and Shoulder of Mutton, *v. supra* 207.

TWICKENHAM. Moor Mead (cf. *le Moore* 1431 *Ct*, *v.* **mor**). South Fd (*Suthfeld* 1436 ib.). Old field-names noted by Cobbet include Bancroft (*Bannecroft* t. Hy 6 *Ct*, *Ban-* 1436 ib., *v.* **croft**). Birch Furlong (id. ib., *v.* **furlang**). Coney Furlong (i.e. 'rabbit furlong'). Crab Tree Shot (cf. *Crabtree* ib. and sceat). Ditch Furlong (*Dichfurlong* 1343 AD v). East Fd (*le Estfeld* 1436 *Ct*). Lym Mead (*Linmede* t. Hy 6 *Rental*, perhaps 'flax mead,' *v.* lin, mæd). North Fd (*Northefeld* 1458 ib.).

Elthorne Hundred

COWLEY. Adcroft (cf. *Adecroft* 1315 Cl in Ealing).

CRANFORD. For Horsleys *v.* læs.

GREENFORD. Birch Fd (*Birchfeild* 1625 *Ct*). Blacklands (*Blacklond* 1537 ib.). Church Fd (*Church feild* 1625 ib.). Lady Mead (*Lady meade* 1537 ib., *v.* mæd). Long Croft (*Longcrofte* 1625 ib.). Mill Hill (*Mylhyll* 1537 ib.). New Fd (*Newfeild* 1625 ib.). Pepper Close (1537 ib.). Pescot Fd (may be *Peasecroft* 1625 ib., *v.* croft). Ridding Fd (*Reddingfeild* ib., cf. *greate Readinge* 1537 ib. and ryding). Town Fd (*Townefeild* 1625 ib., *v. supra* 204). West Mead (*Westmeade* ib.). For Culvers Close, Pen Holme, New Leys, Hill, Home, Long and Wood Pightle, Roundabout, *v.* culver, holm, læs, pightel, roundabout. For Paradise, Poors Land and Thirst Close, *v. supra* 201, 207.

HANWELL. For Bittoms, Home Meadow and Little Harp, *v.* bytme, ham, harp. For Strawberry Meadow cf. Strawberry Hill *supra* 30.

HAREFIELD. Botts Hill (*Botushull* 13th LMxAS iii). Readings (*Little Reddings* 1624 Redford, *v.* ryding). Were Mead (*Wearemead* 1636 ib.). For Dell Fd, Sandy Hearns, Ogbourn and Shire Ditch Aits, Kitchen Fd, the Pightle, Platt, the Slipe, Stockings, *v.* dell, hyrne, iggoð, kitchen, pightel, plott, slipe, stocking.

HARLINGTON. Old Fd (*Oldfelde* 1540 FF). Stony Lands (*Stonyland* t. Hy 8 *AOMB*). For Butt Pond, Home and Town Mead, *v.* butte, ham, mæd, tun. Whim Wham is a nickname of contempt, cf. *supra* 207.

HILLINGDON. In the EnclA 1816 (printed by Redford) we have Bradshaws or Bratchetts Mead (*Bradshaws* 1624 Redford), Chequer Close (id. ib., *v.* checker). Croskey Meadow (*Croskey meade* ib., probably from an inn-sign). Grubb's Croft (*Gubbes close al. Gubbes croft* 1583 Ipm). Lady Mead (*The Lady meads* 1624 Redford, *v.* mæd). Moor Fd (*Moorfields* 1648 ib., *v.* mor). Pen Fd (cf. *Penn close* 1727 ib.). Press Fd (id. 1624 ib.). Long and Run's Readings (cf. *Long Reddings* ib., *Greate, Little*

Readinge 1641 Ipm and **ryding**). For Lynch Close *v.* **hlinc** and
for Shoulder of Mutton *v. supra* 207. Present-day fields noted
by de Salis include Hide Fd (*v.* **hid**), Padcroft Fd, perhaps
'toad croft' from ME *pade, pode*.

ICKENHAM. For Home Close, Pightles, Reedings, the Slips,
v. **ham, pightel, ryding**. For Shoulder of Mutton *v. supra* 207.

NORTHOLT. For Butts Piece, Green Furrows, the Hearn, Horse
Leys, the Pightle, Stroud Fd, *v.* **butte, furh, hyrne, læs, pightel,
strod**. For Fortunes Close *v. supra* 207.

PERIVALE. Horse Close Butts, Home Meadow, Kitchen Fd,
v. **butte, ham, kitchen**. Thrift Meadow is ambiguous. *thrift* may
be the common metathesised form of **fyrhōe**, 'woodland,' or it
may be the common word *thrift* and the name be a complimentary one.

RUISLIP. In Faden (1800) we have Bone Fd, earlier *Borne Field*
(1643 KCR) (near Bourne Fm *supra* 48, *v.* **burna**), Mapit Fd (sic)
(*Marlputfeld* 1436 *MinAcct, Marlepete felde* 1565 *Kings, Mapit
Field* 1754 R, i.e. marl-pit field).

Gore Hundred

HENDON[1]. Asmands Fd (*Assmans* 1685). Banlands (*Bandlands
al. Britelands* 1635, probably 'bean-lands'). Barn Croft (*Berne
croft* 1574). Bell Martins (*Bella Martins* ib., 1635). Black Acre
(id. 1574). Blessbury (*Blessbury Hole* 1685). Boar Mead (id. ib.).
Bolster (id. 1754). Bone Croft (*Bournescroft, Bournelond* 1321
BlBk, *Bonecroft* 1754. Cf. Bone Field *supra*). Breach (cf.
Brachemed 1316–29 *WAM, v.* **bræc**). Broad Fd (*Brodefeld* 1321
BlBk). Brook Fd (*Brokefeild* 1574). Buttericks (*Boterwyk* 1316–
29 *WAM, Butterwicke* 1635. 'Butter farm,' *v.* **wic**). Chalkland
(cf. *Chalke hills* 1635 and Chalkhill Ho *supra* 62. There is no
chalk here). Clay Fd (*Clayfeilde* 1574). Cowbridge Close (id.
1754). Crouch Fd (*Crowche feilde* 1574, *v.* **crouche**). Dean Hook
and Mead (cf. *Denes* ib., *Deene crofte* 1635, *v.* **denu** and cf. Deans
Brook *supra* 3). Deer Fd (*Derefeld* 1321 BlBk). Dell Fd (id.
1754, *v.* **dell**). Duck Mead (id. ib.). Eel Mead and Shott
(*Eel Mead* ib., *v.* **sceat**). Farthing Hill (cf. *Farthing* 1685, *v.*
feorðung). Great, Little Forty (*Forty* 1574, cf. Forty Hall *supra*
73). Fox Hole Wood (cf. *Foxholes* 1754). Fryan Grove (cf.
Fryers londe 1574. *Fryan* probably stands for earlier *Friern*,
cf. Friern Barnet *supra* 99 and Fryant Fm *supra* 62). Gadoby

---

[1] Forms given here are, unless otherwise stated, taken from HendonSurv.

(cf. *Godbesfeld, Goodbeys crofte* 1574). Grove Fd (*Grovefeilds* 1485 ECP). Hatch Croft (id. 1685, *v.* hæcc, croft). Hen Mead (id. 1754). High Fd (*High feld* 1574). Hill Fd (*Hill feild al. Browne croft* 1635). Horn Croft (*Hornecroft* 1574). Holmes (*Homes corner* 1685, *Holmes* 1754). Horse Croft (*Horscroft* 1574). Hungerlands (cf. *Hungerhill* 1574. *v. supra* 206). Kitchen Croft (*lane called Kitchen croft* 1635, *v.* kitchen). Lamb Pits (*Lamput* 1321 BlBk, i.e. probably 'loampit'). Leatheridge (possibly *Leverichescroft* ib. '*Leofric*'s croft'). Lemon Hill (id. 1754). Upper, Lower Ley (*The Leye* 1685, *v.* leah). Long Croft (*Longecroft* 1446 *All Souls*). Malkin Mead (*Makin meade* 1635). Mancroft (id. 1574). Mead Shott (id. 1754, *v.* sceat). Merry Croft (id. ib.). Moor Land (*Morelands* 1574, *v.* mor). Mucknell (*Mucknell Hill* 1575). Needs Hill (*Need Hill* 1754). Nut Fd (*Nuttefeld* 1574). Oldberry (*Oldberries* ib.). Orange Hill (id. 1754). Perry Fd (*Perry feild* 1635, cf. Perivale *supra* 46). Placketts Well (*Plocketts Well* 1754). Plumb Croft (id. ib.). Reets (*Rekes* 1574, *Reades* 1635). Great, Little Riddings (cf. *le Rudyng* 1321 BlBk, *Reddings* 1635, *v.* ryding). The Roundabout (id. 1754, *v.* roundabout). Rowlands (id. 1574). Rushworth (id. 1754). Saffron Fd (id. ib.). Salmon Slades (id. ib., *v.* slæd). Scrubbs (id. ib., *v.* Wormwood Scrubbs *supra* 110). Sheep House Fd (cf. *Schepecoteschot* 1321 BlBk, *v.* sceat). Sheffield (*Shuffield* 1754). Shelk Fd (id. 1685). Sherrock Fd (id. 1754). Shirk Mead (*Sherk Mead* ib.). Slay Lands (*Sley landes* 1574). Slipe Mead (*The Slipe* ib., *v.* slipe). Stains Fd (cf. *le Stane, Stanes* ib., *Stains* 1754 and Staines *supra* 19). Stockings (cf. *Stockinge meade* 1574, *v.* stocking). Stony Plat (*Stonyplotts* ib., *v.* plott). Thorn Fd (cf. *Thorne shotte* ib., *Thornfeilds* 1635, *v.* sceat). Tuttle Fd (may be *Tothill* 1685, cf. Tothill *supra* 174). Up Croft (id. 1434 *WAM*). Water Furrows (id. 1754, *v.* furh). Well Fd (*Wellfeild* 1635). West Fd (*Westfeild* 1574). West Lands (*Westlande* ib.). Whelm Mead (cf. *The Whelme* 1574, probably from OE (æ)wielm, 'spring, source'). Widmore (*Wedmores* ib., *Widmores* 1635). Wool Mead (*Woolemeades* 1635). For Long Breach, Coney Borough, White Gall Fd, Home Meadow, Hanging Fd, Intake, the Pingle, Long Reddings, Saint Foyne Fd, the Shotts, Long Slipe, Slough Fd, *v.* bræc, coneyborough, gall, ham, hanginde, intake, pightel, ryding, sainfoin, sceat, slipe, sloh. For Shoulder of Mutton, *v. supra* 207. Hundred Acres may be ironical, the field being only 16 perches, *v. supra* 207.

KINGSBURY. Bayford Hole (cf. *Boyverd* 1518 HarrowRec, *Boyfordhole* 1632 *All Souls*). Bean Croft (id. 1446 ib.). Church Fd (cf. *Churchcroft* 1632 ib.). Croach (cf. *Crouchfeld* 1381 Harrow-Rec, *v.* crouche). Gore Mead (*v.* Gore Hundred *supra* 49–50). Hill Fd (*Hilfeld* 1445 HarrowRec). Home Fd (*Holmefyld* 1593 *All Souls*). Long Down (*Longdowns* 1632 ib.). Newlands (*Newland* ib.). Old Fd (*Ofeldes* 1445 HarrowRec). Pigs Land (cf. *Pygges* 1546 ib.). Reddings (*Redynges* 1391 AD i, *v.* ryding). Stone Croft (*Stonecrofte* 1584 *All Souls*). West Croft (id. 1632 ib.). Wheat Croft (*Wheatecroft* 1593 ib.). For Long Cutts, Colemans Dean, Honey Sloughs, Cowleys, Horsleys, Pightle, Petfield, the Slipe, *v.* croft, denu, honey, læs, pightel, pytt, slipe, sloh. For No Mans Land cf. *supra* 102.

STANMORE. Clarks Staples (*Clerkes staples* 1680 Davenport, *v.* stapol). High Fd (*High Feilde* 1546 LP). Hooked Mead (*Hoke-mede* 1541 Druett, *v.* mæd). Old Fd (*Oldfeild peice* 1671 Davenport). North, South Park (cf. *Parke pales* 1680 ib.). Old Stockings (cf. *Stockin grove* ib., *v.* stocking). For Home Fd, the Pightle, Long Slip, *v.* ham, pightel, slipe). For All Stones *v. supra* 207.

WHITCHURCH. Anmers (*Anne Marsh* 1541 Druett, *Annemershe* 1552 Pat). Barn Fd (*Barnfeld* 1277 *Rental*). Church Fd (*Churchfeld* 1552 Pat). Down Fd (*Dunfeild* 1680 Davenport). Lurspit (*Lugpyt* 1306 RecStBarts, *Luddepittes* 1541 ib., *Ludpit* 1552 Pat). Potters Mead (*Potters Meade* 1541 Druett). For Home Fd, Pound Fd, Townsend Fd, *v.* ham, pund, tun.

Edmonton Hundred

EDMONTON. Church Fd (*Cherchefeld* 1387 *Walden*). Crabtree Fd (cf. *Crabbtree* 1636 *DuLa*). Gould Shots (cf. *Goldfeld* 1223 AD i and *v.* sceat). Hag Fd (id. 1662 RobinsonEd). Home Meadow (cf. *le Homfeld* t. Hy 7 *Rental*, *v.* ham). Hoppet (*The Hoppitt* 1679 RobinsonEd, *v.* hoppet). Long Fd (*Langefeld* 13th AD ii). Nuckolls (*Nockholes* 1586 Sess, possibly 'goblin hollow'). The Slips (id. 1679 RobinsonEd, *v.* slipe). Scotch Fd (id. 1662 ib., cf. *Scottesgraf* 13th AD ii, *v.* græfe). Starks Nest (*Storkes-nest* 13th AD ii, 1387 *Walden*). Tile Barrow Fd (*Tichelberch* 1252–7 AD i, *v.* beorg). Wood Pightle (cf. *le Wodereding* t. Hy 7 *Rental*, *v.* pightel, ryding). For Bury Fd, Larks Leas, Ox Leys, Man Mead, the Pightle, Bridge Pightle, Overshotts, *v.* burh, læs, mæd, pightel, sceat. For Great Virginia *v. supra* 206.

ENFIELD. From the EnclA (1801) printed by Robinson we have Ayland Green (c. 1686 *DuLa*). Bedwell Fd (*Bedewell in Enefeud* 1274 *Ass*, cf. Bedwell Cottages *supra* 37). Brick Kiln Fd

(*Brickell feild* 1636 *DuLa, v. supra* 205). Broadfield (*Est-*, *Westbrodefeld* 1228 RecStBarts). Charcroft (*Chalkecroft* 1464 *DuLa, Challcrofts* 1627 Robinson, cf. Chalkhill Ho *supra* 62. There is no chalk here). Colwell (*Colwell Longa* 1552 FF). East Fd Hoppet (*Estfeld* 1275 RecStBarts, *v.* hoppet). Goldown (*Couldedowne* 1636 *DuLa*). Gongs Fd (*Congfeild* (sic) 1635 RobinsonEn). Holdbrook (*Holebrooke* 1686 *DuLa*. Cf. Holborn *supra* 4). Holmes (cf. *Holmefeild* ib., *v.* holm). Honey Lands (cf. *Honylane* t. Ed 3 *Rental* and honey). Horsey (*Horshey* 1464 *MinAcct, Horsey* 1636 *DuLa, v.* (ge)hæg). Kings Hole (*Kingshould* 1627 RobinsonEn). Leathersey (*Lethersey* 1484 ib., *Lethersea* 1636 *DuLa, Lethersey* 1686 ib., *v.* eg). Long Ley (cf. *Longlease* 1572 RobinsonEn, *v.* læs). Mapleton Fd (*Mappledon* 1485, 1561 ib., *Maypleton* 1592 ib., *Mapleton feild* 1619 *Ct*, 'maple-down'). Masket Leys (may be *Baskegate* 1619 *Ct*). North Fd (*Northfeild* ib.). Platts (*la Plottes* 1275 RecStBarts, *v.* plott). Stockings (cf. *Stokkynglane* 1464 *MinAcct, v.* stocking). Stonards Croft (cf. *Stonardesfeild* 1636 *DuLa*). Stronglands (*Stronglond* 1619 *Ct*). Strouds Fd (cf. *le Strode* t. Ed 3 *Rental* and Stroud Green *supra* 124). Timber Mead (cf. *Tymberfeld* 1464 *MinAcct*). Well Reading Platts (cf. *Wellreadye, Wellreddie* 1619 *Ct, Wellready* 1686 *DuLa*. The second element is probably riðig, 'streamlet,' cf. Fullready (PN Wa 253), with later confusion with *reading* from ryding). Wick Fd (*Wykefeld* 1464 *MinAcct, v.* wic). For the Butts, the Dole, Devils Dell, the Flash, Mill Holme, Moor and New Leys, Pightle, Pound Fd, Town Meads, *v.* butte, dal, dell, flash, holm, læs, pightel, pund, tun.

SOUTH MIMMS. Biggles (possibly for *biddles*, and if so perhaps to be related to *Bedell mede* 1475 *AddCh*). Hunts Fd (cf. *Huntesgate* 1636 *DuLa*). Roundabouts (*the rounde aboute felde* 1574 AD v, *v.* roundabout). Sheep House Fd (cf. *Shepecotefeld* 1375 Hust). Taffy Dells (possibly *Taperdelle* 1474 *AddCh, v.* dell). For Castle, Hunting, Lime, Rabbit and Shepherds Dell, Home Fd, the Lees, Cow Pasture, Parsons and Scotch Pightle, Pound Fd, Sain Foin Close, Slades, the Slipe, Stockings, *v.* dell, ham, læs, pasture, pightel, pund, sainfoin, slæd, slipe, stocking. For Shoulder of Mutton, Nicelands and Halfpenny Bottom, *v. supra* 207.

TOTTENHAM. Alder Gutter (id. 1789 RobinsonT). Bow Lands (cf. *Bowewode* 1467 ib., cf. Bowes *supra* 68). Broad Mead (*Brodemede* 1546 *Rental*). Cain's Piece (id. 1789 RobinsonT, *v. supra* 207). Gilders Acre (*Geldenacre* 13th AD i, i.e. 'golden acre'). The Holmes (cf. *Sutholm* 1318 Pat, *v.* holm). Home Fd

(*Homefelde* 1467 RobinsonT, *v.* **ham**). Hoppet (*Hoppitt* 1789 ib., *v.* **hoppet**). Lock Mead (*Lokemede* 1502 *Rental*). May Fd (*Meyfeld* ib.). Mockings (from the manor of *Mokkynges* 1419 IpmR, held in 1348 (Ipm) by John de *Mockyng* whose family probably came from Mucking (PN Ess 163)). Slip Grove (cf. *The Slype* 1619 ib., *v.* **slipe**). Well Fd (*Welfeld* 1502 *Rental*, cf. *Welpightil* 1467 RobinsonT, *v.* **pightel**). For Hanging Fd, Lammaslands, Mill Hoppet, the Roundabout, *v.* **hanginde, hoppet, lammas, roundabout**. For Handkerchief Fd cf. *supra* 207.

In a Survey of 1821 printed by Robinson we have Awle Fd (*Awlefeild* 1619 RobinsonT, perhaps from its shape). Rattenscroft (so named in 1620 ib., cf. *Ratonerowe* 1413 ib., 'rat-row,' a term of contempt, *v. supra* 203). For Harp Shot, *v.* **harp, sceat**.

Ossulstone Hundred

ACTON. Broom Croft (*Bromecroftschote* 1380 Cl, *v.* **croft, sceat**). The Heath (may be identical with *Bruerie* 1229–37 StPaulsCh, *Bruiere* c. 1234 ib., the French equivalent). Reddings (cf. *novum Rudingum* 1234 ib., *Ruding'* 1237 ib., *v.* **ryding**). For Petty Croft, New Leys, the Pightle, Saintfoin Fd, *v.* **croft, læs, pightel, sainfoin**. For Friday Fd *v. supra* 206–7.

CHELSEA. Coney Close (i.e. 'rabbit close'). The Slip (*v.* **slipe**). Whitelands (preserved in *Whitelands* College) may have been named in distinction from Blacklands (*v.* Blacklands Terrace in Chelsea *supra* 86). Cf. *White Lands, Black Lands* 1797 Stockdale.

CHISWICK. For Home Fd and Meadow and the Slip, *v.* **ham** and **slipe**.

EALING. Brook Shott (*Brookshot* c. 1490 *Ct, v.* **sceat**). Lot Mead (*Lotmede* 1547 Pat, cf. Lots Rd in Chelsea *supra* 87). Minny Croft (cf. *The Menecroft* 1401 Cl, *v.* **(ge)mæne**). Nova Scotia (so named in 1819 (G), cf. *supra* 206). Potters Fd (id. 1787 Faulkner, cf. *Poteteresriding* (sic) 1315 Pat). Shrubbenhaugh (cf. *Shrobbenhill* 1447 *Ct, le Shrubbyn* 1470 ib. and Wormwood Scrubbs *supra* 110). For Bell Fd, Folly Fd, Furlong Shott, Home Fd, Ferry Aite, Kitchen Meadow, Horse Leys, Pickett Fd, Pickle, Home Pightle, Reddings, Long Shott, the Slads, *v.* **bell, folly, furlang, ham, iggoð, kitchen, læs, piked, pightel, ryding, sceat, slæd**. For Shoulder of Mutton, Nova Scotia and Starve Acre *v. supra* 206–7. Nothing is known of the history of Deadman's Grave.

FINCHLEY. Church Fd (id. 1683 MxNQ i). Ducksetters Fd
(cf. *Ducksitter Lane* 1800 ib. iii, *Duxeter Lane* ib. iv). Long Fd
(*Langefeld* 1294 *Ass*). The Pigeans (*Pigensland* 1629 *Ct*). Rye
Fd (id. 1683 MxNQ i). Wall Grove Fd (*Wellgrove* 1492 *StPauls*).
For Hop Garden, Summer Lands, Ox Leys, Stack Plat, Cus-
combe Shott, *v.* garden, land, læs, plott, sceat. For Thriving
Land *v. supra* 207. Spaniards Fd is named from the Spaniards
Inn *supra* 111.

FINSBURY. Lost minor names from the ParReg include *The
Brickills* (1618), *The Buttes* (1633), *the Cadge* (1608), *Ye Pest
House* (1724), *The Puter Platter* (1679), *Vineger Yeard* (1669),
v. brickkiln, butte. The *Cadge* was the village cage or lock-up.

FRIERN BARNET. Long Slip (*le Slype* 1492 *StPauls*, *v.* slipe).
For Dell Fd, Dial Fd, Pound Fd, *v.* dell, dial, pund. For
Shoulder of Mutton, *v. supra* 207.

FULHAM. Charley Mead (*Cherlowmede* 1447 *Ct*, cf. *Cherlou-
mersh* 1489 FF). Fan Meadow (*le Fen* 1271 ib., *Vanne* 1377
Cl, *v.* fenn). In 1738 (Feret) we have Church Fd (*Cherchfeld*
1457 *Ct*). Stroud Mead (cf. *Stroda* t. Ric 1 StPaulsCh, *v.* strod
and cf. Stroud Green *supra* 124).

HACKNEY. Old field-names noted by Robinson include Home
Close Fd (cf. *Homefeld* 1441 *MinAcct*, *v.* ham). Paradise Fd
(*close called Paradise* 1652 RobinsonH). Pickwell oth. Pigwell
oth. Pitwell Fd (*Pykewell* 1542 ib.). For Hanging 5 Acres,
Hoppit, the Slips, Slipe Mead, *v.* hanginde, hoppet, slipe. For
Shoulder of Mutton *v. supra* 207.

HAMMERSMITH. Hill Fd (cf. *The Hills* 1600 HammSurv). For
Joy Leys and Cow Pasture *v.* læs and pasture. New England is
perhaps a nickname of the type noted *supra* 206.

HAMPSTEAD. Summer Leys (*Somerlese* 1312 *WAM*, *v.* læs). The
Temples (id. 1574 HendonSurv). For Bell Fd, Hemstall,
Hanging Fd, Lawn Pits, the Pightle, Long Slip, *v.* bell, ham-
steall, hanginde, launde, pightel, slipe. In 1761 (Surv) we have
Brockhill (*Brockehole* 1312 Barratt, 'badger hole').

HOLBORN. Among old field-names we may note (i) in the
Kingsway district: Cup Fd (*Cuppefeld* 1529 StGilesSurv, perhaps from its shape). Ficketts Fd (*Ficatesfeld* 1232–5 Williams,
Fikettesfeld 1252 ib., *Fyketesfeld* 1294 *Ass*, perhaps from some
early owner). Leyfield (*Leyfeld* t. Ed 1 Parton). Oldwitch Close

(*Oldwych close* 1607 StGilesSurv, *v.* Aldwych *supra* 166). The Pightles (*le Pightells* 1634 ib.). Purse Fd (*Pursefeld* 1527 ib., perhaps from its shape). Rose Fd (*the Rosefelde* 1567 Parton, from an inn, *messuage voc. le Rose* 1537 ib.). (ii) north of High Holborn: Lambs Conduit Fd and Red Lion Fd (*v. supra* 118, 119). (iii) in the St Giles district: Bear Close (*The Bere close* 1570 Parton, from an inn). Colman Hedge Fd (*Colmanhedge Felde* 1537 ib.), for this hedge *v.* Whitcomb St *supra* 184. Conduit Fd (*The Condute Feld* 1550 Pat). Marshland (*Mersland* 1222 Parton, *Mersheland* 1537 ib.). Newlands (*le Newelond* t. Hy 3 ib.). Pittance Croft (*Pitaunce croft* t. Ed 1 ib., probably belonging to the *pittancer* of St Giles Hospital, cf. Pittensarys Fm (PN Wo 94)). (iv) from the Bloomsbury district: Culver Close ('dove close,' *v.* **culver**). Great, Little Pingle (both 1668, LnTopRec xvii, *v.* **pightel**). Earlier field-names of which the locality cannot be determined include *Conyngerfeld* 1529 Parton, 'rabbit-warren field,' *v.* **coninger**, and *Longesmale acre* t. Ed 1 ib., i.e. 'long narrow acre.'

HORNSEY. Modern (19th century) names noted in HornseyCt include Cocks Fd (*Coxefeildes, Cocksfeild* 1603 HornseyCt, *Cockefeilds* 1605 ib.). Farne Fields (*Fernefeld* 1489 AD vi, *Fernefildes* 1549 Pat, 'fern or bracken field'). Hollam Beech (*Hollon Beeches* 1626 HornseyCt, *HollamBeech* 1652 ib.). Lightland (*Lyghtlondeslane* 1400 AD vi, *Lightlonde* t. Hy 5 AD ii, 1489 AD vi). Newgate Fd (cf. *Newgate lane* 1605 Sess). Oakfield (*Okefeild* 1603 HornseyCt). Oxleas (*Oxe leaze Hawte* 1647 ib.). Pitmans Acre (*Pickmans acre* 1608-39 ib., *Pitmans Acre* 1646 ib.). Pond Fd (cf. *Pondecroft* 1397 AD i, *Pondfeild al. Longefeild* 1608 HornseyCt). High Readings (cf. *Redynges* 1397 AD i, *High Reddinges al. Roote Reddinges* 1647 HornseyCt, *v.* **ryding**). Tanners Scrubbs (cf. Wormwood Scrubbs *supra* 110). Tilekiln Fd (cf. *Tylekilne* 1608 HornseyCt, *Tilkill fild* 1624 ib.). Trundle Mead (*Trundle meades* 1647 ib., probably 'circular meadow,' from OE *tryndel*, 'circle.'

KENSINGTON. For New Leas, Long Shott, *v.* **læs, sceat.**

PADDINGTON. Knights Fd (*Knytesfeld* 1312 *WAM, Knightfeld Grene* 1557 Pat, cf. Knightsbridge *supra* 169). Coney Hole (i.e. 'rabbit hole'). For Bread and Cheese Lands *v. supra* 206–7.

ST MARYLEBONE. From an estate-plan of 1708 in Clinch we have Dove House Park (cf. *Dufehousemedowe* 1538 LMxAS (N.S.) iv). For Bell Fd, Pightle, Pound Fd, the Slipe, *v.* **bell, pightel, pund, slipe.**

ST PANCRAS. In the StPancSurv we have mention of the following old field-names: Culver Meadow (*Culverclose* 1649, *v.* **culver**). Conduit Shot (*Conditeschote* 1405, *v.* **sceat**). The Forties (cf. *Fortie acre* 1649, in Kentish Town near the Fleet, and Forty Hall *supra* 73). Gilden Fd (id. ib., probably 'golden field'). Morwell or Murrels (*Morwellfeld* 1405, 'spring in the marshy spot,' *v.* **mor, wielle**).

SHOREDITCH. 18th-century field-names in the parish include Fairfield (*Faire feild* 1537 ShoreSurv). High Elms (*le Hygh Helmes* 1545 LP). Land of Promise (*v. supra* 207). Millfield (*Mylfeld* 1545 LP). St Nicholas Field (*Nicholes feld* 1258 ShoreSurv, *Saynt Nicholas Felde* 1545 LP, *Nichollfeld* 1550 FF. *Nichol* was probably an early owner, the *Saint* being a later addition). Star Close (*le Starre close* 1503 ShoreSurv, from an inn *The Sterre* 1501 ib.). In a Survey of 1767 we have Milkwives Bridge Fd (*Mylkwyfbridge* 1543 ShoreSurv, *Mylkwyvesbridge-ffilde* 1564 ib.). Earlier names from the ShoreSurv include *Abraham or Apron Field* 1648, *Brenthawe* 1464, i.e. 'burnt **haga**,' *Gore Close* 1648 (cf. Gore Hundred *supra* 49–50), *Laysterne Field* 1683, *close called the Pingells* 1636, *v.* **pightel**, *Shroggs Close* 1601, cf. *Clipstone Shroggs* (PN Nt 74), from *shrogg*, 'bush, thicket.'

STOKE NEWINGTON. In 1734 (RobinsonSN) we have Berry Meadow (probably near the manor house, *v.* **burh**). For Home Stall, Long and Short Slip, *v.* **hamsteall, slipe**.

WILLESDEN. From a list of 19th-century field-names quoted by Potter we have Church Mead (cf. *Chirchefeld* 1416 *AllSouls*). Long Fd (*Longgefeld* 1309 AD v). The Marsh (*la Mersche* 1416 *AllSouls*). Great and Little Sheepcotts (*Shepcote* ib.). By the Rood must have been near some cross or rood. For Butts Green, Horse Cutts, Dyal Fields, Gore Fd, Mapes Hearn (probably near Mapesbury *supra* 162), Oxleys, the Pightle, Acre Plat, Roundabout, Long Reddings, Knowles Shot, *v.* **butte, croft, dial, gara, hyrne, læs, pightel, plott, roundabout, ryding, sceat**. For Friday Fields and Hunger Hill *v. supra* 206.

City of Westminster

WESTMINSTER. From a map of the Ebury estate (c. 1663–70) we have Brickhill feild (*v.* **brick-kiln**). Horseleys (*v.* **læs**). Great and Little Rombelowe (*v.* Pimlico Rd *supra* 181). Tiborne Close was near the present Marble Arch, *v.* Tyburn *supra* 137. For Homeadow al. Homefeild and The Slip, *v.* **ham** and **slipe**. For The Shoulder of Mutton *v. supra* 207.

APPENDIX

I. THE THREE HENDON CHARTERS

BCS 994 is a grant of land by King Edwy to his thegn Lyfing of land at *loceresleage* and at *tuneweorðe*. The estates are not distinguished and the boundaries are not easy to follow, but they seem to include the present parish of Kingsbury and the northern part of Hendon. They begin at *tate burnan* which, from the bounds of BCS 1290 (*infra* 220), would seem to have been the southern of the two headstreams of the Brent. Cf. further PN Herts 49–50 where it is noted that this small stream, a tributary of Dollis Brook, contains the same personal name as Totteridge and here forms the county boundary between Totteridge (Herts) and Hendon (Mx). The bounds then go along the *mearc* (here the county boundary) to *wiðimære*, probably a bad form for *wiðigmere*, i.e. withy-pool, and then along the *mearc* to *holan riðe*, i.e. 'hollow streamlet.' The bounds of BCS 1290 show this to be the small unnamed stream which joins Silk stream by the present Burnt Oak railway station. The bounds then follow the *holan riðe* to its junction with *suluc*[1], i.e. Silk stream. From there the bounds lead by the withy-pool along the boundary to the *tunsteall* on Watling Street (i.e. Edgware Road). The *tunsteall* here is mentioned also in BCS 1290 as 'the old' *tunsteall*, and may have reference to a Roman station on Watling Street, cf. IPN 152. (It can hardly have reference to *Sulloniacæ* as suggested in *Crawford Charters* (97), for that is much too far to the north.) From there we go (south) along Watling Street to *tunwæorðinga gemære*, i.e. the boundary of the people of *tunweorð*. *tunweorð* was an old name for part of Kingsbury parish (*supra* 62–3) and the boundary must be the southern boundary of Kingsbury, which runs west from the Welsh Harp. Thence the bounds strike west from Watling Street by *liuyssace mere* to the *wicstræte*. *liuyssac* may possibly be the same as the Cool Oak of the adjacent Cool Oak Lane (*supra* 56). It is clear that *wicstræt* is an early name for the lane now known as Honeypot Lane which forms the western boundary of Kingsbury parish. It was later known as *Oldstrete* (*supra* 11, n. 1). Then the bounds go along this street to the *hredes* (? for *hiredes*) *mærce æt Sancte Albane*. This seems to be the point where the parishes of Harrow, Great and Little Stanmore and Kingsbury meet and clearly has reference to the fact that Stanmore anciently belonged to the Abbey (*hired*

---

[1] This is the correct reading as shown by the O.S. facsimile, and not *sulue* as given by Birch.

or community) of St Albans. The bounds then go along the *mearc* (east) back to Watling Street, following the present north boundary of Kingsbury parish. Then south along Watling Street to the *deopan fura*, i.e. deep furrow, no doubt the later Collindeep, now Colindale (*supra* 57). Then by Silk Stream and the apple tree and the *gemearceden stocce* back to *tataburnan*. The apple tree and the stock cannot of course be identified, but it is clear that in addition to the present parish of Kingsbury the bounds include a strip of Hendon parish extending from Silk Stream valley to Holcombe Hill. As *tunweorð* would seem to have been co-terminous with Kingsbury (*supra* 62–3), the lost *loceresleage* (*loðeresleage*) would seem to have been the old name for the north part of Hendon parish.

BCS 1290 gives the bounds of an estate called *Lo(h)ðeresleage* granted to Westminster Abbey by King Edgar. This estate is clearly the same as the estate of *Locereslege* granted with *Tuneweorðe* by King Edwy to Westminster Abbey (BCS 994). The bounds run from the old *tunsteall* on Watling Street of that grant to *Æcges wer*, i.e. Edgware, which must be the spot where the present Edgware Brook crosses Watling Street. Then along *stanburnan*, i.e. stony stream (Edgware Brook *supra* 3) to *sulh*, i.e. Silk stream which it joins some 300 yards to the east and so to *yburnan*, i.e. Dean's Brook which unites with Edgware Brook at this point. Then along *yburnan* to *Iccenes ford*, i.e. probably the point farther up Dean's Brook by Hemmings Wood where the boundary between Edgware and Hendon leaves the main stream. Thence it goes along a *sihtre* to the *haga* or boundary hedge and along the *haga* to *grendeles gatan*, i.e. Barnet Gate (*supra* 57). The *sihtre* is the small feeder of Dean's Brook up which the boundary runs, the *haga* is the Hendon-Elstree parish and county boundary. From Barnet Gate it goes along *kincges mearce* to Brent and from Brent follows the boundary to *tatanburnan*. The King's boundary is the stretch of the Hendon boundary from Barnet Gate to the spot where Hendon Wood Lane crosses the upper waters of Dollis Brook (i.e. Brent). Thence it goes south to *tatanburnan*, i.e. the stream which forms the southern boundary of Totteridge (cf. *supra* 219) and so to the boundary of Hendon at *holan riþe*, i.e. probably the small stream which joins the Silk near the present Burnt Oak station, and from the *sulh* or Silk back to the old *tunsteall*.

BCS 1351 gives the bounds of an estate called *Blecceanham* (*supra* 57) granted by King Edgar to Westminster Abbey. It is clear that this included much of the south part of the present parish of Hendon. The bounds begin at *Sandgæt* where the three boundaries meet, i.e. the boundaries of the three ancient parishes of Hendon, Hampstead and Finchley which meet 300 yards west-north-west of the Spaniards Inn. Thence they go west along *Hemstedesmearc*, i.e. the Hendon-Hampstead boundary, to *Mærburnan*, i.e. boundary stream, the old name of Westbourne Brook (*supra* 8) and so along that same stream to Watling Street somewhere near Cricklewood. Then up the *stræt* to the Brent, i.e. the spot where the main road crossed that stream just east of the present Welsh Harp. The bounds then go up the Brent to *fihte burna* which must be the present Mutton Brook (*supra* 5), which joins the Brent at the east end of Bell Lane and then forms the boundary between Finchley and Hendon. From the Mutton Brook the bounds go to the *wogan æpsan*, i.e. the crooked aspentree, thence to the old *hagtreow*, i.e. *haga-treow* or (boundary) hedge-tree, and from that tree to the triple boundary at Sandgate from which they started. The two trees probably stood at two of the sharp angles which the Finchley-Hendon boundary makes on its way from Mutton Brook to Sandgate.

II. THE HAMPSTEAD CHARTERS

BCS 1309 gives the bounds of Hampstead. They are very brief and practically only include the four angles of the parish. They start at *sandgatan* (*v.* the bounds of *Blecceanham supra*), then go south to *fox hangran* which must be the present south-east corner of the parish near Chalk Farm, then west to Watling Street, i.e. the south-west corner of the parish at the south end of West End Lane where it joins Kilburn High Road, then north along the main road to *coc cinge pol* which must be the northwest corner of the parish near Cricklewood Lane, then east back to Sandgate.

BCS 1351 gives more detailed bounds of Hampstead. They start at *sandgæt* (*v. supra*) and go east to *bedegares spicleage* (sic) which must be the point near Ken Wood Farm where the Hampstead borough boundary turns south, then south by *Deormodes wican* (cf. Dormers Well Fm *supra* 45) to *medeman Hemstede*[1], which was probably near the present Gospel Oak on the Hampstead-St Pancras boundary (*supra* 141). Then the bounds go by the *haga* and the rush-*leah* west to the *bæruwe*. This last is Barrow Hill (*supra* 111) on the Hampstead-St

[1] The significance of *medeman* here is obscure. Its usual sense is 'moderate-sized, small,' but it is also used in the sense 'middle in position,' cf. *s.n.* Meadfield, PN Sr 205.

Marylebone boundary. The bounds then go by *stangrave* west to
Watling Street (Kilburn High Road), then north along Watling
Street to *mær burne*, 'boundary stream,' the old name for the
Westbourne Brook near its source (*supra* 8), then east back to
sandgæt.

III. THE WESTMINSTER CHARTERS

BCS 1048 gives the bounds of the Abbey lands of Westminster.
Another version, differing but slightly in details, is given in
BCS 1351. The bounds do not include the western part of the
present City of Westminster, i.e. the later manors of Ebury and
Hyde. They start at the Thames and go up *merfleot* to *pollene
stocc*. *merfleot* must be the Tyburn (*supra* 6) which formed the
boundary between the manors of Ebury and Westminster. It
joined the Thames near the present Vauxhall Bridge. *pollene
stocc* cannot be identified but may have been somewhere near the
present Victoria station. Then the bounds go by *bulunga fenn*
(*-inga* in BCS 1351), presumably the low-lying land in the present
Pimlico, and so by the old dike or ditch (where the stream was
canalised) to *cuford*. *cuford*, i.e. cowford, which was certainly the
spot where the Tyburn crossed the present Piccadilly, as shown
in the Crispin charter (*infra*). The bounds then go up the
Tyburn to the wide *here stræt* (i.e. 'army street'), the present
Oxford Street. They then go along that street and High Holborn
to the old church of St Andrew (*on Holeburne* added in BCS
1351), i.e. near the north end of Shoe Lane, then to *lundene
fenn*, i.e. London fen or marsh, which must have been the tract
of marshy land along the Fleet valley to the west of the City of
London. The bounds then go south along the fen to the Thames
to the middle of the stream and then back by the strand or
shore, i.e. the bank of the Thames (cf. The Strand *supra* 173)
to the *merfleot* where they began.

Armitage Robinson in his *Gilbert Crispin* (167–8) gives the
text of another charter of Ethelred setting forth a *berewic* of
two *mansas* belonging to Westminster. The details differ in some
respects from those of BCS 1048, though in both the western
part of the present city is excluded. The bounds of the Crispin
charter seem to start farther east, i.e. they exclude the marshy
ground by the mouth of the Tyburn. They begin at the *hlaw*
which may be the later Tothill (*supra* 174). This was certainly
on dry ground between the Tyburn and the Abbey. Then into
teoburnan and then north along *anlang* (sic) *teoburnan* to *cuford*.
cuford occurs also in BCS 1048 (*supra*) and is still indicated

by the dip in Piccadilly by Half Moon Street. From *cuford* the boundary presumably follows the Tyburn, as in BCS 1048, to Oxford Street, called however, in this charter, Watling Street. Thence the bounds go east along the street to the *setle*[1] and then to *hinan croftes gemære*, i.e. the boundary of the monks' croft. It is probable that this last was the spot where the present Oxford Street, Tottenham Court Road and Charing Cross Road meet. The bounds must then have gone north, to include the newly added *berewic*. This was the Westminster part of *Totenhale* (*supra* 143 n.), represented later by the parish of St Giles in the Fields (LnTopRec xvii, 25). The northern boundary of the monks' croft would be at the northern end of the berewick, perhaps corresponding, more or less, with the southern boundary in this area of the parish of St Pancras, south of the present Tavistock Square. The bounds then went southward to an unidentified *eald strǽt*, probably the remains of some Roman highway. They then returned to Watling Street, i.e. the later High Holborn, and go along this to the *werhrode*, i.e. felons' cross or gallows. No later mention has been found of this. If one may assume that the old boundaries of the Parish of St Giles (*v.* StGilesSurv ii, pl. 6) correspond with those of the berewick, and that at the gallows the bounds again turned southward, this point would be a little way west of Chancery Lane, and the next landmark mentioned, the 'alderman's boundary', would be in New Square, Lincoln's Inn. The bounds then go south to *akemannestrǽte*; this is undoubtedly the thoroughfare later known as Fleet Street and the Strand (*supra* 10). The bounds then run west along the Strand to *cyrringe*, i.e. the present Charing Cross, where the *strǽt* turns north-west (*supra* 167). Thence, turning south, they follow the bank of the river, crossing *Thorney* (*supra* 165) and including the Abbey and its precincts; and so back to the *hlaw* where they started.

[1] *Setl* denotes primarily a settle or seat, but secondarily an abode or residence.

INDEX

OF SOME WORDS OF WHICH THE HISTORY
IS ILLUSTRATED IN THIS VOLUME

INDEX

OF PLACE-NAMES IN MIDDLESEX

The primary reference to a place is marked by the use of Clarendon type.

With the exception of certain names of special interest, street-names are not included in this Index, nor are those names (again with a few exceptions) which at once suggest the parish in which they are to be found, e.g. Staines Bridge and Moor (in Staines).

In grouping names together no distinction has been made between names written in one or two words, e.g. North End and Northend are grouped under North End. Parish- and river-names are given separately.

No attempt has been made to index the field-names.

INDEX

OF PLACE-NAMES IN COUNTIES OTHER THAN MIDDLESEX

[References to place-names in Beds, Bk, D, ERY, Ess, Herts, Hu, NRY, Nt, Nth, Sr, Sx, W, Wa and Wo are not included, as these have been fully dealt with in the volumes already issued upon the names of those counties.]

CAMBRIDGE: PRINTED BY
W. LEWIS, M.A.
AT THE UNIVERSITY PRESS